Conservation of
Library Materials

A Manual and Bibliography on the
Care, Repair and Restoration of
Library Materials

by

George Daniel Martin Cunha

Conservator
Library of the Boston Athenaeum
Boston, Massachusetts

The Scarecrow Press, Inc.
Metuchen, N. J.   1967

41360

This book has been printed
on permanent/durable paper
with a neutral pH to insure
a life expectancy of at least
one hundred years.

To

Dorothy

without whose help
and encouragement
this book could
not have been
written

A 16th-Century Book Before Restoration

The Same After Restoration At L'Istituto
di Patologia del Libro, Rome
Courtesy of: Istituto di Patologia del Libro, Rome

Preface

This is not a book on bookbinding. The history and technique of that craft have been well covered by many highly qualified authorities.

This volume provides an introduction to the various facets of conservation as well as bibliographical data of permanent value. In addition to being a critical description of the literature on the historic and technical aspects of the care, repair and restoration of books, prints, maps, and manuscripts and other important records, it is a manual of practical guidance for librarians, archivists, curators, conservators, restorationists and bookbinders.

It is paradoxical that in the past thirty-five years there has been much study of the causes of the decay of library materials and means to prevent it, yet at the same time so little has been done to utilize the knowledge made available. In Europe and in other parts of the world, restoration centers, usually with government support, are making organized and coordinated efforts to further conservation of library materials. In the United States, what little is being done is privately financed. The United States, for some inexplicable reason, does not support the International Centre for the Study of the Preservation and the Restoration of Cultural Property (the Rome Centre).

This book is the result of many years of work and study by the author, aided by some of the foremost restorationists and conservators in the United States and Europe. I wish to particularly acknowledge the generous cooperation of the membership of the Guild of Book Workers; Mr. William J. Barrow of Richmond, Virginia; Mr. Harold Tribolet in Chicago; Mr. James Gear, Document Restoration Branch, U.S. National Archives; Dr. Richard Buck, Intermuseum Conservation Association, Oberlin, Ohio; Dr. A. E. Werner and his associate, Mr. David Baynes-Cope of the British Museum

Research Laboratory; Mr. W. Pointer, Officer-in-Charge, British Museum Bindery; Mr. G. Ede, Principal Technical Officer, Public Records Office, London; Mr. Roger Powell, Petersfield, England; Mr. Sidney Cockerell, Granchester, England; Mme. Kleindienst and M. Desbrosses at the Bibliotheque Nationale; M. Pierre Durye, Assistant to the Director, Archives of France; Mme. Francois Flieder, Laboratoire de Cryptogamie, Paris; Mme. J. R. Houres, Chief du Laboratoire du Louvre; Dr. H. J. Plenderleith, Director of the Rome Centre; Dr. Ludovico Santucci and Drs. Piero and Fausto Gallo at the Institute of Book Pathology in Rome; and Vice-director D. Alfredo Colombo at the Vatican's Istituto Restauro Scientifico del Libro.

Last, but by no means least, my appreciation to Mr. Walter Muir Whitehill, Librarian and Director of the Boston Athenaeum, and Mr. Marion V. Brewington, Director of the Kendall Whaling Museum, Sharon, Massachusetts, for their continuing support and encouragement in all matters pertaining to the preservation of books.

G. D. M. C.

Boston Athenaeum

Table of Contents

Illustrations

"There is no such thing as the absolute
ownership of a work of art or of a document
of historical value.   ...So in the case of a
fine illuminated manuscript, or a copy of a
scarce printed book, the owner is at the most
in the position of a life-tenant, with the implied duty of handing on the property to the
next tenant in as good or in better condition
than it was when it came into his possession."

(Douglas Cockerell - Some Notes on
Bookbinding.   London, Oxford
University Press 1929, p. 72)

Chapter I
Historical Background

> (Books) -- compact compositions of fairly well
> defined contents and considerable length, possess-
> ing cultural, historical or literary significance.
> Testaments of Time, New York, Alfred A. Knopf,
> 1965.

A book is a book, but its form is ever changing. Neither
its physical shape nor its material are in any way fixed. The term
properly includes prehistoric rock carvings and scratchings on bone
and antlers, ostraka, painted hides, carved amulets, notched sticks,
runic calendars, clog almanacs, bronze plaques and many other artifacts on which men since earliest times have left a story in pictures, phonetic symbols, carved letters or writing. It is only a
matter of convention that sound recordings and tapes, film strips,
and microfilms and cards are not called books. From a practical
point of view, however, it is useful to consider as books the codex
and those forms which closely antedated it in the West or have per-
sisted as record keeping devices in the East almost to the present.
These include clay tablets, papyri, linen, silk, leather or parchment
scrolls, waxed writing tablets, bundles of palm leaf strips, slips of
wood and ivory or sheets of bark.

The Saxons wrote runes on pieces of beech board. The deri-
vation of the English word book is from the Anglo-Saxon boc, bece,
beech. The Latin word for book, liber, is derived from the Latin
for bark, once used almost universally as a writing material. The
Greek word for book, dipthera, means skins, which were often used
in ancient times.

Regardless of the form or materials of their books, collectors and librarians have always had the problem of preservation.
Deterioration of books is not unique to the twentieth century. The
early Mesopotamians were bothered by bookworms (earth worms)
which bored tunnels through soft clay writing tablets before they

1

were hardened in the sun and even nibbled the surface of the baked
tablets, defacing the markings.   Clay tablets were easily chipped
and broken by rough handling, and to preserve these brick books,
they were sometimes stored in covered jars.   The jars were la-
beled with clay markers affixed with straw and were shelved in an
orderly manner.   Records of major importance received even greater protection; for example, some Assyrian terra cotta tablets now
in the British Museum were encased in clay wrappers that had to
be broken before the records could be reached.   It can be argued
that these clay covers functioned as envelopes, but since each wrapper bears an inscription similar to that on the tablet within, it
seems more logical to call them book covers.   Sargon I, founder of
the Semitic Empire in Chaldea, established a library of clay tablets
which existed until the fall of Nineveh, when it was destroyed by
burning.

In ancient China, before the invention of paper, wood was
the favorite writing surface except for silk.   Narrow slips of wood,
originally bamboo, were used for all kinds of records.   For length-
ier communications these bamboo and wooden slips were joined together at their long edges.   They could be conveniently folded into
rectangular bundles for storage.   Elsewhere in the East custodians
soon learned to protect fragile palm leaf books by fastening strips
of wood to each side of the bundles of palm.   When ornamentation
was desired, carved ivory was often substituted for the plainer
wood.

Clay was not available in the Nile Valley so the early Egyptians used their abundant papyrus to manufacture a paper-like material.   Although superior to clay for writing, papyrus was less durable.   For convenience, the papyrus sheets were glued into long
strips which were then rolled on wooden cylinders and wrapped in
skins or cloth.   It is not known when the Greeks adopted papyrus
for their books and records.   They could have received the knowledge through the Phoenician/Syrian port of Gebel (Byblos) at about
the same time they adopted the Phoenician alphabet.   The Greek
word for book, dipthera, suggests that they first used skins for
writing, but according to Herodotus, by 500 B.C. papyrus was the

preferred material on the Grecian peninsula.

The library of Rameses II (1200 B.C.) undoubtedly contained books made of all of the library materials available to the Pharoahs at that time: clay from other lands, papyrus, palm leaves, wooden pallets, bark, linen, skins and stone. Parchment did not come into use until much later, about 200 B.C. With the exception of stone, all were vulnerable: clay to worms; papyrus to insects, moisture and desiccation; bark, wood and palm leaves to termites; skins and linen to rot and to the cockroaches, silverfish, beetles and mud wasps that infested that hot, dry land. For protection against vermin, dirt and dampness, the Egyptians, Greeks and Romans stored their tightly wrapped scrolls in cylindrical boxes of wood and ivory.

Scrolls continued in common use for centuries and the techniques for making these volumes are well documented. When an author finished his manuscript, it was copied as many times as required by the librarii, or transcribers, and the copies sent to the librarioli who ornamented the texts and supplied the titles and colophons. The scrolls then went to the bibliopegi who bound them by cutting even margins and square ends then polishing the blank sides with pumice. Next they attached wooden cylinders at each end for rolling and added a title, either by affixing a tag to one of the wooden rolls or by pasting a label to the outside of one end of the scroll. Decoration was plain or elaborate, according to the importance of the text or pride of ownership. Catullus describes a book bound for a poet named Suffenus as follows:

> His paper is royal, not common or bad
> His wrappers, his bosses are totally new;
> His sheets, smoothed by pumice, are all ruled with lead,
> And bound with a ribbon of rose colored hue.

Later, in the Alexandrian Library and in others in Greece and Rome, after parchment and vellum had become common writing materials, the conservation problem eased somewhat because of the greater durability of lime-treated skins.

As recorded knowledge increased, the problems of storage increased in proportion. Even under ideal conditions, scrolls were not easy to handle or shelve and in excessively moist or dry areas

there were serious conservation problems.   A dry tightly rolled
parchment crumbles when unwound.   Excessively moist parchment
cockles badly, defacing any writing on it.   Hence it was only natural that those concerned with the making and keeping of records
and books should investigate alternatives to the scroll and the codex
form began to emerge.

It is generally agreed that shortly before the emergence of
Christianity, when desk type furniture was first used in Greece and
Rome, writers began to use oblong sheets for convenience.   These,
after being inscribed, were gathered into bundles and fastened along
one edge by sewing.   The few papyri extant today in codex format
are stabbed at one edge and laced through the stabbed holes.   This
is a clumsy method of binding and is very hard on the pages.   Perhaps that is why early record keepers soon resorted to fastening
their pages with glue.   Cicero, in his Epistles to Atticus (56 B.C.),
has an orator ask a friend for two of his librarians who might
"conglutinate" his books.   This could mean to glue the papyrus
sheets into rolls, but it is interpreted by others as evidence of the
early existence of books in codex form.   There are also indications
that the early Christians favored papyrus sheets over parchment
rolls for reasons of economy.

Another influence in this evolutionary process was the popularity among scribes of the Roman pugillaria.   These wax-coated
wood or ivory writing tablets were convenient in size and had a
firm writing surface.   Even when two or more were hinged together (diptychs and triptychs) to record lengthy data, they were
easy to handle and, more important, the written surfaces, pressed
flat when the book was closed, protected each other.

Another factor was the increased use of parchment because
of the ever increasing scarcity of papyrus.   Papyrus sheets could
be fastened end to end in rolls or in bundles by a combination of
edge stabbing, sewing and gluing.   Parchment, on the other hand,
did not roll easily and when edge bound, the sheets in the books so
formed did not fold back easily.   A more practical method of binding was soon devised.   The scribes folded rectangles of parchment
down the center, inserted several of these folded sheets within each

other to make a gathering of pages and then sewed through the common center fold exactly as single signature note books are made today. The next logical step was to fasten several of these sewn
gatherings together by chain stitching at their spines (folds) to make
books of as many pages as were necessary.

As this new book form increased in popularity, it became
apparent that chain stitching, while suitable for thin volumes, was
not strong enough for books of a dozen or more gatherings. The
spines would cave in as do thick, cheaply made volumes today.
Sometime around 500 A.D., probably in a monastery workshop, an
inventive binder developed a technique for fastening the gatherings
of vellum pages to several cords as well as to each other and bonding the sewn gatherings by applying glue to their common back.
This resulted in a book that would hold its shape, open and close
easily, lie flat when open and, above all, provide maximum protection for the written pages.

The folding of pages, gathering them together, sewing the
gatherings to cords or vellum slips and then gluing is basically the
same as modern binding of Western books. All subsequent operations are to provide protection for the binding or to decorate the
protective covers. The simplest and most obviously needed protection was to glue a skin over the spine to protect the exposed cords
and sewing. There was also a need to protect the sides from wear
and tear, dirt and dampness. Extending the leather spine covering
over the sides helped, but boards were better. At first the boards
were simply glued to the leather at the joint, but it was soon realized that the cords to which the pages were sewn, if long enough,
could be laced into the protective boards. This securely fastened
them to the book, formed hinges for the covers and made a rigid
base for subsequent covering. The protective leather could then be
cut to the taste of the owner, either to cover only the spine and
the joint or to extend entirely over the boards. The net result was
a durable volume that not only protected the manuscript, but also
was pleasant to handle, handsome in appearance and well suited for
subsequent decoration. This new binding technique spread rapidly
through the Western Mediterranean countries and Europe and is

still, with little change, used by fine binders in Europe and America. Experimentation with new materials, minor innovations in sewing technique, clasps and ties, headbanding, etc., are all merely
variations of the basic binding technique originated by ingenious
craftsmen 1500 years ago.

The Greeks and Romans, and later the Byzantines, were
much interested in the decoration of books as well as their form.
Sumptuous bookshops existed in the major cities and bibliophiles
sought out skillful book makers. In one of his letters Cicero requested a friend to send him two slaves who were very clever
binders. The evidence from Pompeii, Herculaneum and elsewhere
is that many book collectors had large libraries of beautifully bound
and exquisitely decorated volumes. In Greek and Roman times
these were mostly scrolls, many in protective cases. Later the
Byzantines added elaborately decorated and jeweled codex form
books to their collections.

In the Near East, the codex developed along slightly different lines. There craftsmen emphasized lightness and suppleness as
distinguished from the more massive oaken boards and thick leather
covers of the West. The Islamic practice, still in use today, is to
protect sewn gatherings of pages with thin wallet-type covers of
leather, sometimes stiffened with cardboard, pasted to the spines.
Often a fabric liner is inserted between the spine and leather to reinforce the hinge. No cords are used in the sewing to stiffen the
spine, support the gatherings or to fasten the boards. The flap extending from one cover around the fore-edge and tucking into the
other cover is a distinctive feature. This Islamic style culminated
in the great school of binding in Persia in the fifteenth century,
which in turn greatly influenced European craftsmen.

Far Eastern civilizations developed independently their own
variation of the codex: the orihon, which is still in use in China
and Japan. To avoid the clumsiness of rolled documents, Asiatic
calligraphers wrote in short lines along the horizontal axis of strips
of writing material, grouping words in about the same way as in
modern books. The lengthy strips were folded accordion fashion
(making pages that could be flipped over with the fingertip) and

these pleated sheets were then stabbed along one edge and laced
between protective covers of heavy paper or cardboard. They were
easy to handle and shelve, opened easily, could be identified on the
spine, and the covers invited decoration. The chief disadvantage
was the waste of writing surface on the reverse of each page,
which was unusable because of the accordion folding and sewing.
Today Chinese and Japanese publishers, in addition to making books
which in form and style are very similar to ours, have developed
a compromise between the Western style and the orihon. The
sheets of paper are printed on both sides, gathered into bundles,
stabbed along one edge and tightly laced between protective covers.
No adhesive is used on the spine or to fasten the covers to the
book. The result resembles the orihon in appearance, but provides
the maximum available printing surface.

     During the development of the book as we know it, decora-
tion has always kept pace with advances in binding techqnique. Gold
and silversmiths, enamelers, jewelers, ivory carvers, and wood
carvers vied with leather workers to ornament the covers of books.
Pride of ownership, as well as the desire of craftsmen to demon-
strate their skills, resulted in a wide variety of adornments. Many
of the very early books still in existence reflect the Byzantine influence by their heavy ornamentation in gold, silver and precious
stones. The decorations on monastic bindings were often ornate re-
ligious symbols. It is interesting to note, however, that ostenta-
tious decoration was not universally accepted. Saint Jerome, for
one, criticized sumptuously decorated books and their owners with
this comment, "Your books are covered with precious stones and
Christ died naked before the gate of his temple." Nevertheless,
when the circumstances of the owners permitted, lavish decoration
was often applied. In Notatia Dignitatum Imperri (circa 450 A.D.)
there are descriptions of volumes of the Emperor's instructions
bound in brightly colored leather and ornamented with the sovereign's
portrait. The Carolingian influence is reflected in the few remaining examples of the ninth to eleventh-century French books which
were often covered with velvet and studded with pearls, gold nails
and rubies as well as with tooled leather. Much of the elaborate

book decoration during the later Middle Ages resulted from new
skills brought back by the Crusaders.   It was also at that time
that the art of enameling was introduced into Western Europe from
Persia through Constantinople.

Although most Celtic book decoration was fairly simple,
some volumes belonging to parish churches were kept in elaborate
reliquaries.   The ornamentation on these shrines (cumdachs) more
than compensated for the plain covers on the books.   Meanwhile,
across the Irish Sea, the English style of bookmaking, which emphasized strength and durability, was coming to the fore.   The English, rather than emphasizing plainness, made use of blind stamping (i.e. designs impressed into moist leather with warm tools).

Islamic book decoration was developed from the highly skilled
leather crafts of Christian Syria and Egypt.   In their period of
greatness, (600 to 1200 A.D.) the Mohammedan invaders carried
their skills and crafts into Europe by way of Spain and Sicily.   Islamic ornamentation, until artistic leadership passed to Persia at
the beginning of the fifteenth century, was austerely geometric.
In Persia elaborate decoration was deemed more suitable to the refined sensuousness of their luxurious and courtly life.   Craftsmen
in Herat developed the techniques for exquisite filigree work, painted landscapes, all-over gilding and inlaying that spread eastward
into India and west through Venice into Europe.

Concurrent with the movement of people and goods in the
Middle Ages, came the inevitable migration of the enemies of
books.   Bookworms and fungi thrived in all the temperate climates
bordering the Mediterranean and were not uncommon even in the
colder countries to the north.   Librarians joined forces to combat
the enemy.   A thirteenth-century manuscript, "Remedium Contra
Vermes Librarum," was widely circulated.   In 993 A.D., Sabur
ibn-Ardashir's librarians in Bagdad used chemical in an attempt to
control termites.   At a very early date the Chinese were using
"huang-neih," an extract from the seeds of the cork tree, to ward
off insects and Chinese law required that this extract be an ingredient in all paper manufactured in the kingdom.   In 1221, after papermaking had been established in southern Europe, the Holy Roman

Emperor, Frederick II, because of the disastrous effects of moisture and insects on the new material, decreed that all new Acts
had to be transcribed on parchment or, if originally on paper, be
transferred to parchment within two years. Cedar oil was a widely used insect repellent and, for extra protection, volumes smeared
with cedar oil were stored in tightly covered jars. Other early insecticides and protective devices were alum, chests of cypress
wood, clay daubing, camphor, pepper, cloves and clove oil, oil of
eucalyptus, musk and red myrrh. Most were of little value, but
the fact that all these and many others were tried as insect repellents indicates that early librarians were acutely aware of the importance of conservation and made intelligent efforts in that direction. As early as the fourth century A.D., in the first organized
Christian monastic community (at Tabenna in Egypt), the concern
for books was so great that its founder, Saint Pachomius, made
book preservation one of the cardinal rules of his organization.

     Wear and tear from normal use was also a problem. To
resist abrasion, heavy books, which were normally shelved on their
sides and often on top of each other, were fitted with metal bosses
on the corners and sometimes in the center of each cover. Fore-
edge clasps and ties were used to keep the books tightly closed.
These fastenings prevented dust and dirt from sifting between the
pages and kept moisture out, thus helping to reduce cockling. The
leather flaps on Islamic bindings served the same purpose. To protect their elaborate, costly and delicate covers, French bookbinders
made wrappers (chemises) of leather, silk or sandalwood. The
Celts across the sea, where living was more austere, gave their
books hard use. Owned mostly by churches and often loaned to
traveling friars, they were probably exposed to the elements as often as they were under a roof. For protection against dirt, moisture and the rigors of traveling, the churches had some of their
volumes bound as "girdle books." These were unusual in that the
leather covers extended about a foot beyond the fore-edge of the
boards and were cut and sewn so that they could be tied in a knot
for convenient fastening to a traveler's belt. The Celts also made
use of "polaires," which were stout cowhide "satchels" with straps

long enough to sling over one's shoulder or hang from a peg at
night. These seem to have originated in the East, coming to Ireland through Gaul.

During the Middle Ages and the Renaissance, in a world
where communication was slow and the time and distance between
centers of learning was great, there was continuous but very gradual improvement in bookmaking, quality of materials and decorative
techniques. Craft leadership passed from one place to another as
cultural, political and economic conditions changed. By the end of
the Middle Ages the European book had come to be essentially
sewn parchment pages, protected by wooden boards that were covered or partially covered with leather or vellum. Backs were flat
and were without decoration or lettering, but the sides were often
stamped and variously decorated. Ties of leather thongs were used
as often as edge clasps. Whereas hides were used for heavy book
coverings, on smaller books the covers were often parchment or
doeskin, devoid of all decoration. Sometimes these light skins were
used as limp covers without boards.

Paper boards came into use early in the sixteenth century
along with the occasional introduction of paper as a covering material on smaller books. By this time, calf was almost the univer-
sal book covering because of its suitability for blind tooling, which
had become the vogue. It was sometimes colored bright red as a
change from the monotonous brown.

The trend in the fifteenth and sixteenth centuries was to smaller books (the influence of printing) and as librarians acquired more
of them, they were stood on end on library shelves to utilize better
the available space. This established a requirement for identification of the book elsewhere than on the sides. At first titles and
authors were inked or painted on the fore-edges of the pages of
text, but soon it was general practice to letter and decorate the
spines. Rounding and backing of spines, originally devised for
strength and to accommodate the boards, also provided more suitable surfaces for lettering and decoration. Edge gilding was decorative, but of equal importance was the fact that it facilitated
cleaning of the top edges of standing books and helped to keep dust

and dirt from falling between the pages.

Gold tooling (gilding), with or without blind tooling, appeared on the scene in the 1500's and had become quite sophisticated by the 1600's. It was also about this time that the usefulness of goatskin and pigskin for quality book covering began to be appreciated. Goatskin was popular with craftsmen for inlaying and they began to turn out beautifully decorated books using a combination of inlaying and gilding. Pigskin was most popular in Germany where it was usually used over sturdy wooden boards and decorated by blind stamping. White pigskin on old books is often confused with alum tawed skin which was prepared by an entirely different process. (See Chapter II.)

The changes in decoration over the past three hundred years have faithfully reflected the changes and refinements in national tastes. Colored labels first appeared on the spines of books in the 1600's. Silk headbands, marbled papers, paste papers and woodblock printed papers were all in use before 1700. One of the most significant innovations in the seventeenth century was the use of paper sides with leather spines in lieu of all-leather coverings on book boards. In France, at this time, lavishly tooled rich red morocco was very popular, although morocco in other colors had begun to appear.

In the eighteenth century the use of decorated paper for interior and exterior construction became firmly established. Hollow backs made their appearance as did the first "publishers' bindings," which were almost always solid colored paper covers over light weight paper boards and flimsy sewing. The trend toward cost cutting by the use of cheaper materials and shortcuts in workmanship had begun.

In retrospect, up until the beginning of the industrial revolution, the most significant events in the development of the book as we commonly regard it were:

    a. The evolution of the codex book form in the beginning of the Christian era.

    b. The impetus given to bookmaking by the introduction of paper into Europe at the end of the Middle

Ages.

    c. The printing of books from movable type.

Each had a profound affect on the making of books and simplified some conservation problems while introducing others.

    After the adoption of the codex, with its simplification of handling and storage, the general trend in conservation was for the better. Medieval books written on parchment, sewn on vellum cords, laced to wooden boards and covered with tough leather or vellum were reasonably resistant to all of their enemies except man. Parchment and vellum could be cockled and mildewed by exposure to moisture, but with reasonable care this could be controlled. These materials were relatively immune to insects. Oak and other hard woods were not termite-proof, but wooden book boards managed to stand up quite well for hundreds of years. Vegetable tanned and alum tawed skins lasted for centuries.

    The advent of paper for bookmaking reduced cost, increased the availability of writing materials and simplified the work of scribes and bookbinders. At the same time, when dampness and unsanitary conditions were the rule rather than the exception, this new material, extremely vulnerable to the ravages of insects and fungi, greatly reduced the average life expectancy of books. The Museum of the Istituto di Patologia del Libro in Rome has on display many early publications with relatively sound leather and vellum covers, but in which the paper contents are either shredded by insects or pulped by mildew.

    With the great increase in the number of books subsequent to the invention of printing, there was a corresponding increase in the problems of caring for them. By this time, however, librarians and collectors were well aware of the disastrous effects of dampness and the importance of warding off insect infestations. They recognized the importance of regular cleaning, frequent airing and drying by limited exposure to sunlight; but other than that, the remedies for book deterioration were few and ineffectual. In the eighteenth century learned societies and universities were offering prizes for practical solutions to the insect problem. In 1774

Dr. Johann Hermann was recognized by the Royal Society of Göt-
tingen for his identification of insects injurious to books and for his
determination of the parts of books most susceptible to the insects
identified and how to repel and kill these insects. By the late nineteenth century the reasons for book deterioration, with the exception of acid in paper and leather, had been quite thoroughly identified (see Blades--The Enemies of Books) but it was not until well
into the twentieth century that truly effective protective and curative
measures began to appear.

The many changes in technology during the industrial revolution made a great impact on the bookbinding craft. Until about
1800, hand binders, without compromising their traditional high
standards of quality and workmanship, could easily bind all the
books printed. After that time bookbinders, in order to meet the
workload and the competition forced upon them by mechanization,
were forced to mechanize their own shops, to cut corners in workmanship and to economize on materials. In all fairness, however,
it cannot be denied that this has been all to the good except from
the point of view of conservation. Fine binding continued, but the
emphasis in the larger binderies was on labor-saving machinery in
order to meet the ever increasing demand. Librarians and collectors were pleased with the many inexpensive, attractively decorated
books on the market and they were all blissfully unaware that the
preservation of these same books would be the despair of later custodians. The fact that so many books made and bound in the nineteenth and twentieth centuries soon fell apart can only be attributed
to the adoption by the craft of machinery and manufacturing techniques which speeded production, cut costs and improved marketabil-
ity at the cost of quality.

It began as early as 1774 when Karl William Scheele, a Swedish apothecary, discovered chlorine, which, within a short time, was
being used for bleaching paper. This made possible the use in high
cost paper of dirty rags that previously could only be used for cheap
stock. However, all too frequently the residual chlorine bleaching
compounds were not washed out of the finished product. This accounts, in large part, for the situation often encountered by librari-

ans today in which late 18th century book pages made of rag paper
and supposedly long lasting and durable have become acid and brittle.

Early in the 1820's, as an economy measure, some paper
makers began to add rosin size to their paper pulp during the beating operation (i.e., engine sizing) to eliminate the necessity for the
hand dipped gelatin sizing of finished sheets. Rosin is a good size
in that it reduces the absorbency of paper, as does gelatin, but it
adds nothing to paper strength and accounts for much of the brittle
brown-stained paper that occurs in nineteenth and twentieth century
books.

About 1775 tree calfing was introduced as a book cover decoration. Originating in Holland, the fad spread rapidly throughout
Europe and across the sea to America. The treatment to achieve
the tree-like patterns on leather was discovered quite by accident
and utilizes the natural outward warping of book boards before the
linings and end papers are pasted down. When book boards so
warped are tilted so that the heads are higher than the tails, water
sprinkled on them will flow in rivulets towards the center and the
rivulets will join in larger streams converging in a central flow
near the bottom edge. The design is like the trunk and branches
of a tree. If iron sulphate and salts of tartar are then sprinkled
on the covers, a chemical reaction will take place, biting into the
leather where it is wet and forming a permanent pattern. While
tree calfing is pleasing to the eye, the iron and potassium salts introduced into the leather, even in minute amounts, sooner or later
break down into acid. There are many examples of tree calf bindings on which the leather does not appear to have been affected but
they are almost all of relatively recent date. There are many
more examples of earlier vintage in which the leather is disfigured
by "pock marks" and is deteriorated to the point where it is useless as a protective covering.

In the 1800's burgeoning new industries using steam for
power created a heretofore unknown problem for librarians. Sulphur dioxide, a major ingredient in coal smoke, penetrated the in-
nermost recesses of urban library buildings, where it was absorbed

by the leather book covers. Once absorbed, the sulphur dioxide
was eventually converted into sulphuric acid, which destroyed the
leather fibers and turned the covers into the powdery nuisances so
often seen on old books today.

Because of the ever increasing requirement for paper, it
was soon necessary to find and use fibers other than linen and cotton for paper pulp. Ground wood, because of its low cost and
abundance, was soon in general use. It was a disastrous development. Paper made from "ground wood" pulp has a high lignin content. This complex organic acid soon attacks paper, causing it to
darken and become exceedingly brittle. Rare is the library today
where there are not hundreds, even thousands, of books in which
the paper is not safe to handle because it was made of ground wood.
Even "chemical wood" pulp is not entirely satisfactory for book paper because all too frequently the chemicals used in removing the
lignin and natural resins in the manufacturing process are themselves not removed. It was not until eight years ago that researchers developed a formula for making durable wood pulp book paper
with a long life expectancy.

For hundreds of years prior to the nineteenth century the
manufacture of leather had remained almost unchanged. It took
months to convert an animal's skin into leather but the finished product was supple, tough, handsome to look at, and above all, lasting
and durable. During the 1800's the time to convert skins to leather
was reduced from months to days. As a result of this "improvement," the useful life of leather book covers was reduced from centuries to months.

Michael Faraday studied the causes of leather deterioration
as early as 1843. Although the problem had been investigated several times since, it was not until about 1930 that it was completely understood. At that time R. Faraday Innes of the British Leather Manufacturers' Research Association began a series of studies
on the mechanism and prevention of decay in leather. His findings
made possible the manufacture of vegetable tanned leather that is
highly resistant to acid decay. The British Museum, using Innes'
data, developed procedures for the use of potassium lactate to de-

acidify and protect book covers from decay by sulphuric acid.
Paradoxically, although acid resistant leather is now available to
the book trade, it is rarely used except by specialty hand binders.

An interesting sidelight to some studies of leather deterioration by the Royal Society of Arts in 1901 was the conclusion that
an important factor contributing to early deterioration of book covers was that book binders, in order to obtain neatness and to facilitate gilding, were paring the leather excessively. The leather applied to many books was so thin that in a very short time, and
with only routine handling, the edges and corners were worn through,
the joints split and headcaps torn off.

Sheepskin, never very durable, came into wide use in the
1800's as a cheap covering material for law books and for circulating library books. Manufacturers began to copy good but expensive
goatskin by artificially graining and coloring sheepskin. The imitations were difficult to detect short of careful examination in a
laboratory. This subterfuge was probably encouraged by the fact
that Russia, an artificially grained cowhide, had been popular with
binders and collectors for almost a hundred years.

As part of the industrial upheaval, the almost complete
mechanization of bookbinding was inevitable and should not be deplored. Without the assistance of machinery, binders could never
have kept pace with the ever increasing number of books coming
from the printers, nor would it have been possible to keep costs
within reason. The first bookbinding machine was a rolling press
introduced in 1827 to compress folded gatherings of pages before
sewing. Since then one machine has followed another until today
folding, pressing, sewing, rounding and backing, gluing, cutting,
trimming, making covers, gold stamping, fastening the covers to
the book and even pasting down the end sheets is all done by machinery. However, there has been a price to pay. Machine sewn
books are just not as strong as hand sewn books. Machine sewn
books cannot be tightly laced to protective boards. A casing of
paper or cloth over cheap cardboard fastened to the spine of a book
with flimsy cheesecloth hinges is hardly more than a dust cover.
Even the better grades of chemically treated wood pulp paper can

be expected to last only a decade or two.

In retrospect, one must conclude that the Industrial Revolution, instead of destroying an ancient craft, created a new industry. Commercial bookbinding should be considered as separate and distinct from extra binding, which is the binding of books by hand in accordance with the traditional techniques of the craft, using the finest of materials and with the highest standards of quality and workmanship. There will always be a requirement for fine hand binding and for the skillful repair and restoration of rare and valuable library materials.

Chapter II
The Nature of Library Materials

Neglect accounts for as many irreparably lost volumes as does loss by natural causes. This chapter provides general information about the nature of library materials and suggests avenues for further study.

CLAY--Pure clay is almost indestructible. When oven baked, or hardened in the sun, it will withstand hard usage indefinitely. Its durability is due to the fact that the principle ingredient in the compound is the inert mineral kaolin (alumina, silica and water). Other ingredients are small amounts of iron, lime, magnesia, soda and potash. The material is plastic when wet because it is made up of minute hexagonal plates which slide over each other when kneaded. When used for brick books by the ancient Assyrians, clay was first moistened then kneaded into dough, shaped by hand, inscribed with a stylus while still soft and finally hardened.

PAPYRUS--This writing material made from the marrow of the papyrus plant was smooth enough when new to be written on with the Egyptian's raveled fiber brush pen. It took their thin carbon black ink and red iron oxide ink well and retained the pigments for long periods of time. To make sheets of papyrus the Egyptians cut the stalks of the plant to lengths of about sixteen inches, split them lengthwise to remove the marrow and split the marrow into thin strips which were laid side by side to form one ply of a sheet. A second ply was laid over the first with the strips at right angles to the first layer. The sheets were then saturated with a gum solution, pressed until dry and polished by rubbing with a bone or with ivory. There were several grades of papyrus, depending upon the part of the plant stalk used and the skill of the makers. Papyrus, being a laminated product bonded by an adhesive, is not paper, which, by definition, is made of shredded and matted vegetable fibers without an adhesive bonding agent.

18

BARK--The Latin word for book, _liber_, is derived from the Latin for inner bark. The material is the layers of tissue surrounding the woody cylinders of trees and shrubs. It is used mainly in tanning, medicine and cookery. Bark (that of birch and the inner bark of some other trees) was used almost universally as a writing surface at one time or another. In the seventeenth century letters were often sent to Europe and America on birch bark. Bark books were common in Central Asia and the Far East until recent times. The epidermis, or cork layer, of most trees becomes weather beaten, seamed, cracked and dark as a tree grows, but birch bark remains light in color and smooth. Bark is vulnerable to dampness and when wet the leaves of bark books stick together and often roll up and become extremely fragile. When dried after being wet, the leaves of bark books and manuscripts split and powder easily when handled.

PALM LEAVES--The epidermis of a palm leaf consists of cells with rather thick walls. When written on with a stylus the point cuts through the epidermis. To accentuate such writing, scribes rubbed the surface of the marked leaf with a mixture of lampblack and oil, either du-du-tel, which is pressed from the fruits of the heart pea, or dummala-tel, distilled from fossil resin. The blacking filled the scars left by the stylus and the oil penetrating into the interior through the scars lubricated and preserved the leaves. In addition to palm the leaves of the olive, talipot, aloe and palmyra trees have at one time or another been used for writing. When desiccated with age these leaves become brittle and crumble easily.

WOOD--In ancient China, before the invention of paper, wood was second only to silk as a writing material. It has been popular throughout history. According to Chaucer, wooden tablet books were still in use in England in the fourteenth century. Wood is the compact tissue that constitutes the main part of the trunks, branches and roots of trees and shrubs. The plant cells of hard woods are thick walled and closely packed together. Soft woods have thin walled, loosely packed cells. Wood is not permanent (neither is iron), but if properly prepared and reasonably cared for, it will last for centuries. Its most perishable part is the sapwood between the bark of a tree and the interior of the stem. This is a soft spongy mass containing fermentable saps which, if not removed, allow dampness to penetrate very easily. Rot develops and worms and insects appear in the sapwood and penetrate the whole substance. Chemical preservatives are effective and desirable for industrially used wood. However, removal of the sapwood and thorough drying is all that is required for wood used for book boards, book boxes, library shelves and cabinets. Hard wood is preferable to the softer varieties.

IVORY--Ivory has always been a favorite medium for writing and decoration because of the fineness of its grain, warm tone, the polish it easily acquires, its incorruptibility and its adaptability to carving and writing. Ivory is the substance of the tusks of elephants, although the tusks of other animals are sometimes used. These are greatly enlarged teeth formed of vertical plates of dental bone, separately covered by enamel and welded together by a cement. It is almost industructible, but the ink on ivory can be worn off.

BONE--This compact, hard, chemically complex material is used in the arts for decorative and writing purposes. Part of its commercial importance is the fact that it is one of the raw materials for gelatin and glue. It is essentially an organic substance infiltrated with mineral salts. The former makes it tough and the latter makes it hard. The principle organic ingredient is collagen and the inorganic salts are those of calcium and magnesium. When traces of fat are eliminated and the water content of bone is removed by drying, it can be polished, carved, engraved, written upon or painted and the finished product will last almost indefinitely. Whalemen's scrimshaw is a good example of the suitability of bone for the arts and crafts.

STONE--Sandstones are grains of sand cemented together by silica, iron oxide and carbonate of lime. Silica sandstones are most durable--those of iron oxide and lime carbonate are easier to work. Slates are hardened clays. All sandstones and slates absorb water, making them vulnerable to damage by freezing. Lime-

stones and marbles are carbonates of lime and differ only in qual-
ity--not in chemical composition.   Marbles are harder and take a
high polish, but are difficult to carve.   Limestones are deteriorated chiefly by chemical impurities in the air and in rain.   Gran-
ites are of great hardness and strength and suffer little from chemical action, but are susceptible to damage by temperature changes.

BRASS, COPPER, BRONZE AND LEAD--Metals have been
used by man for recording as well as decoration ever since his
emergence from the Stone Age.   The Bible (Job 19:24) mentions the
use of lead in preserving writings and the works of Hesiod (Greece,
776 B.C.) are supposed to have been preserved on lead tablets.
Recording historical facts on metal has been commonplace since
Roman times.   Lead is soft and soon tarnishes when exposed to
air, but suffers less than most metals from age and weather.   Copper is an abundant element that is malleable and ductile and can
easily be hammered into sheets.   It does not oxidize readily under
ordinary conditions, but becomes tarnished with a coating of oxide
that resists the subsequent deteriorative action of water and air.
Brasses (alloys of copper and zinc) are equally resistant to corrosion and are more suitable for casting.   Bronzes, mixtures of copper and tin, are often badly corroded when recovered from the
earth, but can be restored to almost their original state by careful
treatment with suitable chemicals.

SKIN--Animal skin is a continuous membrane of fibrous tissue.   The outside has sweat glands and hair follicles which determine the grain.   The flesh side is lined with fat, muscles and
blood vessels.   The variation in physical structure of the skins of
various animals influences their quality for utilitarian purposes.
The inner, or true skin (the corium), is composed of protein fibers
made up of a complicated chain structure of atoms and molecules.
The principle protein fiber is collagen which, when boiled in water,
turns to glue.   Because of its chemical nature, the skin of a
slaughtered animal rapidly putrefies unless steps are taken to preserve it.   Skins are preserved either by tanning (leather), treatment with lime (parchment and vellum), or treatment with alum
(tawed skins).   Even in prehistoric times man knew how to utilize

animal hides and skin preservation was a well established craft in
early Egypt. Whether the Nile dwellers tawed or tanned their skins
is hard to say because of the desiccated condition of these artifacts
when found in tombs.

PARCHMENT AND VELLUM--The process for making parchment and vellum is supposed to have been developed about 190 B.C.
at Pergamum in Asia Minor. It is said to have been developed at
the behest of Emperor Eumenes II, founder of a 200,000 volume library, to provide a substitute for papyrus, which had been denied
him by Egypt. The terms parchment and vellum are often used in-
terchangeably, which is an error. True vellum is the skin of a
young, usually not over six weeks old, calf which has been cleaned
of adhering flesh, hair, fat and muscle, preserved by soaking in a
lime solution, and carefully scraped and polished. Parchment is
ordinarily made from the skins of sheep, ewes, or lambs, but the
skins of other animals are sometimes used. Like vellum, parchment is limed for preservation. It costs more to produce vellum
than parchment, but the finished product is more delicate, has more
polish, shining whiteness and semitransparent beauty. Both vellum
and parchment are strong and long wearing, but they cockle when
damp, become horny when too dry, are difficult to work and are
seldom ornamented. Vellum has always been the choice of craftsmen for luxurious manuscripts and for expensive bindings. Parchment was used for bindings and manuscripts of lesser quality.

TAWED SKINS--Probably the most durable book covering material known is alum tawed skin. It is often seen on seventeenth
and eighteenth-century books and mistakenly called vellum or "vel-
lumized" pigskin. Tawed skins are preserved in solutions of alum
and salt. The result is a tough, flexible, white "leathery" substance which is remarkably suited for blind tooled decoration.
Alum tawed pigskin over oak boards was particularly popular in
Germany. Many such bindings, now hundreds of years old, are
still in almost perfect condition. The impressions made on them
by delicate rolls and stamps still show marvelous definition on the
hard, white surfaces even after centuries of handling. Tawed
leather is now used primarily in glove making and to a very minor

extent in hand binding.

LEATHER--Until the nineteenth century the most common
covering for books was animal skin preserved by tanning after the
hair and flesh were removed. For two thousand years or more
"vegetable tanned" leather was made by infusing skins with extracts
of the bark of trees, usually oak, sumac or hemlock. The chemicals in the bark solutions (tannins) combined with the protein fibers
of the skins, replacing the water and modifying the chains of molecules. This changed the skin to leather, with greatly superior
qualities of wear, water resistance and flexibility. The complete
process consisted of washing the hides; loosening the hair in lime
pits; scraping off the epidermis, hair and flesh; soaking in bark solutions; and, finally, drying and finishing, coloring, polishing and
graining, etc. The process took months but the finished product
was supple, tough, long wearing and handsome. Of even more importance these vegetable tanned leathers were highly resistant to decay and acid. This was because certain water-soluble organic
salts were deposited in the leather in the tanning process. These
salts, called "non-tans," were naturally resistant to atmospheric
pollutants.

In the nineteenth century tanners, because of competition and
the demand for a greater variety of colors, more even hues and
better matching of shades, initiated practices which shortened the
leather making process from months to days and which, in addition
to cutting costs, made it possible to provide a whole rainbow of
colors. As early as 1813 sulphuric and acetic acids were being
used in the pretanning process of cleaning, dehairing, etc., and by
1875 skins, after the bark infusion, were being "degreased" with
dilute acid so that they could be colored with aniline dyes. These
acids dissolved the non-tans in the leather and in their stead left
dangerous salts which immediately began to destroy the fibers, reducing them in a few years to the useless coverings on so many of
the books standing on library shelves today. Even if tanners had
realized what they were doing and had taken steps to rinse out all
of the acids used in the pretanning and degreasing operations, it
would not have helped. With the non-tans gone, the leather would

have had no protection from atmospheric sulphur dioxide and the result would have been the same--powdered leather, annoying to handle, unpleasant to look at and absolutely no protection for the book.

Within the past fifty years chrome tanning (also called chemical tanning) has become industrially important. In this process the skins are preserved by a complex series of chemical reactions involving the use of sulphuric acid, glucose, sodium thiosulphate, soda ash and chrome salts. It makes a good quality, durable leather that is highly suitable for boots and shoes, ladies' purses and many other uses, but because of its stiffness it is completely unsuitable for book work. Perhaps one day leather chemists will find a way to make chrome leather supple.

BOOKBINDING LEATHERS--Up to the end of the eighteenth century calf was used for bindings more commonly than any other leather. It was abundant, easy to decorate and it mellowed with age to a rich mahogany brown. Vegetable tanned calf is still one of the most satisfactory skins for fine bindings.

Russia was an artificially grained cowhide (sometimes calf) tanned with willow bark and scented with birch oil. It was commonly diced by all-over diagonal rulings on the outer surface. Although it was a popular material for many years, it was not as durable as calf.

The cowhide often sold today as "calf" sometimes has the appearance of true calf, but is inferior due to the fact that the hard, thick hides are split twice and sometimes three times before finishing them for book work and for other decorative purposes.

Pigskin, because of its thickness and coarse grain, is most suitable for large books. ‑It wears well and remains strong even after centuries of use. Pigskin is often counterfeited by embossing cheap cowhide, but the forgery can be easily detected because the bristle holes in real pigskin go right through the skin, whereas in the imitation they barely penetrate the surface.

Goatskin, also known as morocco, niger, cape, levant or persian, is the finest of all leather for bookbinding. These small skins are soft but strong, and when vegetable tanned they last for centuries. They color beautifully and have a distinctive texture identified by ridges and furrows in the grain and hair dots in groups all over the surface. Imitation goatskin, made from split cowhide and sheepskin, is inferior in quality and appearance. Straight grained goatskin is made by rolling damp skins until all the furrows in the grain run in the same direction. Crushed goatskin is just that--skins in which the ridges have been flattened by ironing, rolling or pressure.

Next to calf, sheepskin has been a favorite for bookbinding because it was always available and, above all, cheap. Until the introduction of machine made cloth and paper covered books a hundred and thirty years ago, plain sheepskin was the low cost bookbinding material in common use. It is soft and does not wear well and should never have been used for fine binding. Because of similar size and thickness, sheepskin is often worked up to imitate goatskin. These imitations, when new, can deceive even the experts, but in the course of time the artificial texture flattens out and the forgery is exposed. Roan is a low grade sheepskin tanned with sumac and colored to imitate ungrained morocco. Basil is a heavy bark-tanned sheepskin. It is sometimes smooth surfaced but is often embossed with a grain to imitate either goatskin or Russia. Skiver is a cheap, soft material made of the grain side of split sheepskin. It is usually tanned in sumac and dyed and embossed to imitate expensive leathers.

Other skins that have been used for book coverings are kangaroo; sealskin; sea otter; deer skin; shagreen (skins of wild asses, horses and camels prepared in Russia and the East and characterized by small round granulations on the surface); sharkskin (sometimes also called shagreen because of the similarity of its grain to the Russian product); horsehides and even human skin. None are as satisfactory as true calf, goat or pigskin. Suede, sometimes used decoratively on books, is the French word for Swedish, where the velvety material is supposed to have originated. Suede is made by buffing the flesh or grain side of leather on an abrasive wheel to raise the fine nap. Suede calf, the skin of a very young calf buffed on the flesh side, is the best suede leather for fineness and durability.

PAPER--Paper is a thin tissue of any fibrous material, the individual fibers of which, after being separated mechanically and suspended in water, are then matted into sheets by dipping screens into the water suspension and lifting the fibers out. Paper can be made from animal fibers (wool, fur, hair, silk), mineral fibers (asbestos), synthetics (rayon, nylon, glass, etc.) and even ceramics, stainless steel and other metals, but it is normally made from plant fibers (cotton, esparto, straw, wood, flax, hemp, bamboo, jute and many other reeds). The cells of plant fibers are rich in cellulose, the most important ingredient in paper. Cellulose, a white substance insoluble in water and having a high tensile strength, is composed of hydrogen, carbon and oxygen. Other ingredients in plant fibers are sugar, starch, carbohydrates and lignin. Lignin is a very complicated organic acid surrounding and impregnating the fibers. It occurs only in living cells and is vulnerable to oxidizing agents, a fact which is very important in the manufacture of paper and from the point of view of conservation. The plant fibers are microscopically small units, which, because of their complexity, can be given controlled treatment which ultimately determines the physical characteristics of the finished paper (tearing, handling, absorbency, porosity and color).

In living cells the fibers are hollow and filled with protoplasm. In the paper making process the cell walls collapse and the tubes become flat ribbons. The strength of a paper sheet is determined by the strength of its fibers. The bonding power is in the cellulose itself (fabrillation). Fabrilles are hair-like strands which separate from the cell walls when the fibers are soaked and beaten in the pulping process. It is the interlocking of these fabrilles when the pulp is matted, plus the surface tension between the fiber ribbons, that causes the paper to hold together.

The cellulose fibers in paper are subject to damage by oxidation, by action of acids and alkalies and by exposure to sunlight or artificial light.

Paper can be classified according to the sources of the fibers from which it is made. One such arrangement is:

The cotton group ... Cotton, flax, ramie, hemp.
The grass group ... Esparto, straw, bamboo.
The rope group ... Used only for rough paper in the
East.
The wood group ... Ground wood pulp, which is simply
macerated wood chips; and chemical
wood pulp in which the intercellulose
matter in ground wood fibers has
been considerably dissolved, leaving
much purer cellulose.

In each of these categories the chemical characteristics of
the fibers are constant, but the other characteristics vary considerably.   Cotton group papers are of high quality and are strong
and stable.   Wood group papers, which include most of the papers
made today, cover the complete spectrum of quality; most of them,
however, are subject to early deterioration.

The first paper, according to Dard Hunter, the foremost authority on the subject, was a direct result of ancient Chinese economy and inventiveness.   Before the time of Christ, Eastern scribes
were making books and scrolls of cloth.   To utilize the waste material from cutting and trimming the cloth, Chinese artisans, applying an earlier knowledge of felt making, devised a way to pulp the
cloth scraps, making a slurry of the fibers and from it producing
crude sheets of paper.   To augment their rag pulp these ever practical people soon learned to mix shredded bark and hemp with
cloth.   By 105 A.D. the process was sufficiently perfected for one
Ts'ai Lun to report it to the Emperor.   Although Ts'ai Lun is often called the inventor of paper and 105 A.D. is given as the date
of his great discovery, both assumptions are open to question.
Such a monumental accomplishment was more probably achieved only after a great many years of trial and error.   To Ts'ai Lun,
however, should go the credit for recognizing its importance.

The knowledge of paper making spread to Korea and Japan
by 600, to Bagdad in 793, Damascus and Cairo in the tenth century,
Spain in 1151, Italy 1276, and England by 1494.   Russia, the Netherlands, Scotland and Hungary did not acquire the craft until well
into the sixteenth century and Scandinavia in the seventeenth.   William Rittenhouse set up the first North American paper mill in
Pennsylvania in 1690 a little more than a hundred years after paper

was first made by Europeans in Mexico.

From Ts'ai Lun's time until the present, the technique of
making paper by hand has changed very little. The precise methods used in various parts of the world differ somewhat and there
have been refinements in the design of vats, presses, drying cloths
and felts, macerating equipment, drying racks, etc., but it is safe
to say that a medieval paper maker would feel at home in a modern handmade paper mill and vice versa. The general procedure
has always been to make a pulp, dip a mold in the pulp and bring
it to the surface laden with the fibers, and mat the fibers by shaking as the water drains out of the mold. The newly formed wet
sheets are then laid in a pile and more water squeezed out before
drying the sheets on boards in the sun or by hanging them in a drying room. There is no other way to produce handmade paper.

As with so many other crafts, the introduction of machinery
for paper making was inevitable once the industrial revolution got
underway. Nicholas-Louis Robert invented the first practical machine for matting paper in 1798. Subsequent improvements in technology have been such that once logs enter a modern paper mill,
they are reduced to a pulp, cooked, treated with chemicals, picked
up in a continuous sheet on drums, colored, sized, dried and pack-
aged for delivery by a continuous, automated process. Today's requirement for paper is such that the demand can be met only by
using wood as the cellulose source. If the wood is reduced to a
pulp by grinding only, the yield is very high, but the lignin is retained (about 25% of the mass). Early breakdown of the lignin by
oxidation causes serious deterioration of the paper in a short time.
For better grades of wood pulp paper, the pulp is chemically
treated and bleached. Although removal of the lignin gives the paper longer life, the process may introduce other chemicals which,
in some cases, cause the breakdown of cellulose fibers. Alum,
which aids in the dispersal of plant fibers in the water slurry and
also precipitates rosin size on the fibers, is acid and is a common
cause of acidified machine-made book paper.

Modern machine-made paper is classified in terms of its
use. Those most frequently encountered by librarians are news-

print, book, text, cover, bond, offset and coated papers.

Newsprint is mostly machine-finished ground wood pulp.
It is not intended to last and it begins to deteriorate in a few
months. Book papers are made of inexpensive chemical wood pulp
in a wide range of weights and finishes. They are intended for
text books and others of short life expectancy. Text papers are
designed for high grade printing such as expensive books, booklets
and brochures. They are appreciated for their texture and attractive colors, and, because of rather stiff sizing, are better suited
for offset printing than for letterpress. Cover papers are similar
to text stock, but are heavier. As their classification denotes,
they are primarily for booklet covers and come in a wide range of
textures, colors and special finishes. Bond paper, commonly used
for letters and business forms, often shows up in libraries in typed
manuscripts. Cheap bond paper is made from wood sulphite pulp,
but the better grades have 25% to 100% rag content and a proportionally longer life expectancy. Offset papers are similar to book
and coated papers, but with additional sizing to resist the moisture
in offset printing. Their durability and life expectancy are the
same as that of non-offset paper made from the same pulp.

The introduction of the halftone process and the printing of
illustrations in color necessitated the development of china clay or
coated papers. The paper normally used for book work was not
smooth enough even when calendered and super-calendered for the
new printing processes. To get clear impressions china clay mixed
with barytes was added to the wet pulp. The resulting glossy,
smooth, glaring, white material was excellent for fine printing but
for bookbinders and librarians, it was a disaster. Although 10%
clay was enough for excellent illustrations and art work, these "art
papers" were all too often made with far higher percentages of
filler. As a result some are little more than sheets of clay supported by a skeleton of wood, straw or esparto fibers. This paper
is difficult to bind and being hygroscopic is readily damp stained.
Furthermore, it sticks together when stored in humid atmospheres
for any length of time.

Once the difference between the texture, surface and charac-

ter of handmade and machine-made paper is realized, the two can
rarely be confused. Although it is claimed that some machine-
made papers (mold made) have the quality and appearance of the
handmade product, there is no substitute for the strong, durable,
good-looking sheets made from pure cotton and linen rag pulp laid
on a vatman's mold.

In the last three decades paper technologists have made
great strides in improvement of the quality and appearance of machine-made paper. An event of particular significance to librarians
has been the development of a permanent/durable wood pulp paper
that is guaranteed to have a life span of hundreds of years. The
word permanent here stands for the property of paper to retain its
original characteristics. The word durable means resistance to deterioration by use. The term permanent/durable is a connotation
of quality in wood pulp paper in the same sense that all rag denotes
quality in handmade sheets.

In 1959, the Council on Library Resources, being concerned
about the generally unsatisfactory book paper used in the United
States, requested William J. Barrow at the Virginia State Library
to examine these papers from the point of view of permanence and
durability. His findings were discouraging. Ninety percent of the
paper had a life expectancy of less than fifty years and only one
percent could be considered durable. Mr. Barrow then undertook
to develop a formula that would produce paper with a life expectancy
equal to or better than the early rag paper. Since the use of rags
in modern paper making is economically unfeasible, he experimented with various wood pulps and found it possible to make a
permanent and durable product if the fibers were carefully selected
and washed and if all the acid ingredients, particularly alum rosin
size, were eliminated. Paper made according to Barrow's formula
is now commercially available at competitive prices. It has good
texture and appearance, good printing qualities and can be made in
a wide range of tones and weights.

Japanese handmade papers, considered by some to be the
finest in the world, are produced by craft techniques that have not
changed in hundreds of years. They are made by farmers as a

part-time occupation in remote mountain villages where there is a
plentiful supply of water and of natural vegetable fibers. Strength
and permanence are the chief characteristics of these sheets. We
have many well preserved specimens of thousand-year-old Japanese
paper. The most common vegetable fibers used are Gampi, a wild
mountain shrub; Kozo, a tough sinewy shrub of the mulberry family;
and Mitsumata. All are excellent for printing. Mitsumata papers
are noted for elegance and Kozo for toughness and both seem almost to improve with age. There is a wider choice of tones, finish, weight, texture and design in these papers than in those from
other sources. The most serious objection is that their surface becomes rubbed more readily than does that of European handmade
paper.

The so-called rice paper of the Orient is not a true paper
nor is it made from rice. This material, so well suited for Chinese paintings, is cut spirally from the pith of Formosa's (Taiwan's) fatsia papyrifera. The sheets of pith when first cut and
dried are quite brittle, but when saturated with water become tough
and somewhat pliable.

European handmade papers, although lacking the variety
available in those from the East, are generally excellent. Some of
these are being produced in mills that have been operating continuously for several hundred years. However, labor-saving appliances
have, by necessity, been incorporated in the traditional paper making process in the hand mills of Europe. Most of these mills still
use only pure rag pulp made from the finest linen and cotton rag.
The rags are cleaned by boiling followed by rinsing in clear water.
When bleach is used great care is exercised to eliminate residual
chlorine. Although there have been many refinements in the preparation of the pulp and in the later pressing and drying of the sheets,
there is still no substitute for the skill and dexterity of the vatman
in the actual forming of the paper. Finesse in scooping a portion
of the pulp out of the vat, tilting the mold to cause a wave to flow
across it to level the pulp, shaking the mold to set the fibers in
crisscross directions while draining off most of the water is something that is acquired only after a long apprenticeship. It is this

skill that imparts much of the extra quality to handmade paper, and which can not be duplicated by machines.

In addition to their greater strength European handmade papers have been shrunk naturally (not dried on heated cylinders) and their behavior when wet is more predictable. They are excellent for restoration of old volumes and for luxury printing, but are not generally suited for modern bookmaking. The sheets are not square and the rough deckled edges are awkward for printers. There is a disparity in thickness (even in the finest quality material) between sheets in the same run and sometimes even in the same sheet. Sizing in European hand mills is still done by passing the formed sheets through baths of heated animal gelatin and then drying them in a loft. Much paper is sized too heavily for dry printing. This is not too objectionable for hand printing because dampening the paper ever so slightly reduces the resistance of the paper to taking the ink.

For many reasons, including labor cost, the only sources of real handmade papers in the United States are the mills of "hobbyists" who, with great care and attention to detail, are able to make paper approaching in quality the best that has been made in the past. However, their output cannot begin to provide even a token amount of the fine paper needed by restorationists and fine printers.

Ancient American paper--Pre-Columbian craftsmen in Central and South America manufactured a vegetable-fiber writing material that resembled true paper, but was not. This hunn and amatl-paper was prepared from the inner bark of several species of fig trees. The bark was treated by cooking, laid in parallel strips, pressed and beaten and then sized with some kind of gum or starch. Finally the flattened sheets were given a thin white coating of lime or gesso. This process was also known in the Pacific Islands, Southeast Asia and parts of Africa. In some parts of Mexico today the craft is still practiced in the traditional way.

The tapa cloths (bark papers) of the Pacific Islands were the product of great skill; but when European cloth and paper became available the Islanders quickly abandoned making their own. Although in the same general category as papyrus and the early Amer-

ican hunn and amatl, the Polynesian technique for making tapa was
unique.   Each of the hundreds of island groups had its own form of
tools, its own specialized operation, and its own preference in design; but the general principles for the manufacture of the material
were the same from one end of the Pacific to the other.   In the
Tonga Group, for instance, the inner bark of the paper mulberry
was stripped from cut saplings, bleached in the sun, and then by
wetting and repeated beating and folding back over itself was
stretched in width from about three inches to eighteen inches and
shortened in length proportionally.   These small sheets were sometimes made into larger ones by pasting the edges together with
boiled arrowroot.   When this was done the joints were often almost
invisible.   This paper-like cloth (or cloth-like paper) was used only decoratively since writing was unknown in the South Pacific before the coming of the missionaries.

Decorated papers used for book coverings and end papers
fall into three categories: marbled, paste and printed.   Marbled
papers originated in the Near East in the fifteenth century and came
into use in Europe in the sixteenth century.   Hand marbling is done
today almost exactly as it was four hundred years ago.   Colors
are floated on the surface of a gelatinous size, patterns are made
in the floating colors by combing, raking, spattering or other means
and then a sheet of paper is floated momentarily on the size to
pick up the colors and pattern.   The combinations of hues and design obtainable are infinite and there are few things more handsome
than a sheet of fine rag paper marbled by hand in rich, warm colors.   Unfortunately cheap paper was often used in the 1800's.   The
results were decorative enough, but the paper did not last.

Early printed papers (sixteenth-century) were made by im-
pressing designs carved into pearwood blocks onto small sheets of
paper.   These papers were closely related to wallpaper and were
made in many designs and colors.   At first they were used for
household decoration, playing cards, boxes, etc., but later came
into limited use for book covers and end sheets.   The printing of
decorative paper has continued and the quality has constantly improved.   Many beautiful designs are available today, particularly

from Sweden and Italy. A variation of the early printed papers
were the Dutch gilt and flowered designs in the eighteenth century.
These, printed from patterns on wood blocks or metal plates, often
copied the design and texture of expensive fabrics. One well-known
type, particularly popular for end sheets in books, was impressed
in gold on smooth paper and favored pastoral scenes, leafy scrolls
and birds and animals.

Paste papers, very similar to those made by children in
kindergartens, were often made by early bookbinders in their own
shops. These "pulled" papers were made by applying colored paste
to the surfaces of two sheets of paper, placing them together face
to face and then pulling them apart. Variations in designs were obtained by rubbing the backs of the sheets when they were together
or placing string or other objects between the pasted sheets.
Combed paste papers were made by drawing a flat comb across the
surface of freshly pasted paper. Often the fingers were used to
whorl or spot the wet paste. Sometimes they were brushed to create patterns or sponges were used to get a stippled effect. Later
the colored paste was spattered onto dry paper from a brush. This
permitted the use of many colors on a single sheet. Later still
thin "runny" paste was applied generously to a sheet which was then
hung up to dry permitting the colors to run across each other for
decorative effect.

Printed paste papers were more professional and required
more elaborate equipment. In making these, colored paste was applied to a sheet of paper and then a metal plate or wood block impressed on it. When the block designs were cut in relief, the design forced the paste through the paper. With the intaglio plate the
smooth part picked up some of the paste from the sheet, thus leaving a design.

In the early nineteenth century heated embossing rollers were
used to make "moire" paper as a cheap substitute for the popular
but expensive silk covering material. Late in that century calendered marbled paper began to come off machines in Europe and
America. They were (and still are) usually done on paper of poor
quality that was made smooth and glossy by hot rollers. Cheap

machine-made marbled papers look just like that (cheap), but handsome decorative book papers can be printed on roll presses. Many end sheets in use today have been created by eminent artists and are excellent. The pictorial end sheets so often seen on twentieth century volumes, too, are usually the work of prominent artists. They are reproduced from the artist's drawing or painting in black and white or colors by conventional printing techniques. Photographic end papers can be attractive, but all too often are not.

FILM AND PHOTOGRAPHS--Motion picture and still films are thin transparent flexible sheets of cellulose acetate, cellulose nitrate or analogous material coated with a dispersion of light-sensitive chemicals in gelatin which after controlled exposure and subsequent processing, retain an image. Glass is sometimes used to support the emulsion. The chemistry of photography is complex but from the point of view of conservation it is important to know that film, while now usually fire-resistant, is sensitive to extremes of heat, cold, moisture and dryness. It is also easily damaged by improper handling. Its life expectancy, even with minimal handling, tends to be short from the archivist and librarian's viewpoint (i.e., twenty to thirty years). With proper processing and care they can be preserved indefinitely if not damaged by use. Photographic papers are high grade paper stock coated with emulsions which are either dispersions of finely divided silver halide particles in gelatin or color sensitive chemicals in gelatin. Properly processed photographs are free of active chemicals and when carefully stored in tight dust-proof containers in an atmosphere of optimum temperature and humidity should last for a great many years. Photographs, which because of improper processing have not been rid of all active chemicals, soon turn brown and what is worse, their images fade due to continuing chemical action in the gelatin coating.

AUDIO TAPES AND DISCS--The principle sound recording systems in use today are grooved patterns, magnetic patterns and photographic patterns. The bulk of sound recordings in libraries and archives are phonograph discs, magnetic tapes and motion picture sound tracks.

Phonograph records can be made of wax, cellulose nitrate

or acetate, shellac, polyvinyl chloride or styrene. The base of
magnetic tapes can be cellulose acetate, mylar, polyvinyl chloride,
paper or wire. The sound track of motion picture film is on the
same base as the pictures. All of the plastics used as a base are
high molecular weight organic compounds capable of being formed
by heat, pressure, the evaporation of a solvent or by the use of
plasticizers. All are thermoplastics, which means they are materials which repeatedly soften when heated and harden when chilled
and all are soluble in certain liquids.

Sound recordings are made for play-back quality with emphasis on low manufacturing cost. Long life has never been a primary
consideration. The short life expectancy and low resistance to degradation are properties "built into" sound recording devices at the
time of manufacture and even unusual care cannot extend the normally expected life of a disc or tape. Of course, good care can
reduce the probability of premature failure.

The quality of audio tapes and discs varies greatly depending upon quality control in manufacturing the basic resins or plastics and in the sources and quality of the raw materials. Variations in formula, contamination of materials in the factory, slight
variations in heat and pressure during production and innovations in
processing techniques all effect the finished product and it would be
unusual if these comparatively low cost discs and tapes did not differ widely between brands (and even within the same brand) in storage life and resistance to degradation. If they were made under
controls sufficiently rigid to achieve longer life and constant high
quality, their cost would probably be prohibitive.

What is of major importance to custodians is the fact that
plastics are susceptible to damage by environmental changes. Of
equal importance is the fact that this damage (chemical and physical changes within the plastic) which causes sound degradation is not
evidenced by visible changes in the appearance of the tapes and discs.

INK--India Ink, a simple suspension of lampblack in gum, was
used as early as 2500 B.C. It makes permanently indelible marks
on porous writing surfaces because the gum suspension penetrates
the material and the carbon becomes entrapped amongst the fibers.

Carbon ink was widely used for writing in the West until the nineteenth century and still is preferred for fine calligraphy. It has always been the favored writing fluid in the East. There it is prepared by the incomplete combustion of pine wood or oil. The soot
so formed is mixed with fish glue size, scented with musk or camphor; it is molded into sticks and then dried. These sticks are
dissolved in water when a supply of ink is required.

The gum arabic used in the manufacture of the Western variants of "India Ink" emulsifies the oils in the soot (carbon), gives
viscosity to the fluid, holds the carbon particles uniformly in suspension and acts as a binder to fasten the black particles to the
fibers of paper or the surface of vellum. After drying, the carbon
is unaffected by light or by other bleaching agents. Neither carbon
nor gum arabic is injurious to paper.

In about the seventh century iron gall ink came into use for
writing on vellum and parchment because carbon inks did not adhere
well to these materials. This ink was made by mixing copperas
(ferrous sulphate) with oak galls and water and after straining off
the extract, thickening it with gum arabic. When the ingredients
were combined in the proper amounts the pale ink resulting flowed
easily and penetrated deeply. After a few days it darkened to a
black insoluble compound that was difficult to bleach. Although the
early users did not understand the chemistry of the product, the
tannins extracted from the oak galls combined chemically with the
ferrous sulphate to make ferrous tannate; the solution of ferrous
tannate was almost colorless, but after drying on paper, it oxidized
to ferric tannate, which is black.

Iron gall writing inks remain legible for centuries, but they
often fade from dark black to brown. Causes of the fading are
light, residual bleaches in the paper, or an excess of ferrous sulphate converts to oxides of iron (rusty browns), which in turn, act
on the black ferric tannate turning it brown.

Sulphuric acid in iron gall ink (the by-product of the oxidation of copperas) causes the ink to "bite" into paper and vellum to
make a permanent record. Early scribes are known to have added
spirits of salt (hydrochloric acid) or oil of vitriol (sulphuric acid)

to improve their writing fluids. This had no adverse effect on vellum because of the alkaline nature of that material, but it was disastrous on paper. The acid burned through the paper under the ink and that accounts for the "lacy" manuscripts sometimes seen in old collections. The acid also migrated to the adjacent non-inked paper causing it to become dark and brittle. It also migrated to adjacent sheets, contaminating them and causing the reverse brown writing sometimes seen on old manuscripts.

When aniline dyes first became known they were mixed with iron gall inks for color and to facilitate writing on vellum and heavily sized paper. Modern ink is made from various synthetic dyes, all of which are inferior to the two earlier types. Their chief defects are ready solubility in water and other liquids and fading when exposed to light. "Ball point" inks are the least satisfactory because these materials (dye in an oily medium) are very easily soluble in many non-aqueous fluids and the color lies on the surface of paper instead of penetrating deeply into the fibers.

Early printing inks were a mixture of carbon (soot) in boiled linseed oil and were more like paint than ink. Because carbon is one of the cheapest of pigments, it is still the basic material in modern printing inks, which are essentially lampblack and varnish with quick-drying agents added. Most printed material has remained black and permanent regardless of its age. This is because in addition to the blackness from the soot, the oil, after bonding the pigment to the paper, oxidized and polymerized into insoluble black compounds. When early printed papers show evidence of damage from ink (discoloration between the printed lines, embrittlement of the paper, etc.), it can be attributed to the fact that early printers sometimes substituted fish oil or other vehicles for linseed oil or added rosin size to their linseed oil to accelerate drying.

ADHESIVES--Undoubtedly primitive men made use of the adhesive properties of saliva, waxes, resins, egg whites and bitumen in their everyday living. No one knows when they first learned that by cooking animal skins in water one can obtain a sticky substance (glue) useful for holding things together. The Egyptians are supposed to have used the mud of the Nile as a bonding agent for papyrus sheets. Perhaps they did in the beginning, but before long they were using more effective gums and resins, gelatinous materials of animal origin or vegetable matter. It is interesting to note that there was very little change in the technology of adhesives between the time of the Egyptian civilization and the advent of synthetic adhesives in this century.

Adhesives can be classified in several ways--by temperature (hot or cold types), by type of solvent, by type of application, or by origin, which is more commonly used. This categorization includes:

Animal matter.... hides, bone, cartilage, casein
Fish glues.......
Vegetable matter.. gums, natural resins, starches and
                   dextrins, latex, cellulose
Synthetics........

Glue is the result of the hydrolysis of the protein collagen, the main constituent of the inner skin of animals. Glue can also be extracted from the connective tissues, cartilage and bones of slaughtered animals. Glue and gelatin, both colloids and chemically alike, merge into one another by imperceptible degrees. The difference is one of purity--the less pure being the glue. Gelatin is an excellent adhesive, but is even more valuable as an additive to paper. Animal glue is sold commercially in a wide variety of forms and colors. Hide glue, the best grade, is made from hide scraps and trimmings, the wastes from tanneries. Bone glue is an inferior product and should not be used for fine work. The glue-making process, regardless of the source of protein, consists of washing the stock, crushing or shredding it, soaking in lime to eliminate hair and flesh, boiling to extract the gelatinous stuff, gelling and finally drying on screens. The resulting hard, brittle sheets are then broken into flakes or ground into powder. Ground and flake glue is too stiff for some bookbinding uses. Flexible glue is made by adding glycerin, diethylene glycol or sorbitol syrup to flake glue. Diethylene glycol, because of its lower specific gravity, greater affinity for water and lower viscosity, is best for this purpose. Glue, being an organic material, is susceptible to mold. Preservatives, such as beta naphthol, are added to prevent

mold and bacterial growth. Deodorants, such as terpineol, are also a necessary ingredient in commercial glue. However, all glues
putrefy in time and lose their adhesive properties.

Gelatin extracted from fish bladders is called isinglass.
Wastes from fish processing plants are also made into liquid glue.
These wastes are washed and the gelatin extracted with steam. The
product, after clarification, concentration and bleaching, is a viscous, sticky material that can be used directly from its container
without the preliminary soaking and heating required with animal
glues. It is inferior to animal glue and is more easily spoiled by
bacterial decomposition.

Casein glue, made from milk and lime, is one of the strongest adhesives known. It has been used for centuries in woodworking, but is not suitable for book work because the films are hard
and brittle, the casein is naturally acid, and the working life of the
glue is limited to ten to forty-five minutes.

Gums and resins are complex mixtures obtained from various plants. The gums can be dissolved in water--the resins must
be dissolved in spirits. Gums and resins contain essential oils,
natural coloring matter and various impurities. Gum arabic, one
of the better known natural adhesives, is obtained from "acacia
arabica," a tree common to India and Arabia, and from other aca-
cias. These trees exude transparent white tears (gum) which at
times are discolored by impurities. This brittle gum is soluble in
water. When hydrochloric acid is added to water solutions of the
gum, sticky arabin is precipitated. This adhesive, still used in
some library work, is rapidly being supplanted by synthetics.

Paste, the most common substance for joining paper, is made
from the flour of grain (glutins and starches). Cooking flour in
water makes a sticky colloidal substance which sets on drying, can
be spread in thin films and does not stain fibers. Since flour consists of various mixtures of glutin and starch, flour pastes differ
materially in their working properties from pure starch pastes, and
there are differences among pastes made from different varieties
of flour. Wheat paste, the simple flour and water mixture used by
children, is one of the most important working materials of librar-

ians, archive repairers and conservators. Fungicides and insecticides are added to the mixture to inhibit insects and mold, both of
which thrive on the rich nourishment provided by the grain. Rice
flour produces a whiter paste than other grains and because of this
is more suitable for some work.

Starches are carbohydrates occurring in plants as white
granules of varying size and shape. The percentage of starch varies from plant to plant (75% in rice, corn 50%, potatoes 20%). It
is almost insoluble in cold water, but when a suspension of starch
granules in water is heated, the granules swell and form a viscous
solution which gels on cooling. Starch paste films become brittle
with age, due probably to a gradual loss of moisture and from the
growth of molds and micro-organisms. Dextrin is commonly prepared from starch by heating the dry starch to $200^{o}C$. It dissolves
in water to yield a syrupy solution with strong adhesive properties.

Commercial wallpaper pastes are usually made of wheat
flour. Although more expensive than grocers' flour pastes, they are
convenient to use because insecticides and fungicides have already been
added. Cellulose type wallpaper pastes form translucent mixtures
which are easy to handle, are clean and can be stored almost indefinitely without spoiling. Since flour and starch pastes will not
adhere to pyroxylin coated and impregnated book cloths, certain
chemicals are added to them in commercial binderies to overcome
this difficulty. Diethylene glycol, for instance, when mixed with
wheat paste, dissolves the pyroxylin on the surface to be fastened
allowing the paste to stick. Glucose is sometimes added to wheat
paste to reduce the water content, and thus to control the shrinkage
of paper.

Synthetic adhesives--Among the many synthetic materials developed in the past fifty years the thermoplastic structural adhesives are of most interest to restorationists and conservators. A
thermoplastic is a resinous material which is soluble in various
non-aqueous liquids and which remains permanently fusible. A
structural adhesive is one which solidifies on setting as distinguished from those which remain permanently tacky (i.e., that on
adhesive tapes). An important characteristic of the group is that

many shrink on setting because of the evaporation of their solvents.

Polyvinyl acetates (PVA's) are synthetic resins (polymerized vinyl acetate molecules) first made in Germany in 1913. These odorless, tasteless, non-toxic, non-corrosive, non-crystalline, durable materials adhere well to both porous and non-porous surfaces and remain flexible after setting. When dry, they swell in water, but will not dissolve. After setting, they can be liquefied in certain solvents, but even so, are extremely difficult to remove from leather and paper. PVA's, now manufactured and sold widely under a variety of brand names, are not panaceas and when used injudiciously can do irreparable harm. These products, so enticingly advertised, are not uniform in quality, stability, flexibility, durability and bonding strength. They are also sometimes loaded with starches, clays, other resins and plasticizers in addition to the solvents. Although a low pH (high acidity) is common to all PVA emulsions, it has been determined at the W.J. Barrow Research Laboratory that the acidic gaseous decomposition products liberated during aging are volatile and do not remain in the bonded material. PVA's are certainly useful for book repair in circulating libraries, but they should be used with extreme conservatism in the care and repair of more valuable materials. The manufacturers do not make known the various ingredients in their products and there is the possibility that some ingredients could have an adverse effect on leather, parchment, paper and other library materials.

Polyvinyl alcohol is a material produced by the hydrolysis of polyvinyl acetate. It is resistant to most organic solvents, but is completely soluble in water. It has been used in museums but is infrequently used in library work, probably because it is not prepared for commercial distribution as is polyvinyl acetate.

Polyvinyl acitals and polyvinyl butyrals are prepared by treating polyvinyl alcohol with certain complex chemicals. They are used in museums but as yet are untried for library work.

Acrylates (resinous compounds used by museum conservators for spray coating and consolidation of fragile objects) are esters of acrylic and methacrylic acids. They have a potential as adhesives, but so far have been used only as protective coatings for book cloth and paper. Their properties are similar to those of polyvinyl acetate adhesives and they are available commercially.

Synthetic rubber adhesives have an important role in commercial bookbinding (i.e. manufacture of paperbacks) where low cost, good bonding strength, flexibility, but not long life, are required.

One of the earliest of the synthetic resin adhesives was cellulose nitrate, which has been used extensively in adhesives for pottery and glass. Other cellulose derivatives are cellulose acetate, cellulose caproate and ethyl and methyl cellulose. The latter two are general purpose adhesives used in the textile and paper industries.

Soluble nylon is a chemically modified form of nylon produced by treating nylon with formaldehyde. It is soluble in alcohol or alcohol mixed with water and is particularly useful when flexibility and penetration are required. Of great importance in repair work in libraries and archives is the fact that soluble nylon does not exert contractile forces on the bonded material when setting.

The epoxies, an important group of thermosetting synthetic resin adhesives (i.e., those which remain liquid until they are caused to set by the addition of chemical hardeners), have no application to conservation of library materials.

BOARDS--The term boards has several meanings in book making. When used in connection with the material in a book, it means the hard covers to which the decorative covering is glued and applies whether they are made of wood, cardboard or any other material. Until about 1500 almost all boards were wood. At that time pasteboards came into use and within a short time wood was the exception. Pasteboards were of three kinds: (a) those made by pasting together sheets of low quality paper or printing spoilage, (b) a better grade made by matting together wet sheets of new paper as it was lifted from the vatman's mold and (c) an inexpensive pulped board made from paper shavings and often even floor sweepings. Each of these is easily recognizable when an old book is disassembled. They all wear fairly well until the leather covers wear off and then they rapidly crumble at the corners. About the beginning of the eighteenth century boards made from shredded and matted rope fibers became popular for quality work and continued in use through World War II. These are hard and tough and easily distinguished from pasteboards. Even after a hundred years or more of use they remain flat and can often be reused when binding the volumes they originally covered.

Today's boards are usually made of paper and they are available in many weights and sizes. There are three qualities: best black millboards, machine boards and strawboards. The tough, heavy black millboards are made from rope and will stand hard usage. Machine boards include a wide range of boards made by machine from various fibers. Wood pulp, waste paper, waste chips and some fibrous by-products of other industries all go into machine boards. They are not as heavy as best black millboards, but certain of them are fairly tough. They should be used with caution on valuable books because of uncertainty about their composition. Strawboards, as the name implies, are made of straw and are the cheapest available. They are soft, have little strength, and warp easily. Strawboards should not be used on anything of value. Chipboard, a very cheap machine-made product of old chips and waste, like strawboard has no strength and also warps easily. Ragboard is a high quality, clean, fine textured material made from pure rag stock and is used for mounting prints, art work, etc. It is generally too expensive for book covers.

CLOTH--Cloth is fabric made from a variety of animal, vegetable and synthetic fibers spun into yarn and woven. The animal fibers are (1) those in which animal hair is the source (wool, etc.) and (2) those which come from insects (silkworms, etc.). Among the vegetable cloth-making fibers are: (1) vegetable hairs (cotton, vegetable silks), (2) bast fibers from the stems of certain plants (flax, hemp, jute, etc.) and (3) fiber bundles, such as in sisal, esparto, straw, wood, paper mulberry, etc. The fibers most commonly used in book making are flax, silk and cotton.

Cotton, the seed hair of the cotton plant, consists of single hair-like cells and is over 90% cellulose. Being almost pure cellulose, cotton fibers are readily affected by acid and by moderately

strong oxidizing agents. Alkali compounds in moderate amounts
and at ordinary temperatures have little effect on them.

The cellulose content of linen fibers ranges between 70 and
80%. They are very tough, can be bleached white and take dyes
more readily than cotton.

Silk is the natural product of certain moths. In appearance
it is a solid thread resembling a glass rod, but the fiber is really
composed of three layers surrounding a tube filled with a fatty matter. This fatty substance helps to preserve the flexibility of silk
fabrics. Silk has great absorptive powers for dyestuffs. It is dissolved by strong acids, but is resistant to weak ones. Dilute alkalies do not effect it. Silk is commonly weighted for decorative purposes by dipping in solutions of metallic compounds such as tin.
This results in great loss of strength and extreme vulnerability to
sunlight.

BOOKCLOTH--is a generic term for all of the fabric goods
used for book covers. They are usually woven cotton fabrics and
can be bleached and mercerized, dyed, filled with pigment colors,
gelatinized, starched, coated or impregnated with plastics, calendered and embossed. They are divided into classes according to
their relative costs and qualities. Manufacture of cloth for book
covers began in Germany and England in the early 1820's and for
the rest of the century these countries enjoyed a world monopoly of
the material. These early book cloths were starch filled muslins
colored and embossed for decoration. More expensive book cloths
were sized with gelatin. The starch filling gave body to the material, permitted graining with metal plates or rolls and facilitated
stamping with gold. Starch filled book covers wore fairly well, but
were extremely vulnerable to insects and molds and water was disastrous to the covers.

Canvas is a coarsely woven cotton cloth with no filler. It is
durable, but soils readily and has little esthetic appeal. Edition
book cloth is closely woven, lightweight, starch filled cotton, sometimes lightly embossed to conceal the weave of the fabric. It is often very attractive but having no strength or durability, it is not
long wearing. Buckram is a heavier fabric with a clay or starch

filler and is sturdy enough for hard-used circulation library bindings.   It is not attractive and soils easily and unless coated is easily water stained.

The invention in the United States about 1910 of pyroxylin
treated fabrics was a major breakthrough in binding material and
soon many manufacturers were using this and similar chemical
coatings to improve the appearance and durability of book cloth.
The term pyroxylin-treated as applied to book cloth means either
pyroxylin impregnated or pyroxylin coated cotton fabric.   The difference between these is in the quantity of protective coating applied
and the manner of application, and the type of material treated.
The pyroxylin composition consists of gelatinized nitrocellulose, a
plasticizer to confer softness and flexibility, coloring matter and a
solvent.   The fabrics used for impregnation are lightweight muslins, whereas those used for coating are the heavier drills, twills,
and sheetings.   Coated fabrics are sometimes embossed to imitate
leather.   The surfaces of impregnated fabrics retain the texture of
the base material.

Pyroxylin impregnated fabrics are superior to starch-filled
materials because they are washable and resistant to insects, fungi
and dampness.   They wear well and are particularly suitable for
use in tropical and semi-tropical areas.

Pyroxylin coated fabrics are popular with edition binders because of the decorative effects obtainable.   They are water repellent and immune to insect attack, but they do not wear as well as
the impregnated material because of cracking at the hinges and occasionally peeling of the coating.

Silk has been used on book covers primarily for luxury editions.   It is very expensive because silk covered books generally
require boxes to protect them.   The material, however, is frequently used in expensive bindings for handsome doublures (i.e., the luxury coverings on the insides of book boards).   When used with
leather joints and gilded edges, the decorative effects are magnifi-
cent.   Silk on the inside of book covers is protected from the deteriorative effects of light and air and it often outlasts the covers.

Pure silk is one of the best fabrics for reinforcing paper.

This thin, lightweight, strong and flexible material, also called
Japanese silk, silk chiffon, resille de soie, mousseline de soie,
organdie or organza, readily absorbs paste within its fibrous structure to make a strong bond and when properly applied is almost invisible. It is stronger than Japanese tissue paper or European and
American lens tissue, but its useful life (approximately 25 years)
is much shorter than that of paper. Artificial silk, rayon, nylon,
dacron, etc., although possessing many of the properties of real
silk, are not suitable for reinforcing paper because they lack
strength and deteriorate rapidly; and what is of most importance,
the threads of these synthetic materials repel paste instead of absorbing it.

Velvet--Book covers of velvet, often studded with jewels,
were made for royalty as early as the Middle Ages. A few have
survived to the present. Velvet is a textile made of silk and covered on one side with a close, short, fine, soft shag; the other side
is a very strong close tissue. The shag is formed of loops of the
threads of the warp. Cutting these loops during the weaving of the
fabric forms the pile. Uncut velvet, called terry, is sometimes
woven simultaneously with the cut to create figures on the cloth.
Velvet brocades, the most luxurious of all, are made with gold and
silver threads as extra weft, the figures being wrought by hand as
with embroidery. Velveteen and plush are cotton or wool fabrics
which are woven in much the same manner as true velvet.

STAMPING MATERIALS--In the United States gold leaf for
book decoration is beaten from gold bars 999.9 fine. A one-ounce
cube of the precious metal is worked by skilled craftsmen into a
sufficient number of thin leaves (1/275000-inch thick) to cover 175
to 200 square feet of surface. This pure gold, properly applied to
leather by the traditional techniques of the "finishing" craft, retains
its brilliance and luster for a great many years. For use in gold-
stamping machines pure gold is bonded in leaf or powder form to a
plastic base. Gold foil facilitates handling the metal in the machine
and the plastic also serves as an adhesive between the gold and
book cover material when heated letters are applied to it. Bronze
stamping leaf (imitation gold) was first used in Germany in 1905.

This yellow metallic powder on a foil base is actually brass, an alloy of copper and zinc. Its color varies in accordance with the
proportions of the two metals in the alloy. As the amount of copper is increased, the color becomes deeper. Unlike pure gold,
which stays bright and clean until the last traces of it are worn off,
all imitation gold discolors sooner or later (and mostly sooner).
When applied to leather, bronze stamping foil turns green in a matter of a few weeks. Even when applied to cloth or paper covers,
bronze foil will eventually discolor. This discoloration is due to
the action of the gases in the atmosphere and heat and light on the
various metal alloys. Great differences exist in the rate of tarnish
among the various bronze foils and for some unknown reason flat
bronze foil discolors less than rolled bronze. This is attributed by
Kantrowitz and Blaylock to the fact that the high melting-point waxes
used on the flat material (but not the rolled) coat the metallic particles after they are deposited on the leather or fabric in the stamping process. This coating acts as a seal against the deteriorative
effects of the atmospheric gases. Because of the chemical action
of the plasticizers in pyroxylin-coated fabrics, bronze stamping leaf
corrosion is more rapid on these cloths than on starch-filled binders cloth.

Colored stamping foils are also used for decorating paper
and cloth book covers with very attractive results. Colored foils
are preferred over ink for stamping letters and designs on these
books because of the greater covering power of the foils. Their
disadvantage is the tendency to chip off with use.

SEWING MATERIALS--The best thread for sewn books is
linen. Silk, cotton, nylon, dacron, rayon and other threads can be
used, but none has proved to be as uniformly satisfactory as linen
from Belgium and Ireland. Silk is advantageous when a hand-sewn
book has many signatures. The fine silk helps to minimize thickening of the spine. Cotton and synthetic fiber threads are quite satisfactory for use in book-sewing machines.

Linen thread is made from the straw of the flax plant. The
seeds are first separated from the stalks and the stems are then
steeped in water to remove resinous matter and allow fermentation

to take place. After fermentation is complete, the fibrous material is separated from the woody matter and spun into the strong,
even thread so long preferred by hand bookbinders.

Synthetic threads are made by extruding plastic material into chemical baths where it is coagulated into a continuous thread
before being dried and taken up on spools. Like cotton threads,
they are highly refined products of uniform quality, but without the
strength and durability of linen.

The gatherings of pages in better grade cased books and all
handbound books are sewn to each other and then to tapes or cords.
These tapes and cords serve the double purpose of holding the gatherings together and of providing a means for fastening the boards
to the books. Bookbinding tapes should be made of high quality cotton or linen. Synthetics should never be used because they repel
paste and glue and make it difficult to fasten the boards to the
book. Hemp cord, the preferred material for bands in hand-sewn
books, is made from an annual plant native to China, India and
Iran. The fiber from which the cordage is made is produced in the
bark of the plant's straight stiff stalks. The best hemp now comes
from Italy; the fiber is white, very well prepared and of superior
strength. There are many machines for beating the stalks of the
plant, extracting the fiber and ridding it of its resinous matter
(retting); but the highest grade hemp is still produced by hand. No
entirely satisfactory substitute for hemp has ever been discovered.
Manila, sisal, cotton, jute, linen and nylon cords have been used
in bookbinding but none has the combined strength, durability and
"workability" of the Italian hemp.

MISCELLANEOUS MATERIALS--Spine reinforcing materials
include crash and flannel. Crash, known also as super, is glued
to the spines of some books to strengthen them and reinforce the
hinges. On some machine-made books it is the only hinge. The
open weave of the fabric permits the glue to strike through easily
and the lining gets a good grip. When greater strength is desired
canton flannel, which is fleeced on one side, is used in place of
super.

Machine-made headbands are purely ornamental and do not

strengthen the book as do handmade headbands of linen, silk or cotton which are braided on strips of cord and laced into the signatures of hand-bound volumes.

Varnishes are sometimes applied to finished book covers to give gloss and to provide some protection against insects and fungi. Varnish also keeps oil from hands away from leather book covers. This is not desirable because it has been conclusively proven that the leather on frequently handled books (which is regularly lubricated by oil from the user's hands) outlasts identical leather on books which are rarely handled. Varnished book covers are also impervious to other leather preservatives.

Glair is egg or blood albumin, which for centuries has been used by gilders to bond gold leaf to various surfaces. The traditional gilder's glair is the white of an egg, mixed with a little vinegar, then beaten and strained.

Gilding powder serves the same purpose as glair. This finely ground rosin, when dusted into blind-tooled impressions on leather before gold is applied, is melted by the heat of the gilder's tools to bind the gold.

Shellac sizes used commercially as gold-stamping adhesives are made by reducing shellac flakes with alcohol. After being painted into the "blinded in" impressions on leather, the alcohol evaporates, depositing a thin layer of shellac which then serves the same purpose as gilding powder.

Paper sizes--To make paper suitable for writing and printing, it is necessary to give the matted fibers a hard surface; otherwise the paper would absorb the ink like a blotter. This is called sizing. Asiatic paper makers have applied thin coatings of gypsum and pastes of lichen, starch, rice or wheat to the finished sheets. In early European paper making the sheets, after drying, were passed through a bath of gelatin made by boiling scraps of leather and vellum. The paste or gelatin impregnated and stiffened the cellulose fibers in the paper and glazed the surface. High quality modern paper is still sized with gelatin but alum and soap, or rosin and potash are used more often. Gelatin is harmless to paper; alum, rosin and potash are not. Gelatin is a typical colloid that

swells to many times its normal volume in cold water and the swol-
len jelly goes readily into solution at temperatures above 95°F.
This is important to remember in the restoration of paper. Parchment size is an almost pure gelatin made from parchment waste.

Rosin is a natural resin obtained from turpentine by distilla-
tion. There are several varieties varying in color and transparency. It makes paper stiff, resistant to water and more suitable
for receiving ink. At the same time rosin in paper has a catalytic
effect in the action of light on cellulose fibers and it accelerates
the deterioration of paper.

Alums used for sizing paper (also for tawing skins) are
aluminum sulphate. These substances seem to have the same effect on cellulose as rosin. Commercial alum (potash), which is
aluminum potassium sulphate, is used in modern paper making to
precipitate rosin size on cellulose fibers.

Chapter III
The Enemies of Library Materials

Men are unquestionably the greatest enemies of the materials on which they record their thoughts. To the long list of great libraries vandalized by conquering armies or burned in hate, must be added the incalculable loss and damage caused by petty theft, malicious mischief, and careless handling by individuals. This is all the more distressing because it is almost impossible to control, short of imposing security measures that would deny access to books to all but a select few. The continuing loss due to misinformation, lack of information or failure to use available methods of library conservation by the custodians of books is equally serious.

In the past hundred years science has learned how to keep insects and fungi under control and has accumulated much information on more recently identified enemies--heat, light, and acid. But with a few exceptions (such as Plenderlieth's Conservation of Antiquities and Works of Art; Langwell's The Conservation of Books and Documents; Lydenberg and Archer's The Care and Repair of Books; Plumbe's The Preservation of Books; and the noteworthy series of publications by W. J. Barrow) such knowledge rarely gets further than reporting in technical papers and professional journals of limited distribution.

The foes are as follows:

1. People	5. Moisture
2. The air we breathe	6. Vermin
3. Light and darkness	7. Fungi
4. Heat	8. Acid

All are now well understood and means are available to restrain most of them before damage is done. Prevention is not inexpensive but it is reasonable compared to the cost of later repair and restoration and it is cheap compared to the costs of rare and valuable items destroyed by neglect.

PEOPLE--Thoughtless users have dog-eared leaves of books, mangled them with improvised bookmarks, and stained them with everything from perspiration to tobacco juice and shoe polish. There are probably more indelible fingerprints on volumes in the average public library than there are in the files of the F. B. I. The problem of minimizing the wear and tear on circulating volumes will always be difficult.   On the other hand, much avoidable damage is done to books by well-meaning but uninformed librarians by:

   a. Use of pressure sensitive tapes.
   b. Indiscriminate use of polyvinyl acetate and other synthetic adhesives.
   c. Use of highly acid paper for protective wrappers.
   d. Use of wood backing in print, picture, and map frames.
   e. Amateur lamination.
   f. Improper storage.

Pressure sensitive tapes are perfectly satisfactory for sealing packages, but should never be used for repairs on anything but the most inexpensive books.   At best, these repairs are only temporary and the chemicals in some adhesives soon discolor the paper with a stain that is impossible to remove.   Some tapes now available claim to be nonstaining and more permanent, but since there is little information available on the materials in these tapes, it would be unwise to use them on anything other than books and papers that are expected to be discarded after a reasonable period of use.

Extravagant claims have been made by some manufacturers of polyvinyl acetate (and other synthetic resins) regarding the alleged capability of these materials to make old books like new. These white emulsions, generously painted on worn-out books, are claimed to fasten separated covers, consolidate rotted leather, and rejuvenate cloth.   Large numbers of fine volumes have been ruined by the improper use of these products.   What must be remembered is that polyvinyl acetate emulsions are good adhesives and nothing more.   When used as one would use paste or glue, they make very strong bonds which can rarely be separated without damaging the fastened materials.   Since one of the basic principles of rare book and archive restoration is that nothing shall be done in the restoration that cannot be undone if necessary, these irreversible adhesives should be avoided for all except general library work.

The use of newspapers and cheap wrapping paper for wrappers and dunnage for books in storage will protect them from dust and dirt, but, at the same time, will do infinitely more damage than will dust, by acidifying the materials they are intended to protect. The lignin in inexpensive paper is highly acid and this acid migrates rapidly to any other organic material in contact with it. Newsprint absorbs and retains atmospheric moisture, creating conditions conducive to mold growth. Boxes and cartons stuffed with paper are also favorite nesting places for insects and rodents.

It would seem to most conservators that all of the prints, maps, broadsides, and watercolors framed in the past century have been backed with thin, freshly cut soft pine boards, often with a padding of newsprint. The resins and lignin in the wood darken and weaken the paper so "protected." Frequently the stains in the prints mirror the grain and knots of the boards. The unseasoned boards invariably split, allowing sulphur dioxide-laden air to get behind the glass. The result is dark streaks across the face of the print (corresponding to the cracks in the wood), due to the conversion of the absorbed sulphur dioxide to sulphuric acid.

Because old frames were rarely tight (i.e., snugly fitted glass set in putty with a strong, high-grade waterproof paper dust cover on the back), air-borne moisture had free access, thus accounting for the heavy water stains so often seen on the edges of old framed prints.

Lamination by specialists in restoration laboratories has an important place in the conservation of library materials; but it is not a cure-all. Many items have been laminated that could have been restored to near pristine condition by less drastic methods. Expert lamination will provide excellent protection if one is willing to sacrifice the texture and feel of fine paper, and accept in its stead a document with the appearance of a plasticized identification card. On the other hand, when paper has been damaged by acid, fungi or any other destructive agent to the point where it is beyond

repair by traditional methods, lamination by specialists using sci-
entifically designed and engineered equipment and preceded by deacidification of the paper is right and proper. Many important
nineteenth and twentieth-century newspapers and other items printed
on wood pulp paper have been thus saved. Amateur lamination in
library workshops using inexpensive do-it-yourself kits should be
avoided. The results are rarely satisfactory in sealing out the atmosphere and unless the paper is first deacidified, the sulphuric
acid entrapped between the laminating sheets will continue its destructive action.

Glass enclosed bookcases are of questionable value. They
provide some security from petty theft and protection from dust and
aerosols in the atmosphere. They also provide undisturbed nesting
places for insects and rodents, and stagnant air that is conducive to
mold growth, particularly during the summer months in non-air-
conditioned buildings. The high temperature which sometimes pre-
vails in these glass cases also accelerates acid deterioration and
auto-oxidation in leather and paper.

THE AIR WE BREATHE--Pure air, a mixture of oxygen and
nitrogen with traces of carbon dioxide, is responsible for some of
the damage to organic materials. It provides the oxygen and water
vapor necessary for combustion, fermentation, hydrolysis, and auto-
oxidation. Since there is little that can be done to exclude air
from library materials, other than encasing them in boxes filled
with inert gases, it would be unreasonable to include clean air in
the category of enemies of books. It is the impurities in air, particularly city air, that are the real enemies. These are sulphur
dioxide, hydrogen sulphide, ammonia, nitrogen dioxide, ozone, and
aerosols.

The amount of sulphur in the sulphur dioxide annually released into the atmosphere by the combustion of fuel (residential
heating, industrial furnaces, automobile engines, etc.) exceeds sulphur production in all other forms by the entire chemical industry.
Sulphur dioxide is absorbed by porous materials in libraries. Once
absorbed, it reacts with absorbed water, along with the minute
quantities of iron which are almost always present, to form sul-

phuric acid. Acid, particularly sulphuric acid, stains and embrittles paper, causes loss of strength in textiles, decomposes
leather, bleaches dyes, erodes plaster, limestone, and marble and
corrodes iron, copper, bronze and silver.

The hydrogen sulphide in contaminated air is produced by industrial activities in cities and by biological activity in swamps,
lake regions and tidal flats. Significant amounts of hydrogen sulphide are sometimes given off by rubber found in many forms in
modern offices and buildings. Hydrogen sulphide attacks silver,
bronze and copper; but the destructive effect of hydrogen sulphide
on these metals is less than that of sulphur dioxide. The bronze
leaf stamped on many cloth book covers is tarnished by hydrogen
sulphide and sulphur dioxide.

Ammonia released into the air by man and also naturally
generated is harmful to cellulose (alkaline hydrolysis), but because
of the greater amount of acid usually present from sulphur dioxide
in the air, ammonia absorbed by leather, textiles or paper will act
only to reduce the acidity of the material. Ammonium sulphate,
the reaction product of free ammonia with water vapor in the presence of other chemicals, forms a "bloom" on the surfaces of materials varnished with natural resins.

Ozone and nitrogen dioxide are less well-known, but dangerous, impurities in air. Ozone is generated in the upper atmosphere by the action of ultraviolet light on oxygen. Most of the nitrogen dioxide in polluted air comes from automobile exhausts.
The action of sunlight on nitrogen dioxide generates more ozone
and in city smogs the percentages of these two poisons rise to
dangerous levels. Ozone destroys organic materials by breaking
the bonds between carbon atoms. Damp cellulose is particularly
vulnerable to ozone in the concentrations normally found in polluted
air; after prolonged exposure to it, paper and textiles lose their
strength. Ozone fades the colors in fabric book covers, although
such fading is less serious than that caused by photo oxidation (the
action of light). Ozone oxidizes natural resin varnishes--the kind
frequently used by early bookbinders to give a high gloss to leather
covers. The now dark yellow and brittle surfaces of many old maps

which were at one time varnished for protection, resulted in part from the action of ozone. Leather, gelatin, paste and glue, particularly in humid atmospheres, are susceptible to the action of ozone and natural rubber is extremely vulnerable to it. The effect of nitrogen dioxide seems to be mainly bleaching dyed leather and fabrics.

The aerosols include all of the minute solid particles suspended in air (i.e., dirt). In cities they are chiefly carbon from the incomplete combustion of fuel, made sticky by the tarry materials generated in the same process. They include suspended ash, building and soil dust, fiber fragments, sodium chloride (salt from sea spray), and volatile aromatic matter exuded by plants. Sea salt aerosols are of little concern to librarians, archivists and museum curators except near the seacoast. Salt, being hygroscopic, retains water in sufficient quantities to support the growth of molds in buildings exposed to sea air.

The industrial aerosols, in addition to being dirty, absorb and carry with them sulphur dioxide, hydrogen sulphide and iron. When they settle on exposed materials, the sulphur dioxide and other contaminants immediately start their destructive chemical reactions. Abrasive aerosols, together with the dust and dirt within a building, act like sandpaper on books and paper.

In heavily forested parts of the country terpenes and esters are exuded from foliage in vast amounts. Esters are reaction products of alcohols and acids, terpenes are hydrocarbons. Both are aromatic organic aerosols, which often react unfavorably with organic materials.

The water vapor in air provides much of the moisture necessary for the conversion of sulphur dioxide to sulphuric acid; the growth of molds; the rusting and corrosion of metals; the hydrolysis of organic materials; and the water necessary to support insect life.

In summary: the air of our cities contributes to the decomposition of gelatin, paste, glue, bark and palm leaf manuscripts, wood tablets, textiles, leather, vellum, and paper. The impurities in it also corrode metal, tarnish bronze leaf on book covers, erode stone, rot rubber, oxidize some varnishes, bleach dyes, and abrade contiguous surfaces. No library material is safe from the impurities in polluted air, not even in the country or at the seashore.

LIGHT AND DARKNESS--The cycle of day and night, as well as artificial control of light and darkness, has an effect on library materials that, until recently, has been little understood outside of the scientific community. Visible light, either natural or artificial, bleaches writing ink, book covers, and the colors in prints and maps. Prolonged exposure to ultraviolet light causes paper to become brittle and lose its strength. Although light oxidizes paper, it does not act directly on the cellulose molecules; instead it reacts photochemically on the other ingredients and impurities in paper (acid, lignin, resins, glue, starch, dyes, etc.). The products of those reactions then attack the cellulose, breaking the molecular chains, and weakening the material. Cellulose is bleached by light, but lignin and other undesirable matter in paper are generally yellowed. After prolonged exposure to light (resulting in photo sensitized oxidation) paper is more vulnerable to other forms of deterioration and is particularly sensitive to damage by alkalies in subsequent restorative processes.

Ultraviolet light is most damaging to paper and textiles. Daylight and light from fluorescent lamps, both of which contain ultraviolet rays, are destructive. The damaging rays can be filtered out of fluorescent light, but ordinary window glass does not block all of the ultraviolet component of sunlight. Incandescent light is the least damaging to cellulose.

On the other hand, light hinders the growth of fungi and routs vermin from their hiding places. From this point of view, it would be desirable if every nook and corner of libraries and archive buildings could be constantly bathed in light. Roaches, silverfish, firebrats, etc. are rarely seen unless a darkened room is suddenly illuminated. Rats and mice are encountered even less frequently, although it is doubtful that any building is free of them. It has been said that the rats in any city considerably outnumber the human beings. These pests invariably do their damage at night in regularly inhabited places. They roam freely in attics and cellars when they are protected by darkness.

HEAT--Heating libraries is necessary for human comfort,
but at the same time it increases the librarians' problems. Heat
(along with food and moisture) is one of the three conditions necessary for mold growth.   Insects and rodents thrive in warm buildings.
Heat accelerates the chemical deterioration of paper, leather and
textiles.   In overheated libraries, the paste and glue on the covers
of books dry out and cease to bind.

The heat from accidental fires does great damage to books
and paper even though they may not have been close enough to the
flames to be charred. Such damage causes paper to lose most of
its fold strength. It is possible to measure the reduction in strength
of paper which has been stored for long periods over a radiator or
in unventilated, uninsulated attics. Electric lights in display cases
raise the temperature enough to accelerate the photochemical action
of the same light on the paper on display. Such an arrangement
approximates the conditions in an artificial aging oven in a laboratory. In a lighted display case the temperatures are lower than in
the aging oven but the exposure time is longer and the results are
the same.

Papyrus, bark, and palm leaf manuscripts are desiccated by
heat and become fragile and brittle. Motion picture film and photographs are sensitive to changes in temperature as are audio tapes
and discs. The films, tapes and records, being thermoplastic,
soften when heated and harden when cooled. When in a soft state
in overheated buildings or in tropical climates, they are very readily damaged by rough handling. Of even more importance are the
chemical and physical changes (affecting image or sound) which take
place within these thermoplastics when they are subjected to marked
variations in temperature.

The strength of paper is determined by the strength of the
fibers and the bond between them. Cellulose fibers are deteriorated by hydrolysis (decomposition by chemical reaction with water),
oxidation, and photosynthesis and each of the processes is accelerated by heat in the presence of minute quantities of iron, copper
and the other impurities which are always found in paper. Low
temperatures (and low humidity) decrease the rate of degradation.

The useful life of even inferior library materials could be extended
by a great many years if they could be kept refrigerated.

MOISTURE--As do heat and light, moisture works both for
and against the preservation of library materials.   A certain amount
of moisture is necessary for flexibility in paper.   Excessive moisture in paper encourages mold growth and too little makes paper
brittle.   Bark books and manuscripts that have been wet crumble
when dried.

Too much moisture in leather encourages mold growth,
which first changes the colors of dyed skins, then attacks the leather
itself.   Too low humidity desiccates leather.   Prolonged exposure
to low humidity (i. e., many years in the desert) will ultimately convert leather into a bituminous-like material, such as that found in
Egyptian tombs.

Mold spores are in the air everywhere, but they can only
establish themselves on a surface when moisture is present.   The
naturally high humidity in tropical and semitropical regions is of
the gravest concern to librarians and archivists.   Fungi can be destroyed by high temperatures (oven heat) and fungicides, but the
most effective treatment is to control the moisture so necessary
for the growth of these micro-organisms.

Moisture in the form of water from leaking roofs, defective
plumbing, and clogged drains all too frequently finds its way to
shelved books, print and map cases and manuscript files, where it
cockles vellum, stains paper, obliterates writing ink, ruins cloth
book covers, rots leather and wood, and rusts metal.   The water
runs between walls, under bookcases and filing cabinets and into
basements, to the great joy of the insects and vermin inhabiting
those places.   In the case of a fire in a building, the damage done
by the water from the fire hoses often exceeds that done by the
flames.   Old paper wet by spilled water is unpleasantly stained and
if not soon dried out becomes soft and spongy.   Saturated leather,
cloth, and paper book covers are usually a total loss.

VERMIN are noxious and disgusting animals of common oc-
currence and they are difficult to control.   From the viewpoint of
librarians, there are two categories--those that live on and destroy

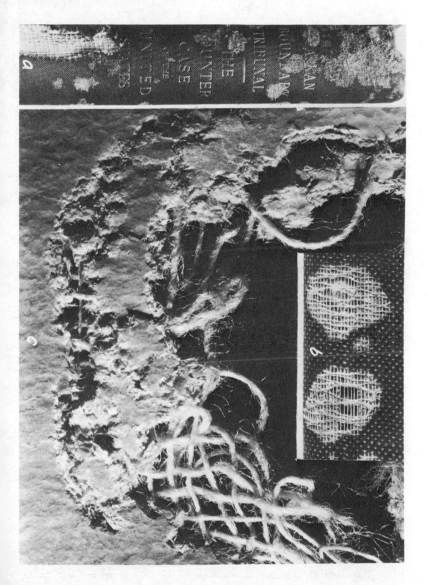

Fig. 1. Damage to cloth-bound books by the American cockroach (Periplaneta americana). (a) Back of book injured (natural size); (b) eaten spots enlarged to show the removal of the sizing by the cockroaches from the cloth; (c) damaged spot of a cover greatly enlarged to show not only removal of sizing, but also destruction of cloth foundation. (Smithsonian Inst. Report for 1939, plate 2) USDA Photo.

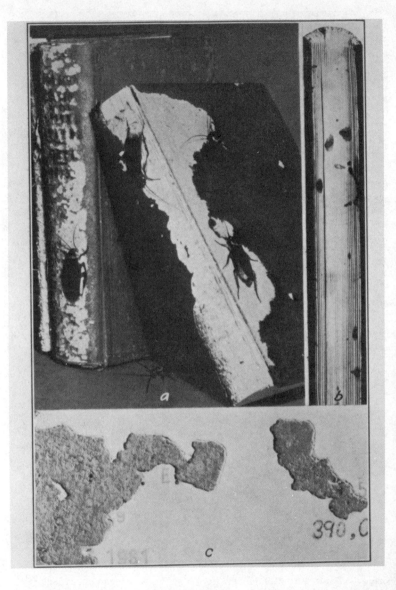

Fig. 2. Damage done to books by the American cockroach "periplaneta americana." (a) Showing the cloth binding eaten from the backs of two books; (b) ink-like stains on edges of pages; (c) label of book file damaged by cockroaches. (Smithsonian Inst. Report for 1939, plate 13) USDA Photo.

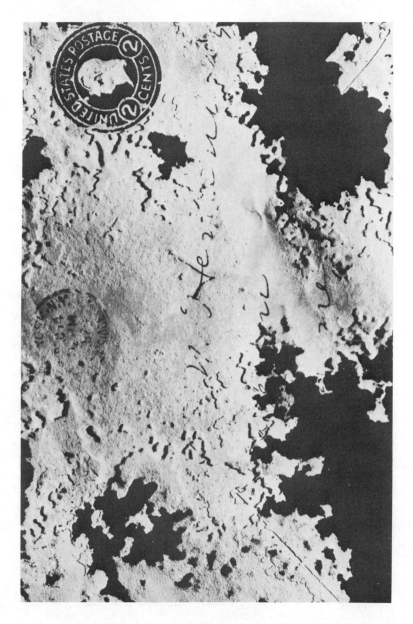

Fig. 3. Silverfish damage to envelope. USDA Photo.

63

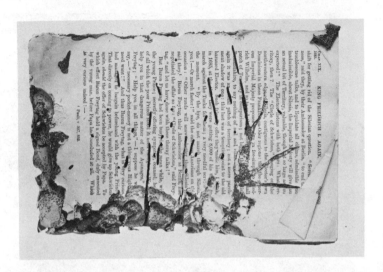

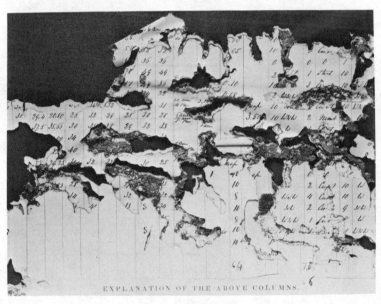

EXPLANATION OF THE ABOVE COLUMNS.

Fig. 4. Indicating how thoroughly subterranean termites can destroy records not properly guarded. Note thin deposit of mud lining burrows in this and above illustration. (Smithsonian Inst. Report for 1939, plate 10, No. 2) USDA Photos.

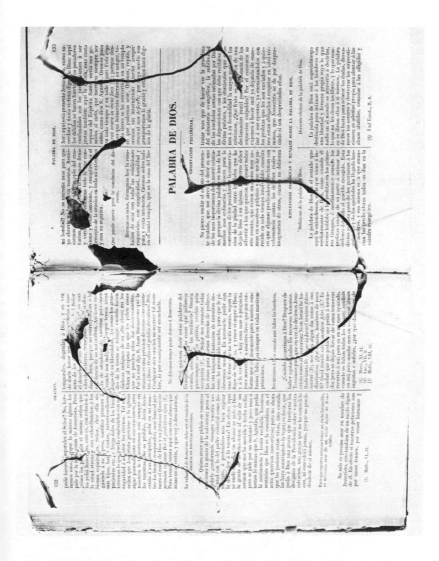

Fig. 5. Book opened to show the ever-varied feeding chambers of dry-wood termites. (Smithsonian Inst. Report for 1939, plate 11) USDA Photo.

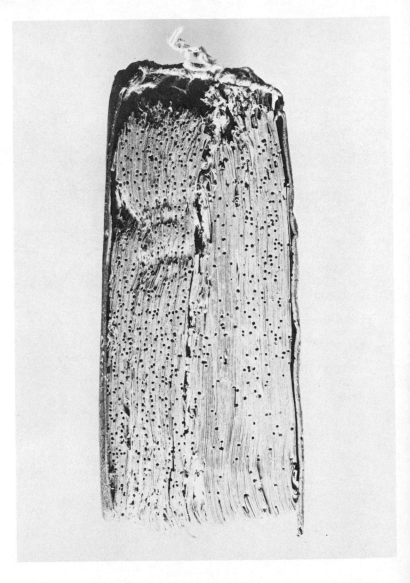

Fig. 6. End view of book infected badly with "neogastrallus librino-cens." The pages of this book were so badly honeycombed and cemented together by bookworm grubs that they could not be turned. The book had to be torn open through the center by main strength. (Smithsonian Inst. Report for 1939, plate 16)   USDA Photo.

Fig. 7. Book, natural size, showing the destructive burrowing of the Hawaiian catorama bookworm. (Smithsonian Inst. Report for 1939, plate 4)   USDA Photo.

library materials and those that are occasional visitors. In the
second category there are those that are imported by various means
and those that live in the dark recesses of the buildings from which
they make forays into book stacks, file drawers, cabinets, etc.

More than seventy species of insects have been identified as
enemies of library materials. The most common of these inverte-
brate pests are the cockroaches, silverfish and firebrats, termites,
book-lice, bookworms, mud wasps, moths, and bedbugs.

Cockroaches--Over one thousand species of these loathsome
creatures exist in the world, with the majority living in tropical or
semitropical climates. Fortunately only five varieties are likely to
be found in libraries. They carry filth on their bodies and are sus-
pected of spreading cholera, poliomyelitis, typhoid fever, and dys-
entery. They conceal their broad, flat, brown or black bodies in
cracks and crevices by day and emerge at night to forage. A favorite food is the paste and glue in book covers and they will eat
through the cloth and paper spines of shelved books to get at it;
they rarely penetrate into the interiors of bound books. They ex-
crete a dark liquid which discolors any material over which they
crawl. The females carry their eggs in pouches on their bodies
and deposit them where food (filth or otherwise) is available and
where temperature and humidity are favorable.

Silverfish and firebrats are slender, wingless, scaled insects
that grow to lengths of one-half inch at maturity. Silverfish are
pearl gray and firebrats are mottled gray--both can easily be recognized by two antennae and three tail-like appendages. Although
they are sometimes seen in the daytime, they are most active at
night. They are found everywhere in buildings, but silverfish prefer damp, cool basements, whereas firebrats relish heat and abound
near furnaces, fireplaces, and heat conductors. Both can go without food for months, but when exposed paper is available, they devour it for the starch and gelatin size. Like roaches, they eat
through book covers to get at the glue beneath. Both insects are
continually producing young. The dark spaces behind the books on
library shelves and behind paper in cabinets and drawers are favorite egg laying places. The eggs hatch in two weeks and if tempera-

ture and humidity are favorable, another generation can be spawned within three months. Silverfish are also known as silver moths, sugar lice, sugar fish, fish moths, and slickers.

Termites thrive in tropical and subtropical climates, but it is not unusual to find them as far north as New England. Although superficially resembling ants and sometimes called "white ants," they are neither white nor ants. Almost nineteen hundred species have been identified. Their remarkably efficient communities of soldiers, workers, and reproducing males and females sometimes number a million or more individuals. Earth-dwelling termites invade buildings by constructing mud tunnels across masonry foundations and between walls and floors. After gaining access to a building, they can do terrible damage in a matter of days. They are difficult to detect because they attack from the backs of cupboards and bookcases and eat their way through wooden shelves and into the interiors of books. After having taken possession of a book or a drawer of paper, they do not stop eating until the contents are shredded and digested and the waste excreted, leaving a mass of pulp where once were printed pages.

Wood-dwelling termites are common to the United States and have spread to all parts of the world. Living above the ground, they enter buildings through any opening available and are as voracious as their earth-dwelling counterparts in destroying any material containing cellulose.

Book lice, also called psocids, are minute gray or white insects no larger than a pinhead that sometimes exist by the thousands between the pages of musty books. They appear in buildings in great numbers in late summer and fall and seek damp, dark areas. Eating almost anything, they are found wherever vegetable or animal matter is allowed to collect. In musty books they prefer the microscopically small fungi in the paper rather than cellulose, gelatin or glue. They are a nuisance, but do little actual damage to library materials. However, their presence should be a warning that conditions are developing that will soon attract the more dangerous library pests.

Bookworm is a generic term that includes the larvae of one

hundred and sixty species of beetles found throughout the world.
These larvae and the adult beetles are inconspicuous and are seldom seen unless their hiding places are disturbed.   In libraries
the beetles lay their eggs on the edges of books and seem to prefer the bottom edges, next to the shelves.   After the eggs are
hatched, the larvae eat their way into the books, making tunnels in
the pages and boards.   These grubs exude a glue-like substance (to
line their tunnels), which often cements the pages together.   Their
excrement is a fine dust which is found in the tunnels and on book-
shelves.   While in the pupal state the animals are in the tunnels,
but after emerging from the cocoons the adult winged insects eat
their way back to the surface to propagate another generation.   This
latter tunneling is less destructive than that done by the larvae.
Bookworms devour printed pages until the text is unintelligible.
Even minor tunneling makes book paper tear easily and sometimes
the dried mucus-like lining in the tunnels sticks the pages together
so firmly that they are badly damaged when pulled apart.

The bookworms in the United States (larder beetles, carpet
beetles and furniture beetles) breed and thrive in granaries and
food processing establishments whence they fly or are carried by
pigeons and rodents to other buildings.   In libraries they often find
ideal conditions for propagation and unless checked can easily get
out of hand.

A common bookworm in India is the powder post beetle, the
Hawaiians are plagued by the Mexican book beetle, and woodworms
are book-eating library pests in Italy.

Moths--The brown house moth is abundant everywhere in the
world except Africa and South America.   The larvae are white,
hairless, dark headed, half-inch-long worms that eat cloth and calfskin covers on books.   For some unknown reason goatskins are immune.   The winged adults lay their eggs in cracks in floors and
walls and any other concealed places.   Four generations a year are
not uncommon in warmer climates.

Mud wasps, if they gain access to a library in those parts
of the world where they are common (Caribbean Islands, all of
Africa, and many parts of Asia), will cement their nests to the con-

cealed fore-edges of shelved books and to the bookcases themselves.
They do no damage to the interiors of books, but the mud cement
on the fore-edges is tenacious and unsightly.

Bedbugs live in cracks between boards, in furniture and in
fabrics, and exist on blood. Although not normally considered to
be a library pest, these minute, flat wingless insects can be introduced into libraries in returned books from infested houses. Once
in, they will multiply (as long as the temperature remains high
enough) by laying eggs in cracks and crevices. They can go without food for a year and will attach themselves as parasites to domestic animals and pet birds. Their natural enemies are cockroaches and ants.

Rodents--These gnawing, biting animals found all over the
world include mice, rats, beavers, porcupines, squirrels, rabbits,
lemmings, and many other species. Some are beneficial to man;
others, rats in particular, are disease carriers (bubonic plague and
trichinosis) and destroyers of property. The black rat of light and
slender build (often seven inches long) has been largely displaced
by the brown (Norway) rat, which is larger, more vicious and more
voracious. Female brown rats have as many as fifty offspring a
year and an old building often harbors thousands of them. Because
they are rarely seen, it is difficult to realize how abundant they
really are. In libraries and museums they eat anything made of
paper, leather, vellum, glue, paste, gelatin, etc. Once established in a building, particularly an old one, they are very difficult
to exterminate. Although they prefer to nest between walls and in
dark recesses of cellars and attics, they have been known to rear
their young in infrequently opened closets, desk drawers, bookcases, and cabinets. When surprised in such places and unable to flee,
they will bite in self-defense. Such bites are extremely dangerous.

Over three hundred species of mice are known to exist in
the world (everywhere except in the Pacific Islands). They are universally domesticated and find in human habitations safety from
their natural enemies, materials for nest making and plentiful food.
House mice are blue-gray in color and, including their tails, reach
a length of four inches. They, too, produce as many as fifty young

a year, all of which can fend for themselves in a fortnight. They
are not as loathsome or dangerous as rats, but are a nuisance in
libraries because of the damage they do to paper which they fancy
for nest making and because of the droppings they deposit.

Squirrels are typical rodents. Friendly and pleasant as they
are in the woods and parks, in public buildings they are pests. Although strict vegetarians, normally living and breeding in warm
lined nests in hollow trees, when trapped in buildings the damage
they can do with their teeth is surprising. All too frequently they
are cultivated as pets and encouraged to sit on window sills and
desks to beg for food. This seemingly harmless trick can be the
means by which vermin (beetles, grubs, fleas, etc.) are introduced
into libraries. It has been established that insect infestations in at
least one New England library originated in just this way.

Although not classified as vermin, pigeons living in and
around public buildings often get out of hand. In addition to depositing their excrement everywhere, they transport insects from place
to place in their feathers. They roost and nest in air shafts, attics
and anywhere else they can escape from inclement weather, fouling
these places with manure. The origin of an infestation of bookworms (carpet beetles) in one New England library was traced directly to a pigeon roost in an internal air shaft. These beetles,
brought into the shaft by the birds, made their way between the
walls to the interiors of glass enclosed bookcases containing some
of the library's most important acquisitions. Fortunately they were
discovered and destroyed before much damage was done.

FUNGI--Fungi are the most numerous of living things, occurring wherever there is organic matter upon which they can sub-
sist. Most are too small to be seen with the naked eye. These
plants are quite diverse in structure, but all lack chlorophyll, the
green coloring matter of other plants. They are either parasites,
living on and absorbing food from other living plants, or sapro-
phytes which live on dead or decaying organic matter. The difference between fungi and plants of higher order is physiological, resulting from these food habits. Green plants absorb carbon dioxide
from the air and with the aid of their chlorophyll in the presence

of light and moisture, convert it into carbohydrates for tissue building and growth. Since fungi have no chlorophyll, they must get
their carbohydrates from other organic matter. Another distinguishing characteristic of these plants is that they grow much better in
darkness than they do in light.

Mildew and mold are interchangeable terms to describe those
fungi which, living in or on organic tissues, obtain their food by
sending root-like organs into the host's cells. They are recognized
by the powdery masses (colonies) of spores which they form on the
surfaces of infested materials. Mold is found where dampness pre-
vails, such as in cellars and other inadequately ventilated spaces.
The slightest trace is a warning that the temperature and humidity
are above the limits of safety for library materials.

Fungi spores, always present in great numbers in the air,
are quite harmless until they find an environment in which the humidity is high, temperature warm, light subdued and nourishment
abounds--conditions which exist in many libraries and archives.
At first the problem is only a nuisance and the mold spores can be
removed easily by vacuum cleaning or by brushing when the material can be carried outdoors. However, if the conditions favoring the
mold growth are not remedied, the second stage of fungi deterioration (staining) takes place. This is evidence that the micro-organisms are beginning to digest the host material. If, at this time,
positive action is not taken to kill the spores and reduce the humidity and temperature, serious damage will result. Leather will rot;
paper will be eroded on the surface, then become soft and as absorbent as blotting paper and will ultimately be reduced to a crumbling pulp.

When fungi attack the starches and glues in paper these sizes
are converted to other materials lacking the strengthening properties of the sizes. After the starches are digested, the mold attacks the cellulose fibers making the paper soft and weak. It is
easy to distinguish between acid deterioration in paper and fungi deterioration. Acid embrittles the sheets (causing them to crack
when folded); paper weakened by fungi, although very soft and weak,
can still be handled and folded without breaking.

The same molds which damage paper cause certain iron gall inks to fade. In extreme cases this fading can obliterate the writing in manuscripts. It is difficult to restore writing faded by fungicidal action.

In recent years it has been learned that papers vary in their resistance to fungi, depending upon the chemical treatment during manufacture. Machine-made wood pulp papers are much more vulnerable than handmade rag papers. Sized papers, because they are less hygroscopic, are more resistant than unsized papers. Paper with a pH of 5.5 to 6.0 is extremely resistant to mold. Papers bleached with chlorine are particularly susceptible to one species of mold that assimilates free chlorine and synthesizes its products. Calendered paper, because it is smoother, cleaner, and less hygroscopic, resists mold, whereas the rougher textured papers more easily harbor the spores. Certain resin sizes in paper inhibit mold and on the other hand, gelatins and starch sizes encourage it.

Certain dangerous bacteria also live on organic matter, but fortunately they are rarely found in libraries. When this does occur, it is because the library materials have been contaminated by saliva, mucus, grease or other unsanitary substances.

Foxing, the annoying brown spots often seen on old paper, is evidence that fungi have been at work in the paper even though the mold and the conditions causing it may long since have been corrected. In 1935 Thomas Iiams and T.D. Beckwith (at the Huntington Library in California) conducted an extensive investigation of foxing and concluded that it is independent of the intensity of development of mold (i.e., foxing can happen even though the fungi present are too few to be observed by the naked eye).

They further concluded that:

(a) The moisture necessary for foxing is far less than that required for the development of visible molds.

(b) The extent of foxing in paper is influenced to a high degree by the methods of manufacture (namely: the iron salts and other impurities added).

(c) Fourteenth-century paper of almost pure cellulose is generally less foxed than late eighteenth or early nineteenth-century paper.

(d) Foxing stains are the result of chemical action between the iron impurities (iron hydroxide and iron oxide) in paper and the organic acids released by the fungi.

Although Iiams and Beckwith admitted that their study did not resolve the problem of foxing, it is the best available information on the subject.

Chemists have also discovered that vegetable-tanned leathers, which are preferred for fine binding, are more susceptible to mold growth than chrome-tanned skins. Microscopic examination of mildewed leather has revealed that the fungi, rather than attacking the collagen fibers, invade the substances incorporated in the skins during tanning. Rose and Turner's experiments in England have proven that water in excess of that molecularly bound in leather must be present to support destructive mold growth.

Kanagy and others at the U.S. Bureau of Standards (Journal of Research 36/1946) proved that the loss of strength in mildewed leather is due to decomposition of the grease in the material and is not due to breakdown of the hide substance. These findings suggest that the cause of the breakdown of mold-infested leather is not the same as the cause for the destruction of moldy wood, paper or other cellulosic material. More recent experiments by Mme. Flieder in Paris (Laboratoire de Cryptogamie) proved conclusively that mildew in its advanced stages will cause leather to stain and discolor and degenerate into a rotten mass.

Bark books, palm leaf manuscripts and vellum, parchment, and papyrus are just as vulnerable to the attacks of fungi.

ACID--The archenemy of librarians and archivists is acid. Because of the various means by which acid can be introduced, no library is safe from this insidious foe. Other enemies are easily recognized and some are relatively easy to curb before much damage is done, but the acidification of paper and leather often passes the danger point before those most closely concerned with the care of these materials are aware of what is taking place. In many instances the leather or paper is acidified during manufacture and fiber deterioration has already begun before the books, prints, maps or manuscripts become the responsibility of librarians.

Principle sources of acid in paper are sulphur dioxide in
polluted air, lignin in wood pulp, alum-rosin sizes, residual bleaching chemicals, iron gall ink, and migration from other materials.
Leather is acidified by chemicals added during manufacture, by ab-
sorption of sulphur dioxide from polluted air or by migration of
acid from other acidified materials. Parchment and vellum, because of their alkaline nature, resist acid.

Sulphur dioxide alone, even in relatively high concentrations
in city air, is harmless to library materials. However, in the
presence of even minute traces of copper and iron, the catalytic
action of these metals causes the sulphur dioxide to react with water
(moisture in the material) to form sulphuric acid, which completely
destroys cellulose and collagen fibers by breaking down the molecular structures. This causes paper to become so brittle as to crumble when handled and so badly stained as to almost obliterate printing and illustrations. The amount of acid present is not as important as the fact that it is there, because in time even the weakest
concentrations will accomplish the same destruction.

The chemical activity of acid present in materials is measured in terms of pH, which expresses the hydrogen ion concentration. For library work the pH of a material can be determined
with sufficient accuracy by spot testing with certain chemical indicators. The pH scale is an arbitrary one. It is numbered from
one to fourteen with 7.0 the neutral point, 14 the limit of alkalinity,
and 3.0 an indication of extreme acidity. It is important to remember that because the scale is logarithmic, the increase in acidity
between 7.0 and 6.0 is only one-tenth of the increase between 6.0
and 5.0 and so on up or down the scale. Sulphuric acid is the
most injurious because it is not volatile, but even the weakest acids
have a measurable deteriorating effect on paper. Sulphuric acid in
leather makes it brittle, causing book joints to split and backs to
tear off. Acidified leather will eventually deteriorate to a red
powdery substance (red rot) totally lacking in strength or protective
value.

The quality controls in the modern paper making industry
are sufficient to insure removal of all bleach residues. This was

not always the case. In the early nineteenth century papermakers
relied heavily on chlorine to whiten pulp made from soiled rags.
The chlorine residues left in these papers were ultimately converted
to hydrochloric acid, which is almost as destructive as sulphuric
acid. This accounts for the staining and embrittlement of some rag
paper that should have retained its whiteness and original strength
for centuries. Contrary to popular belief, good paper does not naturally become old looking with age. Many papers made in the sixteenth and seventeenth century from clean, white rags with nothing
added have, with normal care, remained as crisp and clean as the
day they were made. Stained paper is the result of contamination
and abuse and not of age. Even paper made with cellulose derived
entirely from wood will remain crisp and clean for great lengths of
time if the impurities are completely removed from the pulp and it
is not sized with rosin. Durable wood pulp papers of high quality
are now being made by some papermakers.

The principle source of acid in modern paper is the use of
alum to precipitate rosin size and to overcome other manufacturing
problems. Rosin sizing reduces the cost of paper production. Alum,
a weak acid, is required to precipitate the rosin and to cause clay
particles, the loading in many book papers, to adhere to the pulp
fibers. The combination of the acid action of the alum and its oxidation of the rosin causes early embrittlement and darkening of
many machine-made papers. Starch and gelatin sizes, which are
applied to the finished sheets, are relatively harmless to paper.

Most of the early iron gall inks and almost all modern inks
are acid. India ink, a suspension of carbon black in a liquid, is
not. The number of early written manuscripts on which the ink has
eaten through the paper is ample evidence of the acidity of iron gall
writing fluids. About 1930 the National Bureau of Standards tested
all of the inks then in use by United States government agencies
(and also several made to the specifications of early iron gall formulas) and found that all of them appreciably weakened the papers
on which they were tested. Again, the villain is acid.

In the case of iron gall ink, sulphuric acid is formed by reaction of ferrous sulphate with gallic and tannic acids. In addition

to burning through the paper directly under the writing, this acid
migrates into the paper around the writing and into adjacent sheets
as well.   The destructive action of the acid continues for a long
time, discoloring and weakening page after page of the paper as the
migration progresses.

  Lignin is a highly complex organic acid which surrounds and
impregnates the cellulose fibers and which gives weight and substance to woody plants.   If it is not removed from wood pulp in the
paper-making process, it is a major source of trouble for librarians.   Even today, after many years of study by paper chemists,
the chemical is not completely understood.   It is subject to oxidation and is affected by light.   After degeneration by either or both
of these two processes, the acid organic by-products that result attack cellulose fibers.   In the case of newsprint, in which little of
the lignin is removed during manufacture, staining and embrittlement begins to take place in just a few days.   Cheap paper made
for inexpensive books often has a high lignin content and it, too,
soon deteriorates.   After the perfection of the process for making
paper from wood pulp (mid-nineteenth century) and before chemists
had identified the reason for the inferiority of the product and developed means to improve the quality, most books and magazines
and many prints, maps and broadsides, etc., were printed on paper
with a high lignin content.   The hundreds of thousands of almost
useless books standing on library shelves today are mute evidence
of that practice.

  Unfortunately for library conservators, acid in paper, like
acid in ink, migrates to other paper, cardboard, textiles, or leather
in contact with the contaminated sheets.   Because of this, manuscripts written with the best carbon ink on high quality rag paper
can be seriously damaged by storing them in document boxes made
of inexpensive cardboard or by keeping them in file folders made of
cheap paper.   Manuscripts bound in books with cheap end papers
and boards are soon weakened and discolored.   At first only the
manuscripts at the beginning and the end of the books are effected,
but after a number of years every sheet will be contaminated.   The
practice of mounting manuscript collections in blank books, with

each manuscript fastened to a separate blank page of what was often the cheapest of wood pulp paper, was even more destructive.

Summary: Much knowledge is available about the enemies of all library materials, rare or otherwise. It behooves the librarian, regardless of the function of his organization, to familiarize himself with those he can be expected to enounter and to use the means at his command to control them.

Chapter IV
General Care of Library Materials

Libraries are following the lead of museums in the scientific approach to preservation. Researchers are isolating the enemies of books and examining library materials to discover exactly what they are and why they act as they do. Preservation, no longer empirical, now emphasizes prevention to avoid costly repairs and restoration. Rapidly increasing knowledge in this field cautions us not to rely too heavily on the older methods of conservation.

Northeastern University's Dr. T. N. Ferdinand in speaking of the problem of obsolescence in science and engineering said, "Obsolescence exists when an individual uses viewpoints, theories, concepts and techniques that are less effective in solving problems than others currently available in his field of specialization." (American Scientist, 54 No 1 (1966) page 46.) This applies to librarians and archivists.

Knowing the nature of the enemies of library materials, the first objective is the creation of an environment in which these enemies cannot exist. This includes temperature and humidity control, the removal of aerosols and noxious gases from polluted air and good housekeeping. Other factors to be considered are lighting, storage conditions, control of vermin, the use of fungicides, ventilation, and the routine care of library materials.

ENVIRONMENT CONTROL--In terms of conservation, nothing will give greater return than an investment in air-conditioning and a carefully planned and rigidly supervised program of housekeeping. Air-conditioning is expensive and the wages of cleaning personnel are high, but the costs of bookbinding, repair, restoration, and replacements are higher. Cellulose is subject to deterioration by hydrolysis, oxidation and photosynthesis. Each is accelerated by heat. Paper degradation is minimized by low temperatures and dryness, which, however, make parchment and vellum horny and are not

80

beneficial to leather and other library materials. It has been determined that temperatures between 60° - 75°F and relative humidities between 50% - 60% are optimum for the preservation of library
materials. However, control of temperature and humidity is only
half the problem in regulating the atmosphere in which library materials are kept. Air admitted to libraries and archives in urban
areas should be free of contaminating aerosols and noxious gases to
reduce the accumulations of grime and to minimize the chemical deterioration of materials.[1]

Air Conditioning--The most practical way to control temperature and humidity and clean air is by central air-conditioning.
These systems are most efficient when designed into new construction, but they can be installed in existing structures. The four
functions of air conditioning are ventilation, filtration, temperature
control, and humidity control.[2]

Ventilation--From the point of view of conservation, oxygen
must be classified as a noxious gas. It supports the lives of
people in libraries, but it reacts degeneratively with paper, leather,
film and other materials. Fortunately, this oxidation, with the exception of certain films and other plastics, is a slow process under
the conditions normally encountered in libraries.

Filtration--It is possible by filtering to clean urban air of
its contaminating aerosols and noxious gases, minimizing the grime,
abrasion, and chemical deterioration they normally introduce. Suspended aerosols are screened from air by filters, spun out by cy-
clone devices, or precipitated electrostatically. All can be effective, but filters are the least expensive. Because contaminated air
is let into a building every time a door or window is opened, it
would be pointless to require 100% effectiveness in air filtration.
Such efficiency would also be extremely expensive because of the
power required to pump air through the denser filters that would be
required and the cost of their frequent cleaning. Sulphur dioxide
can be partially removed from air by frequent recirculation through
activated charcoal filters. A more effective system (used at the
Folger Shakespeare Library, the National Archives in Washington
and the National Gallery in London) is to pass incoming air through

a water spray. Pure water will remove about half the sulphur dioxide. An alkaline water spray (pH 8.5 to 9.0) will remove all of
the gas.

Ozone can be removed from air only by expensive electro-
static precipitation.

Temperature Control--For the health and comfort of people,
indoor temperatures must be kept between 65° - 75°F but this range
of temperature is about the point at which accelerated deterioration
of library materials begins. Whereas 50°F is an excellent temperature for books, common sense dictates that rooms be kept at about
68°F, the threshold of human comfort.

Humidity Control--People can tolerate wide ranges of change
in humidity, but because of the sensitivity of organic materials to
moisture changes, relative humidity in libraries should be kept within reasonable limits. Forty-five to sixty-five percent is desirable
--above that mold is encouraged; below it, paper and papyrus become brittle and vellum horny, wood warps and leather reacts un-
predictably. Modern air conditioning systems, room air condition-
ers, and dehumidifiers can easily control relative humidity between
50% - 60%. Regardless of the type of control, it must be operated
continuously, day-in and day-out, to maintain a constant moisture
level.

The cost of complete air-conditioning (temperature, humidity
control and filtration) is reasonable in new construction. It is expensive in old buildings, but it should be installed in every library
if at all possible. If treating the entire area is out of the question,
consideration should be given to isolated humidity control. (See
Amdur, E.J. "Humidity Control - Isolated Area Plan" Museum
News Technical Supplement December 1964/No. 6.) Such modifi-
cation would provide protection for the library's treasures.

The operation of air-conditioning equipment should be checked
frequently by engineers. In the northern United States, where sea-
sonal temperature changes can be as much as 110°F, the relative
humidity may fluctuate between 10% and 90% in a very short time.
Unless the equipment continues to keep humidity between 50% - 60%,
the money spent for air conditioning will be largely wasted insofar

as conservation is concerned.

Housekeeping--The hundreds of thousands of individual dust collecting items in libraries, plus all of the dirt catchers normally found in large public buildings, make housekeeping doubly difficult. Regular cleaning personnel rarely understand the great importance of cleanliness in libraries. A cleaning schedule establishing orders of priority, sequences of operations, and daily and weekly routines should do much to insure that all of the spaces in a library get their share of attention. Additional specific instructions for getting into remote corners, behind cabinets and under desks to remove dirt and refuse which harbor vermin, would be equally useful, if supervision is close enough to ensure compliance. Frequent inspections by key personnel are of great value in the battle against dirt.

The regulations governing book storerooms in the Lenin Library in Moscow (translated into English in Collection of Materials on the Preservation of Library Resources, USSR State Library 1953 U.S. Department of Commerce OTS Publication 64 - 11053) provide an excellent example of what can and should be done to control dirt and vermin.

Librarians should give serious consideration to good, old-fashioned spring cleaning in a different part of the attic, basement and closed stacks at least once a quarter to remove every vestige of dirt that will attract insects and rodents. Paralleling the work of the cleaning staff, the building superintendent should make sure that leaks in plumbing and heating systems and in the walls and roof are promptly repaired; that basements are kept dry and that holes in walls and foundations, particularly around sewer pipes, are plugged with cement. Books should be cleaned with a vacuum cleaner rather than by dusting; formalin or other disinfectants should be used in all cleaning water; trash should never be allowed to accumulate anywhere; and snacks and beverages should be prohibited except in designated dining areas.

Since most libraries have no more cleaning personnel than is necessary to keep the offices and public areas presentable, there are alternative solutions. For instance, the manuscript division at the Library of Congress keeps one man fully employed at cleaning

books and book shelves, oiling leather-bound volumes, and doing
simple repairs. Operating with a library cart carrying cleaning
supplies and equipment, his work is a model of efficiency as he
moves from row to row and stack to stack, keeping tens of thousands of bound volumes in clean and serviceable condition.

When it is impossible to provide even one full time book
cleaner, consideration should be given to the use of students or vol-
unteer help for occasional cleaning of selected areas. One library's
procedure is to set up a working space to which the books from the
area selected for cleaning are temporarily removed for cleaning by
student employees who are available during the summer. The
walls, floor, ceiling and shelving in the emptied space are scrubbed
with detergents, following which everything is painted. After this,
if there has been any evidence of vermin, insecticides are painted
or sprayed in the cracks and crevices and in other areas normally
blocked by the books. Before the books are returned to their original shelves, they are individually vacuum cleaned and inspected for
evidences of mildew and other damage. Then the leather-bound
volumes are treated with a good dressing, vellum covers are
washed carefully with saddle soap, and worn and frayed clothbound
volumes are sprayed with acrylic resin. The pages of any books
with traces of mildew are sprayed with a 5% solution of thymol in
alcohol. Books that show other signs of chemical or physical damage are set aside for further repairs.

Light--Light bleaches colored paper, leather, and textiles;
it fades colors in prints and maps; and it accelerates the chemical
and physical degenerative processes in all organic materials. Since
it is not feasible to keep libraries completely dark, the alternative
is to reduce the exposure to light as much as possible. Sunlight
should be prevented from falling directly on book shelves, framed
material or exhibition cases. Window lighting should be diffused by
Venetian blinds, curtains or louvers of opal glass. The ultraviolet
component of fluorescent light can be filtered out by inexpensive
sleeves slipped over the cylindrical tubes. Window glass that ex-
cludes the most harmful of the sun's rays is available for new construction. Although it is too expensive to replace all the glass in

an older building, it might be well to consider this for the windows
of rare book rooms.

Display cases should have protective glass that absorbs both
heat and ultraviolet rays.   Lacking these, cases should have plastic
filter sheets taped to the inside of glass surfaces to eliminate the
ultraviolet component from the light falling on the items being shown.
These cases should always be illuminated from the outside or by
concealed fluorescent lamps that are screened by plastic ultraviolet
filters.

When a library is closed, it should be kept in darkness.
Regardless of the fact that darkness encourages mold growth and at-
tracts vermin, all document rooms, storerooms and closed stacks
should be darkened except when in actual use and illumination in
these places should be by incandescent bulbs or filtered fluorescent
lights.

Housing--Few librarians are fortunate enough to have new
buildings incorporating the latest air-conditioning engineering, lighting design, physical security, and construction features.   The great
majority must make do by incorporating modern conservation and
security measures in older buildings as funds become available.
Guidance for this is available in Neal Harlow's discussion of the design of special library facilities in his essay, "Physical Housing
and Equipment."   (Rare Book Collections, Association of College
and Research Libraries Monograph No. 27, Chicago, American Library Association 1965.)   Clara LeGear describes an ideal library
map room in Maps: Their Care, Repair, and Preservation in Libraries (Washington, Library of Congress, 1956), and other construction and renovation guides are available in professional library literature.

The National Archives in Washington probably incorporates
as much built-in storage protection for library materials as any
building in the world.   A description of the design of the building,
together with the scientific justification for its various features, is
contained in Kimberly & Scribner's Summary Report of Bureau of
Standards Research on the Preservation of Records, Washington,
U.S. Government Printing Office, 1934.

The considerable literature on museum protection (fire, burglar proofing, etc.) should be of particular interest to archivists and keepers of rare book collections.   An example is H.P. Scott's "Lighting and Protection for an Art Museum" (Electrical Construction and Maintenance, New York, 1956).   It describes the measures installed at the Clarke Art Institute, Williamsburg, Massachusetts for alarms, smoke detection, temperature and humidity control, lighting, etc.

The National Fire Protection Association in Boston, an independent, nonprofit, technical and educational clearing house, is the best source for fire safety information.   Their Fire Protection Handbook (1965), and Standard For The Protection of Records (1963) are both important and they list six hundred titles on various aspects of fire prevention.

It would be interesting to know how many libraries depend primarily on sprinkler systems for fire protection.   Except in fires that completely destroy the building, the damage done by water usually far exceeds that done by the flames.   Where local ordinances require standpipes in public parts of library buildings, fog making devices are as effective as spray nozzles and the fog is far less destructive to books and paper.   The use of foam for fire control produces a minimum of moisture damage to records and it warrants serious consideration.[3]   The advantage of low water content, lightweight, high-expansion foam is that it can be generated in massive 1000:1 volumes from small quantities of liquid.   When used in conjunction with an automatic fire detection system, it provides fast extinction with no damage to records in closed cases, boxes and files.   With the exception of plastic materials, foam does relatively little damage to unpackaged items.   Since motion picture film, photographs, microfilm, film slides, phonograph records, and audio discs are usually in some sort of protective covering, this should not disqualify foam for fire protection in libraries.

When a building is not of fireproof construction, dry type extinguishers should be in every room.   These emit carbon tetrachloride, methyl bromide or carbon dioxide, all of which are effective. The larger carbon dioxide extinguishers on wheels can even contain

fires that have gotten a good start.   Acid-type extinguishers should
be avoided.   Asbestos blankets, strategically placed, should be a
part of every library's protection.   It was learned after a fire at
the Baltimore County Branch Library (Library Journal 87, 1962)
that tightly packed books, phonograph records, and card catalogues
suffered relatively little damage, whereas loosely packed items were
badly scorched or burned.   Protective coverings such as book
jackets, boxes, and envelopes were surprisingly effective in keeping
the flames away from their contents.

Theft during working hours is controllable by efficient security guards and a careful check-out system.   Burglary is discouraged
by the many excellent alarm devices obtainable from protection
services.   Museum News 43 (1965) No. 10 describes an inexpensive
alarm system utilizing a $32. 00 radio transmitter and receiver.
This is equally applicable for the protection of special collections
in libraries.

In 1956, at the request of the International Council on Museums, Interpol (the international police organization) investigated
the measures museums might take against theft.   Their report, in
UNESCO's Museum 17 (1964), analyzes the problem and gives a
plan of action for detection and defense and operational procedures.

Infrequently as it occurs, when the time comes for moving
a library, the problem is not as simple as hiring a moving con-
tractor or calling on volunteers.   Serious damage can be done unless the work is supervised by personnel experienced in the handling of books.   Before a move is made, the operation should be
carefully planned, based on the information in Peter Spyer-Duran's
Moving Library Materials, Chicago, Library Technology Project,
American Library Association 1965, and William Kurth, Moving
a Library, Metuchen, N. J. , Scarecrow Press, 1966.

Storage--The benefits of expensive air-conditioning systems
and the most meticulous attention to housekeeping will be of little
avail if the containers for library materials are not well designed.
File folders, document boxes, slip cases for books and portfolios
for prints, maps, and broadsides which are made of inferior cardboard, or are lined with cheap ground wood pulp or rosin sized

paper, contaminate the material they are "protecting" by the migration of their acid into the paper or leather they contact.   Flimsy
document boxes with loose, ill-fitting covers are nesting places for
vermin.   They also admit dust and mold spores which find them
ideal places for growth.   Wooden boxes are gnawed by rodents,
bored by bookworms, are high in lignin content, and are hygroscopic.   Tin and steel boxes rust.   Plastic envelopes, other than those
of cellulose acetate, may seriously damage photographs, negatives,
and film slides.   Containers for library materials, whatever their
size and shape, should be made only of high quality acid-free paper
and cardboard, pyroxylin coated book cloth, aluminum, stainless
steel, cellulose acetate, or acid resistant leather.   Covers should
be dust tight, but not air tight.

It is relatively easy to test folders, document boxes, and
portfolios to see if replacement is required.   A drop of phloroglu-
cinal solution applied to paper or cardboard will turn red if lignin
is present.   Another drop of a pH test solution will give an indication of the degree of acidity.   A pH of less than 6.0, or evidence
of lignin, requires replacement.   Permanent/durable acid-free file
folder stock[4] is available from several sources (See Appendix G).

The Institute of Paper Chemistry has completed a study for
the Council on Library Resources on the suitability of protective
boxes.[5]   The conclusions were that control of acidity in box material is a simple matter, but that good housekeeping is more effective
in repelling insects from boxes than is the incorporation of chemical ingredients in the stock.   Plastic coating and aluminum lamination of the cardboard improved resistance to mold, but built-in fire
resistance was difficult to obtain.   The findings of this report indicate that although some boxes are better than others in this respect
permanent/durable document boxes are not available.   The alternative for those needing such receptacles is to select a sturdy, high
quality box for storage purposes, but to slip the actual documents
in acid-free file folders cut to fit before placing them in the boxes.
The specifications for storage boxes developed for the National Archives are given in American Archivist v. 13 (1950) and v. 17
(1954).

Book boxes are useful for protecting luxury bindings, old
bindings with important decoration and tooling, and rare books in
contemporary, but dilapidated boards.   Boxes with fall down covers[6]
are much better suited for this purpose than the traditional slip
cases and solander cases, because books can be removed from them
easily without subjecting the spines to strain or the sides to abrasion.

Any member of the Guild of Book Workers or any reputable
commercial bindery is capable of making protective cases that are
as simple or as elaborate as may be desired.   They should be fab-
ricated only with best quality millboards or commercial black boards,
acid resistant leather, pyroxylin impregnated book cloth, and handmade rag paper or permanent/durable machine-made paper.

The most practical and economical method for storing pamphlets is in document boxes made to sizes convenient for shelving.
This preserves the slender volumes in their original state.   Luxury
bindings for valuable pamphlets, regardless of how pleasing to the
eye, or bulk bindings of runs of pamphlets are never entirely satisfactory.   Luxury bindings are too often out of keeping with the contents.   Bulk bindings, if oversewn, are awkward to handle and difficult to read because of the reduced inner margin.   When miscellaneous pamphlets are bound together and the edges trimmed, it is
inevitable that one or more will have dangerously cropped margins.
Pamphlets required for circulation must be bound.   However, they
should not be expected to last as long as other books in circulation.
Important and valuable pamphlets should be individually boxed.

Collections of manuscripts are best stored in acid-free wrappers in flat document boxes with the documents unfolded and lying
flat.   The use of acid-free file folders in steel drawer filing cabinets is more convenient but is less satisfactory from the point of
view of preservation.   Documents standing on edge are likely to be
injured when removed from crowded drawers.   The nineteenth century practice of binding manuscripts in book form, has largely been
abandoned for many reasons.   Owners of manuscript collections in
nineteenth-century bindings will invariably find that inferior binding
materials have badly contaminated the records.   It is most impor-

tant to remove such damaged records from the bindings as soon as possible and to place them in acid-free wrappers. These should be stored in document boxes until such time as they can be deacidified, old paste and glue removed, and other necessary repairs made. When stored in boxes several manuscripts can safely be kept in each wrapper and ten to twenty wrappers will fit into each box, making thirty to seventy documents per box.

Assuming that librarians are able to store all their manuscripts in acid-free wrappers in sturdy boxes, there is still danger to their collections:

    a. if ground wood pulp paper or rosin sized documents are in the same folder with good quality paper.

    b. if news clippings are attached to written or typewritten records.

    c. if cardboard separators are used for convenience.

News clippings should be deacidified if they must be filed with good paper; otherwise they should be filed separately. Records that have become dark and brittle with age should be removed and tested for acid and lignin, and restorative measures taken before they are returned to the files. When highly acid documents are discovered, it would be well to test other papers with which they may have been in contact for extended periods.

Prints[7]--The disparity in the physical conditions of prints of any period is due as much to improper maintenance as it is to chemical and physical deterioration. The proper care of prints includes careful handling as well as the provision of a safe and healthful environment. Prints should be filed in flat boxes or flat drawer metal filing cabinets and should be in individual acid-free paper wrappers. To minimize the probability of damage, handling should be reduced to a minimum. Use two hands when it is necessary to remove them from their wrappers. When matted for exhibition, 100% rag content cardboard with rag paper hinges should be used. Pressure sensitive tape should not be used. Sheets of cellulose acetate in the window of open-face mounts will provide extra protection.

Broadsides are best protected in acid-free paper wrappers in flat document boxes. When handling is necessary, the same precautions should apply as for prints.

Maps--Maps in any form are awkward to handle. They are
rarely of uniform size; many are rolled on wooden rods or have
been clumsily folded. The rolled maps are usually dirty, embrittled by acid, darkened by varnish, and backed by rotting fabric.
Folded and flat maps are often as bad.

The best protection for maps is to file them in acid-free
wrappers in flat drawer steel blueprint files (about 35" x 45" x 2").
Up to ten sheets can be put in one wrapper and ten filled wrappers
will conveniently fit in a drawer. Such map cases are used in the
Library of Congress and British Museum map rooms. Blueprint
files will receive most maps without folding and almost all sheets
with no more than one fold. A single fold does little harm to a
map. Double or triple folds are particularly damaging where the
creased edges meet and should be avoided. Extra-large sheets can
be wrapped around three-inch diameter mailing tubes which have
been covered with a good grade of acid-free paper. The bundle can
then be wrapped in linen for dust protection and stored on top of
the cabinets. Some early maps, particularly those of seacoast
areas, were made by irregularly pasting together several smaller
printed sheets. When too large for the cabinets, they can be soaked
apart, dried and pressed, and filed in a single wrapper with appropriate labeling.

It has been discovered by experience at the British Museum
that it is false economy to file modern reference maps without previously backing them with high quality paper or fabric. They are
too easily damaged even by normal use and are soon rendered un-
serviceable unless reinforced.

Examination of framed maps, prints, broadsides and related
material will reveal that they are frequently backed with pine boards,
often with old newspapers or cheap cardboard as padding between
the boards and pictures. These should be removed. The paper has
undoubtedly been damaged, even if it is not already stained and
darkened, and will require deacidification to arrest the deterioration. If these items are to be reframed, professional picture restorers can reduce the stains and resize the paper if necessary.

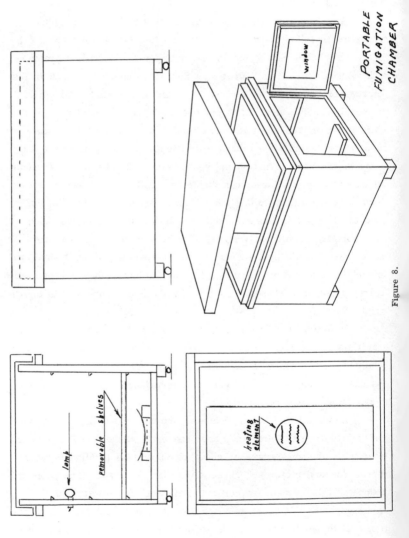

window

PORTABLE
FUMIGATION
CHAMBER

lamp

removable shelves

heating
element

Figure 8.

92

Portable Fumigation Chamber

(design based on that of the Bibliotheque Nationale)

1. Cabinet of wood (metal lining optional); interior unpainted and unvarnished.

2. Soft rubber gaskets on door and between cover and box.

3. Three removable shelves.

4. Wired for 110 volt alternating current. Heating element, covered by large watch glass, is rheostat controlled.

5. Interior is illuminated by a twenty-five watt lamp.

6. Dimensions are optional - 30" width, 48" length, and 30" height are convenient.

7. Suitable for use with thymol, formalin, ethylene oxide, camphor, naphthalene, and para-dichlorobenzene.

8. WARNING: Do not use with carbon disulphide unless all electrical fittings are disconnected. CARBON DISULPHIDE EVAPORATES TO FORM AN EXPLOSIVE MIXTURE WITH AIR.

Items not intended for display are safer in acid-free wrappers in
document boxes or map cases than in frames.

Pest Control--In the United States chemists and entomol-
ogists are experimenting with infra-red, ultraviolet light and high
frequency sound waves in a continuing search for new pest control
methods.   The Japanese are investigating heat and reduced air pressure for the same purpose.   These methods warrant increased attention because of growing concern about the effect of pesticides on
people and animals, the increasing resistance of insects to chemical poisons, and the sensitivity of some organic materials to strong
chemicals.   It is probable that these experiments will some day provide new controls, but for the present we must depend upon proven
techniques.   All insecticides are poisonous to human beings and
must be used with great care.   Recommended precautions in using
these chemicals are discussed on page 99.

The problem of insect control consists of (a) keeping insects
out,   (b) containing them once they gain access to a library, and
(c) destroying them.   Insects need not be a problem in libraries
where good housekeeping and sanitation are the rule if all incoming
materials, including returned books as well as new acquisitions and
donations, are examined carefully.   It would be ideal if all new items
could be vacuum fumigated as is done at the Huntington Library, the
National Archives and some other libraries, but the cost of the
necessary equipment rules that out for most.   Effective fumigation
is obtainable by the use of less expensive, but also less efficient,
chambers.   A third alternative is to examine each incoming book
page by page and to scrutinize all other incoming material and supplies.   When this searching uncovers winged insects, larvae or pupae, they can be destroyed by spraying.   The same can be accomplished by placing the infested material in a tightly closed container
with a tray containing a mixture of three parts ethylene dichloride
to one part carbon tetrachloride.   Paradichlorobenzene or carbon
disulfide are equally effective.   Such an atmosphere will kill all
winged insects and larvae in twenty-four hours, but the box should
not be opened for three weeks to insure that larvae subsequently
emerging from eggs are also destroyed.   This is a slow process,

but the probability of 100% kill is greater than by spraying.

When in spite of all precautions insects do get into a library, they can be eradicated if prompt, positive action is taken. Cockroaches, silverfish, firebrats, bookworms, termites, and moths are all vulnerable to one or more of the many powerful insecticides available. If applied according to instructions, or better still by a professional exterminator, the pests can be eliminated without endangering personnel.

Air-conditioned steel and concrete buildings are generally safe from earth-dwelling termites. Older buildings are not, unless protective measures are taken by professional exterminators. Earth-dwelling termites that do gain access are quite readily poisoned by the application of insecticides near their tunnels, on top of their nests, or in cracks and crevices in floors and walls. Because termites lick each other's bodies and devour their own dead, they assist in their own destruction if enough chemicals are placed near the nests or tunnels.

Wood-dwelling termites can be excluded by tight building construction and window screens, but once they gain access, only fumigation will rid a building of them. This calls for professional assistance. If hydrocyanic gas is used, the building will have to be sealed for forty-eight hours and then aired for forty-eight more before it is safe for human entry. If it is not feasible to close a building for four days, a less effective job can be done in twenty-four hours with methyl bromide.

When termites are known to have gained access to a library, a temporary measure to keep them out of the books is to move the wooden shelves aways from the walls and stand them on plates of metal or in dishes of coal tar or creosote.

Cockroaches, silverfish, firebrats, bedbugs, mosquitos, and bookworms in the beetle stage can be controlled effectively by spraying the walls, woodwork, floors, ceilings, interiors of closets and cupboards with dieldrin, using one-half pint of 20% solution per gallon of water. This spray stays lethal for at least two years and will kill any insect on contact. Other effective sprays are oil solutions of five percent DDT, two percent chlordane, two percent ma-

lathion, or one-half of one percent lindane.   Because of the oil,
these are less desirable.   Insecticide powders containing ten percent DDT, five percent chlordane, four percent malathion, or one
percent lindane or dieldrin may be used when they can be dusted
into cracks and crevices or in other places where they will not be
swept up or be visibly objectionable.

There is no effective chemical spray or powder for bookworm larvae because of their burrowing.   They must be destroyed
by fumigation in a vacuum fumigation tank, fumigation chamber, or
a sealed area, with hydrogen cyanide, methyl bromide, carbon disulfide or other lethal gases.   Book varnishes containing insecticides are no longer necessary.

Book lice (psocids) are soft-bodied insects that succumb when
they are subjected to heat and dryness.   Hence, thorough airing on
a hot, dry day of an infested room and everything in it will usually
eliminate a mild infestation of these mites.   If they persist, look
for their breeding places, such as a mass of damp paper or old
rags, or upholstered furniture.   Persistent book lice can be killed
by fumigating the room or building, but this will rarely be necessary.

The aerosol and spray-type insecticides now available eliminate the necessity for sodium fluoride mixed with wheat flour, so
long a stand-by for silverfish control.   That poison--inconvenient to
use, unsightly, and above all hazardous--should be abandoned.   For
display cases, tablets of paradichlorobenzene, inconspicuously
placed, will repel silverfish and other insects.

The Centre National de la Recherche Scientifique in Paris
sells a book wax (CIRE 212) incorporating insecticides and fungicides.   This wax, which comes in several colors, dresses the leath
er covers on books and makes them insect repellent.   The wax is
particularly useful for tropical climates, where complete eradicatior
of insects is almost impossible.

When insects are detected in a library and have probably
been imported in a single book, staff personnel can safely handle
the situation by:

a.   vacuum cleaning all the books in the immediate

vicinity of the contaminated one(s) to remove
dust, dirt, eggs, etc.

b. placing these books, opened fanwise, in a tightly
closed box containing paradichlorobenzene crystals
(one and one-half ounces per cubic foot of box) or
chloroform (one-half ounce per cubic foot) and letting them fumigate for ten days.

c. reshelving the fumigated books and watching them
carefully for at least six months.

The best protection from rodents is to deny them access by
sound building construction, tight screens, and by plugging all holes
in foundation walls, particularly around water and sewer pipes and
gas mains.   Implementing this, it is important to eliminate conditions conducive to multiplication of rats and mice.   Dark, damp
basements, pools of water, accumulations of waste and debris, and
spilled food particles in eating areas all attract these pests.   Once
established in a building a professional exterminator is needed to
eradicate them.

Control of Mildew--Gamma radiation, ultraviolet light, high
frequency currents, and ultrasonic vibrations have all been used
with some success to prevent microbiological deterioration of library
materials.   These are interesting developments and some will no
doubt be in general use one day, but for now it is still necessary
to rely on chemicals and air-conditioning.

Excellent analyses of the problems of fungi and their control
have been made by Fausto Gallo at the Institute of Book Pathology
in Rome[8] and L. A. Belyakova, S. G. Rybakova, and others in Moscow.[9]   Dr. Plenderleith's The Conservation of Antiquities and
Works of Art is also authoritative on this subject.

Fungicides for mildew control are palliative only and in temperate climates should be used only until the heat and dampness en-
couraging the growth of spores are brought under control.   In tropical countries where air-conditioning is not available or its use not
feasible, librarians must rely on chemicals to keep mildew under
control.

Mildew is eliminated permanently only when temperature is
kept at 65 - 75°F and relative humidity at 50 - 60% and when there
is free circulation of air.   These temperature limits are a com-

promise between what is necessary for human comfort and the lower
levels that are optimum for the conservation of library material.
Ventilation is particularly important in buildings that are not air-
conditioned. Even in high humidities, good ventilation will often inhibit the growth of mold. The maintenance of constant temperature
and humidity, even when not within the desired limits, is more desirable than fluctuating readings.

When it is not possible to air-condition a building or selected
rooms, water vapor in the air may be reduced by mechanical units
or chemicals. (Relative humidity can also be increased mechanically.) Moderately priced mechanical dehumidifiers can control
moisture to fairly close tolerances, but have no control of the associated temperature. Anhydrous calcium chloride and silica gel
are effective. Seven pounds of silica gel dehumidify one thousand
cubic feet of air by absorbing moisture. When the gel is saturated,
it is made reusable by heating in an oven. When calcium chloride
is used, it should be exposed, in several locations in the room, in
wire cylinders six inches in diameter and fifteen inches high, standing in shallow pans. This, too, is reactivated by heating. When
using chemical dehumidifiers, all windows must be kept closed and
doors to the spaces being treated should be opened as little as possible.

In non-air-conditioned buildings librarians should have a direct reading hygrometer. When the relative humidity of the outside
air is below 50% (and the temperature permits) all windows and
doors should be opened wide for maximum circulation of drying air.

Mildew inhibitors include phenyl mercuric nitrate, pentachloro
phenol, betanaphthol, para-nitro-phenol, thymol, and salicylanilide.
These, when painted or sprayed on leather, parchment, paper,
papyri, cloth, etc., will help prevent the growth of mildew. They
should be used with care because of their varying effect on materials. Thymol, for instance, dissolves some inks and varnishes, and
para-nitro-phenol stains.

Sometimes, particularly in temperate climates, there are instances of mildew occurring in some parts of libraries (even air-
conditioned ones) and not in others. This can usually be traced to

improper ventilation. Remote rooms with a single door for access
and no outside venting are particularly susceptible. Mildew occurs
often in stack areas where books are tightly packed close to the
floor, walls and ceiling. Glass-enclosed bookcases are also vulnerable. The remedies are to open windows and circulate the air
with fans, provide outside louver-type vents in windowless rooms,
redesign the air-conditioning ducting, reshelve the books to allow
at least six inches of space above, below and behind each stack and
to substitute wire screening for glass fronts in musty cases.

Precautions in Using Fungicides and Insecticides--The advent
of synthetic chemicals for pest control has enabled man to overcome insect infestations that would heretofore have been irrepres-
sible. Unfortunately these controls are not always permanent, for
insects rapidly develop resistance to pesticides. The ever increasing number of poisons of ever greater toxicity, and the danger of
adverse effects on the human system have complicated the problem
of their use. However, this does not mean that libraries and archives should prohibit the use of chemicals for pest control. Rather,
it calls for indoctrination of all personnel in their importance as an
aid to library conservation.

A brief but scholarly analysis of the subject, with a lengthy
bibliography, is Piero Gallo's "Problems in the Use of Insecticides
on Occupied Premises."[10] This is a straightforward presentation
of the dangers involved in the use of insecticides. It is not intended to discourage their application, but to assist in their intelligent
use.

Insecticide poisoning can happen during application or by subsequent contact with the chemical residues. Since toxicity is much
greater for some chemicals than others, librarians should always
specify the use of low toxicity materials for any disinfestation of
their premises. The more important chemicals and their degree of
toxicity, according to Dr. Gallo; are

Insecticides
    Low toxicity: gammexane, chlordane, DDD, DDT,
        dipterex, malathion, methoxychlor, mineral oils,
        pyrethrine, rotenone, chlorbenzide.
    Intermediate toxicity: aldrin, chlorthion, diazinon,

dieldrin, heptachlor, lead arsenate, phenkoptone,
toxaphene.
Very toxic: demeton, dimefox, dinitrobutylphenol,
dinitrocresol (DNC), endrin, fluoroacetamide,
guthion, methylparathion, phosdrin, schradan,
sulphodex, TEPP.

Fungicides
Low toxicity: antibiotics, copper compounds,
dithiocarbamates, TMTD.
Very toxic: concentrated organic mercury compounds.

Repellents
Low toxicity: naphthalene, paradichlorbenzene.

Concentrated chemicals requiring dilution with water or other solvents are most dangerous and they must be prepared with
great caution. It is best that their application in libraries be done
only by professional exterminators. Commercial mixtures are less
hazardous than the concentrated chemicals, but they also must be
treated with respect. Their toxicity is influenced by the nature of
the basic poisons, the solvents or additives and the impurities present. The listing on a package of the chemical constituents of an insecticide mixture or formula does not necessarily indicate its potential effect on the human organism. The safest disinfestations are
carried out in the open air or in well ventilated spaces indoors.
Application of insecticides in small rooms or confined spaces requires extra precautions because of the ease with which dangerous
concentrations of chemicals can be built up.

The probability of insecticide poisoning decreases with added
training. Users must know the risks associated with the work.
They must frequently be reminded of safety precautions and must be
thoroughly familiar with first aid measures for each insecticide
used. The selection of chemicals to be used, the designation of
spaces to be treated, and the routine to be followed must be the responsibility of a specially trained staff member. It may not be left
to the discretion of general maintenance personnel.

Toxic residues from fumigants can persist for several days
after fumigation of a room. Spaces so treated should be sealed off
for at least seventy-two hours. Liquid and aerosol sprays applied
to materials and surfaces inside buildings evaporate slowly. Although not as serious pollutants as gases, their after-effects should

not be ignored. Twenty-four hour isolation of sprayed spaces is prudent. Step-by-step check lists must be mounted beside the controls of vacuum fumigation tanks. Failure to seal the tank door or improper manipulation of the controls could release odorless methyl bromide into the building. Since the symptoms of poisoning from this gas do not appear for several hours, lethal doses could be inhaled.

In 1935 the National Bureau of Standards determined that the following pesticides are harmless to paper: hydrocyanic gas, ethylene chloride, carbon tetrachloride, carbon disulphide, ethylene oxide, carbon dioxide, and methyl formate-carbon dioxide. It has since been learned that acidic gammexane gas, even in minute doses, has a deleterious effect on paper and iron gall ink. Thymol in heavy doses is safe on any library material not coated with oil paints or varnish, except palm leaves.

General precautions in the use of insecticides and fungicides in libraries are:

    a. Read and heed all instructions on the container label.

    b. Keep insecticides stored under lock and key.

    c. Never transfer chemicals to unlabeled containers.

    d. Mix pesticides out-of-doors.

    e. Do not use food-handling utensils for insecticides.

    f. Do not smoke when handling insecticides.

    g. Do not use oil base sprays near an open flame or sparking electric equipment.

    h. Use a respirator and protective clothing during prolonged handling of insecticides.

    i. Do not use malathion, lindane, diazinon, chlordane, or dieldren to treat an entire room. Use only where insects are known to hide.

    j. Isolate rooms treated with insecticides and fungicides for twenty-four hours.

    k. When pesticide containers are empty, wash them, punch holes in cans and break glass containers.

    l. Keep dusting and spraying equipment in good condition. Use wire to clear obstructed nozzles--never try to blow them clear.

    m. Wash hands and face thoroughly with soap and

water after using pesticides.

n.   If pesticides are accidentally swallowed, induce
vomiting and call a doctor.

o.   If fumes are accidentally inhaled, remove person to
open air, call a doctor, administer artificial respira-
tion if necessary.

Leather--Most leather made after 1800 needs frequent attention, depending on the quality of the original skins and the process
of tanning.   Books bound in vegetable-tanned leather which has not
been contaminated by city air normally require only an occasional
dressing to keep them in good condition.   On those volumes covered
with acid-tanned skins or which have had continued exposure to polluted air, one will find splitting joints, worn edges, loose backs and
powdered leather.   Some can be salvaged, a great many cannot.

Leather-bound volumes which have become dirty can, unless
they are powdered, be washed before further treatment.   Castile
soapsuds or frothed-up saddle soap applied with a sponge or soft
cloth will remove most surface dirt.   The suds should not be wet
and they should be wiped off promptly so as not to saturate the
leather.   Thorough drying is important.

Sponging new leather, or sound old leather, with a solution
of potassium lactate (7%) in water will neutralize any acid present
and deposit residual salts in the skins to inhibit subsequent acid
contamination.   Potassium lactate is available from bookbinding
supply houses and chemical suppliers or it can be compounded by a
druggist to this formula:

Water	92. 75%
Potassium lactate	7. 0%
Paranitrophenol[11]	0. 25%

After the deacidification of leather-covered books, a good
dressing will improve their appearance, provide a protective coating
to help seal out polluted air, consolidate powdered leather and lubri-
cate the fibers by restoring lost oils.   Each of the mixtures in Appendix E can be used safely on all types of leather.   Neat's foot
oil, Turkey Red Oil, pure lanolin, glycerin, vaseline, mineral oil
and even unsalted butter have all been used as leather preservatives.   Each will help to keep leather supple, but none is as satis-

factory as the compounded formulas.

CIRE 212, the French book leather preservative previously mentioned, is, because of incorporated insecticides and fungicides, of particular importance to libraries in humid regions where insects and fungi are a persistent problem. The wax is easily applied, but there is a tendency for the wax to coagulate on the surface of any leather with a pronounced grain. Some of the commercial leather dressings are quite satisfactory, but none are in any way superior to the formulas in Appendix E.

There is little that can be done for powdered leather other than to apply an oil or wax dressing to improve appearance. Sponging with potassium lactate is of no benefit, because the acid damage has been done.

Loose backs and split joints can be repaired by rebacking the volumes with new leather. They cannot be mended by painting with book repair liquids which are claimed to "restore old books and make them as new." These will not make good joints and they give leather a plasticized appearance.

Paper--Cellulose fibers are damaged by high temperatures, light, acids, alkalis, and strong bleaches. Other paper ingredients, such as rosin, contribute to its degeneration. It is impossible to prevent auto-oxidation (with attendant darkening and embrittlement) of the resins in machine-made paper, but the life expectancy of the sheets can be extended if they are protected from heat, humidity and light. Good quality rag paper will be effected less by heat, light, and humidity unless it is contaminated by acid gases or chlorine bleach residues, in which case the rate of degradation will approach that of chemical wood pulp paper.

Book paper is safest in a windowless, air-conditioned room having good air circulation and lighted by incandescent lamps. Windows should be painted or curtained to diffuse daylight and every effort should be made to keep air circulating and the temperature and humidity constant. Fifty-percent relative humidity is optimum, but a range of 50 - 60% is more realistic. In the care of books, indoctrination of all staff personnel in the fundamentals of conservation is of greatest importance. The most elaborate provisions are

of little avail if protective measures are ignored or the reasons for
them are not understood.

Newsprint--Microfilming has resolved some of the problems
in connection with the care of filed newspapers, but there will always be a requirement for the preservation of some originals even
after they have been filmed. Newspapers should be stored in dark
rooms, which are lighted, by incandescent light, only when it is
necessary to retrieve an issue for reference. More than any other
paper, newsprint should be protected by filtered air-conditioning.
Again, if this is not possible, the best possible alternatives are
warranted. Binding these awkward sheets is unquestionably good
protection against wear and tear, but newsprint, unless deacidified
before binding, degenerates between the covers almost as rapidly
as in the open air. Bound or unbound, nineteenth and twentieth-
century issues are all too often unsafe to handle.

Manuscripts--The pamphlets by Adelaide Minogue[12] and Lucille Kane,[13] together with Chapter III of Dr. Plenderleith's important book [14] contain practically all the information needed by the
average librarian for the care of written records. Although Miss
Kane's guidance places undue stress on plastic lamination (... "the
only process that has yet been devised which restores and preserves
documents adequately..."), the chapter on preservation is replete
with practical advice on routine care of manuscripts, as is Miss
Minogue's entire effort. Dr. Plenderleith's emphasis is on care
and restoration of more valuable material.

As for all other paper, the useful life of manuscripts is prolonged by protecting them from heat, light, acid gases and mildew.
They are safest when filed in acid-free wrappers in durable boxes
in fireproof cabinets. Folded manuscripts should be opened and
flattened for convenient handling and to minimize damage by flexing.
Microfilming will often more than pay for itself in the saving of
wear and tear, and subsequent cost of restoration of the originals.

Maps--In 1956 Clara LeGear described the care and repair
of maps as practiced in the Library of Congress for more than sixty years. [15] The booklet is outdated in regard to deacidification
and might lead one to think, erroneously, that plastic lamination has

supplanted all other preservation techniques. Otherwise, it properly emphasizes the importance of careful handling and of protection of maps from heat, light, moisture, vermin, fungi and polluted air.

Parchment maps should always be kept on a flat surface under a light weight to keep them from cockling. Very valuable maps
should be mounted in open-face mats with cellulose acetate windows
to protect them from abrasion and soiled hands. Because of strain
on their bindings, large atlases should never be shelved standing on
edge.

Contrary to general impression, cloth backing on maps is
not superior to paper. Cotton, linen and silk will deteriorate in
twenty to thirty years, contaminating the paper to which the fabrics
adhere. Map backings of pure rag paper of about the same weight
and texture will, with reasonable care, last as long as the map itself.

Plastic lamination of maps will give a great deal of protection from dirt, fungi, moisture and rough handling. For frequently
used reference material, or for fragile items on crumbling ground
wood pulp paper, lamination is probably the most sensible preservative. Such treatment for exquisitely engraved and colored antique
maps is unthinkable. Regardless of their present condition, it is
seldom that early items on rag paper cannot be cleaned, cleared of
stains, deacidified, resized and mended to return them to very
near original condition.

Prints and Drawings--Before the general application of insect sprays and fungicides, the ink and colors on exposed prints
and drawings should be tested by applying a drop of water (or the
spray solvent) to an inconspicuous part of the picture. Fugitive ink
or colors will be picked up when the wetted paper is blotted with
white absorbent paper.

Poor fastness to light is common in colored pictures, particularly older ones done with alum lakes. A picture's resistance
to light should be determined before it is selected for exhibition.

Book illustrations and prints are often done on heavily coated
paper to permit the printing of colors. These loaded art papers are

vulnerable to dampness and have been known to shed their pictures
under extreme humidity. Even under less drastic conditions, they
often stick together. The only remedy is to keep them away from
moisture in any form. When circumstances permit, it is sometimes of help to spray the faces and backs of pictures on coated
paper with acrylic resins or acrylic resins and silicones. Before
this is done a part of the picture must be tested to determine the
effect of the spray.

Parchment and Vellum--Parchment and vellum are extremely durable materials. They are stronger than leather, paper and
papyrus, but are cockled by moisture and made horny by lack of it.
Normal aging causes yellowing and some deformation results from
humidity changes. These deformations warp book covers and cause
ink and colors to flake off.

The primary consideration in the care of parchment and vellum is to stabilize the storage atmosphere. If air-conditioning is
not available, then mechanical or chemical humidity control is ad-
visable. Because it is almost impossible to make parchment and
vellum unpalatable to rodents, documents on parchment should be
kept in strongboxes or steel cabinets with tight drawers.

Vellum covered books become grimy and should be cleaned
periodically. Regardless of protest from those who lament the loss
of a book's old look, there is no virtue in dirt. Dirty vellum at-
tracts vermin and dirt should not be confused with the patina of age.
Cleaning is relatively simple. When the froth from whipped castile
soap suds, not the liquid, is wiped on with a sponge and rubbed off
with a clean flannel cloth, much of the surface dirt will come off.
If thoroughly dried in the open air and then polished with a lanolin
leather dressing, the material will take on a pleasing mellow hue.
Saddle soap applied as a paste and then rubbed off removes surface
dirt from vellum and handsomely polishes it. These treatments
should never be attempted on vellum manuscripts because of the
danger of removing the writing and illuminations.

Parchment and vellum are stained by mildew, but these
stains should never be washed out. A safe treatment is to brush
off the loose spores and kill the embedded fungi by painting the ma-

terial with benzene, or better still, fumigating it in a thymol chamber for several days. If a thymol cabinet is not available, books with parchment pages or loose parchment documents can be interleaved with papers which have been impregnated with a ten-percent solution of thymol in alcohol. In humid regions, these thymolized papers can also be wrapped around vellum bindings to provide continuous protection from mold. Always test ink before using thymol.

Cloth covered books--Plain cloth and paper covered books require little care other than an occasional dusting. When they become badly worn or frayed, their appearance can be considerably improved by spraying lightly with acrylic resins, or acrylic resins and silicone, both of which are sold in convenient aerosol cans. Cloth covers that are sized with starch or gelatin are susceptible to mildew, easily stained, ruined by water and devoured by insects. They must be kept dry and should be shelved in subdued light to minimize bleaching of their spines. Pyroxylin-covered book cloths, being resistant to moisture, insects, mildew, and acid and extremely durable, withstand hard usage.

New books in hard boards, but with plain cloth (not pyroxylin) or paper covers should, as a general rule, be sprayed with acrylic resin before going on library shelves. If carefully applied, this spray will give an almost invisible, but tough, finish to the cloth and paper which will be moisture, insect, and mildew resistant and also act as a barrier to polluted air.

Unusual Book Materials--Records on metal, stone, clay, bark and leaves, in the United States at least, belong in museums. Librarians who have such materials in their collections should seek advice from the nearest museum conservation laboratory in regard to the care of these pieces. For general information Dr. Plenderleith's The Conservation of Antiquities and Works of Art (London 1962) will be useful. More specialized knowledge is available in the Fogg Art Museum's quarterly, Technical Studies in the Field of the Fine Arts (1932-1942), and the International Institute for Conservation's Studies in Conservation (quarterly 1956 to the present). The IIC's quarterly, Abstracts of the Technical Literature on Archeology and the Fine Arts reports a surprising amount of material on

the conservation of exotic library materials, as well as paper,
leather, parchment and vellum.

Cuneiform tablets of unbaked clay contain water soluble
salts which, during storage, sometimes migrate to the surface and
crystallize.   These salts then obscure and sometimes damage the
inscriptions.   Although the remedial treatment--baking the tablets,
followed by washing in water--seems simple it is more than kitchen
chemistry.   Prudent librarians will send their "brick books" to the
nearest museum laboratory when treatment is necessary.

Palm leaf manuscripts are particularly vulnerable to insects
and become desiccated and brittle with age.   Keeping them in boxes
with camphor or naphthalene will repel insects.   A constant temperature (70^OF) and humidity (50 - 60%) will arrest deterioration until
restorative treatment can be arranged.   The Danish Centre for the
Study of Oriental Manuscripts in Copenhagen restores the strength
and flexibility of their palm leaf records by spraying them with
walnut oil. [16]   Crumbling palm leaves are best preserved between
plates of glass until they can be repaired.

Bark manuscripts last best when kept at a temperature of
70^OF and relative humidity of 50 - 60%.   When too dry, the layers
of bark separate and curl, defacing the writing; when too moist,
mildew sets in.   Birch bark is naturally resistant to insects.   The
best protection for these items is in individual acid-free wrappers
in document boxes.   Crumbling bark should be protected between
sheets of glass sealed on the edges with wax.   Complete information on the care of bark manuscripts appears in Bhargava's Repair
and Preservation of Records.   (New Delhi, National Archives of
India, 1959.)

Bone and ivory are so similar that, except under a microscope, it is difficult to tell them apart.   Book covers and tablets of
these materials are warped by heat and dampness and should be kept
in air-conditioned surroundings.   Other than that, an occasional
cleaning with fresh water and mild detergent followed by drying with a
soft cloth is about all that can be done to preserve them.   Washing
will remove grime and grease.   Removal of any other foreign matter or stains should not be attempted except in a conservation lab-

oratory.

Wood--The most important consideration in the conservation
of wood is to protect it from extreme fluctuations in temperature
and humidity.   This will inhibit mildew, eliminate the internal
strains due to swelling and shrinking, and minimize the possibility
of rot.   An occasional application of linseed oil will keep out un-
wanted moisture.   When mildew does occur, it is easily removed
in a thymol cabinet or by vacuuming.

Insects are the greatest problem for librarians who have
wooden materials.   Wood worms, termites, carpet beetles, etc.,
often inflict great damage before they are discovered.   Small, coni-
cal piles of sawdust under wooden objects are the telltale warnings,
but the absence of these does not mean insects are absent.   Frequent inspections are necessary.

It is a good precaution, when wooden objects are displayed
in glass cases, to set a small dish of paradichlorobenzene in the
cases.

Stone--Museum conservators rely primarily on cleaning and
impregnation with wax, lacquers and silicone esters to retard the
decay of soft stone.   The techniques are complicated and require
considerable equipment and skilled personnel not normally found in
libraries.   Because of its hardness, marble can be cleaned by library employees by the use of vacuum cleaners (not dusting cloths).
Occasional washing with mild soap and a little ammonia in water,
followed by a thorough rinsing with clear water, will remove all deposits of grime.   The removal of stains from marble is another
matter, and unless they can be removed by soap and water, it is a
job for a conservator.

Metals--Corrosion of metals is best prevented by eliminating
the cause.   Badly corroded metal is restored in museum laboratories by special solvents, electrochemical treatment or washing,
brushing and polishing.   Except for brass and silver tarnish, and
perhaps rust on some articles made of iron, librarians should again
rely upon museum assistance for the preservation of metal.

Tarnish is safely removed from decorative silver on book
covers, engraved plates, etc. with a soft cloth, French chalk and

alcohol followed by a soap and water bath. With these, there is no danger of wearing off inscriptions or decorative marks. Commercial polishes and rouge cloths are effective cleaners, but are also abrasive. A shiny black patina (silver sulphide on old silver) is chemically stable and highly protective and need not be removed except to decipher information. Patina is protective and corrosion is not, but the two are easily distinguished. Freshly cleaned silver can safely be coated with any one of the lacquer sprays sold for that purpose. These coatings are almost invisible and provide excellent protection against further tarnish.

Copper is oxidized in clean air and oxidized and tarnished by hydrogen sulphide in polluted air. After polishing, copper and its alloys should be coated with a protective lacquer. This, plus atmosphere control, will effectively check deterioration.

Lead, tin and pewter oxidize, creating a dull, protective patina on their surfaces. Corrosion by organic acids is another matter. When corrosion, as distinct from a dull patina, appears on coin collections, etc., the problem should be referred at once to a conservation laboratory.

Iron rusts in the presence of moisture and oxygen. Iron, rusted or otherwise, is also deteriorated by electrochemical action when certain salts are present in the air. Deterioration of iron can be prevented by protective coatings if the surface is properly prepared. Chemical rust inhibitors also help, but this calls for more than painting them on the metal. The best recourse for a librarian, in regard to the preservation of iron and steel objects, is to keep them clean and dry.

Film, Photographs and Sound Recordings--In the past twenty-five years technology has made great improvements in photographic materials for the preservation of records. These are now highly stable and much more satisfactory from the point of view of reproduction. Accelerated aging tests suggest that cellulose acetate film, under normal storage conditions, will endure as long as rag paper. Its useful life depends upon storage conditions, the care with which it is handled, and its chemical characteristics. Deterioration will occur and the only way to detect it in time is inspection at regular

intervals. Inspection, to be effective, must include opening each
container, running motion picture and microfilm through splicing
reels and examination of cut film, plates, slides and transparencies on a light table to look for indications of damage.

Motion Picture Film--Acetate films are fire resistant and
chemically stable, but they can be ruined by heat, moisture, fungi,
acid gases in polluted air, and gases released by deteriorating nitrate film. Nitrate films are chemically unstable and flammable.
They slowly decompose, even under ideal storage conditions, releas-
ing nitrogen dioxide (which forms nitric acid) and nitric oxide. The
film first turns yellow, then darkens and becomes brittle and finally decomposes to a powder. Nothing can be done to arrest this
process.

For fire prevention and to preserve the photographed information, all data on nitrate film should be copied onto acetate stock.
Although the words "nitrate film" have, for many years, been
printed on nitrate stock and "safety film" on the edges of acetate
stock, this is not infallible identification.[17] Print-through of the
identifying words from negative to positive (and vice versa) has
been known to take place. The safest and surest means of identification is to have all motion picture film made before 1952 examined
in a photographic laboratory, but librarians can make a rough check
on their old films by the trichloro ethylene test[18] and the ignition
test.[19]

Control of temperature ($70^{o}F$) and humidity (50% - 60%) are
of major importance in film storage, as is removal of acid gases
from urban air. In lieu of full air-conditioning, mechanical or
chemical humidity control will help. Lacking this, only storage in
sealed cans, after laboratory conditioning for at least two weeks,
will insure longevity. All film, regardless of type, should be kept
standing on edge in flat cans in metal cabinets, which, in turn, are
positioned for maximum air circulation around them. Cabinets for
sound film should not be near electric motors, emergency generators or heavy duty wiring.

Nitrate film should be kept in unsealed cans to permit release of gaseous decomposition products. It should be stored one

film to a can, in a vented metal cabinet or a fire resistant vault
conforming to the requirements of the local fire code or the National Board of Fire Underwriters standard for such vaults.[20]

Special standards and specifications for long-time storage
(hundreds of years) of archival film are available from the American Standards Institute, 10 East 40th Street, New York, N.Y.

Film storage of any sort should always be on the main floor,
never in the basement or on the top floors or in the attic, to avoid dampness and high summer temperatures.

Microfilm--Although acetate base microfilm is expected to
last for centuries, the unexpected appearance of minute blemishes
on some of these records is cause for concern. These have been
under intensive study since 1961, but are not yet fully understood.
So far there has been no information loss, but until the matter has
been resolved, librarians should think twice before discarding old
newspapers and other records which have been transferred to film.

Librarians having microfilm files should have them examined
periodically for aging blemishes in accordance with the inspection
procedures recommended in Bureau of Standards Handbook 96, Inspection of Processed Photographic Record Films for Aging Blemishes (U.S. G.P.O., 1964). They should be handled in accordance
with the recommendations of the National Bureau of Standards[21] and
preserved in accordance with the American Standard Practice for
the Storage of Microfilm.[22]

Photographs--Desirable conditions for the storage of photographs are the same as those for film. However, because of the
different sizes and shapes, the details must differ. Because wood
and cardboard absorb moisture, boxes for negatives and slides
should be made of metal, polyethylene or styrene. A small amount
of silica gel, one ounce for fifty negatives, will keep the humidity
low. The gel must be reactivated occasionally, but this can easily
be done in an oven. Snug, but not airtight, covers on the boxes
will keep out dust and grime. Negative boxes should be shelved in
a well ventilated metal cabinet with an electric lamp in the bottom
to keep the temperature a few degrees above room temperature.
This arrangement will practically assure freedom from mold and

reduce the probability of other damage.

Fading of colors on prints or in film transparencies is caused by the ultraviolet components of light, humidity, heat and chemical action in the material. Light-absorbent glass mounts or thin plastic sheets over the faces of the photographs help to filter the light. In lieu of air-conditioning or humidity control, pictures can be coated with cellulose ester or polyvinyl phthalate to seal out moisture and acid gases from polluted air or from the cements used in mounting them.

Assorted films and prints of miscellaneous sizes, which do not fit the usual slotted boxes, should be kept in individual seamless cellulose acetate envelopes complying with the "American Standard Requirements for Photographic Filing Envelopes for Storing Processed Photographic Films" (American Standards Institute, 10 East 40th Street, New York, N.Y.). All-rag paper envelopes are also good. Kraft and other machine-made paper containers are not, because of their alum and rosin content. Selection of a filing cabinet is of secondary importance after the photographs or films have been individually enveloped for protection.

Sound Recordings[23]--Phonograph records and magnetic tapes deteriorate in storage. In the case of the discs, it is because of the economic impracticability of manufacturing long lasting, durable, chemically stable phonograph records to sell for a reasonable price. The problem with audio tapes is less serious. Intensive care will not prolong the short life expectancy of these two recording devices, but it will prevent premature failure.

Phonograph records become brittle with age. They warp, crack and undergo chemical changes, all affecting the sound. All a librarian can hope to do to minimize the inevitable is to:

    a. Keep records clean of fungus nutrients.

    b. Select packaging materials free of fungus nutrients.[24]

    c. Stabilize the environment at $70^{\circ}F$ and 50 - 60% relative humidity.

    d. Keep discs away from sunlight and fluorescent light.

    e. Keep discs standing on edge in smooth surface envelopes.

    f. Provide waterproof gas-tight cellulose acetate envelopes

for the discs.

g. Keep dust and dirt in the playing and storage areas at an absolute minimum.

h. Establish rigid procedures for handling the discs.

As a precautionary measure, rare and valuable records should be rerecorded and the copies stored apart from the originals.

Magnetic Sound Tapes--Tapes are chemically stable but differ considerably in strength. The strongest and most durable are those made on polyester and polyvinyl chloride bases. The most serious problems seem to be stretching and shrinking of the base, which affect the quality of sound, the danger of accidental erasure, induced noise due to external magnetic fields, and print-through which results in the signal on one layer being repeated on adjacent layers of tape in the rolls. Recommended procedures for preservation and storage of magnetic tapes are:

a. Keep tapes on metal reels in metal cans or sealed polyethylene boxes standing on edge on wooden shelves in wooden cabinets.

b. Cabinets must be well clear of electric motors, emergency generators, heavy-duty wiring, and radiators, and should not be stored in the basement or attic.

c. Stabilize environment at $70^{o}F$ and 50 - 60% relative humidity.

d. Use only on immaculately clean, high quality playback equipment in dust free rooms.

e. Examine all tapes at least once every two years on a rewind-type inspection device. After inspection leave the tape on the reversed roll to minimize creep, induced curvature and print-through.

In the Tropics--Wilfred J. Plumbe's The Preservation of Books in Tropical and Subtropical Countries (London, Oxford Press, 1964) reflects his experience as librarian at the University of Malaya and at Ahmadu Bello University, Nigeria. This excellent book shows evidence of much research, but for some reason does not include acid among the enemies of books. Those who use the book must be aware that acid gases in polluted air may not be as common in the tropics as elsewhere, but that acid from other sources can be even more troublesome. Plumbe does include some minor enemies found in tropical libraries--rats, mice, squirrels, bats,

General Care   115

birds, snakes, mongooses, meerkats, and lizards, calling them a
"...distraction for those who are trying to read. "

Other reliable sources are the National Archives of India
(New Delhi) and the proceedings of the Indian Historical Records
Commission. Scientists in that country, to implement their own
studies in the preservation of library materials, are adapting to
tropical conditions the findings of American and European researchers in library conservation. K.D. Bhargava's Repair and Preservation of Records (New Delhi, Archives of India 1959) and Y.P.
Kapthalia's Care of Books in Tropical Libraries (New Delhi, Archives of India 1955) are both important. With Plumbe's book they
provide basic guidance for the librarian in the tropics.

The general use of air-conditioning would not automatically
solve the problems of equatorial libraries. The plight of individuals alternately exposed to hot, humid air and then cool, dry air
must be considered, as must the fact that in remote areas electric
power is not always reliable. Nor would massive applications of
modern fumigants eradicate insects and mildew. In humid climates,
the choice of toxicant is less important than the choice of a vehicle
for it and chemicals powerful enough to control tropical insects and
fungi may have a deleterious effect on paper, leather, vellum, bark,
palm leaves, etc.

No protective treatment for library materials in the tropics
is ever permanent nor is it even long lasting. Frequent examinations must be the rule if disastrous damage is to be avoided. Paper requires more protection against moisture than against heat.
Simple things, such as ring fasteners and metal clasps, are sources
of rust stain. Buckram, linen and cotton book covers entice insects
and fungi. Glues get soft and sticky and adhesives must be poisoned
to repel vermin. Artificial resin adhesives, in most instances, are
more suitable than traditional glues. Similarly, pyroxylin plastic
book covers are superior to leather, vellum or buckram. Leather-
bound volumes require constant attention and the only sure protection for them, and for valuable books in general, is to seal them
in tight metal boxes, with silica gel and an insecticide as additional
safeguards.

Photographic materials are even more sensitive to tropical conditions. For some reason glossy prints attract more bacteria and fungi than do matte finished pictures. Microfilm spots appear there more frequently than elsewhere. Storage of all processed film, photographs, slides, transparencies, etc., in plastic bags in tight metal containers is almost mandatory. Acetate film deteriorates in the 90°F and 90% relative humidity that prevail for months at a time. Even in the dry tropics, the excessive heat damages the plastic base and gelatin coating. Fungi attacks are particularly severe and extra care is required to keep motion picture film clean, dry and well lacquered.

Four alternatives for prolonging the life of processed film are:

a. Automatic air-conditioning.

b. Mechanical dehumidification of selected areas, which is more complicated than in temperate regions because of the requirement for air-tight, vapor-sealed construction.

c. Conditioned film storage (an expensive highly technical process for stabilizing the moisture content of film in controlled atmospheres and then sealing it in metal cans.) This is practical only for long-time storage.

d. Desiccation with silica gel (a complicated process requiring the services of a photographic technician.)

Notes

1.   Thomson, G. "Air Pollution - A Review for Conservation Chemists." Studies in Conservation Vol. 10, No. 4, (1965).

2.   Buck, R.D. "A Specification for Museum Air Conditioning." Museum News Technical Supplement December 1964/No. 6.

3.   Beers, R.J. "High Expansion Foam Fire Control for Record Storage" Fire Technology, May 1966.

4.   Barrow, W.J. "Archival File Folders" American Archivist 28 (1965) 125-128.

5.   Piez, Gladys T. "Archival Containers - A Search for Safer Materials" American Archivist 27 (1964) 433-438.

6. See A Rod For the Back of the Binder. Chicago,
   Lakeside Press, 1928, page 29. See also Harrison, T.,
   Fragments of Bookbinding Technique. London School
   of Printing, 1950.

7. See Zigrosser, C. & Gaehde, C.M., A Guide to
   the Collecting and Care of Original Prints. New York,
   Crown Publishing Co., 1965. See also Schraubstadter,
   C., Care and Repair of Japanese Prints. Cornwall,
   N.Y., Idlewild Press, 1948.

8. "Biological Agents Which Damage Paper Materials in
   Libraries and Archives," Recent Advances in Conservation, 1963.

9. New Methods for the Restoration and Preservation of
   Documents and Books (trans. from Russian) National
   Science Foundation, Washington, 1964 and Collection
   of Materials on the Preservation of Library Resources
   (trans. from Russian) National Science Foundation,
   Washington, 1964.

10. Recent Advances in Conservation. London, Butter-
    worth's 1963.

11. This disinfectant and mold inhibitor is quite satis-
    factory on dark colored leather, but it will stain light
    shades. Alternative disinfectants are betanaphthol,
    2-hydroxi-dyphenyl, phenyl mecurie acetate, O-phenyl
    phenol, and p-chloro m-cresol.

12. The Repair and Preservation of Records. Washing-
    ton, U.S. National Archives Bulletin Number 5, 1943.

13. A Guide to the Care and Administration of Manu-
    scripts. Nashville, American Association of State
    and Local History, 1966.

14. The Conservation of Antiquities and Works of Art.
    London, Oxford Press, 1902.

15. Maps/Their Care, Repair and Preservation in Li-
    braries, Washington, Library of Congress, 1956.

16. Nordstrand, O.K. in Studies in Conservation, No. 3
    (1959) pp. 135-140.

17. See Storage and Preservation of Motion Picture Film.
    Rochester, N.Y., Eastman Kodak Company, 1957.

18. One-quarter-inch diameter test pieces of acetate
    film will float in a test tube of trichloro ethylene.
    Nitrate film test pieces sink.

19. One-inch strips of nitrate film lighted by a match
(in an ashtray out of doors, ignite easily, burn with
a bright yellow flame and are consumed in fifteen
seconds.   Test strips of acetate film are ignited
with difficulty and are only partially consumed.

20. Pamphlet No. 40 (1953).   National Board of Fire
Underwriters, 85 John Street, New York.

21. McCamy, C.S. and Pope, C.I., Summary of Current Research On Archival Microfilm, National Bureau
of Standards, Technical Note 261, Washington, U.S.
G.P.O. 1965.

22. American Standard Practice for Storage of Microfilm.
PH5.4-1957 American Standards Association, New
York.

23. The most authoritative information on this subject
is Pickett and Lemcoe's Preservation and Storage of
Sound Recordings.   Library of Congress, 1959.

24. All commercial record packaging today is unsatisfactory on these points.

Chapter V
Repair and Restoration

General librarians can turn to the excellent publications of
the American Library Association, the Council on Library Resources
and the Library Binding Institute for aid in the solution of many of
the basic problems of preservation, care and repair. Their responsibility is primarily to prolong the useful life of books that will
ultimately be expended or replaced. Others, particularly the keepers of rare books, are confronted with a different situation. They
must preserve the materials in their custody so as to pass them on
to their successors in the best possible condition.

The decision to restore a unique item as against spending
the same sum on lesser repairs to a number of important, but less
valuable pieces, is difficult. In 1941 Dr. Hellmut Lehmann-Haupt
reviewed this dilemma.[1] His essay lacks information on damage by
acids, light, mildew, heat, etc., but is, nevertheless, an outstanding analysis of whether or not to rebind and an excellent introduction, in librarian's language, to the mechanics of bookbinding. In
1929, Douglas Cockerell, one of the foremost twentieth-century bookbinders, made this comment:

> Generally speaking, if books of value must be re-
> bound, everything possible should be done to strength-
> en the actual leaves of the book. The nature of the
> binding itself is not a matter of such vital importance,
> provided it forms an adequate protection to the book
> and is not incongruous in style. An aggressively
> modern decorated binding on an old book seems to
> be sadly out of place, but what is right and what is
> wrong is a matter of taste and feeling, and cannot be
> laid down by rule.

> Cockerell--Some Notes on Bookbinding. London, Ox-
> for University Press, 1929. p. 77.

This insight is probably the secret of Mr. Cockerell's success.
His appreciation of the overriding importance of conservation was
not shared by all his contemporaries.

The practice of conservation has come a long way since
Cockerell's time, when restoration methods were mostly empirical.
Dr. Ludovico Santucci, chemist at the Istituto di Patologia del Libro in Rome, outlined the scientific approach to the conservation of
archival materials in a paper addressed to the 1961 Rome Conference of the International Institute for Conservation.[2]   Reporting
from the scientific point of view, Dr. Santucci described the potential danger in some empirical procedures in conservation and
restoration and concluded that the closest cooperation should be established among scholars, custodians and scientists.   He suggested
that those in charge realize the importance of combining scientific
discoveries with the traditional techniques of restoration.   Finally
he reminded his readers that this cannot be achieved without a great
deal of effort and considerable expense.

This chapter will examine the pros and cons of some of the
recent innovations; it will emphasize certain techniques considered
to be of particular importance.   Binding and restoration of library
materials cannot be learned quickly from do-it-yourself manuals.
There are some things that should be done by the library staff, others
require the skill of bookbinders and conservators.   Most libraries must
seek outside assistance for the bulk of their repair requirements.   The
agencies and associations to which libraries can turn for advice on conservation, expert restorations and high quality workmanship are described in Appendix D.   Costs for these services are higher than the
cost of routine repair and maintenance of library materials, but in view
of tools and equipment required, the value is good.

An alternative is a cooperative approach.   Small and medium
sized museums have pooled their resources to establish regional associations for clinical assistance, information, and advice and have
supported a single conservation laboratory for their joint use.[3]
The organizational experience of the highly successful Intermuseum
Conservation Association is reflected in the proposal for regional
library conservation associations in Chapter VI, which, with foundation assistance, could be established in several centrally located
cities in the United States.   These would make available to member libraries, at minimum cost, a clinic for the care and treatment

of library materials. Such centers, in addition to expert restoration and repair service, would provide information, advice and training for personnel; thus contributing to better conservation of library materials.

Paper--Salvage of disintegrating paper is not new, but it is only within the past forty years that scientific methods have been applied to the problem. Successful paper repair depends upon an understanding of conservation, training in special skills and techniques, the availability of tools and equipment and experience. The labor involved often makes it costly. In libraries and archives, it should be confined to less valuable and expendable items until the personnel doing the work gain the skill and confidence that come only with long practice. Librarians should establish a working relationship with a reputable conservator, who will agree to examine document collections and suggest what can be done safely on the premises and what should be done in laboratories with more elaborate equipment.

Reliable guidance on paper repair is available in

a. Plenderleith, H. J. The Conservation of Antiquities and Works of Art. London, Oxford, 1962.

b. Minogue, A.E. , The Repair and Preservation of Records. Washington, D.C. , U.S. National Archives, Bulletin No. 5. 1943.

c. Kane, L.M. , A Guide to the Care and Administration of Manuscripts. Nashville, Tenn. , 1966.

d. Werner, A.E. , "The Preservation of Archives." Journal of the Society of Archivists, Vol. 1, No. 10 (1959).

e. Anthony, D.C. , "Caring for Your Collections; Manuscripts and Related Materials." Technical leaflet No. 8, American Associations for State and Local History, Madison, Wisc.

f. Cockerell, S.M. , The Repairing of Books. London, Shepard Press, 1958.

g. Lydenberg and Archer, The Care and Repair of Books. New York, Bowker, 1960.

h. Langwell, W.H. The Conservation of Books and Documents. London, Pitman, 1957.

Miss Minogue's pamphlet is replete with practical information on paper repair as it is done in the National Archives. The

subject treatment by Langwell and by Dr. Plenderleith is scientific.
Miss Kane's booklet is an important contribution to paper conservation, except that she overemphasizes lamination. Dr. Werner's essay should be read for an understanding of some of the scientific
solutions to archival repair. Sidney Cockerel describes paper repair as it has been done by him and his father for seventy years.
John Alden's 1960 revision of Lydenberg and Archer stresses what
can be done by librarians without recourse to special skills or machinery.

       Testing paper--Acidity of paper is determined with great ac-
curacy in paper laboratories by shredding samples of a sheet, treating the shreds with hydroxides and then measuring the acidity of the
extract. An alternative method is to make a direct reading of the
acidity of the paper with an expensive electronic indicator. For
laboratory purposes these measures are desirable, but such accuracy is not necessary for librarians or archivists. They are interested only in the general conditions of the paper (i.e., is it very
acid, slightly acid, neutral or alkaline) and they need to know only
the approximate acidity on the pH scale (i.e., 3.0, 3.5, 4.0, 4.5,
5.0,---8.0, 8.5 etc.). This can be done by spot testing with any
of several pH testing solutions available from chemical supply
houses. The most useful is a so-called wide neutral range indicator. A drop of one of these applied to a piece of paper will give
an indication, by the color it assumes, of the approximate acidity
of the cellulose fibers. After a little experience in reading the colors, librarians will find these spot testers extremely useful.

       Prior to any repair or restoration, it is important to know
whether a deteriorated paper was made entirely, or in part, from
ground wood. This can be determined by placing a drop of phloro-
glucinol solution on the paper. This will turn red if any lignin is
present, indicating that untreated ground wood was used in the paper
pulp.

       Chemists determine the pulp content of paper by identifying
the fibers under a microscope with the aid of various stains. A
crude, but sometimes useful, identification of pulp content can be
made by applying a drop of Herzberg's Stain to a piece of paper.

Cotton or linen rag content will turn the spot red; chemical wood
pulp blue; and mechanical wood (ground wood) pulp yellow.   This
test is not infallible and when precise identification is important, it
is best to have it done by a laboratory.

Mildew--No one fungicide is capable of destroying all of the
hundreds of species of mold spores that infest organic materials.
The logical solution is to have several available that will be effective on leather, paper, parchment, papyrus, etc., without damaging
these materials.   Chemicals with a high chlorine content will damage paper.   Some chemicals discolor materials, others soften varnishes, etc.   In Latin America, it is not uncommon for booksellers
to soak old volumes in gasoline to kill fungi.   This definitely is not
recommended.   The following compounds are safe, chlorine free,
fungicides for general library use:

> Salicylanilide
> Mercapto benzothiazole
> Copper oxinate
> Thymol
> Formaldehyde
> Para-nitro-phenol
> 2-hydroxy biphenyl (O-phenyl phenol)
> Ethylene oxide
> 2-hydroxy-diphenyl amine

Salicylanilide is colorless, odorless, non-volatile and long
lasting.   Available in aqueous and non-aqueous solutions, it has
proved useful as an inhibitor for brown stain and foxing.   Mercapto
benzothiazole is sometimes mixed with salicylanilide for increased
effectiveness.   Para-nitro-phenol is effective, but it leaves a green
tinge and is useful on dark leather only.   2-hydroxy biphenyl is not
soluble in cold water.   Copper oxinate is a superior fungicide that
is available in water and oil solutions for spray gun application.

Formalin (40% formaldehyde) is effective for sterilizing papers, but it cannot be used on parchment, vellum or leather.   One
method for utilization of formalin is to expose mildewed paper in a
covered box in which the formalin is heated in a shallow plate over
a 25 watt light bulb.   Sterilization will be complete in twelve hours.
A simpler method for single sheets, such as pastel or charcoal
drawings and water colors, is to lay them on a piece of muslin sus-

pended over blotters which have been saturated with a two-percent
solution of formaldehyde in alcohol. The operation is more efficient if the formaldehyde vapors are contained by placing a box
over the arrangement.

Thymol, although not permanent, is an effective, easy to
use, general purpose sterilizer. Mildewed materials can be exposed to the vapors in simply constructed fumigation cabinets (see
Figure 8) in which the chemical is melted in watch glasses over
25 watt bulbs. The cabinet is designed to accommodate loose papers, books, manuscripts, maps and prints. Thymol is toxicologi-
cally safe, but should be used with caution because it dissolves
some inks and attacks paint and varnish. Because it does not im-
pregnate the material, it will not reduce mildew stains nor will it
provide lasting protection.

When a fumigation chamber is not available, books and loose
papers may be sterilized by interleaving them with tissue (or blotting paper) that has been impregnated with 10% thymol in alcohol.
These papers inserted between every ten sheets will in a few weeks
completely destroy all mold growth. Thymol-impregnated file folders and document boxes will inhibit formation of mildew on their
contents. Thymol-impregnated paper has been used successfully to
sterilize papyrus.

Mold spores and bacteria can be destroyed by two hours' exposure to ultraviolet light, but because of the adverse effect of ultraviolet light on organic materials, such treatment should be reserved for those items which cannot be handled by other methods.

When there has been a widespread attack of mold on the contents
of a library, it can be brought under control by fumigating entire rooms
(if the rooms can be sealed). This seldom-required procedure is described by Plenderleith, Conservation of Antiquities etc. page 55.

Mildew stains can sometimes be washed out of paper; if not,
bleaching will reduce them. In either case, it is important to resize the paper to replace the gelatin (or rosin) leached out of the
paper in the restoration or digested by the fungi.

The most useful fungicides for leather are para-nitro-phenol
and pentachloro phenol. Used separately or together in exceedingly

diluted solutions (0. 35%para-nitro-phenol in alcohol or 0. 25% pentachloro phenol), they will protect leather from fungus attacks even
under the most adverse conditions.   Stronger concentrations of para-
nitro-phenol stain leather.   When stronger applications are desired, a
2% solution of sodium pentachloro phenol in alcohol or water is safe
for use on leather.   It should not be used on paper because of its
chlorine content.

Insects--When insects are discovered, eradication is no problem.   Vacuum chamber fumigation, when this equipment is available,
is the quickest and most positive treatment.   Impregnating wood
with liquid fungicides is very effective. aerosol sprays are not.   Insects in wooden book covers (and books) can be destroyed by deep-
freezing them.   A home-type freezer will do the job very well.
The cold is perfectly safe for all organic materials for the short
periods of time required.

A simple fumigation chamber can be improvised by placing
books opened fanwise in any covered container with a saucer of
para-dichloro benzene crystals (1. 5 oz. per cubic foot of air space)
or a dish of chloroform (1/2 fluid oz. per cubic foot).   The container is then sealed with masking tape and set aside for two weeks,
after which it must be opened outdoors.

It should be noted that one treatment may not be sufficient
to eliminate all the insects, as the eggs and pupae of the insects
are resistant to insecticides.   The treated books should, therefore,
be kept under observation for at least a year; if insects reappear,
fumigation should be repeated.

Museum News 44, No. 5 (1966) describes an air-tight, sheet
metal, portable fumigation chamber on rubber casters suitable for
heavy books and wooden objects.   This $108. 00 device is highly
suitable for most librarians.   For ordinary work it is charged with
carbon disulfide in a concentration of 6 fluid ounces for 23 cubic
feet of air.   Ninety-six hours of fumigation is required.   For wood-
boring beetles a heavier concentration is used.   For safety, ethylene oxide or carbon tetrachloride can be used instead of the highly
flammable carbon disulfide.

Cleaning and Removing Stains -- Grime can be removed from

the surface of paper with soft erasers, ground art gum, the commercial preparations used by draftsmen, or wallpaper cleaning
doughs.

Methods for removing stains from fabric are thoroughly covered in the Department of Agriculture's Home and Garden Bulletin
No. 62 (Washington US GPO 1964). Stains in paper can be reduced
by the use of absorbent materials, washing, solvents, and by bleaching with chemical stain removers.

Fresh stains, such as grease and oil, can be removed when
still wet by cornstarch, corn meal, talc or powdered chalk. These
should be dusted on, allowed to absorb the staining substance, vacu-
umed or brushed off and fresh powder dusted on repeatedly until
the action is stopped. Blotters, cotton, soft cloths and absorbent
paper will soak up wet stains and will sometimes remove most of
a grease stain if it has not yet oxidized. Heat from a warm iron
applied to blotters sandwiching a paper stained with oil or grease
sometimes drives the spots into the more absorbent sheets.

Washing--Soaking in hot (almost boiling) water will often
clean very stained and dirty paper. The hot liquid will dissolve
the paper size, but that can be replaced. The addition of a small
quantity of synthetic detergent increases the effectiveness of the
wash water, but the detergent wash must be followed by several
rinses in clear water. Manipulating the paper under the water with
a soft brush (good quality shaving brush) will help loosen the embedded dirt. A surprising amount of foxing, brown stain, and mildew stain can be removed by soaking in cold water overnight. Frequent changing of cold water baths until the run-off water is clear
gives better results. In the process of washing, paper is often revitalized. This is undoubtedly due to some mechanical rearrange-
ment of the cellulose fibers.

Before paper is immersed in water, all ink and colors should
be tested for solubility. Carbon and iron gall ink stand up well in
water. Modern liquid ink, ball point ink and indelible pencil marks
do not. Printer's ink and most printed colors are usually safe.
However, reds should be doubly checked before they are moistened.
A drop of water on the color will soften it enough to be picked up

by a blotter if it is not fast.   A damp white blotter will also pick
up traces of inks if they are soluble in water.

Aged water colors behave erratically.   Some are as fast as
printed hues, but in general they should not be bathed for cleaning.
Occasionally lithographs or engravings decorated with water colors
are so badly stained and deteriorated that washing, bleaching, and
deacidification are the only remedy.   In such cases, it may be
found that most of the pigments (red excepted) will survive the
treatment.   As a precaution, however, notes and a diagram of the
color pattern will be of help in replacing lost colors after the operation is completed.

The selection of a solvent for paper stains depends upon the
nature of the foreign matter.   A liquid that is effective for one type
of stain may make another more persistent.   Water is the most
useful solvent and the safest, being neither flammable nor poisonous.   Also useful are benzene, toluene, alcohol, gasoline, xylene,
turpentine, pyridine and many others.   The solvent is usually applied with a soft brush or a tampon of cotton wool against the back of
the stained paper, which is face down on a clean white blotter.   Repeated application of the solvent and frequent blotter changes are required
until the blotter absorbs no more dirt.   By this time, if the solvent
has been correctly chosen, the stain should have been removed completely.

Some typical stains and solvents are

STAIN	SOLVENT
Adhesive tape	Carbon tetrachloride* Benzene†
Pressure sensitive tape	Benzene† or trichloro ethylene Toluene†
Duco cement	Acetone†
Glue	Warm water
Paste	Water
Lacquer	Acetone†
Tar	Gasoline† Carbon tetrachloride* Pyridine* Benzene†

STAIN	SOLVENT
Paint	Alcohol and benzene mixed† Pyridine* followed by water Turpentine
Rubber Cement	Carbon Disulphide* Benzene and toluene mixed†
Wax	Gasoline† Chloroform* Carbon Disulphide*
Shellac	Ethyl alcohol†
Iodine	Ethyl alcohol†
Mildew	Ethyl alcohol† Benzene†
Fly specks	Hydrogen peroxide
Tea and coffee	Potassium perborate
Rust	5% Oxalic acid
Mud	Water or ammonia
Grease, fat, oil	Alcohol† Trichloro ethylene Gasolene† Benzene† Pyridine*
Lipstick	5% Tartaric acid followed by water
Varnish	Alcohol† Acetone† Pyridine*
Natural Resins	Alcohol†

† Flammable
* Objectionable odor

It must be remembered that most solvents strong enough to remove stains are either highly flammable or have a strong odor. Many of them have a noxious effect on the human body, particularly where ventilation is poor.

Pressure-sensitive mending tapes, never intended by their manufacturers for use on valuable records, have unfortunately been used all too frequently by well meaning, but misinformed, individuals. When soaking with water is possible (either by immersion or with a damp cloth), the tape will sometimes wrinkle and curl, making it possible to peel it off. The adhesive residue can then be removed by sponging with benzene or trichloro ethylene. When water does not loosen the tape, it can be worked off by painting the edges with benzene or trichloro ethylene and lifting the plastic with a pair of tweezers. Painting the underside of the paper with the solvent will hasten this. These methods will remove even badly deteriorated tape but will not remove the stain the tape invariably leaves. Final sponging of the residual adhesive with the solvents may reduce these stains. If not, there is nothing that can be done.

A device for increasing the effectiveness of solvents on persistent stains has been in use at the National Archives for many years. Designed by Arthur E. Kimberly, formerly head of the Document Reproduction and Restoration Branch, it is a Soxhlet Extraction Apparatus, (Figure 9) which repeatedly drenches a document suspended in the cylinder (A) with freshly distilled solvent until it is clean.

Bleaching--Chemical stain removers include oxygen and chlorine bleaches, acetic acid, ammonia, oxalic acid, and sodium thiosulphate. Chlorine and its compounds are superior to the others.

The simplest and safest (but not the most effective) chlorine bleach is Chloramine-T. This mild reagent, which does not harm cellulose, is normally used in two-percent aqueous solution but concentrations up to ten or fifteen percent are more effective. Contrary to previously published information, the residual chlorine does not evaporate into the air, and unless the print or document is washed thoroughly after treatment, bleaching will continue.

One or two-percent solutions of sodium hypochlorite will remove even the most stubborn stains in paper, but must be used with great care because of the effect of this chemical on cellulose. Paper treated with hypochlorite must be neutralized with an antichlor (1% sodium thiosulphate) followed by prolonged rinsing in running water. Bleaching with diluted hypochlorite should normally be avoided.

The sodium chlorite bleaching process described at length in Museum, Volume V, Number 2 (1952) is powerful, but absolutely safe for paper. Although requiring rather elaborate laboratory equipment, it is preferred by some conservators because of the degree of control available. Paper so treated must be deacidified at the end of the process.

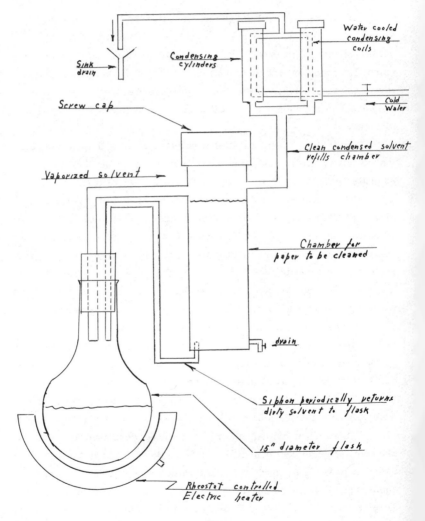

Sink drain

Condensing cylinders

Water cooled condensing coils

Screw cap

Cold Water

Clean condensed solvent refills chamber

Vaporized solvent

Chamber for paper to be cleaned

drain

Siphon periodically returns dirty solvent to flask

15" diameter flask

Rheostat controlled Electric heater

130

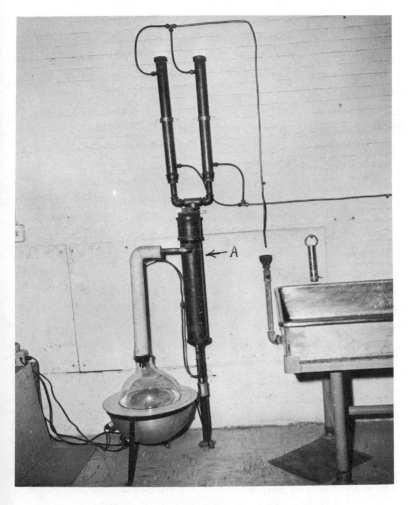

Figure 9
Soxhlet Extraction Apparatus
In use Document Restoration Branch, U.S. National Archives

131

A safe and effective bleaching process that is within the capability of anyone who has developed his own photographic prints is that described by Sheldon Keck in the Fogg Art Museum's Technical Studies, Volume V, Number 2 (1936). This method of cleaning prints leaves no trace of acid, alkali or salts in the paper. The essential ingredients are sodium hypochlorite, hydrochloric acid and ammonia. Three large photographer's trays are required. The chemical reactions are rather complicated as a print or document is passed through three separate solutions, but the result is highly satisfactory.

Mild stains can sometimes be removed from fragile paper, charcoal drawings, pastels, water colors, etc., by placing them in a tightly closed box with a block of plaster of Paris that has been saturated with hydrogen peroxide.

Deacidification--In spite of certain shortcomings, the most satisfactory method available today for the deacidification of acid paper is that developed by William J. Barrow.[4] The process, which is in general use throughout the world, comprises soaking the paper in a solution of magnesium bicarbonate, which neutralizes the acids and deposits buffering salts in the cellulose fibers to preclude reacidification. This is suitable for single sheets of paper, but is not suitable for deacidification of books. It would be necessary to take the books apart for treatment and then rebind them. The required apparatus is not customarily available in a library workshop and it requires considerable space. However, the outlay of money and space is warranted when rare books and important prints, manuscripts and maps need deacidification.

The process requires a sink with at least 30" x 48" washboards, racks for drying paper, assorted large photographic trays, a glass carboy, a carbon dioxide cylinder with appropriate valves and pressure gauges, plus tubing, clamps, etc. The bicarbonate is obtained by bubbling carbon dioxide gas through a mixture of light magnesium carbonate and water for two hours, letting the residue settle and siphoning off the clear liquid.[5]

The Barrow laboratory is developing a spray technique, using magnesium bicarbonate, to deacidify books without having to take them apart.

Because of the great importance of deacidification in the
preservation of archival and library material, considerable research
is being done to improve control of and eventually eliminate this problem. Promising alternatives, currently being explored, warrant
notice. It may be some time before they are sufficiently developed
for general use.

Calcium hydroxide solutions (lime water) were first used by
Barrow in 1939 to neutralize acid in paper. This process, requiring a second solution of calcium bicarbonate to carbonize the residual hydroxides in paper, has all but been abandoned.

Baynes-Cope, in the British Museum, is working with solutions of barium hydroxide (1.9%) in methyl alcohol to deacidify
documents, which, for one reason or another, cannot be wetted by
water. Alcohol solutions also offer promise for the spray deacidification of books.

In the Barrow laboratory 6% solutions of magnesium acetate
in alcohol used for spray deacidification have raised the pH of
book paper above the danger point, but do not provide buffering
against future acidification as does magnesium bicarbonate.

Richard D. Smith, fellow at the University of Chicago Graduate Library School, has been successfully deacidifying paper with
5% solutions of magnesium methoxide in methyl and ethyl alcohol.[6]
His experiments confirm that alcohol solvents are the logical avenue
of approach for further experiments in the deacidification of bound
volumes.

In 1965 investigators at the Washington State University College of Engineering developed a process for simultaneously neutral-
izing and strengthening paper by impregnating it with the sodium
salts of carboxymethylcellulose.[7] These salts neutralize the acid
and at the same time significantly increase the folding strength of
aged paper. Because of the potential for simultaneous strengthening and deacidification, this approach warrants much more study.

The Chemical Section of the Research Laboratory at Moscow's Lenin State Library has conducted extensive experiments in
connection with the preservation of old newspaper.[8] Using poly-

methyl acrylate emulsions they have been able to strengthen old
newsprint and make it resistant to moisture. What is disappointing
in the Russian experiments is that the polymethyl acrylate does not
reduce the acidity of the aged paper (neither does it increase it),
and there is no suggestion in the report as to what the acid may do
to the protective coating as time goes on.

In England W. H. Langwell has reported a process for vapor
phase deacidification of books and documents.[9] Essentially this
consists of exposing the items to an alkali gas. Langwell uses cy-
clohexylamine, carbonate (CHC), an organic derivative of ammonia,
for this purpose. Papers so treated are not only deacidified but
they also resist reacification. Documents are treated with CHC by
placing them in a tightly covered box with a sachet of the chemical.
Neutralization of the acid is accomplished in about two months.

Acidified books are treated by interleaving them with sheets
of paper impregnated with the chemical (one sheet every fifty pages).
It is not necessary to remove the impregnated paper when deacidification has been completed. The Langwell experiments suggest a
preventive measure for paper that has not yet deteriorated to the
point where it is unsafe to handle.

Sizing--Resizing during restoration replaces the original sizes
which have been leached out of the paper during the washing, bleaching and deacidification operations, or which were previously digested by fungi.

Immersing the individual sheets in hot solutions of glue,
boiled parchment trimmings, or gelatin restores their original crisp-
ness and body. One ounce of gelatin per quart of water, heated to
$135^{O}F$, is most commonly used.

The successful use of synthetic resins as size for the new
acid-free permanent/durable papers indicates that soluble nylon,
polymethyl acrylates, carboxymethylcellulose and other similar compounds will one day be in general use as sizes.

Mending--One of the more important requirements for successful mending is to keep the paper "relaxed. " Repairing long
tears is not easy because of the difficulty in bringing the separated
edges together for fastening. If, however, the cellulose fibers are

relaxed by immersing the torn document in water on a piece of
glass, the edges can be manipulated into position. When the glass
is then lifted out of the water, the relaxed paper will hold this
position during repair.

When repairing tears in books, or other paper that cannot
be relaxed with water, it is sometimes possible to use philatelists'
"peelable stamp hinges" to hold torn edges together on one side of
the paper while repairing the other. The adhesive on the hinges
should be tested before use, to be sure the hinges do not skin good
paper when being peeled off.

Skill in mending comes only after long practice. There are
many techniques for paper repair, all of which have merit. For
those who wish to try their hand at some, these relatively simple
sequences are suggested:

1. This is a method used for apprentice training in
   Great Britain.

   a. Select a mending paper to match damaged sheet in
      weight, tone, texture (and chain and wire marks if
      possible).

   b. Pare edges of damaged paper with a surgeon's
      scalpel.

   c. Lay damaged paper on repairing paper, matching
      chain and wire marks, and outline the missing
      area with a bone folder (not a pencil).

   d. Tear out the repairing piece 1/16th inch outside
      of the folder mark.

   e. Turn the repairing piece over and pare the edge
      with the scalpel.

   f. Apply paste to both pared edges, then place them
      together (pare to pare), rub with a bone folder and
      let dry.

   g. When dry, tone the repair if desired.

2. The secret of expert silking[10] and tissuing is to relax
   the paper by working on a wet surface. One of the
   many alternatives is as follows:

   a. Wet the working surface with water.

   b. Lay the damaged sheet on the wet surface and
      paste it with very thin (watery) wheat paste.

   c. Lay on tissue (or silk) and paste it down with the
      thin paste.

    d. Turn the damaged piece over and paste the reverse side.

    e. Lay on tissue (or silk) and paste it down.

    f. Lift the reinforced document from the wet surface and place on chipboard to dry.

3. A procedure much used in Italy for mending holes or missing corners is this:

    a. Select a mending paper to match that in the document.

    b. Apply paste generously to the edge of the hole or missing corner.

    c. Place the mending paper over the hole or missing corner so as to match the chain marks.

    d. With a razor blade or scalpel scrape the surplus paper away from the mended area, leaving a 1/16th inch overlap. (Damp the mending paper if necessary.)

    e. With a camel's hair brush lightly paste the joined edges and burnish with a bone folder.

4. Document backing with wove or laid paper is done as follows:

    a. Select a backing paper to match as near as possible the weight, tone, and texture of the document, print or map to be backed.

    b. Lay the sheet to be reinforced face down on a flat surface and relax it by spraying with water.

    c. Lay the backing sheet on another flat surface and paste it thoroughly with wheat paste.

    d. Pick up the backing paper and lay it, paste side down, over the sheet being reinforced.

    e. Cover with wax paper and rub down thoroughly.

    f. Remove the wax paper and let dry.

When entire printed pages (or large section of printed pages) are missing, very satisfactory replacements can be made if a full size photo-copy of the missing material can be obtained. First select a sheet of new handmade rag paper of tone, texture, wire marking, etc., to match the original. Then have the photo-copy of the missing material reproduced on this paper by the Xerox flat plate process. The result will be a facsimile page, which can be tipped into the book in its proper place or used to fill in the missing portion of an imperfect page. If the facsimile paper is carefully selected, and the photocopy is good, the restoration will be inconspicuous, but not dishonest.

Lamination--When the deterioration of paper has been ar-
rested in its early stages, resizing with gelatin is normally all that
is required.   When deterioration has seriously weakened paper or
made it brittle or pulpy, some form of reinforcement is needed.
This can be a good quality tissue paper; a laid or wove paper of
appropriate weight and texture; a layer of pure silk (not synthetic
fabric); or sandwiching the damaged sheet between layers of cellulose acetate and bonding them together with heat and pressure.

Tissuing is a relatively simple procedure which, when done
properly, is almost invisible.   For only slightly weakened paper, it
is entirely adequate and will last as long as the paper to which it
is applied.

The preferred reinforcement for weakened rag paper printed
or written on one side is wove or laid paper applied with wheat
paste.   The wide variety of European and Oriental papers available
makes the selection of a suitable backing routine.   The tone, weight
and texture of Japanese SEKISHU (natural) are such that it can be
used as an inconspicuous backing on a great many restorations.

Silk reinforcement is initially stronger than paper, but it
can be expected to last only twenty-five to thirty years.   However,
because when properly applied it is practically invisible, it is useful for strengthening seriously weakned documents printed or written
on both sides, which for esthetic reasons should not be laminated
with plastic.

Plastic lamination is a boon for wood pulp paper records
which are crumbling and are too fragile for any of the other methods of reinforcement.   Laminated paper will unquestionably stand
very rough usage and will undoubtedly last for centuries.   If preservation is the only consideration, its use is warranted.   Many records, however, have been laminated with plastic when deacidification and reinforcement with tissue or rag paper would have been
more than adequate.   Plastic lamination is an important recourse
for librarians and archivists, but the practice of laminating everything is to be deplored.

The evolution of plastic lamination and the current state of

the art have been well documented[11] and the process has been ex-
haustively tested. [12] Cellulose acetate can be expected to last as
long as rag paper and it has no adverse effect on paper. This is
not true of cellulose nitrate or polyvinyl chloride films. Cellulose
acetate is a permeable film. Paper laminated with it is subject to
further contamination by sulphur dioxide unless it has been deacidified with magnesium bicarbonate.

All cellulose acetate films are not suitable for lamination
(see Gear- "Lamination After 30 Years"). The only film that currently meets the performance specifications suggested by the Bureau
of Standards is formula P-911, manufactured by the Celanese Corporation of America.

Although tissue paper is customarily used between the acetate film and the document for extra strength, in the Archives of
France silk is used to reinforce plastic laminations. The minute
loss of transparency is considered negligible compared to the increase in strength.

The Laboratory for the Conservation and Restoration of
Books at the USSR Academy of Sciences has experimented with polyethylene as a plastic laminant for paper[13] and recommends it as
particularly suited for paper with a high ground-wood pulp content.

In an effort to achieve simultaneous lamination and deacidification, W. H. Langwell in England has developed Postlip Duplex
Laminating Tissue, which is a high grade tissue paper impregnated
with polyvinyl acetate which contains magnesium acetate as a de-
acidifier. It is applied with heat and pressure or by pressure
alone after saturating the tissue and document with acetone.

Ink--Faded ink is not always a catastrophe. Illegible carbon
ink writing can often be deciphered by infrared, ultraviolet or sodium light photography. Weak carbon and iron gall inks can be read
more easily with the aid of a convenient hand-held "black light"
magnifier (LITE MITE, Stecker & Yale, Inc., Marblehead, Massachusetts, about $26.00).

The vapor of ammonium sulphide will restore iron gall inks
by creating ferrous sulphide on the paper. Writing restored this
way does not last long because the iron sulphide is oxidized to iron

sulphate in a short time.   This also affects the paper.

A two-percent solution of tannic acid will also blacken the
ferric oxide in iron gall ink as well as some modern inks that are
a mixture of iron galls and synthetic dyes.   This is permanent
darkening and there will be no acid damage to the paper if the surplus solution is rinsed off after the ink has been revived.   However,
the paper will probably be darkened by the iron impurities in it re-
acting with the tannic acid.

Faded synthetic dye inks are extremely difficult to revive
unless the writing fluid was contaminated with iron.   This can be
determined quickly by testing a small portion with tannic acid solution.

Sulphocyanic gas fumes (or an aerosol spray of the same)
will recover iron gall ink that has been chemically treated to obliterate it.   Other means of recovering obliterated ink and detecting
forgeries are treated in detail in Ordway Hilton's An Evaluation of
Chemical Methods for Restoring Erased Writing Ink.   (London,
Swindon Press, n.d.).

Dr. Ludovico Santucci at the Institute of Book Pathology in
Rome has developed a process for regenerating faded ink without
affecting the paper, [14] but it is practicable only for records that are
worth expensive restoration.

Leather--Leather in prime condition is excellent protective
covering.   Deteriorated leather is worthless even when its appearance is still satisfactory.   The preventive measures suggested in
Chapter IV will preserve old vegetable-tanned leather from biological or chemical deterioration indefinitely.   If these same measures
(particularly those for the inhibition of acid damage) are begun on
modern leather when it is new and are continued, the material's
life expectancy should approach that of the earlier tanned skins.

When acid deterioration has taken place, nothing can be done
to restore the protective strength of leather, although its appearance
can be considerably improved by lanolin and wax dressings.

Leather from the eighteenth century or earlier is sometimes
horny.   If it is dampened with a sponge and then oiled with a lanolin leather dressing, it should regain some of its suppleness.   Care

should be taken in treatment of gold tooled covers because a too
generous application of lanolin may result in loss of some of the
decorative details.

Leather which has been water soaked must be sterilized,[15]
dried promptly in air, not in an oven, and treated with potassium
lactate solution and an oil dressing to restore its protective chemicals and to relubricate the fibers.   Failure to do this will result in
total loss.

The surface of powdered leather can be consolidated with a
wax dressing (CIRE 212) or British Museum Leather Dressing,
which contains beeswax.

When it is imperative to preserve leather which has rotted
to the point of falling apart, it can be returned to handling condition by saturating it with polyethylene glycol (i. e. molten Carbowax
1500'' Union Carbide and Chemical Company).   This will not make
book covers usable as such, but it will save decorative patterns and
the details of binder's finishing tool impressions, both of which can
be used to identify the creator of the work.

Vellum--Hermann Smith's report on manuscript repair in
European archives[16] includes detailed information on vellum repair
as he saw it done in the British Museum, Public Records Office,
Archives of France, Vatican Library and other European restoration centers.   With few exceptions the craft techniques described
are still valid.

Vellum and parchment are more difficult to repair than are
other library materials.   Expert, almost invisible, mending can be
done, but only after much practice.   Library personnel, other than
conservators and bookbinders, should confine themselves to cleaning, flattening and removing wrinkles.

The use of water or solvents is hazardous to writing and illuminations on vellum.   When mildew effects vellum, sterilization
in a thymol cabinet or improvised fumigation chamber is the best
remedy.   Vellum book covers are cleaned by erasing the grime and
removing the more persistent soil with saddle soap applied as a
paste, or the froth from castile soap suds.   Never use wet suds.

Mildew stains on book covers can sometimes be removed by painting with alcohol or benzene after brushing off the spores.   Ink
stains have been removed from vellum book covers by repeated
painting of the spot with a solution of 5% Chloramine-T.

Flattening vellum is a relatively simple matter and the necessary equipment is inexpensive.   The secret is to relax the material when feasible, but keep in mind that dampness is fatal to the
color and to adhesion of gold on illuminations.   Horny, dry,
wrinkled vellum documents sandwiched between dampened[17] white
blotters and kept under moderate pressure for at least a week or
two will come out flat, dry and supple.   Documents in hard rolls
and those too badly wrinkled to sandwich between damp blotters can
be made soft and flexible in a relaxing box and then flattened by
pressure.   Relaxing boxes are covered wood or metal chests lined
on four sides with blotters and fitted with wood brackets for sus-
pending books, manuscripts, scrolls, etc., away from the bottom
and sides.   When the blotters lining the sides are dampened with
water containing 0.25% sodium pentachloro phenol and the cover
closed, the humid environment within the box will sooner or later
soften the hardest vellum and loosen the most obstinate folds.   A
handy alternative relaxer for horny vellum scrolls is a navigator's
waterproof chart tube.   These are metal cylinders with screw caps
and rubber seals.   They can be lined by slipping a rolled-up blotter
into them.   When the blotter is dampened with water and fungicide,
it will expand against the sides of the cylinder, making room for
the scrolls (loosely protected by Kraft paper) to be slipped down the
center.

The Austrian National Museum in Vienna has originated an
unusual method for restoring the flexibility of vellum.   Documents
that are free of colored illuminations are first dampened with water
and then dehydrated by displacing the water with acetone or ethyl
alcohol.   The solvent is changed several times to insure complete
replacement of the water.   The last solvent bath includes a small
amount of lanolin to be deposited in the material as a plasticizer
after the liquid has evaporated.

Vellum which has been shrunk and misshapened by moisture

142   Conservation of Library Materials

can be restored to near original dimensions on a stretcher (see
Figure 10) after it has been relaxed either in a box or between
damp blotters.   The stretcher subjects the document to uniform tension in all directions until it is thoroughly dry and flat.   This device is also excellent for removing wrinkles and creases.

The British Museum laboratory favors a glass plate method
for removing wrinkles.   They relax the document, place it on a
clean plate devoid of all grease, cover it with a blotter and weight
down the edges with strips of lead.   As the vellum shrinks on drying, the friction removes the creases very satisfactorily.

Holes in vellum are repaired by roughing the edges and applying a bevel-edged vellum patch.   For particularly neat work the
patch is applied on the back of the hole and a second piece of vellum, cut just big enough to fill the aperture with no overlap, is inserted in the cavity from the front.   The repair is then held under
a weight until dry.

Tears in vellum, if the edges are chamfered, are mended
by pasting the overlapping edges and holding them together under
weights until dry.   Repairing tears or cuts in which the edges do
not overlap requires the greatest of skill.   Formerly such damage
was mended by sewing the edges together with a baseball stitch,
but that technique has been abandoned.

The practice today is to

a. pare the cut edges with a scalpel.

b. cut a patch the length of the tear and a little wider
   and pare it.

c. apply adhesive to the edges and fit the patch over
   the tear.

d. rub down with a folder and dry under a weight.

e. tone the patch to match the document.

Wheat paste or hide glue will not make a good bond on vellum.   Polyvinyl acetate is better, but gelatin with one drop of concentrated acetic acid is best.   The acetic acid pits the vellum and
permits the gelatin to bite in.

In lieu of adhesives, the edges of chamfered tears can be
painted with 10% acetic acid.   This will gelatinize the vellum under

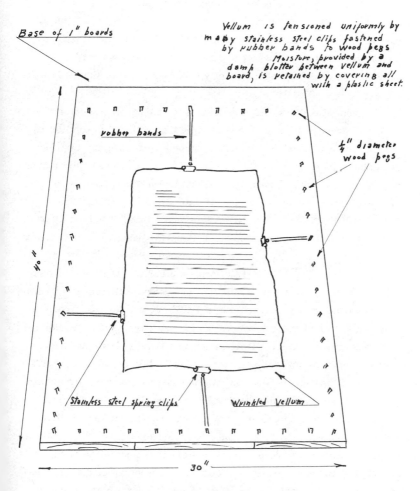

Base of 1" boards

Vellum is tensioned uniformly by many stainless steel clips fastened by rubber bands to wood pegs. Moisture, provided by a damp blotter between vellum and board, is retained by covering all with a plastic sheet.

rubber bands

¼" diameter wood pegs

40"

Stainless steel spring clips

Wrinkled Vellum

30"

Figure 10
Vellum Flattening Device

143

the weak acid so that when the torn edges are rubbed together and dried, the mend will be self-bonding. Such repairs are often less visible than those in which adhesives are used.

Otto Wachter, of the Austrian National Library in Vienna, has devised a method for delicate repairs to illuminated vellum manuscripts using goldbeater's skin.[18] The skin must be real goldbeater's skin, the stomach of an ox, and not the fish skin substitute.

When the ink or illuminations are flaking off vellum manuscripts, they can be refastened by spraying with a 5% solution of soluble nylon in alcohol. The low surface tension nylon and alcohol solution penetrates the minute cracks in the illumination and under the flaking ink, drawing the pigments back into position where they are firmly rebonded as the alcohol dries.

BOOKBINDING AND REPAIR--Handbinding--The best information still in print on fine binding is Douglas Cockerell's outstanding Bookbinding and the Care of Books (London, Faber and Faber, 1956). Many other fine instructional texts have been written on the subject, but they are now available only occasionally in second-hand dealers' catalogues. Edith Deihl's Bookbinding: Its Background and Technique, out of print since 1950 and now very expensive, is well worth the price. Mrs. Diehl, borrowing heavily from the best of earlier works on the subject, assembled in two volumes a wealth of general information as well as detailed instruction for handbinding. Other authors who should be sought by those interested in craft bindings are Zaehnsdorf, W. J. E. Crane, Clara Buffam, William Mathews and Paul Hasluck. These are the classics. There are also quite a few more recent texts written in a popular vein for school use and for hobbyists. Two of these, particularly good because of the excellent illustrations of procedures which accompany the text, are Aldren Watson's Hand Bookbinding and Manly Bannister's Pictorial Manual of Bookbinding.

Repair--Harold Tribolet, in an address before the Society of American Archivists in 1953,[19] spelled out what librarians should expect in the way of quality and workmanship from bookbinders and restorers. This covers the subject except for advice on the treat-

ment of acid paper. Sidney Cockerell's The Reparing of Books.
London, Shepard Press, 1958, is replete with detailed instructions
for the repair of fine volumes. As a general rule, in the restoration of important books, the less done the better. Acidity must be
corrected, mildew deterioration remedied and unsightly insect damage made presentable, but librarians should make sure that whatever else is done is limited to what is absolutely necessary. In
the process, margins should not be trimmed, type impressions
should not be pressed out, paper should not be over-bleached and
contemporary bindings, original end papers etc., should not be discarded. Chemical and bacteriological damage should be corrected
but it is often better to box rare and valuable items than to rebind
them. In this matter, frequent review of Hellmut Lehmann-Haupt's
analysis on the pros and cons of binding will be profitable.

Leather bookbindings almost always can be repaired if the
leather has not deteriorated to powder. Any cover from the
eighteenth century or earlier should be repaired rather than replaced. Fortunately, even the fragments of most of these early
leather covers are still tough and durable, and can be utilized.
Split oak or beech boards can be rejoined with glue and worm holes
can be filled with plastic wood. Dog-eared paper boards can be
hardened with glue and in extreme cases reinforced with plastic
wedges.[20] Warped paper boards can be flattened.

When it is necessary to disassemble an old book because of
acid or mildew deterioration, there is rarely any difficulty in saving the leather on the sides. The backs are a different matter.
Hollow backs come off easily, as do those on spines which have
been lined with paper before the application of the leather. The
back is lifted with a scalpel, minimizing tearing of the leather.
While the paper lining splits in this process, the lining paper which
adheres to the fragile backs does hold them together. Many early
English bindings have the leather pasted directly to the spine of the
book, with no paper liner. These are usually still tightly fastened
and it is extremely difficult to get them off, even in pieces. There
are ways to salvage these tight backs but binders are often reluc-
tant to take the painstaking steps necessary because of the cost in

time. When the tooling is particularly attractive or the cover is
important historically, the binding order should include specific instructions in this regard. In general, all instructions for the repair of old bindings should be specific unless the librarian is absolutely confident that his restorationist is a bibliophile as well as a
bibliopegist.

The leather on warped and dog-eared corners is usually worn
away, exposing the boards. When such damaged corners are reinforced with glue, and sometimes plastic wedges, they must also be
covered with new leather neatly shaped and tucked under the old,
both for appearance and strength. Sometimes binders instead merely stain the exposed boards to match the old leather. This incompe-
tent practice often goes unnoticed when the books are returned.
Again, this can be avoided by specific binding instructions when the
books are sent out.

At the Bibliotheque Nationale in Paris, new gold tooling on
restored bindings is aged by washing it with a mixture of bitumen in
benzene and then speckling it with a toothbrush dipped in bitumen.

Library binding--The difference between edition (publisher's)
bindings and library binding is that although both are "cased in"
coverings (as distinguished from "laced-on" boards in hand binding)
library bindings are sturdier because of the use of more durable
covering material as well as heavier end sheets and reinforced
hinges. The pages in better library bindings are sewn to several cotton
tapes, which provide extra strength and serve as hinges between the
book and the cover. Edition bindings are not sewn on tape and the
stitching through the folds is barely enough to hold the gatherings
together. The overcast sewing on most library binding reduces the inner margins and makes the book less flexible than a handbound book.
This is a necessary compromise between quality and cost.

The Library Binding Manual (American Library Association,
1951), prepared under the direction of the Joint Committee of the
American Library Association and the Library Binding Institute, is
an excellent introduction to the theory and practice of library binding and it provides the justification for the Minimum Specifications
for Class "A" Library Binding long accepted by American libraries

and the binding industry. The latest reprinting of the standards
(including those for rebinding used volumes and periodical binding,
as well as the prebinding of new books) is available in the Library
Binding Institute's Handbook for Library Binding (Boston 1963). This
informative pamphlet, together with the Library Binding Manual,
provides a complete source of information on the care and repair
of circulating volumes.

In 1960 the American Library Association's Library Technology Project undertook a study to recommend performance standards for library binding.[21] The group recommended the development of five separate standards for library binding (i.e., heavily
used material, heavy format material, lesser used material, binding for music, and belles-lettres). They also suggested three separate standards for publisher's bindings as well as a continuing test
program.

Cloth Binding--The United States Government Printing Office's
Bookbinding - Theory and Practice, which is an apprentice training
manual, contains all that library personnel need know about machine-
made cloth bindings. It also contains much information on periodical binding, box-making, slip cases, mechanical and loose leaf binding, adhesives and materials. Too compendious to be used as a
textbook, it is, nevertheless, a useful reference tool.

The rebinding of clothbound books, a major problem in any
library, is best solved by the selection of a reputable commercial
bindery that provides work conforming to the Minimum Specifications
for Class "A" Library Binding.[22] Books so repaired will come
back sturdier and more durable than when they were new.

Important modern books merit better protection than that af-
forded by edition bindings, but do not always require expensive hand
binding. Standard library binding, with reduced inner margins and stiff
spines, is inappropriate for these. Hellmut Lemann-Haupt examined
this problem in 1941[23] and concluded that by eliminating the oversewing and giving more attention to the appearance of library bindings, they can be made appropriate for some important books. This
is still a valid conclusion that might very well be examined further
in any extension of the American Library Association's Library Tech-

Technology Project study on the binding needs of libraries. At the
present time the most sensible treatment for valuable cloth covered
volumes is to box them for protection.

For those libraries fortunate enough to have personnel,
space and equipment to do minor repairs to circulation volumes
etc. , there are several good sources of information. Sidney Cockerell's Repairing of Books includes chapters on repairing cased
books and on repairing unsewn (paperback) bindings. The Care and
Repair of Books by Lydenberg and Archer, revised in 1960 by John
Alden of the Boston Public Library, has an excellent section on
mending. Hand Bookbinding by Aldren Watson, New York, Reinhold
Publishing Corp. , 1963, contains step by step procedures, with detailed illustrations, for repair, rebinding and making slip cases
and boxes. This book provides an excellent list of inexpensive
workshop tools and equipment. Two pamphlets by leading library
supply houses are well worth having for their suggested methods of
book repair. They are the Demcobind Manual (Madison, Wisconsin,
Demco Library Suppliers) and Bookcraft (Syracuse, N. Y. , Gaylord
Bros. , Inc. , 1951).

Maps--Early maps, printed on good quality rag paper with
carbon ink, respond remarkably to procedures for restoration of paper. Many nineteenth and twentieth-century maps, printed on thin,
ground-wood pulp paper, backed with linen or cotton and often
heavily varnished, are another matter entirely. These are a chal-
lenge to any conservation laboratory.

Clara LeGear's out of print Maps; Their Care, Repair, and
Preservation in Libraries (Washington, Library of Congress 1956)
with its abundance of information on all aspects of map care should
be obtained by all libraries, even if photo-copying is required.
This book provides all the information needed on this subject, except for the repair of acid and fungus damage.

Manuscripts--Irreplaceable manuscripts must be handled with
extreme care. These important records are often received at a
library worn, torn on the edges, split at the folds, stained, mildew
infested or embrittled by acid. Regardless of their condition, it is
seldom that they cannot be returned to seviceable condition on the

premises by library personnel.

In the restoration of manuscripts, whether new acquisitions
or older collections, careful examination is the first step.   Mildew
or previous mildew damage is evidenced by a musty odor, circular
stains, living spores or a limp feel to the paper.   Acidified documents are darkened and brittle.   Testing with a spot indicator will
reveal the degree of acidity.   When bundles of paper are opened,
insects, dead or alive, are often exposed.   Dead bodies do not necessarily mean the danger is over.   There can be larvae or thousands of eggs in the inner recesses of envelopes, between the folds
or in the container.   In any case, fumigation is imperative.   Foxing stains are unsightly, but not necessarily dangerous.   On the
other hand, grease stains are food for insects and mold.   Water
stains suggest that the cellulose fibers may have been damaged.

After inspection (and fumigation if necessary), vacuum cleaning will remove dust, loose dirt and foreign matter.   Care must be
exercised to insure that in the vacuuming no fragments of damaged
paper are sucked into the hose.   The alternative is blowing away
the dirt when compressed air and an exhaust hood are available.
Stain reduction and the removal of grime are no problem with manuscripts written in carbon ink.   Iron gall ink can be dry cleaned,
treated with solvents, and washed but it can not be bleached.   Synthetic dye ink should be carefully tested for water solubility and for
reaction to solvents before liquids are applied.   Bleaching is out of
the question and washing is probably dangerous.   Printer's ink offers no problems.   Occasionally, with manuscripts written with carbon or iron gall ink, after removal of the grime and reducing the
stains by washing, the paper has been sufficiently revitalized so as
to require no further attention.   Manuscripts that have been damaged by acid or mildew usually require resizing after they have
been deacidified, sterilized or bleached.

Pencil writing on manuscripts is resistant to treatments for
mildew and acid and is usually not effected by bleaching.   However,
if there is any doubt about the permanence of marginal notations in
pencil, they can be varnished with a solution of cellulose acetate
(5-6%) in a mixture of methyl-ethyl ketone, dioxane, and acetone

(1:1:2). When delicately applied to the writing with a fine tipped
brush, the varnish will protect it during all restorative processes.

Many manuscripts are in good condition except for wrinkles
or multiple folds that complicate filing and storage. Flattening is
a relatively simple operation. This can be accomplished by carefully opening the papers and then interleaving them between blotters
under a moderately heavy weight, not a press, for several weeks.
If every tenth blotter is dampened ever so slightly with water and
0.25% thymol to inhibit mold, the moisture infiltrating the pile will
expedite the process. When there are a large number of documents
to be flattened, they can be handled conveniently by first humidify-
ing them in a relaxing box and then running them through a photographer's drum dryer for matte prints (Figure 11). The paper will
come out flat and crisp and ready for filing. Drying on the heated
drum will facilitate washing, deacidifying and bleaching and will,
at the same time, flatten and remove creases from the documents
being processed.

Manuscripts are mended by tissuing, silking, repairing tears,
replacing missing fragments and backing with rag paper. Lamination with cellulose acetate film is appropriate and is often the only
solution for crumbling documents on wood pulp paper. It is seldom
required for the repair of rag paper.

Practical guidance for the repair of manuscripts is available
in Adelaide Minogue's Care and Preservation of Records; Lucille
M. Kane's A Guide To the Care and Administration of Manuscripts;
and Herman Smith's "Manuscript Repair in European Archives."
American Archivist, vol. I, 1938. More technical data is presented
in Plenderleith, Conservation of Antiquities and Works of Art; Langwell, The Conservation of Books and Documents; and A.E. Werner,
"The Preservation of Archives," Journal of the Society of Archivists, Vol. I, No. 10 (October 1959).

Prints and Drawings--In Zigrosser and Gaehde, Guide to the
Collection and Care of Original Prints, Crown Publishers, New
York, 1965, Mrs. Gaehde, one of the foremost print restorers in
America, emphasizes the damage that can be done by unskilled re-
pairing and improper handling of prints. Carl Schraubstadter's

Figure 11

Photographer's Electrically Heated Print Dryer
(for drying washed, bleached, deacidified or sized paper in quantity)
(Photo courtesy of The PAKO Corporation, Minneapolis, Minn.)

151

Care and Repair of Japanese Prints, Cornwall-on-Hudson, Idlewild
Press, 1948, reflects a lifetime of experience as a collector, artist
engraver, proprietor of an artists' supply house and repairer. This
book is not a definitive authority on the subject of print repair, but
all methods described were learned by the author at firsthand in Japan and are known to be safe. Dr. Plenderleith's Conservation of
Antiquities and Works of Art, Chapter 3, describes the methods for
cleaning, repair and mounting of prints, drawings and manuscripts
developed at the British Museum Research Laboratory. In Feb. , 1949,
R. D. Buck, then with the Fogg Museum, summarized in ICOM News
what he considered to be the best materials and practices for the conser
vation of drawing. Detailed step-by-step procedures for the repair of
prints and drawings are in Morton C. Bradley's The Treatment of
Pictures. The format of this manual is unusual, but it is an excellent source of information on the practices of professional restorers.

The repair of prints and drawings is not simple and, in general, should be left to professional picture restorers. Expert assistance is available from members of the International Institute for
Conservation, many of whom are conservators on American museum
staffs. The combination of a wide variety of papers, all kinds of
inks and colors, and various techniques of application all complicate the problem. Some water colors are almost insoluble after
many years on a picture, others are still fugitive. Pastels, pen
and ink drawings, sepia and charcoal sketches vary to extremes.

The most that should be attempted by library personnel other
than conservators is the cleaning and repair of black and white
prints. These can be washed, sterilized, freed of stains, deacidified, bleached, mended and resized in a well equipped library workshop with a reasonable probability of success.

The sequence of operations would be
   a. sterilization
   b. dry cleaning with art gum, etc.
   c. stain reduction with solvents
   d. soaking in cold water to relax paper
   e. soaking in hot (200°F) water to clean paper

      f. bleaching (preferably Chloramine-T)

      g. deacidifying if necessary

      h. sizing

There can be no assurance that the hues and colors in prints will survive restoration in a library workshop. It would also be extremely hazardous for library personnel to attempt any repairs to pastels, charcoal sketches and colored drawings or water colors, other than sterilization to destroy mildew. In the case of fungi attacks on pastels and crayon drawings which might be effected by thymol or other disinfectants, the spores can be lifted off the surface with a camel's-hair brush dampened with alcohol.

In order to protect a print or drawing, a good backing is essential. Rag board or a good quality rag paper is best for this purpose. Strawboard, cardboard and panels of wood should never be used. All pictures are safer when mounted on rag board and preferably with a rag board overthrow.[24] Mounted prints and drawings, particularly pastels, should always be protected against mildew by inserting under the picture a paper liner, which has been saturated with a 10% solution of thymol and then dried.

Black and white illustrations in books can be considered to be permanent, for they are invariably done with printer's ink which is made with lampblack, the cheapest and most permanent of pigments. Colored inks and some of the very modern quick drying blacks complicate the repair of books with colored plates. Some may be smudged by aqueous suspensions of fungicides or dampness and others are soluble in alcohol and other solvents.

Seals--Wax seals are easily broken and should be repaired immediately to prevent further damage or loss of fragments. A good adhesive for seal repair is a mixture of two-thirds beeswax and one-third rosin melted together. This hot mixture is flowed into the interstices and the pieces are pressed together with the fingers, momentarily, until the adhesive sets. Missing parts can then be filled in with colored plaster of Paris, which, after drying, is scraped with a scalpel to conform to the general contour.

Plain wax wafers, which served only to close the document, are usually of no importance to the record and can be disposed of.

They will usually float off a manuscript during washing, bleaching and deacidification, leaving a soft residue which can be scraped clean without damaging the paper.

Conservators copy official seals by making molds of plaster of Paris or latex, using the original seal for a pattern. For photographic purposes, copies are cast in the mold, using waxes especially colored for maximum contrast on the film.

The Exotics--In the case of unusual library materials, librarians should limit themselves to the procedures for their general care outlined in Chapter IV. The repair of these materials is best left to specialists trained in various aspects of museum conservation.

Papyrus, a laminated writing material, cannot be restored by the same techniques used for paper. The wet methods used on paper would ruin it. Papyrus that has survived the ages is usually wrinkled, creased, dry and brittle. Papyrus scrolls are unrolled by relaxing them with barely damp blotters and carefully flattening them. Fragmented sheets of papyrus are repaired with strips of goldbeater's skin and are sometimes backed with linen or silk after the pieces are reoriented. Papyrus is sterilized by pressing it between blotters dampened with thymol or sodium pentachlorophenol.

Birch bark--One of the few instances in which silk is preferable to tissue in library conservation is in the repair of embrittled birch bark manuscripts. Prior to reinforcing, the bark is cleaned with glycerin and water for waterproof ink, or with carbon tetrachloride or acetone when the ink is not waterproof. If adhering, the bark manuscripts are first separated in a hot solution of paraffin oil, which also washes away much dirt as it separates the leaves. After cleaning and drying on a plate of glass, the bark is silked on both sides, using a thin wheat paste adhesive. After drying, the fabric is trimmed to within 1/16th inch of the edge of the bark. For additional protection, bark manuscripts can be inlaid in a piece of heavy rag paper cut to fit the bark and using the 1/16th inch silk as an overlay. An alternative after the silking is completed is to mount the bark between sheets of glass sealed on the edges.

Palm Leaf Manuscripts--If scratched writing on palm leaves
is faded, it can be restored by rubbing graphite into the stylus
marks with a cotton pad and then removing the surplus with cotton
wool. Faded writing that was not scratched through the epidermis
of the leaf cannot be restored.

Palm leaves that have become brittle regain some of their
flexibility after spraying with walnut oil. Thymol has been found to
be harmful to palm leaves and treatment for mildew should use
para-nitro-phenol. Otherwise, the repair of these records is the
same as for birch bark manuscripts.

A recent innovation at the Baroda Museum and Picture Gallery is to laminate brittle palm leaves between two sheets of polymethyl methacrylate, using acetone as the solvent.[25]

Bone and Ivory--The repair of bone and ivory, other than
the removal of surface dirt with soap and water and chemically removing salt encrustations, is usually done by vacuum impregnation
with nitrocellulose lacquers, polyvinyl acetate emulsion or other adhesives to consolidate the mass of the material.

Cuneiform Tablets--In 1956 the British Museum established
a special workroom for the conservation of their many thousands of
cuneiform tablets. The restoration procedure, as reported in the
British Museum Quarterly vol. 23 No. 2, 1961, is essentially (1)
baking at 400° to 750°C to liberate chemically combined water, (2)
soaking for four weeks in fresh water (changed daily) to remove
water soluble salts and (3) drying in warm air. This treatment
hardens the clay without changing its color. It makes the clay resistant to water and removes disfiguring salt crystals to restore
legibility.

Stone--There is no general agreement as to the efficacy of
preservation measures and no stone preservative so far used has
met with any significant measure of success except when the stone
objects are displayed indoors.

Wood--The first requirement for wood repair is a good adhesive. Casein glues have been used for centuries for rejoining
split wood in book covers. Today's synthetic resin adhesives are
even better and epoxy resin adhesives, which set without change of

volume, are best.   Holes in book covers are filled with plaster of
Paris, putty, glue and sawdust, or plastic wood.   Missing pieces
are replaced with new wood, cut to fit and fastened with epoxy cement.   Damaged veneer is repaired with flexible glues and clamping
irons designed for cabinet making.   Olive oil applied sparingly to
marquetry keeps it from drying out, and almond and lemon oils are
used for cleaning inlaid wooden objects.

Termite-ridden wooden objects or dry rotted wood are consolidated by vacuum impregnation with wax or synthetic materials.
Wooden objects that have been split and warped by dehydration have
been restored to their original shape by soaking in water for two
weeks and then treated with polyethylene glycol, dried and refin-
ished.[26]

FILM AND TAPE--Repairs to film and tape, other than
splicing breaks, require the services of a photographic laboratory.

Magnetic sound tape can be rehabilitated, without affecting
the recorded information, by laboratory machinery which scrapes
the tapes clean of foreign materials.[27]   In Europe, gold compounds
are used to protect microfilm images against oxidation fading.   Da-
guerrotype images are now chemically restored, including the complete removal of oxidation stain, without etching the plates.[28]
Black and white photographic prints are made immune to mold
growth by special treatment with Hyamine 1622,[29] but there is no
known satisfactory fungus protection for color prints.

Library staffs should concentrate their efforts on keeping
photographic materials clean, dry and safe from mildew and polluted air.   When fungus is found, it should be removed from films
and tape only in a laboratory.   The reactions of different photographic material to fungicides are such that only experienced tech-
nicians can safely do this work.

Dirt can be removed from moving picture film and microfilm by wiping with a lintless fabric pad moistened with a special
cleaner.[30]   However, the cleaning operation should be carried out
in an atmosphere of 50% relative humidity to minimize static elec-
tricity, which will attract dust.   If an immaculately clean, dust-fre
workroom is not available, this work should not be done.

The repair and restoration of library materials in the tropics is essentially the same as in temperate zones, except that the damage inflicted by the enemies of books is more frequent and more drastic. In equatorial countries prevention must be emphasized.

The care and repair of prints, drawings and manuscripts in Australian museums has been reported by William Boustead.[31] The methods described for deacidification and mildew control are based on American and European practices, but are modified to suit their limited budgets, the continued high temperatures and humidity and the lack of air conditioning in the subtropical climate of parts of the country.

The care and repair of books in the tropics is well covered by Wilfred Plumbe.[32] His lengthy bibliography of books and articles on tropical conservation makes this book of particular interest to librarians in equatorial countries. K.D. Bhargava[33] describes the repair of paper and other records as it is done in India. Except for his guidance in repair of birch bark and palm leaves, the techniques described are little different than those in temperate zones but the materials used are those found to be more suitable in the tropics.

Fire and Water Damage--Intense heat will embrittle paper even though flames do not reach it. Books are naturally resistant to flames and even when their covers and edges are badly charred, the interiors, except for the heat embrittlement, are generally salvageable. Boxes provide considerable protection for manuscripts and other documents, particularly when they are tightly packed. Water damage during a fire is often more serious than combustion.

The immediate requirement after a fire or flood is to separate the water-soaked material from that which is charred only. Vast drying areas are needed. They must provide good circulation of air at normal room temperature. Books dry best when stood on edge with the pages fanned out but this is not practical for even modest numbers of wet volumes. The alternative is to interleave the pages with blotters, paper toweling or any other absorbent paper available. As soon as possible the interleaving sheets should be replaced with dry ones impregnated with thymol to inhibit mold.

Do not attempt to accelerate the drying with artificial heat. When
books have suffered excessive damage from mud and water, as in
the Florence floods in November, 1966, they should be taken apart,
the leaves separately washed in thymol water, dried, flattened and
wrapped in thymol impregnated paper until such time as they can
be rebound.

Charred volumes can often be trimmed at the edges and rebound. For out of print circulating books, this is probably the only
economically feasible solution. It would be less expensive in the
long run to buy new copies if the books are still in print. Rare
and valuable books exposed to heat should be restored even if there
is no evidence of charring.

Water-soaked manuscripts, prints, broadsides and maps
should be separated carefully and should be dried individually to
keep them from being stuck together by their gelatin size. Those
which have been water-soaked only can be restored on the premises
by washing, sterilizing, resizing if necessary, pressing between
blotters in a letter press or drying on a photographer's print dryer.
All manuscripts, etc., which are known to have been exposed to in-
tense heat should be segregated for examination by a conservator.
Badly charred documents, on which the writing or printing is obliterated, can still be deciphered by chemical or photographic processes. These should be handled as little as possible to minimize
crumbling. Do not try to separate charred bundles of paper; rather
lift them from their containers and wrap them in cotton wool until
they can be professionally treated. Pick up badly charred single
sheets on pieces of cardboard and keep them between cardboard for
protection.

Quality Control--Craftsmanship and choice of materials are
the determining factors in the quality of new book production as
well as in the repair and restoration of all library items.

Insistence on adherence to standards and the use of the best
materials will prolong the life of rebound library books. Indiffer-
ence to enforcement of the Minimum Specifications for Class "A"
Library Binding[34] by libraries and by commercial binderies is reported by the American Library Association Technology Project.[35]

The Guild of Book Workers has its own "Standards and Specifications Governing All Work Submitted for Exhibition." (Appendix
C). All Guild workers abide by these specifications. Librarians
might well insist that these standards govern the performance of
all work other than rebinding of circulating volumes.

The papermaking industry can now produce permanent/dur-
able book papers comparing favorably in cost with other book paper.
If used in book production this paper will insure useful life for hundreds of years.[36] Insistence by all those who purchase books that
they be printed on these long-lasting papers would be a most mean-
ingful contribution to conservation of library materials. Some university presses are leading the way in this matter.[37]

Insistence that book binders and conservators use only handmade, high quality, starch or gelatin-sized paper in the repair and
restoration of important items will contribute to extending their life.
There is a wide range of weights, tones and textures in the handmade European and Japanese paper now available, so insistence on
their use is justifiable. In no case should the use of rosin-sized
machine-made paper be permitted.

Books rebound in leather should use alum tawed pigskin or
acid resistant, vegetable-tanned calf, goat or pigskin that will stand
up under the PIRA test. This accelerated aging test for leather,
developed by the British Leather Manufacturers' Research Association, will reveal in the course of a week whether acid-free vegetable-tanned leather will withstand deterioration by polluted air.
Alum tawed pigskin is one of the most durable covering materials
known. Books covered with it hundreds of years ago are still
strong and durable and still show no signs of chemical deterioration.
Chrome-tanned leather is extremely durable and resistant to mold
and acid but it is unsuited for bookbinding. It is difficult to adapt
chrome-tanned leather to the shape of a book because of its water
resistance.

How to Judge a Binding--Late in his life Douglas Cockerell,
an acknowledged master of the art of fine bookbinding, set down
what he considered to be the requirements for quality in his work.[38]
These criteria, based on a lifetime of experience and fine crafts-

manship, could well be adopted by all librarians as modern standards of quality for handbinding and rare book restoration. (Cockerell's specifications for fine hand bindings to meet his standards of
quality are available in his Bookbinding and the Care of Books, 5th
edition, London 1955, p. 308-311.) The method for examining library bindings suggested by the Joint Committee of the American
Library Association and the Library Binding Institute[39] is useful for
determining the quality of rebinding or edition binding without dis-
section. This check list, with slight changes, is also available
from the Library Binding Institute.[40]

Library Workshops--A library workshop can be an isolated
work area, a conventional bindery or a conservation workroom. A
work area for the simplest of book repairs need have little more
than a bench or two, with a cabinet and drawers for supplies, in a
seldom used but well lighted space. Librarians contemplating the
establishment of a workroom can do no better than to refer to Aldren Watson's Hand Bookbinding (Reinhold, N.Y. 1963), which provides sketches of such a space and lists of the basic tools, equipment and supplies that are needed.

The establishment of a bindery is another matter. The necessary bindery tools and equipment for the repair or binding of a
library's important volumes include, in part, large and small
presses, cutters of several kinds, glue pots, a sink, sewing frames,
stove, various knives, scales, gold stamping and finishing tools, a
large assortment of special tools for the general binding operations,
and a sizeable inventory of material. The outfitting of a bindery
should be left to the discretion of the bookbinder who will work in
it, but for the information on the scope of the effort, see Lawrence
Town[41] and Edith Deihl.[42] A well equipped bindery operated by a
qualified binder and one or two assistants can take care of all of
the handbinding required by most libraries.

Conservation workrooms should be separate from a library's
bindery because of the difference in the nature of the work and also
because the degree of cleanliness necessary is impossible to maintain in a bindery. Conservation workrooms should be reserved as
such, even though they are used only occasionally. The functions

of the workroom are to provide space, tools and equipment to permit book restoration and repair operations beyond the scope of
conventional binding practices; to enable selected and trained library
personnel to engage in the examination of prints, drawing, maps,
manuscripts, broadsides and related material; and to house minor
restoration operations such as bleaching, deacidifying, treatment of
mildew and insects, resizing, repair, mounting, etc. Museum conservation laboraties require X-ray apparatus, special lighting, both
ultraviolet and infrared photographic equipment, microscopes, examining tables, vacuum relining apparatus, a thermostatically controlled oven, fumigation chambers and air compressors. A library
conservation workshop can get along quite well with a thymol cabinet, a large sink with broad drainboards, deacidification apparatus,
a fume hood, a photographer's drum-type print dryer for matte
prints, one or two 4' x 8' work benches with drawers and cabinets,
illuminated magnifying glasses, large plastic trays (24" x 30"), a
large sturdy press (20" x 26"), a steel cabinet, safety cans for solvents and a tank type vacuum cleaner.

Notes

1. "On the Rebinding of Old Books" in Bookbinding in
    America. Portland, Maine; Southworth-Anthoensen
    Press, 1941. Repr. 1967, R.R. Bowker, N.Y.

2. "The Application of Chemical and Physical Methods
    to the Conservation of Archival Materials" in Recent
    Advances in Conservation, G. Thomson (ed.). London,
    Butterworth's 1963, pp. 39-47.

3. See Buck, R.D., "An Experiment in Co-operative
    Conservation." Studies in Conservation, Volume 2,
    Number 3, April 1956.

4. Barrow, W.J., The Barrow Method of Restoring De-
    teriorated Documents. Richmond, Va. 1965.

5. A.D. Baynes-Cope of the British Museum Research
    Laboratory produces magnesium bicarbonate in small
    quantities by discharging a CO_2 capsule into a "spark-
    let" type seltzer bottle containing ten grams of mag-
    nesium carbonate. After standing for two hours, the
    solution is diluted for use by adding four quarts of
    water.

162   Conservation of Library Materials

6. "Paper Deacidification: A Preliminary Report."
    The Library Quarterly, vol. 36, No. 4, October 1966.

7. Raff, Herrick and Adams, "Archives, Document
    Preservation." Northwest Science, vol. 40, No. 1
    (1966).

8. Yabrova, R.R., "The Prevention of Aging of Books
    and Newspapers" Collection of Materials on the Pres-
    ervation of Library Resources. Moscow 1963. English
    translation, U.S. Department of Commerce O.T.S. Pub-
    lication 64-11053.

9. Journal of the Society of Archivists, April 1966; also
    American Archivist, vol. 29, No. 4 (1966).

10. Silk, because of its short life expectancy, is inferior
    to tissue, which should last as long as the document.

11. Gear, James L., "The Repair of Documents--American
    Beginning" American Archivist 26:469-475 (Oct. 1963).

    ---- "Lamination After 30 Years: Record and Prospect"
    (ibid.) 28:293-297 (April 1965).

12. Barrow, W.J., "Restoration Methods" (ibid.) 6:151-154
    (July 1943).

    ---- "Deacidification and Lamination of Deteriorated
    Documents 1938-1963" (ibid.) 28:285-290 (April 1965).

    Wilson, W., and Forshee, B.W., Preservation of
    Documents by Lamination, Bureau of Standards, Mono-
    graph 5, U.S. G.P.O. 1959.

13. Belen'kaya and Strel'tsova. "Restoration and Preserva-
    tion of Books and Documents by Thermoplastic Film
    Coating" in New Methods for the Restoration and Pres-
    ervation of Books, Moscow, (Department of Commerce
    OTS 64-11054).

14. Bollettino Dell'Istituto di Patologia del Libro (Roma)
    Anno XXII Fasc I-IV Gennaio-December 1963.

15. 0.25% para nitro-phenol (or 0.25% sodium pentachloro-
    phenate for light colored leather).

16. American Archivist, Volume I, Numbers 1 and 2
    (1938).

17. The water used to dampen the blotters should con-
    tain 0.25% sodium pentachloro phenol to prevent mildew.

18. "The Restoration of the 'Vienna Dioscorides'" Studies
    in Conservation, vol. 7, No. 1. February 1962.

19. "Binding and Related Problems" The American Archivist, volume 16, Number 2 (1953).

20. Available from the bindery, Hunt Botanical Library, Carnegie Institute of Technology, Pittsburgh, Pa.

21. Development of Performance Standards for Library Binding. Phase I. Chicago, American Library Association 1961.

22. Standard for Library Binding, Boston Library Binding Institute, 1963.

23. Bookbinding in America. Portland, Maine - Southworth Anthoensen Press (1941) pp. 254-261.

24. See Plenderleith's Conservation of Antiquities and Works of Art, pp. 88-91.

25. Bhowmik, S., "Conservation of Palm-Leaf Manuscripts" Baroda Museum and Picture Gallery, Bulletin 19:59-65, 1965-66.

26. Forest Products Journal, October 1962.

27. Guidelines for Magnetic Tape Rehabilitation, Waltham, Mass., Cybetronics (1966).

28. Revansway, C. in Image. Rochester, N.Y., George Eastman House 5 (1956) pp. 156-159.

29. Rohm & Haas Co., Washington Square, Philadelphia.

30. Kodak Movie Film Cleaner (with lubricant).

31. "The Conservation of Works of Art in Tropical and Subtropical Zones," Recent Advances in Conservation. London, Butterworth's 1963: and "Deacidification of Prints and Drawings in Tropical Climates," Studies in Conservation, vol. 9, No. 2, May 1963.

32. The Preservation of Books in Tropical and Subtropical Countries. Kuala Lumpur, Oxford University Press 1964.

33. Repair and Preservation of Records. New Dehli, National Archives of India, 1959.

34. Appendix One Library Binding Manual. American Library Association, Chicago 1951.

35. Development of Performance Standards for Library Binding Phase I. Chicago, American Library Associa-

tion, 1961.

36. Permanent Durable Book Paper.   Richmond, The
Virginia State Library, 1960.

37. For example, University Text (S.D. Warren Co.)
is used by the Harvard University Press.

38. Some Notes on Bookbinding.   London, Oxford University Press, 1929 (pp. 78-85).

39. Library Binding Manual.   American Library Association, Chicago 1951, (pp. 50-51).

40. Handbook for Library Binding, Library Binding Institute, Boston, 1963 (pp. 13-14).

41. Bookbinding by Hand.   London, Faber & Faber,
1956 (pp. 19-24).

42. Bookbinding, Its Background and Technique.   New
York, Rinehart & Co., Inc., 1946, pp. 6-23.

Chapter VI
The Cooperative Approach to Conservation

The conservation and restoration of library materials is highly technical and even in the most carefully maintained libraries, it is inevitable that important books and associated materials will, sooner or later, require repair or restoration. Such services are costly, whether performed on the premises or by outside conservators and specialists. Many library budgets do not include funds for restoration and important materials progressively deteriorate. There is an alternative that might well be considered. A cooperative approach to conservation of library materials under which libraries in each region pool their efforts and resources might accomplish jointly what most of them are unable to accomplish individually.

The concept of a cooperative approach to conservation has been proven feasible by the success of the Inter-Museum Conservation Association, which has headquarters at Oberlin College.[1] This group of midwestern museums works together to increase understanding of the care and preservation of art objects, to operate a clearing-house of information on conservation, to provide training for conservators, to make available, at reasonable cost, the highest quality of restoration services and to stimulate scientific research into the problem of conservation.

The establishment of regional library conservation associations can accomplish the same for librarians and archivists. Subjects to be considered in establishing such regional associations are outlined below.

Preamble

Rare books, prints, broadsides, maps and manuscripts in libraries, museums and historical societies are deteriorating owing to the normal aging process and to the effect of acidity, fungi,

165

vermin, heat and dampness.

Libraries and other institutions are handicapped in their battle to preserve important collections by unfamiliarity of their personnel with the theory and practice of conservation, the shortage of skilled restorationists and the high cost of establishing restoration shops on their own premises. A draft of the proposed articles of incorporation and by-laws for such an organization follows:

Proposed Articles of Incorporation for a
Regional Conservation Association

The undersigned, a majority of whom are citizens of the United States desiring to form a Corporation not for profit under the General Corporation Act of   , do hereby certify:

FIRST: The name of said Corporation shall be

SECOND: The place in   where the principal office of the Corporation is to be located is in the City of   ,
County.

THIRD: The purposes for which the Corporation is formed are to improve and disseminate knowledge of the theory and practice of library conservation in relation to rare books, prints, maps, broadsides and manuscripts of historical and cultural interests, such as are now found in libraries, museums, and historical societies of charitable and educational institutions; to investigate materials and equipment and to conduct studies and tests in order to develop methods to protect, preserve, maintain the integrity of and improve the conditions of such library, museum and archival materials of historic and cultural interest; to coordinate and assist in carrying out conservation programs of charitable and educational institutions which may become members and to render conservation services for them; to maintain a laboratory and staff in order to carry out such purposes and to train the staff of member institutions; to receive and accept donations, gifts, and bequests for the furtherance of its purposes; to acquire, hold, operate, lease, sell, mortgage or otherwise dispose of any real estate or personal property or interests therein necessary or appropriate for the accomplishments of its purposes.

FOURTH: The following named persons shall serve as Trustees of the Corporation until the first annual meeting or other meeting called to elect Trustees:

1.

2.

3.

FIFTH: A Member of the Corporation may vote, consent or act by proxy appointed by a writing signed by such member.

No part of the net earnings of the Corporation shall inure to the benefit of any member and no part of the activities of the Corporation shall include disseminating propaganda or attempting to influence legislation.

On the liquidation or dissolution of the Corporation, all assets and property of the Corporation, subject to the payment of liabilities, shall be transferred and conveyed to one or more domestic or foreign corporations, societies or organizations engaged in or proposing to engage in activities substantially similar to the educational activities of this Corporation in accordance with such plan of distribution as may be adopted by a vote of a majority of the then members at a special meeting called for that purpose and otherwise in accordance with such plan of distribution as may be directed by a court of competent jurisdiction.

IN WITNESS WHEREOF, we have hereunto subscribed our hands this_____ day of   , 196 .

_____

_____

_____

STATE OF   )
     COUNTY   )
)

Personally appeared before me, the undersigned, a Notary Public in and for said County, this   day of   , 196 , the above named   ,   , and   who each severally acknowledged the signing of the foregoing Articles of Incorporation to be his free act and deed for the uses and purposes therein mentioned.

WITNESS my hand and official seal on the day and year last aforesaid.

_____

Notary Public

Proposed By-Laws

Article 1 - Membership

Section 1.   There shall be two classes of membership in the Association:

(a)   Institutional membership, which shall be available only to non-profit charitable and educational institutions owning or having custody of books, prints, broadsides, maps and manuscripts.

(b)   Individual memberships, which are created only for the purpose of qualifying individual persons to serve as trustees of the Association by reason of the _____ _____ statutory requirement that trustees of a corporation not for profit shall be members of the corporation.   Any individual person who becomes a trustee or a trustee ex-officio of the Association shall ipso facto become an individual member of the Association, but only during the period of his trusteeship.   There shall be no other individual members.

Section 2.   All voting rights of members of the Association are vested in the institutional members.   Individual members shall have no voting rights as members, shall not be entitled to any privileges as members and shall not be subject to the payment of dues or assessments.

Section 3.   Qualified institutions may be admitted to membership and may be expelled from membership by a vote of a majority of the Board of Trustees at any time in office.

Section 4.   The Board of Trustees may determine from time to time the initial membership fee, if any, of new institutional members and shall determine in each year the dues or assessments for

each institutional member, which may consist of or include minimum amounts to be guaranteed to the Association by the various institutional members for services available to them (whether or not
such services are requested) on such basis as the Board of Trustees may deem fair and equitable. The Board of Trustees may
waive dues, assessments and minimum guarantees from any institutional member which furnishes, without charge to the Association,
use of space for the Association's laboratory and headquarters and
use of equipment acceptable to the Board of Trustees.

Section 5. Any member may resign from the Association by
a writing filed with the Secretary specifying the date (not a past
date) on which the resignation shall be effective. Any such resignation shall not release the resigning member from payment of dues
or assessments or minimum guarantee for the balance of the calendar year in which the resignation is effective, or from payment of
any other obligation to the Association, and no refund of pro rata
dues, assessments or minimum guarantees will be made.

Article 2 - Meetings

Section 1. The annual meeting of the members shall be held
as soon as feasible after January 1st of each year, normally in connection with the meeting of another association or society customarily attended by some or all of the institutional representatives.
Such annual meeting may be held at such time and place as may be
determined by the President of the Association and specified in the
notice of the meeting.

Section 2. Special meetings of the members may be held at
the call of the President or Vice President.

Section 3. Notice of each meeting shall be given in writing
to each member at least ten (10) days prior to such meeting. Notice of special meetings shall specify the purposes of the meetings.

Section 4. Two-thirds of the member institutions represented in person or by proxy shall constitute a quorum. Institutional members may act, vote or consent by proxy appointed by
writing signed by the Institutional member. At each meeting of

members at which a quorum is present, all questions and business shall be determined by vote of a majority of the Institutional members present in person or by proxy, unless a different vote is required in specific matters by law, the Articles or other provisions of these Regulations.

Article 3 - Board of Trustees

Section 1.   Except as otherwise determined by the members and except as otherwise required by law, the Articles or these Regulations, the Board of Trustees shall manage and conduct the affairs of the Corporation.

Section 2.   The Board of Trustees shall be elected by the members at each annual meeting or at any special meeting called for the purpose of electing trustees.   In addition, the Chief Conservator of the Association shall be a trustee ex-officio.   Trustees shall hold office until the next annual meeting of members and until their successors are elected and qualified.

Section 3.   The trustees at any time in office, regardless of their number and although less than a majority of the whole Board of Trustees, may by vote of a majority of their number, fill any vacancy in the Board of Trustees, however occurring.

Section 4.   Immediately after each election of Trustees, the Board of Trustees shall meet at the place of such election for the purpose of organization, the election of officers and the transaction of such other business as may come before the meeting.   No notice of such meeting need be given.

Section 5.   Regular meetings of the Board of Trustees may be held at such times and places as the Board of Trustees may from time to time determine.   Special meetings of the Board of Trustees may be called by the President or Vice President or Chief Conservator or by any two (2) trustees.

Section 6.   One-third (1/3) of the trustees at any time in office shall constitute a quorum and at each meeting of the Board of Trustees at which a quorum is present, all questions and business shall be determined by vote of a majority of the trustees present unless a different vote shall be required on specific matters by law, the Articles, or other provisions of these Regulations.

Article 4 - Officers

Section 1.   The officers of the Corporation shall be a Chief
Conservator, a President, a Vice President, a Secretary and a
Treasurer, all of whom shall be elected by the Board of Trustees.
The Board of Trustees may appoint such additional officers as it
may deem necessary.   Each officer, whether elected or appointed,
shall have such authority and shall perform such duties as may be
prescribed by the Board of Trustees.   Any two offices may be held
by one person but no officer shall sign any instrument in more than
one capacity.   No officer of the Association shall receive a salary
or other compensation unless specifically authorized by the Board of
Trustees.   Every officer as such shall be subject to removal by the
Board of Trustees at any time by the affirmative vote of the majority of the Trustees then in office.

Section 2.   The Board of Trustees may appoint an Executive
Committee or other Committee from its members and may delegate
to any such Committee any powers of the Board of Trustees.   Any
such Committee shall act only in the intervals between meetings of
the Board of Trustees and shall at all times be subject to the direction and control of the Board of Trustees.

Article 5 - Services

Section 1.   The Corporation shall provide to each Institutional member in good standing a periodic inspection of the members'
collections and an adequate record of such inspections.   Additional
services, such as laboratory examinations, analyses, recommendations for treatment, and treatment may be provided to Institutional
members on such terms and conditions as may be determined from
time to time by the Board of Trustees.

Section 2.   Institutional members may request examination
and treatment of only objects owned by them or in their custody or
in which they have an interest.   No object will be accepted for examination or treatment unless accompanied by a request in writing
signed by the Institutional member and reciting that such Insitutional

member owns the object or is duly authorized to make the request.

Section 3. The Board of Trustees may authorize the rendering of conservation services for non-profit charitable and educational institutions which are not members of the Association on such terms and conditions as the Board of Trustees may from time to time determine, but the Association shall not engage in any commercial activity or render any examination or treatment services except to non-profit charitable and educational institutions.

Article 6 - Amendments

Section 1. These Regulations may be amended, added to or replaced by written consent of all Institutional members or by a vote of a majority of the Institutional members at a meeting called for that purpose.

Proposed Organization and Staffing
for a
Library Conservation Association

The Association's Conservation Center could be located in

(a)   Its own building

(b)   Leased space

(c)   On the premises of a member institution

The advantages of owned or leased space would be

(a)   More choice of location

(b)   Probably more space

(c)   Independence

The disadvantages would be

(a)   Acquisition cost (or annual rent)

(b)   Maintenance charges

(c)   Heat, light, telephone charges, etc.

The advantages of occupying space in a member institution's premises are

(a)   No rent, maintenance or heating problems

(b)   Reduced utility charges (perhaps none)

(c)   The use of other facilities at the institution

(d)   Availability of students for part-time work

The disadvantages are

(a)   Probably limited space

(b)   Some danger of losing identity

To compensate an institution for hosting the association's center, it should not be assessed an annual membership fee.   If a member institution hosts the center, it should retain ownership of all furnishings and basic equipment in order to avoid tangles that might arise from corporative ownership.

Regardless of location, the center's work space should include

(a)   An administrative area containing

    1.   An office

    2.   A combined schoolroom/library

    3.   The laboratory

(b)   Storage and layout area containing

    1.   Vacuum fumigation tank*

    2.   A humidifying vault*

    3.   A Barrow laminator

(c)   A wet work area including

    1.   Deacidification apparatus

    2.   Washing and drying equipment

    3.   Stain reduction apparatus

    4.   Fume hood

(d)   A paper and vellum repair room

(e)   A bookbindery

(f)   A map and print shop

The staff to operate the Center would include

	Minimum	Optimum
Chief conservator	1	1
Bookkeeper/secretary	1	1
Layout worker (to operate laminator, humidifier, fumigator, cameras, etc.)	1**	1
Wet workmen (or women)	1**	2
Paper and vellum restorers	2**	2
Map and print repairmen	1**	2
Bookbinders	2**	6
Building custodian	0	1

Staff to operate the Center (cont.)	Mini- mum	Opti- mum
Apprentices	0	4
Chemist	0	1

*   These would double as safes for security.
**   Interchangeable.

     The shops and spaces would be furnished with (in addition to the traditional tools of the bookbinder and archives restorer) those special tools and equipment developed in recent years for the scientific treatment of paper, leather and vellum.

     The laboratory would be furnished with the standard supplies and equipment for testing paper, leather, and vellum and the materials used thereon.

Notes

1.   R.P. Buck, "An Experiment in Cooperative Conservation."   Studies in Conservation, vol. II, No. 3, April 1956.

Chapter VII
In Conclusion

Paradoxically, our competence to care for books has declined steadily as the craft of bookmaking evolved into the major industry it is today. Sixth-century books were lasting artifacts. Pages of parchment or vellum firmly fastened to vellum thongs were laced into stout wood boards and the whole covered with strong vegetable-tanned leather for additional protection. The Book of Kells, at Trinity College, Dublin, and the Codex Sinaiticus, now in the British Museum, are only two of the extant examples of the durability of these early volumes. These surviving books are dramatic proof of the importance of the quality of material in conservation. With the exception of acid and polluted air, they have been exposed to the same destructive agents as are the materials in modern libraries. It was the natural resistance to insects, fungi, heat, and moisture of vellum, oak boards, and vegetable-tanned leather that preserved these treasures against everything except the depredations of people.

In the Middle Ages, when paper rather than vellum became the preferred writing surface, the rag paper used, which was essentially pure cellulose sized with animal gelatin, required only reasonable care for permanence and durability, so deterioration could be kept within tolerable limits. With the advent of printing from movable type and the proliferation of books that followed, the situation began to change and with the coming of the industrial revolution, it got out of control. The ever increasing demands for paper necessitated the substitution of wood pulp for rags, and alum and rosin sizing were substituted for gelatin and starch. The use of acid to hasten the tanning process in order to meet the urgent requirements for more leather in a greater variety of colors and hues was disastrous. The substitution of cloth for leather on edition bindings reduced costs and solved the problem of powdered leather covers but the cloth covers were more attractive to vermin and

175

mold, and much less resistant to moisture and to physical abuse.
The inferior strength of machine-cased books as compared to hand-
bindings had to be accepted if the cost of book production was to be
kept within reason.   The growth of urban industrial areas, their
air polluted by noxious gases and aerosols, further aggravated the
problem.   We have now reached a point at which the Association of
Research Libraries' Committee on the Preservation of Research Library Materials has had to report:

> The imminent danger of losing much of the infor-
> mation that society has gained because of the de-
> terioration of paper on which this has been recorded
> has created a major problem of national concern.
> (Report on The Preservation of Deteriorating Books,
> September 1964.)

It is probable that ninety percent of the books printed since
the beginning of the twentieth century will be lost because of deterioration, unless positive action is undertaken to preserve them.
By any criterion of conservation we are in more dire straits today
than we were a hundred years ago.   This need not be.   The enemies of books have been identified and the means to control them
are understood.   The urgent requirements are to apply the knowledge preventively and to save those materials that have already suffered serious damage.   The cost will be high but these records
represent our heritage.

The most effective deterrent is environment control. Money
spent on air-conditioning, proper lighting and good housekeeping will
do more than anything else to retard the degradation of library materials.   Books kept in space with filtered air which is maintained
at a constant 70^OF temperature and 50% relative humidity; which is
lighted by natural and artificial light from which the ultraviolet energy has been screened; and in which good housekeeping practices
have eliminated insects and other vermin will, if not previously
contaminated by acid, last indefinitely.   Materials which have become acid can be stabilized so as to last equally long.   Current
research indicates that ultimately the Barrow deacidification process,
which is very effective but is currently limited to unbound materials, will be replaced by a spray deacidification technique or by ex-

posure to alkaline gases.

Next in importance is insistence by librarians and others
that books be manufactured only from materials of the best quality.
There is no longer any excuse for printing worthwhile books on
alum/rosin-sized paper or paper which is not free of lignin and
other contaminants. The paper industry can now, at competitive
prices, manufacture permanent/durable book papers with a life expectancy of many hundreds of years. Pyroxylin-impregnated book
cloth is infinitely superior to other fabric covers. Synthetic adhesives are immune to mold and vermin. High quality, acid-free
boards are equally important. However, publishers are in a highly
competitive industry and they cannot be expected to use such materials unless librarians, through their professional associations,
insist that all books other than expendable materials be so made.

Faced with the inevitable problems of repair and restoration,
librarians have three alternatives: they may do nothing, they may
make minimum repairs, or they may provide expert restoration.
Many, because of limited funds, must settle for minimum repairs.
Even the most generously endowed libraries do not have funds adequate to provide all the repair and restoration their collections require. The cooperative approach to conservation (Chapter VI) may
provide a solution. The time has gone when the occasional rebinding of books will suffice. We have been overtaken by the inevitable
and only by concerted action can we regain control of the situation.

Appendix A

Damage to Library Materials

Cause	Effect
By people	
Pressure sensitive tape	Stained and oxidized paper
Polyvinyl acetate	Irreversible bonds; glazed book covers
Newspaper and other ground-wood pulp paper	Good paper acidified by contact; attract vermin
Wood and cardboard supports	Contaminated good paper; stained prints etc.
Amateur lamination	Stains sealed in; acid decay continues; lamination material not stable
Careless habits	Stained and damaged material
Alum/rosin size in paper	Darkened and embrittled sheets
Chlorine bleach residuals	Darkened and embrittled sheets
Nitrates and other chemicals in film	Yellow stains Powdered film
Inadequate heating and ventilation	Too much or too little heat Too much or too little moisture
By the air we breathe	
Sulphur dioxide	Oxidized to sulphuric acid; faded dyes
Hydrogen sulphide	Tarnished silver and copper; corroded bronze stamping leaf
Ammonia	Attacks resins and varnishes (i.e., white bloom)
Ozone and nitrogen oxides	Cracked rubber Darkened varnish Weakened paper and textiles Rotted leather Faded colors Decomposed adhesives Faded images on film

179

Cause	Effect
By the air we breathe (cont.)	
Aerosols	Gummy deposits on flat surfaces Soiled materials Abraded book covers Nuclei for acidic gases
Water vapor	Warped wood Stained paper Moisture for acid hydrolysis Sustains fungi and vermin
By light	
Ultraviolet radiation	Embrittled organic material (photolysis)
Visible light	Faded colors) Yellowed paper) photo-oxidation Hardened rubber)
By darkness	Haven for vermin Precipitates mold growth
By moisture	

Water or too high humidity	Musty odor
	Stained paper
	Flaked paint and ink on vellum
	Cockled parchment and vellum
	Rotted wood
	Smeared ink
	Corroded metal
	Weakened adhesives
	Stained and rotted leather
	Disintegrated papyrus, bark and
	    leaves
	Activates soluble salts in stone
	Sustains vermin
	Hydrolyzes cellulose
	Film and tape stick together
	Softening of gelatin on film and
	    tape

Lack of moisture	Horny vellum Dried out adhesives Desiccated paper, leather, papy- rus, bark and leaves Abnormal stresses in wood Embrittled film and sound tape Curled film and sound tape
By heat	
Excessive heat	Embrittled paper, bark, leaves, papyrus

180

Excessive heat (cont.)	Accelerated mold growth
	Dried out adhesives
	Vermin thrive
	Accelerates other deterioration processes
	Edge buckling on film and tape

By vermin

  Insects

Cockroaches	Odor
	Excretion stains
	Excrement (minute black pellets)
	Eaten cloth and paper book covers
	Carry disease
Termites	Shredded paper
	Devoured wood
Silverfish	Eaten exposed paper (lacy effect)
Moths	Holes in fabric and calf skin
Bookworms	Tunneled paper and boards
	"Cemented" book pages
Book lice	Nuisance

  Rodents

Rats and mice	Carry disease
	Gnawed wood
	Transport insects
	Foul cabinets and drawers with excrement
	Shredded paper
	Eat adhesives, leather, starch and paper
Squirrels	Carry insects
	Gnawed wood
(Pigeons)	Not rodents or vermin, but they carry insects and foul buildings

By fungi

Molds	Spores on paper and leather and film
	Stained paper and leather
	Weakened, but not brittle, paper
	Pulpy paper
	Rotted leather
	Digest organic sizes
	Distorted images on film
Foxing	Brown spots on paper

Cause	Effect
By acid	
Acid	Accelerates cellulose hydrolysis
	Absorbent paper
	Embrittled paper
	Darkened paper
	Rotted fabrics
	Decomposes fats and greases in leather
	Cracked backs and hinges in leather-covered books
	Powdered leather
	Faded colors
	Corroded metal
	Eroded limestone
	Lace work pages under iron gall ink

Photographic Film

	Caused by
Edge buckling	High temperature
Softening of the gelatin	High humidity
Sticking together	Water
Curling	Low humidity
Embrittlement	Low humidity
Yellow stains	Nitrates in film
Powdered film	Nitrates in film
Faded images	Ozone and nitrogen oxides

Appendix B

The Principles of Archive Repair

At the opening of the first course in record and document
repair at the London School of Printing and Graphic Arts in 1951,
Roger Ellis presented the principles of archive repair. With the
permission of Principal Ellis Thirkettle, CBE, MBIM, Ellis' re-
marks are summarized below:

> There is a great deal more in repair of archives than
> the simple application of paper and paste; the whole
> process of repair may defeat its own object unless the
> true nature of the archive--and hence of the repair
> which it is to undergo--is fully understood...
>
> We have called them the principles of archive repair,
> not of manuscript repair simply. The distinction is
> purposely made...
>
> It is this archive or record character of the manuscripts
> with which we shall deal that determines the nature of
> their treatment... Archives are an actual part of the
> activities which gave them birth, material evidences sur-
> viving in the form of writing. ...a manuscript or docu-
> ment of archive character, whatever other qualities it
> may possess, is first and foremost a vehicle of evi-
> dence, of impartial evidence; it is for this quality, in
> the first place, that it has been preserved, and it is
> this quality above all others that any process of repair
> must respect. The record may indeed possess other
> qualities; it may be monumentally large or microscopi-
> cally small; it may be thousands of years old or merely
> a matter of days; it may be an object of great beauty or
> an offence to the eye; its contents--the written evidence
> which it conveys--may be trivial or revolutionary, scan-
> dalous, treasonable, pious, comic, or merely dull; but
> all these qualities are secondary to the prime fact that
> the document conveys, and is, a piece of evidence, and
> that it is on this account that a document has been, and
> must be, preserved.
>
> But if the soul of archives resides in their evidential
> quality, they have also bodies which are hardly less im-
> portant. The message of a document is of little avail

183

if it exists only invisible and disembodied...

How, then, do these qualities of the archive, spiritual and corporeal, affect its repair? In this way: First, that no process of repair may be allowed to remove, diminish, falsify, or obscure, in any way, the document's value as evidence; and this must apply not only to the evidence obviously conveyed by the writing upon the document, but also to those overtones of evidence conveyed by it through other means,... Second, that no process of repair may be used which could in any way damage or weaken the material of which the document is made...an ill-conceived method of repair, or one insufficiently tried, may prove to be a cure worse than the disease. ...Reducing all this to simple practical rules, the repairer must endeavour to put nothing into his document which was not there when he received it, and to take from it nothing which was. And before starting on a repair, he may well ask himself, 'How little need I do to this document to make it fit for use again?'...

First, the writing. Where this has vanished, he will make no attempt to reinsert it. ...Then where the writing is faded, the repairer will best not attempt to revive it by chemical reagents... The only case of this kind in which the repairer can safely intervene is when the writing, though neither lost nor obscured, is becoming loose through, for example, the decay of the prepared surface upon which it is written; here the repairer may and must refix it,...

The greater part of any repair process, however, will be directed towards fortifying, or replacing, the vehicle upon which the writing is borne; and here the repairer must observe three simple but fundamental rules:

1.   As far as possible, to replace missing material with material of the same kind;

2.   To leave the nature and extent of his repair unmistakably evident;

3.   Never to do anything which cannot be undone without damage to the document.

From the first of these rules occasional departures are necessary. Although a repairer must try to avoid adding to a document anything which was not there when he received it, yet clearly he must do this when large parts of the original paper or parchment are missing, in order that the document as a whole may be given back its original strength; but though he cannot avoid

184

adding what is new, he can and will avoid adding what is foreign to the material of the original. He will repair a paper document with paper and a parchment document with parchment; a broken seal with new wax; and where old size has perished from the paper he will add new. The result will be not a patchwork but a homogeneous document, having throughout its constituent parts, old or new, the same properties as the original document, and responding in the same ways to temperature, humidity, handling, and the passage of time. From this rule he may allow himself two departures, in the use of (first) an adhesive for fixing the material of a repair, and (second) some transparent material, through which the writing can be read when the document must be strengthened all over its surface or upon both sides. And perhaps the experienced repairer may add a third: when the material he would prefer is not to hand, and the document will perish if not repaired, he will use an effective and harmless substitute--thus a large parchment membrane may on occasion be backed with linen.

The second rule has its origin equally in the archive character of the document. ...Repair must never become tampering, and never can become so provided that it obscures nothing of the original, and is itself clearly distinguishable. The repairer, then, will never tint his paper or parchment to 'harmonize' with the original; indeed he will encourage a contrast, and will rely upon the excellence of his new materials, and the neatness of his work, to avoid offence to the eye, when the document happens, by chance, to be a thing of beauty. He will also be at pains not to conceal by his operations any portion or feature of the document which is a part of, or could shed light upon, its evidential value; and this means not simply that he will never paste new paper over old writing (though it is easier than you might think to do this, when an endorsement is faint or the edge of a closely-written document is tattered), but also that he will observe, preserve, and on occasion reveal such other incidental features as original sewing-holes, dustings of pounce, marks of folding, traces of seals, watermarks, old end-papers, even on occasion stray blobs of wax or old stains--and a great many more. The applications of this apparently over-fussy rule will appear in the course of practical work, but it is worthwhile to emphasize now how essential it is to preserve all the features of a record--even those, as Sir Hilary Jenkinson has remarked, that you cannot see. Sewing-holes, for instance, when they are found in the document, must be carefully preserved; if the documentation has to be stitched again, the new stitches must pass through the

185

old holes and no new ones must be made; and these holes must not be covered or concealed. For these sewing holes may be the only remaining evidence of a previous gathering or binding, and so of a previous or original order of the document; while a correspondence of these modest holes may establish that two documents now widely separated were once joined. Every archivist in due course discovers his own favourite examples of the value of such incidentals.

Proportionately more must we value the original make-up of a record, when it survives. When dealing with a single document, or a number of documents whose order is of no significance, this question does not arise. When, however, the documents are attached together in order and by design, as a file, roll, volume, or whatever it may be, this original make-up must be treated with the utmost respect. The rule here must be: the archivist or repairer must never interfere with, still less destroy, the existing make-up of a record if he can possibly avoid doing so. Not only does this make-up hold the papers or membranes in an ordered relation, but it is itself part of the record--a form purposely given to it by its creators or custodians. Though venerable, however, it may not be perfect, and it is allowable for a repairer to alter a document's make-up for three reasons, viz., convenience of consultation; convenience of storage; and protection of the document itself.

The third of our rules touches upon another basic quality of the archive, implied if not expressed in the definition which I have quoted--that it is unique. It is the only document, or set of documents, produced by the transaction (whatever that was); it is the record; it cannot be replaced. So to proceed hopefully upon a course of repair from which no retreat is possible may at the worst destroy this record, and will at best irrevocably alter it.

Finally, may I emphasize the importance of the quality of your materials. The task of the archivist is to preserve his records to eternity, and when choosing materials for repair he must be certain that they have at least the same expectation of life as the original material of the record, and that they have no destructive chemical reaction. For these reasons he will be wary of plastic foils and chemical adhesives whose behaviour has not been tested over long periods of time, and he will rely on parchment prepared by traditional methods, paper whose composition and manufacture he knows and approves (with hand-made linen rag paper he cannot go far wrong), natural silk, linen, or cotton fabrics whose life is known to run into many centuries, and--for adhesive--a simple paste of white flour...

Appendix C

The Guild of Book Workers

Standards and Specifications Governing All Work Submitted for Exhibition.

All categories to use best material obtainable.

1. Full leather binding.

    a. Book to be handsewn with unbleached linen thread, cotton, silk, surgical silk (not rayon) or other thread of proven strength.

    b. Repaired with oriental mending tissue, Whatman English banknote mending paper or papers of comparable strength.

    c. It is recommended that only animal glue, shell glue or fish glue of the best quality be used.

    d. It is recommended that only wheat, rye or rice flour or other starch pastes be used.

    e. Boards of strongest quality shall be used (not necessarily in thickness). Commercial black or tar board, English mill board, French "carton bleu" or boards of comparable strength and quality are recommended.

    f. Either tight or hollow back acceptable.

    g. Leather, undyed or dyed, provided it is not sprayed, pigmented or artificially grained.

    h. Leather hinges may be either sewn in or pasted down with end tapes.

    i. All books larger than 16 mo. should be sewn on a minimum of four (4) cords, vellum, leather strips or tapes of comparable strength.

    j. Raised bands may be built up on the backs of books when the back has been sewn on four or five (4 or 5) cords--either to conform to the bands already there or as part of the design. False bands may not be put on the backs of books to simulate real bands.

k. No books accepted with sawn-in cords.

l. Blind tooling should not be colored to simulate the effect of a heated tool applied to moistened leather.

m. Headbands should be handsewn not machine-sewn.

n. Paper chosen for end sheets for all types of bindings should be strong and durable.

Appendix D

Research Centers and Professional Associations

Research centers around the world are constantly striving to better the methods of collection, preservation, study, interpretation and exhibition of antiquities and works of art. Although library science is on the fringe of this area, librarians can benefit by keeping informed on the work of these centers and affiliating themselves with some of the conservation associations dedicated to advancing the competence of their members. Many of the viewpoints, theories, concepts and techniques of museum conservation are equally applicable to the preservation of library materials. The close relationship between the two professions was demonstrated at the meeting of the International Institute of Conservation (American Group) in Chicago in June, 1966. One-third of this three-day gathering of leading United States and Canadian conservators and curators was devoted to the nature of paper; its conservation and restoration; adhesives; and the effects of light, humidity and temperature on organic materials.

Following are some of the conservation centers and professional societies which can assist librarians and archivists in conservation and related matters:

International
    a.   United Nations Educational, Scientific, and Cultural Organization (UNESCO) Place de Fontenoy, Paris VII, France. UNESCO's Bulletin for Libraries frequently contains articles on the conservation of library materials.

    b.   UNESCO's International Council of Museums (ICOM), Paris, publishes ICOM News, which contains many articles of importance to librarians.

c.	International Centre for the Study of the
Preservation and the Restoration of Cultural
Property (Rome Centre), 1256 Via Cavour,
Rome. An independent, intergovernment in-
stitution with 39 member countries connected
by statute and agreements with UNESCO.

Dedicated to the coordination of preservation
and restoration on a world scale, the Centre
provides direct technical assistance and schol-
arships, trains specialists, publishes technical
literature and maintains a library of technical
literature.

d.	International Institute for the Conservation of
Historic and Artistic Works (IIC), c/o The National Gallery, Trafalgar Square, London.

The Institute was founded in 1950 to provide
a permanent organization to coordinate and improve the knowledge, methods and working
standards needed to protect and preserve precious materials of all kinds.

The IIC's News, its Abstracts, and its Studies
in Conservation disseminate information on research into all processes connected with conservation, both scientific and technical, and on
the development of those processes. The London office welcomes queries on technical problems.

American (Including Canada)
a.	The International Institute for Conservation of
Historic and Artistic Works (IIC) (American
Group), c/o Conservation Centre, Institute of
Fine Arts, New York University, One East
78th Street, New York, N.Y. 10021.

Established in 1960 for the purpose of maintaining a regional branch of the IIC, to foster
fellowship among American members, to share
knowledge and to advise the IIC regarding problems and conditions peculiar to the field of conservation in America. It does not have an information service, but questions on specific
problems will be referred to a suitable authority.

b.	The Prevention of Deterioration Center operated
by The National Research Council of The National Academy of Sciences, Washington, D.C.,
ceased operation in 1965.

191

c.   Intermuseum Conservation Association, Allen Art Building, Oberlin, Ohio.

Coordinates and assists in carrying out conservation programs, disseminates knowledge on the theory and practice of conservation in relation to works of art and renders conservation services.

d.   Conservation Center, Institute of Fine Arts, New York University, One East 78th Street, New York, N.Y. 10021.

A four-year course leads to a master's degree in fine arts and a special diploma in conservation.

e.   Guild of Book Workers, 1059 Third Avenue, New York, N.Y. 10021

A nonprofit organization, affiliated with the American Institute of Graphic Arts, dedicated to keeping alive the crafts which were and are the cradle of modern mass book production. The Guild, the only national organization in the United States representing the hand bookcrafts, is a collection center for useful and reliable information on conservation, repair and fine binding. It distributes this information through a journal, published three times a year and through periodically revised lists giving extensive and up-to-date information on American and European supply sources.

f.   American Library Association (ALA), 50 Huron Street, Chicago, Illinois. 60611

Sponsors a Library Technology Project to make available to the library profession technical information and assistance in the areas of equipment, supplies, and systems. Publishes the ALA Bulletin and occasional publications, such as Library Binding Manual; Performance Standards for Library Binding and a forthcoming series of pamphlets on bookbinding, repair and preservation.

g.   Council on Library Resources (CLR), 1025 Connecticut Avenue, N.W., Washington, D.C.

Established in 1956 with Ford Foundation support, the Council is an independent nonprofit body whose objective is aiding in the solution of library problems. The Council conducts its work chiefly through grants or contracts.

h.　Association of Research Libraries, 1775 Massachusetts Avenue, N.W., Washington, D.C.

Its Committee on the Preservation of Library Materials is investigating a plan for the permanent preservation by a national agency of at least one example of every deteriorating record. The committee is also examining the merits of preservation by microfilm vs. restoration of the original.

i.　Library Binding Institute, 160 State Street, Boston, Massachusetts, is a national trade organization of library binders founded in 1935. It has established standards for library binding which are followed by most libraries in the United States. It maintains a quality control program and is a source of information and assistance for librarians and library binders on problems affecting the maintenance of library materials.

j.　The William J. Barrow Research Laboratory, Historical Society Building, Richmond, Va., concentrates on investigation of problems connected with the preservation of library materials. Sponsored by the Council on Library Resources, it regularly publishes its findings on acidity and deacidification, storage, adhesives, book paper, performance standards, etc.

k.　National Archives, Document Reproduction and Preservation Branch, Washington, D.C., maintains a restoration laboratory staffed by personnel highly skilled in deacidification and plastic lamination. Will provide information on request.

l.　National Bureau of Standards, Washington, D.C., has done much research, in cooperation with private and government activities, into the problems of the conservation of library materials.

m.　The Smithsonian Institution, Washington, D.C., has established a conservation department. Plans call for a laboratory for research on the preservation of paper, vellum, and leather.

n.　The services of the United States Department of Agriculture, Washington, D.C., and those of the various state agricultural departments are available to librarians in connection with problems of insect and pest control.

o.   The Metropolitan Museum of Art, New York, N.Y., has done advanced studies, in cooperation with the National Bureau of Standards, on the effect of light on museum objects.

p.   The work of the Technical Association of the Pulp and Paper Industry, New York, New York, (TAPPI) is of much importance in library conservation.

q.   The National Trust for Historic Preservation, 815 17th Street, N.W., Washington, D.C., includes library materials in its scope of interest.

r.   The Extra Bindery of the Lakeside Press, R.R. Donnelly & Sons Company, 2223 South Park Way, Chicago, Ill., has, under the inspired leadership of Harold W. Tribolet, pioneered in the field of rare book conservation.

s.   The Conservation and Scientific Research Division, National Gallery of Canada, Ottawa, Ontario, Canada, does much research on the environment of organic materials.

European
Great Britain

a.   The Research Laboratory, British Museum, London WC1, England, conducts scientific studies of ancient materials, their reactions to various environmental conditions, and methods of preservation and restoration. It includes specialized laboratories and restoration workshops. Emphasis is on the scientific approach to conservation.

b.   The Public Records Office, Chancery Lane, London, England, is charged with the care and preservation of national treasures dating back to the Conquest (1066 A.D.). An ultraconservative policy emphasizes reliance on the traditional procedures for the repair of records. It has a large, well-staffed workshop for paper, vellum, bookbinding and wax seals.

c.   The British Museum Bindery is a trade union bindery operated by H.M. Stationery Office for the sole use of the British Museum. It works closely with the research laboratory and restoration techniques are a mixture of traditional craftsmanship and scientific innovations.

d.   British Museum Map Room operates its own map repair and restoration workshop.

e.   Imperial Chemical Industries, Ltd., Imperial Chemical House, Millbank, London SW 1, England, conducts research on insect and fungi control and welcomes queries on the use of their products.

f.   The Library Association, Chaucer House, Malet Place, London WC 1, England maintains an information service of special value to librarians in tropical countries.

g.   The Forest Products Research Laboratory, Princes Risborough, Aylesbury, Bucks, England, conducts studies on the preservation of wood.

h.   The Imperial College of Science and Technology, London SW-7, England.

i.   British Leather Manufacturers Research Association, Milton Park, Egham, Surrey, England.

j.   Printing, Packing and Allied Trades Research Association, Leatherhead, Surrey, England. (PATRA)

k.   Conservation Department, Victoria and Albert Museum, London, England.

Italy

a.   Istituto di Patologia del Libro, via Milano 76, Roma, is the world's foremost laboratory dedicated to the study of the preservation of books. Publishes the quarterly journal, Bollettino dell' Istituto di Patologia del Libro, in Italian, English and French. Designated by Ministry of Public Instruction to coordinate the work of various libraries in Italy in repairing and restoring books and manuscripts.

b.   Gabinetto Nazionale delle Stampe, Villa della Farnesina, via Della Lingaro 230, Roma, is a state-operated print restoration center charged with the preservation of the prints, etc., in the various national libraries and museums, with emphasis on scientific methods of conservation.

c.   Istituto Restauro Scientifico del Libro, via Rusticucci 13, Vatican City, has modern laboratories and excellent workshops for the repair and restoration of Vatican and church treasures.

d.   The Italian Government has established a Center for Research in Conservation in Florence.

France
a.   Centre National de la Recherche Scientifique, 13 Quai Anatole France, Paris VII, subsidizes research on insecticides and fungicides and on the conservation of paper and leather.

b.   Laboratoire de Musee du Louvre, Pavillon Mollien, Place du Carrousel, Paris I., places emphasis on the conservation of paintings, ceramics, and metal. It does much original work on the use of ultraviolet, infra-red, and sodium light in conservation.

c.   Archives National de France, 60 rue des Francs-Bourgeois, Paris III., has its own bookbindery and restoration workshop for the preservation of the French Archives. It publishes Bulletin d'Information sur la Pathologie des Documents et Leur Protection.

d.   Bibliotheque National, 58 rue de Richelieu, Paris II, has restoration workshops for map repair, bookbinding, parchment and vellum repair, and paper conservation.

A Partial Listing of Other Conservation Centers in Europe and Asia:

a.   State Hermitage Museum, Leningrad

b.   Pushkin State Museum of Fine Arts, Moscow

c.   Department for Book Preservation and Restoration, USSR State Library, Moscow

d.   Department for the Conservation of Antiquities, National Historical Museum, Stockholm

e.   Institut du Patrimoine Artistique, Brussels

f.   The Chemical-Physical Laboratory, Swiss National Museum, Zurich

g.   Laboratory of the Doerner Institute, Munich

h.   Paper Publications Society, Hilversum, Holland

i. National Archives of India, Janpath, New Delhi

j. Indian Standards Institution, Manek Bhavan, 9 Mathura Road, New Delhi

k. Art Gallery of New South Wales, Sidney

l. General Research Laboratory of Objects of Art and Science, Amsterdam.

m. Archives School, Marberg, West Germany

n. Research Laboratory, National Museum, Warsaw

o. Academy of Fine Arts, Warsaw

p. National Research Institute of Cultural Properties, Ueno Park, Tokyo

q. Restoration Laboratory, Royal Archives, Brussels

r. Central Laboratory for Restoration and Conservation of Works of Art, Moscow

s. Laboratory for Preservation and Restoration of Documents of the Academy of Sciences of the USSR, Moscow

t. Central Conservation Workshop, State Library, Prague

u. Industrial Graphic School, Prague, offers a four-year course for training restorers and conservators

Appendix E

Some Useful Formulas

Wheat paste

Wheat flour	4 ounces
Water	1 quart
Formalin	10 drops

(Add flour to water, mix well until all lumps are broken, then cook in a double boiler for twenty minutes. Add the formalin, stir well and let cool.)

Wheat paste is used for leather, flannel, cambric and silk, for paper end sheets and for boxes, portfolios, slip cases, etc., when shrinkage and distortion are not a consideration. Because of the convenience, some book workers prefer commercial wallpaper pastes. These usually contain insecticides and fungicides. Unless the package label includes a formula for the product, wallpaper paste should be used only for routine library pasting. Library supply houses sell wheat pastes that should be free of harmful ingredients. However, unless specific information on the chemical composition of the commercial product is available, it should not be used on rare and valuable library materials.

Rice paste

Rice flour	4 ounces
Water	2 quarts

(Mix the flour with a small amount of cold water to form a thick cream. Bring the rest of the water to a rolling boil and pour about half into the cream while stirring vigorously. Mixture should thin out and become smooth. Add more boiling water to get desired consistency and set aside to cool.)

Starch paste

Laundry starch	4 ounces
Water	2 quarts

(This adhesive is mixed the same way as rice paste. The consistency is right when the mixture is glossy and translucent rather than dough-like. The secret in making rice and starch paste is vigorously boiling water mixed thoroughly into previously wetted powder.)

Rice and starch pastes are white and are useful on very light-toned and white papers which have not become discolored with age.

A paste for pyroxylin-coated fabrics

Water	8.5 ounces
Diethylene glycol	1.7 "
Beta-naphthol	0.02 "
Glucose	3.5 "
Wheat flour	3.5 "

(Add the flour to the water and cook to smooth consistency. Mix beta-naphthol, diethylene glycol and glucose and add to flour-water mix. Stir well and let cool.)

Ordinary wheat paste will not bond pyroxylin-coated fabrics, but the diethylene glycol in the formula acts as a solvent for the pyroxylin. This is a non-shrinking adhesive because glucose has been substituted for part of the water. It can be used on paper when wetting and shrinking must be minimized.

A paste for tropical use

Dextrine	4.0 ounces
Oil of cloves	0.1 "
Safrol (poison)	0.1 "
White arsenic (poison)	0.2 "
Water	1 quart

(Add flour to water, mix until smooth, cook in double boiler for twenty minutes. Add oil of cloves, arsenic and safrol.)

This will repel and destroy insects but it is poisonous so should not be used by unskilled staff.

Glue

Hide glue (flexible)	1 pound
Water	to cover
Terpineol	0.03 ounces
Beta-naphthol	0.03 "

(Cut cake into one-inch cubes and cover with cold water. Let soak for twelve hours and then heat in glue pot or double boiler to 130°F. Add Terpineol and beta-naphthol.)

Flexible glue is brittle hide glue to which has been added a certain amount of softening agent--usually gelatin, sorbitol syrup or diethylene glycol. The terpineol in this formula is to reduce the odor. The beta-naphthol is a preservative.

Glues are normally used on the spines of books and on colored starch-sized or gelatine-sized book cloth. They are also

199

used on paper when wetting must be minimized.

Leather dressings

Potassium lactate 7%

Potassium lactate 50% solution	2. 0 ounces
Water (distilled)	1 pint
Para-nitro phenol	0. 05 ounces

British Museum Leather Dressing

Anhydrous lanolin	7. 0 ounces
Cedarwood oil	1. 0 "
Beeswax	0. 5 "
Hexane (flammable)	11. 0 "

(Melt the lanolin and beeswax, add the cedarwood oil and stir in the hexane.)
British Museum Leather Dressing is available from the

Amend Drug and Chemical Company, 117 East 24th Street, New York, N.Y. , and from the Technical Library Service, 261 Broadway, New York, N.Y.

Another formula

Neat's-foot oil	10 ounces
Anhydrous lanolin	15 "

(Melt these ingredients in a double boiler and let cool before using.)

Another formula

Anhydrous lanolin U.S.P.	7. 5 ounces
Japan wax	1. 25 "
Castor oil U.S.P.	3. 0 "
Sodium stearate	0. 75 "
Distilled water	12. 5 "

(Melt lanolin, wax and castor oil. Add water while stirring vigorously. Add sodium stearate.)

Paper cleaners

A surface cleaner

Tergitol (TP-9)	1. 0 ounces
Hexaline glycol	0. 5 "
Water (distilled)	7. 7 "
Lauryl diethanolamide	0. 8 "

(Mix in a blender.)

A penetrating cleaner

Tergitol (TP-9)	0. 2 ounces
Pine oil	2. 5 "
Potassium hydroxide	0. 2 "
Tall oil	0. 9 "
Hexaline glycol	1. 0 "
Water (distilled)	4. 7 "
Deodorized kerosene	0. 5 "

(Mix in a blender.)

Bleaching solutions
        Chloramine T (2%)
            Chloramine T   2.5 ounces
            Water   1 gallon
        This will reduce mild stains in paper, but the residual
        chemical must be rinsed out of the paper with clear water.

        Sodium hypochlorite (2%)
            Sodium hypochlorite 5.25%   8 parts
            Water   13   "
        This bleach will reduce heavier stains than will Chloramine
        T, but it will also affect some colors and can damage paper
        fibers.   It must be neutralized when the stain is removed.

        (Neutralizer--sodium thiosulphate (hypo) 5.6 oz. in one
        gallon of water.   After neutralizing residual hypochlorite,
        the hypo must be rinsed out of the paper by immersion for
        forty-five minutes in running water.)

Paper sizes
        Gelatin size
            Pure food gelatin   1 ounce
            Water   1 quart
        (Add gelatin to water, soak for twenty minutes, then heat
        to 130°F before immersing paper.)

        Starch size
            Starch   4 ounces
            Water (distilled)   4 quarts
        (Mix the starch with a small quantity of cold water to make
        a paste, then add four quarts of boiling water while stirring
        vigorously.   When cold apply to surface of paper by brush-
        ing.)

        Another size
            Polyvinyl acetate   0.6 ounces
            Water   9.3   "
            Magnesium acetate   0.1   "

        Soluble nylon size
            Soluble nylon powder   1.75 ounces
            Water   10.5   "
            Methy alcohol   24.5   "
        (Mix in a flask and heat to 130°F in a water bath to melt
        the nylon.   The nylon powder must be I.C.I. Industries
        (Great Britain) Maranyl Nylon C109/P DV55 and not the U.S.
        or German equivalent.   This can be obtained from ICC Or-
        ganics, Inc., 55 Canal Street, Providence, Rhode Island.)

<u>Pesticides</u>
General library insecticide and fungicide

Hexachloro cyclohexane	0.05 ounces
Cresol	0.05 "
Mercury acetate	0.05 "
Alcohol	99.85 "

(This is useful for general sterilization of shelves, cabinets, file drawers, etc., but should not be used on paper because of chlorine content.)

A fungicide for impregnating paper by dipping

Salicylanilide	0.5 ounces
Water	1.5 gallons

(Dissolve salicylanilide in a small amount of water, then add the balance of the liquid.)

A fungicide for spraying paper

Salicylanilide	1 ounce
Trichloroethylene	76 ounces
Acetone	4 "

(Mix the solvents then add the salicylanilide. Use only in a well-ventilated working area.)

A moth preventive spray

Pyrethrum extract*	2 ounces
Sesame oil active	10 "
DDT Technical**	4 "
Kerosene	5 gallons

(* 20% weight/volume pyrethrum
(** Not less than 70% DDT)

Appendix F
Soluble Nylon

A New Tool for Restorationista

The British Museum Research Laboratory, in its continuing search for new materials for conservation, has pioneered the development of solutions of nylon in alcohol for the consolidation of fragile materials. This technique is important because it provides a remedy for badly deteriorated paper that is unsafe to handle.

Soluble nylon was used originally to consolidate the surface of ostraka (i.e., potsherds and limestone fragments from ancient Egypt) to protect carbon ink inscriptions thereon during the restoration process. The British Museum laboratory soon realized that the compound had great potential in other fields of restoration. Papyrus documents, for instance, can be treated with the solution, which is readily absorbed, thus insuring that there is no danger of the ink flaking off. Elsewhere the solution has saved rubrications and flaking ink on parchment manuscripts. Soluble nylon possesses good adhesive properties and is particularly useful for the reattachment of flaking paint and ink on illuminated manuscripts. The solution, having a very low surface tension and viscosity, readily penetrates into the minute cracks in deteriorating painted surfaces and flows underneath the protruding flakes of detached paint, drawing them back into position.

The material is a special chemically modified form of nylon manufactured by Imperial Chemical Industries, Ltd., under the trade name "Maranyl Nylon Soluble Polymer C/109/P" and is supplied as a light cream-colored powder in two grades, DV45 and DV55. The DV55 has less tendency to gel and is preferred. The powder is soluble in ethyl alcohol, methyl alcohol or industrial methylated spirits. Isopropanol is not a good solvent. The nylon dissolves in it only with difficulty and the solution gels more readily. The manufacturer's recommended solvent is a mixture of 70 parts of alcohol and 30 parts of water. However, the British Museum laboratory prefers a non-aqueous solvent because it dries more quickly and does not risk the running of water-soluble inks.

Five-percent solutions of the compound are made by mixing 50 grams of the powder in 1000 cc of the solvent and heating in a

203

water bath to 40°C until the powder dissolves. After cooling, the solution will stay fluid for several days before gelling. Reheating to 40°C for a brief time redissolves the gelatinous mass.

The protective film formed on surfaces by painting or spraying with this solution has many desirable properties. It does not exert any undue contractile forces as it dries. It is sufficiently tough to consolidate fragile surfaces and at the same time is permeable enough to permit subsequent restoration operations. It has a marked degree of flexibility. It has good temperature and abrasion resistance and good resistance to both vegetable and animal oils. The film has a matte appearance and does not leave an unpleasant sheen. Of utmost importance is the fact that these nylon coatings are soluble in alcohol and thus, in accordance with the ethics of restoration, the process is reversible.

The material can be used to consolidate book paper, prints, maps and manuscripts that otherwise would be too brittle to treat. It can be applied with an ordinary vibrator-type sprayer. After drying, the paper can be washed, bleached, sized, mended, guarded or sewn, with confidence that it will not crumble in the process. The finished product shows almost no evidence of the nylon reinforcement, which in the case of deteriorated paper appears to penetrate deeply into the sheet rather than to merely coat the surface. The nylon apparently mixes with the paper fibers, consolidating the mass. It can be applied with an ordinary vibrator-type sprayer.

Appendix G

Some Suppliers of Materials

One of the many advantages of membership in the Guild of Book Workers is access to their supply list. This is an annotated register of firms and individuals dealing in high quality materials used in library conservation. It contains over 300 entries, cross-referenced for convenience. The list given below is not the Guild's list even though some of the suppliers are identical.

Adhesives
    Glue   (Consult local directories)
    Pastes
        (a) Arobol Manufacturing Company
             110 East 42nd St., New York, N.Y.

        (b) Samuel Schweitzer
             660 West Lake Street, Chicago, Ill.
    Polyvinyl adhesives
        (a) Delcote, Inc.
             1419 Faulk Road, Wilmington, Del.

        (b) Polyvinyl Chemicals, Inc.
            26 Howley Street, Peabody, Mass.

Boards
    Book boards
             Aurora Paperboard Company
             705 North Farnsworth Road
             Aurora, Ill.
    Bristol board
             J.H. Albere Paper Company
             110 Lafayette Street, New York, N.Y.
    All-rag mounting boards
        (a) Andrews/Nelson/Whitehead, Inc.
             7 Laight Street, New York, N.Y.

        (b) Bainbridge & Sons
             20 Cumberland Street, Brooklyn, N.Y.

        (c) Colonial Paper Company
             201 Purchase Street, Boston, Mass.

Book cloth

    (a) Holliston Mills
        70 West 40th Street, New York, N.Y.

    (b) Gane Bros. & Company
        480 Canal Street, New York, N.Y

    (c) E.I. Dupont de Nemours & Co., Inc.
        Fabrics Division, Wilmington, Del.

    (d) Arkwright-Interlaken, Inc.
        Fiskeville, R.I.

Brass fittings (locks, corners, hinges and clasps)
        H. Mitchel & Company
        36 New Charles Street, London EC1, England

Cellulose acetate envelopes
    (a) Markilo
        902 South Wabash Avenue, Chicago, Ill.

    (b) E.T. Keeler Company
        423 Wisconsin Street, Chicago, Ill.

Chemicals
    (a) Consult local directories

    (b) Amend Drug and Chemical Company
        117 East 24th Street, New York, N.Y.
        (Potassium lactate, British Museum Dressing,
        rice flour, phloroglucinol)

    (c) Technical Library Service
        241 Broadway, New York, N.Y.
        (Potassium lactate, leather dressing)

    (d) Eimer & Amend (Fisher Scientific Company)
        633 Greenwich Street, New York, N.Y.

    (e) Laboratoire de Cryptogamie
        12 rue Buffon, Paris V
        (CIRE 212 insecticide and fungicide book wax)

    (f) ICI Organics, Inc.
        50 Canal Street, Providence, R.I.
        (Soluble nylon)

    (g) Union Carbide Corporation
        230 Park Avenue, New York, N.Y.
        (Detergents, carboxymethyl cellulose gum)

    (h) Rohm & Haas Company
        Independence Mall West, Philadelphia, Pa.
        (Water soluble resins)

    (i) Hercules Powder Company
        Wilmington, Del.
        (Carboxymethyl cellulose gums, resins)

(j) K & K Laboratories, Inc.
121 Express Street, Plainville, N.Y.
(Magnesium methylate solutions)

(k) C.R. Bard, Inc.
Murray Hill, N.J.
(Ethylcne oxide ampules for fumigation)

Dehumidifiers (and humidifiers)
(a) Westinghouse Electric Corporation
Dehumidifier Dept., Columbus, Ohio

(b) Dryomatic Division, Logetronics, Inc.
715 E. Fayette Street, Alexandria, Va.

(c) Cargocaire Engineering Corporation
6 Chestnut Street, Amesbury, Mass.

Document boxes
(a) Consult local directories

(b) F.H. Buffinton Company
134 Thurbers Avenue, Providence, R.I.

(c) Spink and Gaborc, Inc.
26 East 13th Street, New York, N.Y.

(d) Cambridge Paper Box Company
196 Broadway, Cambridge, Mass.

Flat filing cases for maps, etc.
(a) Hamilton Manufacturing Company
Two Rivers, Wis.
(Steel cases)

(b) Miller-Trojan Company
Troy, Ohio
(Corrugated cases)

Heat filtered incandescent lights
Sylvania
60 Boston Street, Salem, Mass.

Heating elements for workshop equipment
Hotwatt, Inc.
128 Maple Street, Danvers, Mass.
(Cartridge, strip, band, and glass heating units)

Lamination Equipment
(a) W.J. Barrow Laboratory
State Library Building, Richmond, Va.

(b) The Arbee Company, Inc.
192 Central Avenue, Stirling, N.J.
(Flat bed type)

Lamination Services
- (a) W. J. Barrow Laboratory
  State Library Building, Richmond, Va.

- (b) The Arbee Company, Inc.
  192 Central Avenue, Stirling, N. J.

Leather
- (a) Andrews/Nelson/Whitehead, Inc.
  7 Laight Street, New York, N. Y.

- (b) Ets. A. Jullien & Cie
  42 Rue Saint-Jacques, Paris V, France

- (c) Rougier et Plé
  13-15 Bd. des Filles du Calvaire, Paris VI,
  France

- (d) Russell Bookcrafts
  Hitchin, Herts, England

- (e) J. Hewitt & Sons, Ltd.
  87 St. John Street, London WC 1, England

- (f) H. Band & Company, Ltd.
  Brent Way, High Street
  Brentford, Middlesex, England

- (g) Edvard Schneidler, A. B.
  Malmskillnadsgatan 54, Stockholm, Sweden

Alum tawed skins
Russell Bookcrafts
Hitchin, Herts, England

Map backing materials
- (a) Russell Bookcraft
  Hitchin, Herts, England
  (cloth-lined paper; Postlip laminating tissue)

- (b) Seal, Incorporated
  Shelton, Conn.

- (c) The Ulster Weaving Company
  432 Park Avenue, New York, N. Y.
  (Linen, etc.)

Paper
Plain and decorated handmade paper and mending tissue
- (a) Andrews/Nelson/Whitehead, Inc.
  7 Laight Street, New York, N. Y.
  (European and Oriental papers)

- (b) Rougier et Plé
  13-15 Bd. des Filles du Calvaire, Paris VI,
  France

208

(c)   De Wailly et Marc
3 Rue de Poitevins, Paris VI, France

(d)   Douglas Cockerell & Son
Riverdale, Granchester, Cambridge, England
(Marbled paper)

(e)   Edvard Schneidler A. B.
Malmskillnadsgatan 54, Stockholm Sweden

(f)   Phillip's
121 O'Farrell Street, San Francisco, Cal.

(g)   Yasutomo & Company
24 California Street, San Francisco, Cal.
(Japanese paper)

(h)   International Inspection Service (IIS Crafts)
Central P. O. Box 1539, Tokyo, Japan

Permanent/durable book paper and folder stock
(a)   B.W. Wilson Paper Company
Carey at Tenth, Richmond, Va.

(b)   Arden-Cortland Paper Corp.
296 Broadway, New York, N.Y.

(c)   S.D. Warren Company
225 Franklin Street, Boston, Mass.

Acid-free lining paper
Charles R. Gracie & Sons, Inc.
148 East 58th Street, New York, N.Y.

Machine-made paper for boxes, slip cases, casing-in,
etc.
Canfield Paper Company
62 Duane Street, New York, N.Y.

Parchment and Vellum
H. Band & Company, Ltd.
Brent Way, High Street, Brentford, Middlesex,
England

Photographer's drum dryers
PAKO Corporation
6300 Olsen Memorial Highway
Minneapolis, Minn.

Reproduction on rag paper
Xerox Reproduction Service (Local directory)
(Specify "flat plate process")

Silk
(a)   Sauzet et Caponat
68 Rue de l'Hotel de Ville, Lyon, France

209

(b)   Transparo Company
      P.O. Box 838, New Rochelle, N.Y.

(c)   Combier Silks, Ltd.
      308 Regent Street, London W1, England

(d)   Government Silk Weaving Factory
      Raj Bagh, Srinagar, Kashmir, India
      (Fungus-resistant silk)

Spray guns
      (a)   Burgess Vibrocrafters, Inc.
            Grayslake, Ill.
            (Electric vibrator type)

      (b)   Maccarl Company, Inc.
            4342 Pearl Road, Cleveland, Ohio
            (Plastic hand operated "Mac-40")

      (c)   Johnson Wax Company (Local directory)
            (Plastic hand type)

Ultraviolet filtering tubes and sheets
            Glass Distributors, Inc.
            1741 Johnson Avenue, N.E., Washington, D.C.

Ultraviolet illuminated magnifiers
            Stocker & Yale, Inc.
            Marblehead, Mass.
            ("Lite Mite" blue-black light)

Tools and equipment
      (a)   Consult local directories

      (b)   William J. McLaughlin & Company
            256 South 23rd Street, Philadelphia, Pa.

      (c)   Ernest Schaefer, Inc.
            72 Oraton Street, Newark, N.J.

      (d)   Craftools, Inc.
            One Industrial Road, Wood-Ridge, N.J.

      (e)   Sangorski & Sutcliffe
            Poland Street, London W1, England

      (f)   N.J. Hill & Company
            Belmont Street, Chalk Farm, London NW 1,
            England

      (g)   Russell Bookcrafts
            Hitchin, Herts, England

      (h)   Rougier et Plé
            13 Bd. des Filles du Calvaire, Paris VI,
            France

      (i)   Wilhelm Leo's Nachfolger
            Christophstrasse 9, Stuttgart, Germany

(j)   Ditta Cosimo Tassinari
        Piazza S. Maria Novella
        Firenze, Italy
        (Engraved rolls and stamps)

(k)   Technical Library Service
        241 Broadway
        New York, N. Y.

Vacuum fumigation systems
     (a)   (Walk-in models)
           Vacudyne Corporation
           375 East Joe Orr Road, Chicago Heights,
           Chicago, Ill.

     (b)   (Portable systems)
           Minnesota Mining and Manufacturing Company
           Medical Products Division
           St. Paul, Minn. 55119

Vacuum pumps (and compressors)
     (a)   Gast Manufacturing Corporation
           Benton Harbor, Mich.

     (b)   Welch Scientific Company
           331 East 38th Street, New York, N. Y.

Vapor phase deacidification paper and sachets
        Russell Bookcrafts
        Hilchin, Herts, England

Appendix H

Measuring Relative Humidity

Because of the importance of temperature and relative humidity in conservation, librarians should have some means of determining these two conditions at any time in any part of a building. Recording thermometers and hygrometers are desirable but they are too expensive except for rare book rooms, vaults, and display cases that contain exceedingly valuable items.

Mercury thermometers are cheap enough to be mounted in a dozen or more places in a library. Direct reading dial type hygrometers will give the approximate relative humidity only in the immediate vicinity of their mounting place. These indicators are of limited usefulness.

Sling hygrometers (psychrometers), on the other hand, will give extremely accurate humidity indications. These instruments consist of a pair of wet and dry bulb thermometers mounted in a frame with a handle so that they can be swung in the air. The difference in temperature, after the water on the wet bulb has been evaporated by moving air, gives a point of entry for prepared tables from which the corresponding relative humidity is taken. The operation is rapid and readings can be made in a few minutes at several places in a room or building to uncover variations in moisture content in the air that result from poor heating or ventilation.

Appendix I

Glossary

Reprinted from the American Library Association's Library Binding Manual by permission of the Library Binding Institute.

All Along. In hand sewing of books, with the thread passing from kettle stitch to kettle stitch of successive sections, one complete course of thread going to each section. Also called One Sheet On, and One On.

Art Book. Any volume, on art or related subjects, which contains many illustrations (particularly in plate form), requiring mounting, sewing through the folds, or other special care in binding.

Artificial Gold. See Imitation Gold.

Artificial Leather. A term used for chemically coated fabrics made to resemble leather, especially in the graining.

Back. 1. The combined back edges of a bound volume, as secured together and shaped in binding. Not to be confused with Backbone, Backstrip, Shelf Back, or Spine (q.v.) 2. The endmost leaves of a volume, usually devoted to the index, appendixes, and the like.

Back or Backing. To shape a ridge on each side of the back of a sewed volume, prior to covering, by way of compensation for the thickness of the boards, and to provide a hinge-line for the cover to swing from without strain.

Back Cover. That part of the book cover following the endmost leaves.

213

Back Edge. The left-hand edge of a recto, corresponding to the right-hand edge of a verso. This is the binding edge in the case of the ordinary bound volume.

Back Lining. 1. Generally, the material (paper or fabric) used to line the back of a book prior to encasing it in a loose back (or hollow back) cover. Specifically, in Class "A" library binding, this must be Canton flannel; in edition binding, crash or crash and paper are used. 2. The muslin reinforcement on the back of some paper-covered books. 3. Sometimes, in library binding, the paper used for stiffening the backbone of the cover. (The preferred term for this is Inlay.)

Back Margin. The left-hand margin of a printed recto and the right-hand margin of a printed verso. In the ordinary book the back margin adjoins the binding edge.

Backbone. That portion of a bound volume which stands exposed when ranged with others on the shelf, cover to cover, in the usual way. Also called Spine and Shelf Back.

Backing. See Rounding-and-Backing.

Backing Boards. Bevelled hardwood boards used in connection with a press for backing volumes in lieu of the more generally used job-backer with its bevelled steel jaws.

Backing Hammer. A hammer with a short handle and a flat, broad face, used in rounding and backing.

Backing Machine. A machine for backing books. See Round and Back.

Backstrip. 1. The Spine (q.v.) of a book. Sometimes called Back. 2. That portion of a cover material which extends from joint to joint. 3. Erroneous usage for Inlay (q.v.).

Bands. 1. The cords or tapes on which the sections of a book are sewed, when not let into prepared saw-cuts across the

214

back. 2. The ridges across the backbone of certain leather-bound volumes. 3. Loosely, gold-creased lines across the backbone of a volume.

Bench Sewing. Sewing through the folds, by hand, on the sewing bench; suspended cords (or tapes), to which the sections are to be sewed, are arranged across the back edges of the sections.

Bind "As Is." A direction to the binder to bind material in the order or in the condition in which it is submitted by the customer, regardless of any seeming imperfection.

Bind In. To fasten securely into the binding; said of any supplementary material.

Binder's Board. A high-quality, single-ply, solid pulp board for bookbinding, made to full thickness in one operation, from mixed papers, and kiln-dried or plate-dried. Sometimes called Millboard.

Bindery Slip. See Binding Slip.

Binding. 1. The process of producing a single volume from leaves, sheets, signatures, or issues of periodicals, or of covering such a volume. 2. The finished work produced by this process. 3. The cover of a volume.

Binding Edge. The edge of a volume (usually the back edge) that is to receive the main binding treatment (sewing, rounding-and-backing, etc.).

Binding Slip. A sheet (large or small) of instructions sent to the bindery with each volume, specifying the binding requirements for that particular volume.

Bleed. In binding, to trim printed matter so that the text or illustration is cut into.

Bleed Illustration. An illustration printed so as to run to the extreme edge of the page, leaving no margin.

215

Board. The binder's board, pasted board, chip board, news board, and laminated board used as a foundation for book covers. So called because wood was originally used.

Board Paper. See Paste-down.

Boards. A form of bookbinding in which the boards are covered with paper. Also called Paper Boards.

Book. From the bindery point of view, any number of leaves in a binding or to be bound. Cf. Magazine. Also, any collection of more than 64 pages, bound in any manner or material. Cf. Pamphlet.

Book Jacket. A detachable wrapper, plain or printed, flush with the covers at head and tail, but folded over between the cover (both front and back) and the book proper. Also called Dust Cover, Dust Jacket, Dust Wrapper, Jacket, Jacket Cover, and Wrapper.

Bookbinding. See Binding.

Bound In. See Bind In.

Break. A parting of adjacent sections due to loosening of the sewing.

Broken. 1. Of a book, tending to open readily at a place or places where the binding has been forced or strained. 2. Of a leaf, folded over.

Buckle. To warp and twist in several directions. Said of boards and folded signatures.

Buckram. A filled book cloth with a heavy-weave cotton base. Originally applied only to a starch-filled fabric of this type; now, also, an impregnated fabric with a heavy base.

Bulk. The thickness of a book between its covers.

Call Number. Letters, figures, and symbols, separate or

in combination, assigned to a book to indicate its location on shelves. It usually consists of class number and book number. Sometimes known as Call Mark or Shelf Number.

Cancel. Any part of a book (a leaf or leaves) intended to be substituted for the corresponding part of the book as originally printed.

Canton Flannel. A soft cotton fabric with a nap on one side; used as back lining material in library binding.

Case. A cover that is made complete before it is affixed to a volume.

Case Binding. A method of binding in which the book covers are made separate from the book and later attached to it; distinguished from those methods in which the cover cannot be constructed as a separate unit. Sometimes called Casework.

Casework. See Case Binding.

Casing-in. The process of putting a volume that has received all of the binding or rebinding operations into its cover or case.

Certified Bindery. A library bindery which has been approved as qualifying under the Certification Plan of the Joint Committee of the American Library Association and the Library Binding Institute.

Chain Stitch. See Kettle Stitch.

Cloth Sides. Having cloth as the side material of the covers of a volume, as in half, quarter, and three-quarter binding.

Coil Binding. See Spiral binding.

Collate. In library binding, to examine a book or magazine volume, page by page, before binding, in order to determine completeness and nature of material, to diagnose material, sewing, and other treatment, and to arrange material in proper sequence, preparatory to sewing.

Compensation Guards. Short stubs bound in a volume to balance the space taken up by bulky inserts.

Concealed Joint. See Invisible Joint.

Cords. Heavy hemp, cotton, or linen strings to which sections are sewed in the process of binding a book by hand. Cf. Tapes and Bands.

Corner. 1. The junction point of two edges of a book cover (usually the outer ones). Various types are: Square Corners, Round Corners, Library Corners, Dutch Corners, and Mitered Corners (q.v.). 2. The leather or other material on the corners of book covers in half binding and three-quarter binding.

Cover. 1. The outer covering of a volume, no matter what material may be employed. 2. Popularly, either of the two side pieces of a cover proper; as, front cover, back cover.

Crash. 1. Coarse, open-weave, starched cotton goods, used in edition binding for reinforcing backs of volumes. Also called Super and Gauze. 2. A pattern peculiar to buckram grades of book cloth, showing a coarse pebbled effect.

Cut. 1. To trim the edges of a book. 2. Of a book, having cut edges. Not to be confused with Opened (q.v.).

Cut Flush. Of a bound volume, having the cover trimmed after binding, so that its edges are even with the edges of the leaves. Also called Trimmed Flush.

Deckle Edge. The rough, feathery edge of handmade paper, caused by a frame called the "deckle" used in molding the paper; or a similar edge in machine-made paper. Also called Feathered Edge.

Decorated Covers. In library binding, bindings in which the front cover, and sometimes the spine, has an illustration, design or special lettering.

Dog-eared. Having leaves turned down at the corners, or corners of covers broken.

Dust Cover. See Book Jacket.

Dust Jacket. See Book Jacket.

Dust Wrapper. See Book Jacket.

Dutch Corner. See Library Corner.

Edition Binding. The kind of bookbinding that is furnished to the book trade, i.e., quantity binding in uniform style for a large number of copies of single titles. Cf. Publisher's Binding.

End-Leaf. See End Papers.

End Papers. (Front and Back). End papers shall consist of three functional parts: a pasted-down or outward end-leaf which becomes the cover lining; at least two free fly-leaves; and reinforcing fabric.

End Sheet. See End Papers.

Extra Binding. The binding of books with more than ordinary care and handling and/or with a higher quality of material, usually with ornamentation. Generally binding in leather, but formerly, binding done by hand as distinguished from case binding.

Fabrikoid. The trade name for a brand of pyroxylin-coated cloth. The term is sometimes used generically.

Feathered Edge. See Deckle Edge.

Fiber Cover. An extra-stiff but slightly flexible cover stock, used on large-sized pamphlet-like material.

219

Filled. Treated with a chemical compound which fills the interstices and/or covers the fibers of a fabric, to give it body, color, or other physical or chemical properties.

Filler. The blank pages added at the back of a thin pamphlet when it is bound as a sizable volume. Also called Padding.

Finisher. The person who does the lettering and/or ornamentation on bookbindings.

Flange. See Ridge.

Flat Back. A book back that is at right angles with the sides; opposed to the usual round back.

Flat Sewing. See Side Stitching.

Flat Stitching. See Side Stitching.

Flexible Binding. 1. Any binding having other material than stiff boards in its cover. 2. Any binding that permits the book to open perfectly flat.

Flexible Glue. An adhesive made of a mixture of glue and some material like glycerine, to keep it from becoming dry and brittle.

Flush. See Cut Flush.

Fly-Leaf. 1. A blank leaf at the beginning or the end of a volume, between the lining paper and the first or last section. 2. Loosely, also the blank free half of a lining paper or a blank leaf which is part of the first or last section.

Foil. Leaf used in stamping lettering in imitation gold, silver, or other colors.

Fold. A bend in any flexible material, such as paper, made by turning a sheet over upon itself.

Fold Sewing. The process of sewing through the central (or binding) fold of section after section of a volume, by hand or machine. Also called Sewing Through the Fold.

Folio Recto. See Recto.

Folio Verso. See Verso.

Fore Edge. The front or outer edge of a book. Also called Front Edge.

Forwarding. In extra, job, and library binding, the group of operations that follow the sewing, except those having to do with lettering and finishing the cover. They include trimming, backing, etc., lining up, headbanding, and covering.

Foxing. The discoloration of paper by dull rusty patches, variously attributed to fungus, impurities in manufacture, sulphur dioxide in the atmosphere and dampness.

Front Cover. That portion of a book cover in front of the foremost leaves.

Front Edge. See Fore Edge.

Full Binding. The binding of a book completely (both back and sides) with any one material. Strictly speaking, this term, and also the term Full Bound, should apply only to leather bindings. Also called Whole Binding. See Also Half Binding, Quarter Binding, and Three-Quarter Binding.

Gauze. See Crash.

Glue Off. 1. To apply glue (flexible glue, in library binding) to the binding edge of a volume, after the other three edges have been trimmed, and just prior to backing (or rounding and backing). 2. Formerly, to apply glue, by hand, to cloth, paper, or leather, in cover making.

221

Gold. Short for Gold Leaf (q. v.).

Gold Leaf. Genuine gold, beaten into a thin leaf, adapted for use in lettering.

Grain. 1. In leather, the markings on the outer surface, after the hair has been removed. 2. In paper and binder's board, the direction in which the fibers of a sheet generally lie. 3. The artificially embossed surface of leather or other material.

Groove. 1. A depression along each side of the back of a volume, formed during the process of rounding and backing. 2. A depression along the binding edge of front and back covers. 3. The space between the board and the back of the volume in an open joint.

Guard. 1. A strip of paper, muslin, or other thin material, on which an insert, leaf, section, or map may be fastened to permit free bending. Also called Stub. 2. Strips of paper or fabric put together to act as a guard and also to equalize the space to be taken up by a folded insert. 3. A strip of paper or other material reinforcing a signature.

Guarded Signatures or Sections. Signatures or sections, usually the first and the last of a volume, that have paper or other reinforcing material pasted around the back (fold) to condition them for sewing.

Gutter. The combined marginal space formed by the two inner margins of facing pages of a volume.

Half Binding. A style of binding having a leather back and leather corners, and cloth or paper sides. The leather of the back should extend onto the boards one-quarter the width of the board, and the corners should be in harmonious proportion. The term Half Binding is applied also to any similar combination of two different materials.

Hard Cover.   Stiff board covers.

Head.   1. The top of a volume or page.   2. By extension, the top portion of the backbone of a bound volume.

Headband.   A small ornamental band (sometimes protective), generally of mercerized cotton or silk, placed at the head and tail of a volume between the cover and the backs of the folded signatures or sections.   (Formerly the two were distinguished as Headband and Tailband; now both are called Headbands.)

Height.   Length of cover from head to tail of volume.

Hinge.   Any paper or muslin stub or guard that permits the free turning of an insert, leaf, section, or map.

Hollow Back.   See Loose Back.

Illustrated Covers.   In library binding, bindings in which the front cover has a decoration embodying an approximate reproduction of the design on the original publisher's cover or book jacket.

Imitation Cloth.   Paper which has been embossed to give it the surface appearance of a fabric.

Imitation Gold.   A metallic composition, much used as a substitute for genuine gold leaf on book covers.   Also called Artificial Gold.

Impregnated.   A term inaccurately used for Filled in the case of pyroxylin-filled fabric, since the filling compound does not penetrate the fibers of the fabric.

Imprint.   1. The name of the owner of a book as stamped on the binding (usually at tail of spine).   2. The name of the publisher as stamped on the publisher's binding (usually at the tail of the spine).

Inlay. In library binding, the paper used for stiffening the backbone of the cover. Commonly, but erroneously, called Back Lining or Backstrip.

Insert. 1. An illustration, map, or other piece, produced separately from the body of the book, but bound in it. 2. In newspapers and magazines, and sometimes other publications, an extraneous piece, not originally an integral part of the publication, slipped in to accompany the publication.

Inside Margin. 1. The part of the turn-in on a book cover not covered by the end paper. 2. The Back Margin (q.v.).

Inside Strip. See Joint.

Interleaf. An extra leaf, usually blank, bound in between any two regular leaves of a volume, to provide space for writing or to protect pictures.

Invisible Joint. A cloth book joint of reinforcing fabric so made that it cannot be seen in the finished book. Sometimes called Concealed Joint.

Issue (of a periodical). See Number.

Jacket. See Book Jacket.

Jacket Cover. See Book Jacket.

Japanese Tissue. A very thin, strong, transparent tissue paper, often pasted on each side of old or worn paper to preserve it. Used also for mending tears in paper. (Strictly speaking, the term refers to such paper made only in Japan, but it applies also to a similar paper made in the United States.)

Job Backer. A machine used for backing a book by hand.

Joint. 1. Either of the two portions of the covering material that bend at the groove and along the flange when the covers of a bound volume are opened or closed. Sometimes called Inside Strip or Hinge. 2. (pl.) The reinforcements applied to the end linings or to the combination of end papers and end sections, designed to strengthen the binding.

Kettle Stitch. A stitch used in book sewing, by means of which each section is firmly united to the preceding one at head and tail. Also called Chain Stitch.

Kraft. A tough, strong paper, made entirely from wood pulp produced by a modified sulphate pulping process.

Label. A piece of paper or other material, printed or stamped, affixed to the cover of a volume. The usual position is on the spine or front cover.

Leaf. 1. One of the units into which the original sheet or half sheet of paper, parchment, etc. is folded or divided to form a book. A leaf consists of two pages, one on each side, either or both of which may be blank, or may bear printing, writing, or illustration. 2. Gold leaf. 3. Thin metallic sheets, other than gold, used in lettering.

Legal Buckram. Trade name for a heavy starch-filled buckram.

Lettering. The process or result of marking a cover with the title or other distinguishing characters (and, loosely, accompanying ornamentation).

Library Binding. 1. A special form of bookbinding for strength and durability to withstand severe library use. Distinguished from Edition Binding. 2. The process employed in producing such a binding.

Library Buckram. 1. A heavy weight cotton fabric having the qualities called for in the Minimum Specifications for Class "A" Library Binding. 2. A trade name sometimes erroneously applied to all cloths of a similar nature.

Library Corner. A book corner in which the covering material is not cut, the excess being taken up in two diagonal folds, one under each turn-in. Also called Dutch Corner, Round Corner.

Line Up or Lining Up. In library binding, to strengthen a volume (after sewing, trimming, and, usually, backing) by applying glue to the back and affixing the flannel and any reinforcing material.

Linen. 1. A book cloth made of flax. 2. A book cloth made of cotton in imitation of genuine linen. 3. A book cloth pattern that resembles the texture of linen.

Lining Paper. 1. A strong paper used for the end papers of a volume. 2. The end papers themselves. 3. The paper used for lining the backs of heavy books, supplementing the lining fabric.

Lining Strip. See Inlay.

Lock Stitch. See Kettle Stitch.

Loose Back. The back of a book in which the covering material is not glued to the back. Also called Hollow Back, Open Back, Spring Back.

Magazine. A publication with a distinctive title, intended to appear in successive (usually unbound) numbers or parts at stated or regular intervals and, as a rule, for an indefinite time. Each number or part generally contains articles by several contributors.

Margin. The space on a page outside the printed or written matter. The four margins are commonly designated as: head, or top; fore edge, outer, or outside; tail or bottom; back, inner, inside, or gutter.

Matching. Reasonably approximate duplication, as to lettering, cover material, paper, etc.

226

Mending. Minor restoration, not involving replacement with any new material or the separation of book from cover.

Millboard. See Binder's Board.

Mitered Corner. A book corner in which a triangular piece of the covering material is cut off at the corner so that the turn-ins meet without overlapping.

Nap. The loose fibers attached to the surface of a fabric.

Newsprint. Cheap paper made largely from wood pulp, on which newspapers are printed.

Number (Publication). A single numbered or dated issue of a series, a magazine, or a serial publication; generally so slight in extent that two or more may be bound together to form a volume.

One On. See All Along.

One Sheet On. See All Along.

Open Back. See Loose Back.

Open-back Case. See Slipcase.

Opened. Of a book in which the folds of the sheets have been slit open so as to separate the leaves for reading. Not to be confused with Cut (q.v.).

Overcasting. Hand sewing in which each section is sewn through and over the binding edge. (In older usage, a generic term, including oversewing and whipstitching.)

Oversewing. Sewing, by hand or machine, through the edge of each section in consecutive order, using preformed holes through which the needle passes.

Padding. See Filler.

Pamphlet. From the bindery point of view, a pamphlet is any collection of leaves, paper bound or self-covered, consisting of 64 pages or less.

Pamphlet Binding. 1. Binding done by a printer or for a printer, in which the sheets, as they come from the press, are wire-stitched. The term applies both to pamphlets and to magazines. 2. The manner in which pamphlets and magazines are bound as they come from the publisher; usually wire-stitched, either side-stitched or saddle-stitched.

Pamphlet-style Library Binding. A style of binding for a pamphlet or a thin group of pamphlets when use is expected to be infrequent. Its characteristics are side-stitching, usually with wire, and covers with cloth hinges, usually of plain boards, heavy paper, paper-covered boards, or thin lightweight cloth, cut flush, without gold lettering. (This style should not be confused with Class "A" library binding, as no process or material is of Class "A" standard.)

Paper-backed. See Paper-bound.

Paper Boards. See Boards.

Paper-bound. Bound simply with a paper cover. Also called Paper-backed.

Paste-down. That half of the lining paper which is pasted to the inner face of the cover. Also called Board Paper.

Pattern. In binding magazines, and the like, a sample volume, sample back, rub-off, and/or other data used for matching the style.

Periodical. See Magazine.

Plastic Binding. A type of flat-opening binding used for pamphlets, commercial catalogs, etc. The single leaves and the separate front and back covers are fastened by means of a special-

228

ly cut piece of synthetic plastic having prongs (combs) that pass through slots near the binding edge and are curled back within the cylinder thus formed by the plastic.

Plate. A full-page illustration on a leaf which normally is blank on the other side. The reverse may, however, bear a descriptive legend, the title of the work, or another plate. The leaf is usually of special (heavy) paper and may or may not be included in the pagination.

Portfolio. A case for holding loose papers, engravings, or similar material, consisting of two covers joined together at the back and usually tied at the front and the ends.

Prebound. Short for Pre-library-bound (q. v.).

Pre-library-bound. Of new books, bound in library binding prior to or at the time of original sale. See Appendix 2, Standards for Reinforced (Pre-library-bound) New Books.

Publisher's Binding. The binding of a book as it is issued by its publisher. It is nearly always identical with edition binding, and commonly implies ordinary cloth.

Publisher's Cover. A case designed for use in an edition binding.

Pyroxylin-coated. Referring to a fabric completely and heavily covered with a nitro-cellulose compound. (Loosely applied to fabrics with cellulose acetate coating.)

Pyroxylin-filled. Referring to a fabric filled but not heavily covered with a nitro-cellulose compound. (Loosely applied to fabrics with cellulose acetate filling.) Frequently called Pyroxylin Impregnated, although the word Impregnated is not strictly accurate.

Pyroxylin Impregnated. See Pyroxylin-filled.

Quarter Binding. Binding in cloth-covered boards, with

229

leather backs (or paper-covered sides, with cloth or leather backs), in which the back material extends only slightly onto the sides. In quarter binding, the leather (or cloth) back should extend one-eighth the width of the boards onto those boards.

Rebinding. The thorough rehabilitation of a worn volume, the minimum of work done being resewing and, if necessary, putting on a new cover.

Reconstructed Binding. Trade name for a pre-library binding on a new book.

Recto. The right-hand page of an open book, usually bearing the odd page number. Also, the front of a separate printed sheet, e.g., of a broadside. Formerly called Folio Recto.

Reinforced Binding. 1. Term loosely used by publishers for edition bindings which purport to be strengthened sufficiently to withstand hard library use. 2. Inadequate term for pre-library binding. See Pre-library-bound.

Reinforced Library Binding. A secondary binding in pre-library-bound style. Properly used only to refer to Class "A" pre-library binding, but sometimes used in referring to a prebound book in which the publisher's original cover is retained.

Reinforcing. Strengthening the structure of a weakened volume, usually by adding material. (For example, the strengthening of a hinge with cloth or the reinforcing of a page by covering it with tissue.)

Reinforcing Fabric. A fabric used for strengthening the end papers at their hinge.

Repairing. The partial rehabilitation of a worn book, the amount of work done being less than the minimum involved in rebinding and more than the maximum involved in mending. Includes such operations as restoring cover and restoring lost corners of

230

leaves.

Ridge. Either of the two outer projections along the sides
of a backed and rounded volume, against which the cover boards
are fitted. Sometimes called Flange or Shoulder.

Rough Edges. A generic term, including Uncut (Untrimmed)
Edges and Deckle Edges.

Round. To form the convex back and corresponding concave
front, in rounding and backing.

Round Back or Rounded Back. A book back that has been
given a convex form by rounding and backing.

Round Corner or Rounded Corner. 1. Same as Library
Corner (q.v.). 2. A book cover in which the board is cut off at
the corner before covering; usually confined to leather bindings.

Rounding-and-Backing. The combined operation of rounding
and backing a book, to shape it preparatory to covering. See
Round and Back.

Rub-off. An impression of the lettering and its position on
the backbone of a book, made by placing a piece of strong, thin
paper, the exact length of the book and a little wider, over the
backbone, exactly even with the bottom of the backbone, and rubbing it with the lead of a heavy pencil or something similar; used
for matching bindings. Also called Rubbing.

Rubbing. See Rub-off.

Saddle Stitching. Stitching together leaves (double leaves inserted one within the other) with thread or wire passing through the
bulk of the volume at the fold line. So called from the saddle of
a stitching machine. Cf. Side Stitching.

Sample Back. A strip of binding material made up like the
backstrip of a volume, to be used as a sample for matching color,

fabric, lettering, etc.

Sand or Sanding. To clean the edges of a volume by hand, with sandpaper, or by a sand-wheel machine, removing the least possible amount of margin from the volume.

Saw Cuts. Grooves in the back of a book, made with a saw, for receiving the cords.

Score or Scoring. In library binding, to make a crease near the edge of a section or leaf, in the case of moderately stiff paper, in order to facilitate easy opening of the volume.

Section. 1. In library binding, a group of leaves of a volume, suitable for sewing. 2. In Class "A" library binding, a group of leaves of a volume, not exceeding .050 inch in thickness, except flexible pulpy paper, which may not exceed .060 inch each.

Serial. A publication issued in successive parts, usually at regular intervals, and, as a rule, intended to be continued indefinitely.

Set Out. To attach an insert to a guard so that it stands out from the bound back or gutter.

Sewing. In bookbinding, fastening sections together, by means of needle and thread, one at a time, until the whole volume is fastened together. (A generic term, including fold sewing, oversewing, and overcasting.) To be distinguished from Stitching.

Sewing Bench. A board having two uprights connected by an adjustable bar between which and the board are stretched the tapes or cords on which the book is to be sewed. Also called Sewing Frame and Sewing Rack.

Sewing Frame. See Sewing Bench.

Sewing Rack. See Sewing Bench.

Sewing Through the Fold. See Fold Sewing.

Shelf Back. See Backbone.

Shelf Number. See Call Number.

Shoulder. See Ridge.

Side. 1. The front (or back) cover face of a bound volume. 2. The paper, cloth, or other material used on a cover face. Also called Siding.

Side Lettering. See Side Title.

Side Stitching. Stitching together single leaves or sections near the binding edge, with thread or wire from front to back through the entire thickness of the leaves or sections. Distinguished from Saddle Stitching. Also called Flat Sewing and Flat Stitching.

Side Title. A title impressed on the front cover of a bound volume.

Siding. See Side.

Singer Sewing. Side stitching with thread. The sewing extends the full length of the volume.

Sizing. The process of applying a suitable bond between binding material and lettering.

Slide Box. See Slipcase.

Slide Case. See Slipcase.

Slip-in Case. See Slipcase.

Slipcase. A box designed to protect a volume, covering it so that its back only is exposed. Also called Slide Case, Slip-in Case, Open-back Case, and Slide Box. See also Solander Case.

Smyth Sewing. Fold sewing done on a Smyth sewing machine.

233

The usual kind of sewing in edition binding, commonly done without tapes, but may be done with them.

Solander.   See Solander Case.

Solander Box.   See Solander Case.

Solander Case.   A book-shaped box for holding a book, pamphlets, or other material, named for its inventor, D.C. Solander.   It may open on side or front with hinges, or have two separate parts, one fitting over the other.   Also called Solander, Solander Box, and Solander Cover.

Solander Cover.   See Solander Case.

Special Volume.   Any undersized, oversized, or odd sized volume, or any volume that requires special handling.

Specification Slip.   See Binding Slip.

Spine.   See Backbone.

Spiral Binding.   A patented form of binding in which a row of fine holes is drilled through the leaves (trimmed so that each leaf is separate), and a continuous spiral-twisted wire is drawn through the holes.   Also known as Coil Binding.

Sponging.   The process of dampening with a wet sponge, as in preparing wrinkled newspapers for pressing.

Spring Back.   See Loose Back.

Sprinkled Edges.   Book edges on which color has been irregularly sprinkled or sprayed.

Square Corner.   A book corner in which a piece of the covering material is cut out at the corner so that one turn-in of the covering material considerably overlaps the other without additional folding.

Squares. The portions of the edges of a book cover that project beyond the paper body of the book.

Stained Edges. Book edges that have been stained with color.

Standardized Lettering. A simplified method of lettering bound magazine volumes, in which all unnecessary words, abbreviations, or decorations are omitted. Years and months are placed in alignment on volumes of all sizes and titles are placed in alignment within each group size.

Staple. In pamphlet and magazine binding, one of the several clinched wire fastenings used in wire-stitching.

Starch-filled. Referring to a fabric the interstices of which are filled with starch.

Stippled Edge. The edge of a volume which has been spotted irregularly with ink or dye.

Stitching. In bookbinding, the fastening together of the leaves by means of thread or wire, each single passage of the threaded needle or wire going through the bulk of the volume. (A generic term, including side stitching and saddle stitching.) To be distinguished from Sewing.

Stub. 1. A narrow strip of paper, muslin, or other thin material sewed in between sections, for attaching folded maps or other material of extra bulk. A cancel is usually mounted on the stub of a canceled leaf. Also known as Guard. 2. The remaining portion of a leaf cut out of a volume.

Super. See Crash.

Tail. 1. The bottom portion of the backbone of a bound volume. 2. The bottom portion of a page.

Tailband. See Headband.

235

Tapes. Pieces of tape, or strips of cloth, to which sections are sewed and whose free ends are pasted to the boards, or inserted between the split boards of the book covers to lend strength to the binding. Cf. Bands and Cords.

Three-quarter Binding. Binding similar to half binding, except that the leather extends further on the sides, theoretically to three-quarters of half the width of the sides. Corners are proportionately large.

Tight Back. The back of a volume in which the covering material has been glued to the back. Confined mostly to leather-backed books.

Tip In or Tipping In. To paste a leaf (or leaves) onto a printed sheet or into a bound book, without guards.

Title Leaf. See Title Page.

Title Page. A page at the beginning of a book or work bearing the full title and usually also author (if any), publisher, place and date of publication, and/or other data. Sometimes called Title Leaf.

Trim. To cut the edge of a leaf or group of leaves of a volume.

Trim. 1. The portion cut off in trimming. 2. The edge after trimming.

Trimmed Flush. See Cut Flush.

Turn-in. The portion of a volume cover formed by turning in the cover material over the outer edges of the boards.

Two Along. In bookbinding, a method of sewing on bands, tapes, or cords that treats two adjoining sections as a single unit, a method generally used for thick volumes composed of thin sections, to avoid making the bound volume too thick at the back. Also known as Two On and Two Sheets On.

Two On. See Two Along.

Two Sheets On. See Two Along.

Uncut Edges. Edges of a volume that have not been trimmed in any way. Also called Untrimmed Edges. Cf. Deckle Edges.

Untrimmed Edges. See Uncut Edges.

Verso. The left-hand page in an open book, usually bearing the even page number. Also, the back of a separate printed sheet. Formerly called Folio Verso.

Visible Joint. A cloth book joint, so made that it can be seen in the finished book.

Volume. 1. Any group of leaves, of a book, magazine or newspaper, bound together. 2. All the issues of a given publication issued within a specified publication period; usually the consecutive numbers of a magazine for six months or a year. 3. For library statistical purposes, any printed, typewritten, mimeographed, or processed work, bound or unbound, which has been catalogued and fully prepared for use. In connection with circulation, the term volume applies to a pamphlet or a periodical as well as to a book.

Warp. The threads that run the long way in fabrics.

Warp. In book covers, to curve away from the plane of the book.

Waterproofing. Lacquer or other waterproof material applied over lettering.

Whipstitching. See Overcasting.

Whole Binding. See Full Binding.

Wire Stitch or Wire Stitching. To sttich (a pamphlet or a magazine) with wire staples, either side-fashion (side stitch) or saddle fashion (saddle stitch).

Wrapper. See Book Jacket.

Bibliography

Probably the first printed work on bookbinding and restoration was Capperonnier de Gauffecourt's now extremely rare Traite de la Reliure des Livres, La Motte (1763). This is cataloged in Brunet's Manuel de Libraire, Paris 1861, Vol. II, page 1502 and described as a seventy-two page octavo volume of which only twenty-five copies were printed. No copies are recorded at the British Museum, Bibliotheque Nationale, or the Library of Congress. Since de Gauffecourt's time there has been a flood of books, pamphlets and magazine articles on the history of binding, binding techniques, binders, collectors and great collections. Wolfgang Mejer's 1925 list of almost 2700 titles in seven languages is considered the best bibliography on bookbinding available up to that time but it is by no means complete. In 1954 A.R.A. Hobson, Director in Charge of the Book Department at Sotheby's, assembled for the National Book League a list of references that he considered sufficient to provide one with a first-rate knowledge of the history of binding. In an appendix to the same pamphlet Hobson included what he regarded as reliable texts in English on the binding craft and industry. In 1963 Max Hettler in Stuttgart published Anneliese Duehmert's Buchpflege, a bibliography of over two thousand titles in several languages on the care and repair of bindings.

In the twentieth century there has been a surprising number of technical papers on the various aspects of conservation as well as important contributions to our knowledge of books. Leo Deuel's Testaments of Time (1965) is a scholarly account of what is being done to retrieve and restore ancient records. This, a good point of departure for the study of the history of books in all the various forms, includes a lengthy bibliography. Douglas McMurtrie's The Book (1957) is unquestionably the best account of the development of the book in codex form. This, too, has a fine bibliography of tech-

nical as well as historical interest. All that any librarian needs
to know about paper is available in Dard Hunter's Papermaking,
New York, 1943.

In regard to technique, the works of Douglas and Sidney
Cockerell will for a long time to come be the standard references,
although Laurence Town's Bookbinding by Hand presents Douglas
Cockerell's teachings in a more comprehensible manner. Bernard
Middleton's 1963 History of English Craft Bookbinding is far wider
in scope than the subject suggests. This edifying volume was written by a master craftsman and reflects his own experience, plus
over ten years of exhaustive research. As a technical reference,
it is unexcelled and it is of particular importance to librarians who,
in deciding whether to rebind or restore old books, must be able to
recognize contemporary workmanship. Middleton documents his
sources in hundreds of footnotes.

Bookbinding in America (1941), containing three essays by
Hellmut Lehmann-Haupt, Joseph W. Rogers and Hannah Dustin
French, gives an excellent description of binderies, materials, and
craftsmen to 1825 and the transition from an ancient craft to a modern industry in the 1800's. The third essay, Lehmann-Haupt's "On
the Rebinding of Old Books," is an analysis of the ethics and aes-
thetics of rebinding and warrants the attention of all librarians who
must inevitably make such decisions. Miss French's lengthy list of
binders appended to "Early American Bookbinding by Hand" should
be of great help in identifying colonial craftsmanship. Mr. Rogers'
discourse on "The Rise of American Edition Binding" would be
more properly titled if the word "American" were not included and
the dissertation were understood to be an introduction to the mechanization of bookbinding on both sides of the Atlantic.

Two Russian publications are of much interest because of
their detailed reporting on library conservation measures and restoration techniques in the U.S.S.R. Translations of these, A Collection of Materials on the Preservation of Library Resources and
New Methods for the Restoration and Preservation of Documents
and Books, are available from the U.S. Department of Commerce,
Office of Technical Services, Springfield, Virginia. N.G. Belan'-

Kaya's "Methods of Restoration of Books and Documents" in New Methods... is an outstanding summary, with much technical detail on the traditional as well as modern techniques for paper restoration in Russia, Europe, and America.

Valuable references from the point of view of practical library conservation are these works:

H. S. Plenderleith, The Conservation of Antiquities and Works of Art

Clara Le Gear, Maps: Their Care, Repair, and Preservation in Libraries

Adelaide Minogue, The Repair and Preservation of Records

H. Richard Archer (ed,), Rare Book Collections

Douglas Cockerell, Bookbinding and The Care of Books and Some Notes on Bookbinding

Sidney Cockerell, The Repairing of Books

Lucille M. Kane, A Guide to the Care and Repair of Manuscripts

W. H. Langwell, The Conservation of Books and Documents

Lydenberg and Archer, The Care and Repair of Books

Gary Thomson, "Air Pollution - A Review for Conservation Chemists" in Studies in Conservation, Vol. 10, November 1965.

Between 1932 and 1942 the Fogg Art Museum published a quarterly journal, Technical Studies in the Field of Fine Arts. These journals, a gold mine of information on materials, craftsmanship and techniques, environmental control, general conservation, etc. were made doubly useful by the publication in 1964 of a subject index to the series done by Bertha E. Usilton, Librarian at the Freer Gallery of Art. In addition to more than 160 articles and notes and many reviews of technical books, Technical Studies contains about 450 abstracts of articles that appeared in other journals. Later Mr. Rutherford Gettens of the Freer Gallery and Miss Usilton compiled Abstracts of Technical Studies in Art and Archeology 1943 to 1952, which was published by the Freer Gallery in 1955. Since that time the technical literature on art and archeology has been abstracted and published under the auspices of the International Institute for Conservation of Historical and Artistic Works, (IIC) with headquarters at the National Gallery in London. Known as the

241

IIC Abstracts until 1966, they are now the Art and Archeology Technical Abstracts, prepared at the Institute of Fine Arts, New York University. Since 1952 the IIC has also published a quarterly journal, Studies in Conservation, which should not be overlooked.

This bibliography, to enhance its usefulness, is organized to correspond with the chapter arrangement of the text. The great many references to publications of museum origin or interest are included because of the close affinity of library conservation to certain aspects of museum science. Environment control as practiced in museums is equally applicable to libraries and archives. Measures developed in museums for the care and repair of paper, textiles, leather, parchment, etc. are of utmost importance to librarians.

A Selective Bibliography on Books and Their Conservation

History

General

Abbott, T. K. Celtic Ornaments from The Book of Kells. Dublin, 1895. Fifty plates.

Alexander, Shirley M. On the Origins and Development of the Luxury Manuscript. New York, Conservation Center, New York University, 1966. A study of gold writing and purple parchment.

"Ancient Books." Art Journal 11:279.

"Ancient Form and Material of Books." Penny Magazine 5:310.

Andrews, William Loring, Jean Grolier de Servier, Viscount d'Aguisy. New York, 1892. 8 v. Account of his life and of his famous library. 6 plates of bindings.

---- Roger Payne and His Art. New York, 1892. 8 v. 11 plates.

Arnett, John Andrews (i. e. J. Hannett), An Inquiry into the Nature and Form of the Books of the Ancients. London, 1837.

---- Bibliopegia or the Art of Bookbinding in All Its Branches. London, Groumbridge, 1835.

---- The Bookbinders' School of Design as Applied to the Combination of Tools in the Art of Finishing. London, 1837. 8 plates engraved by Joseph Morris.

Arnold, Thomas W. (Sir) and Grohmann, Adolf, The Islamic Book. London, The Pegasus Press, 1929. pp. 37, 44, 57.

Audin, Marius. Le Livre. Son Architecture Sa Technique. Paris, Les Editions G. Crès et Cie, 1924.

Barrow, John. Dictionarium Polygraphicum. London, C. Hitch and C. Davis, 1735. 2 v.

Barrow, William J. "Black Writing Ink of the (American) Colonial Period." American Archivist. 11:291-307, 1948. Charts.

Bendikson, Lodewyk. "The House of Magnus, Famous Bookbinders of the Seventeenth Century." Pacific Bindery Talk, Los Angeles, 8(6):94-100, February, 1936.

Bennett, Paul A. (ed.). Books and Printing. New York, The World Publishing Co., 1963. A treasury for typophiles but of general interest to librarians and conservationists.

Beraldi, Henri. La Reliure au XIXe Siecle. 1895-97. 4 v. The standard account, written most entertainingly.

Berger. Histoire de l'Ecriture dans l'Antiquite. Paris, 1891.

Binns, Norman E. Bookbinding, Its Evolution and History: An Introduction to Historical Bibliography. The Association of Assistant Librarians, Chap. 20, 285-318, 1953.

"Books and Bookbinding in Syria and Palestine." Art Journal, 20:41,113.

Bosch, G.K. "The Staff of the Scribes and Implements of the Discerning; an Excerpt." A.O. 4. (1961). Translation of a 1100 A.D. Arab text on bookbinding.

The Bookbinder in Eighteenth Century Williamsburg. Williamsburg, Va., Colonial Williamsburg, Inc., 1959.

The Bookbinders Price List. London, 1812.

Brassington, W.S. History of the Art of Bookbinding, with Some Account of the Books of the Ancients. London, Stock, 1894.

Brassinne, Joseph. La Reliure Mosane. 1912-32. 2 v. Supplemented by Verheyden's few published articles as in Le Livre en Brabant, 1935, and his catalog of the Antwerp Exhibition of 1930. The last is a work of immense erudition, but its usefulness is impaired by being written in Flemish and by its lack of illustrations.

British Museum. "Guide to the Exhibition in the King's Library, Illustrating the History of Printing, Music-printing, and Bookbinding." 1939.

Browne, Sir Thomas. Hydriotaphia. 1658.

Brunet, Gustave. La Reliure Ancienne et Moderne. Paris, E. Rouveyre et G. Blond, 1884.

Bushnell, George Herbert. From Bricks to Books. London, Grafton & Co., 1949.

---- From Papyrus to Print, a Bibliographical Miscellany. Grafton, Chap. 10:79-89, 1947. On Scottish bookbinding.

Carter, John. Publishers Cloth. London, Constable, 1935 (and New York, Bowker, 1935). An outline history of publisher's bindings in England 1820-1900.

---- "The Origin of Publishers' Cloth Binding." The Colophon. Part 8, 1931.

----Binding Variants in English Publishing, 1820-1900. London, 1932.

---- More Binding Variants. London, 1938.

Cennini. The Craftsman's Handbook. New York, Dover Publications, Inc., 1933. Modern translation by Daniel V. Thompson, Jr. of Cennini's 1437 Il Libro dell'Arte.

Černý, Jaroslav. Paper and Books in Ancient Egypt. An inaugural lecture delivered at University College, London, May 29, 1947. London, H. K. Lewis & Co., Ltd, 1952.

Chapman, R. W. "Notes on Eighteenth-Century Bookbinding." Transactions of the Bibliographical Society, The Library. December 1923.

Chiera, Edward. They Wrote on Clay. Chicago, University of Chicago Press, 1938. This description of early Babylonian-Assyrian civilization contains much information on clay tablets.

Child, John. The Society of London Bookbinders 1780-1951. London, 1952.

Cobden-Sanderson, T. J. "Craft Ideals." Transactions of the National Association of the Advancement of Art and Its Applications to Industry, 1888.

---- English Illustrated Magazine, 1891.

---- Cosmic Vision, 1922.

---- Ecce Munde, 1902.

---- The Journals of T. J. Cobden-Sanderson. London, 1926. 2 v.

Cockerell, Douglas. "Fine Bookbinding in England." Art of the Book. Studio, pp. 69-124, 1914. Charles Holme, Editor.

---- "Development of Bookbinding Methods--Coptic Influence." The Library, 4th series, 13(1):1-19, June 1932.

Cockerell, S. C. The Gorleston Psalter. London, Chiswick Press, 1907. Description of the binding on a fourteenth-century manuscript.

245

Commercial Bookbindings. New York, Grolier Club, 1894. A historical sketch of commercial binding in the 19th century.

Couderc, C. Les Enluminures des Manuscrits du Moyen Age. (VIe au XVe siecle) de la Bibliotheque Nationale. Paris, 1927. 119 pages of text and 80 plates.

Cundall, Joseph. On Ornamental Art Applied to Ancient and Modern Bookbinding. London, 1848.

---- Bookbindings, Ancient and Modern. London, George Bell & Sons, 1881.

Dahl, Svend. History of The Book. Metuchen, N.J., The Scarecrow Press, 1958. The first English edition of this book by a famous Danish librarian.

Darly, Lionel. Bookbinding Then and Now. London, 1959. The story of one bindery from its beginning in the 18th century to the present.

Davenport, Cyril James Humphries. "The Decoration of Book-edges." Bibliographica, London, 2:385-406, 1896.

---- Thomas Berthelet, Royal Printer and Bookbinder to Henry VIII, King of England, with Special Reference to his Bookbindings. Chicago, The Caxton Club, 1901.

---- Life of Samuel Mearne. Chicago, Caxton Club, 1907. Howard Nixon at the British Museum has proved that only 11 of the 20 books selected for illustration of Mearne's work are his.

---- The Book and Its History and Development. New York, Van Nostrand, 1908. All of Davenport's work, except his life of Payne, must be used with caution because of questionable research.

---- Roger Payne. Chicago, Caxton Club, 1929. One of the most famous 18th century binders. This is the only biography by Davenport that is considered to be reliable.

Davis, Hassoldt. "Book Binding in the South Seas." Scribners Magazine 99:120-121, 1936. Interesting account of Mrs. Davis' use of local material for book covers.

Design in Bookbinding: As Represented in Exhibits at the Sixth Triennial Exposition of Graphic Arts at Milan, Italy, in 1936, with Illustrations of Eighteen Bookbindings There Exhibited. Chicago, privately printed, 1938.

Deuel, Leo. Testaments of Time. New York, Alfred A. Knopf, 1965.

Devauchelle, Roger. La reliure en France, de ces origines à nos jours. Paris, Rousseau-Girard, 1959.

Dibdin, Thomas Frognall. The Bibliographical Decameron. London, 1817. 3 v. Illustrated. Dibdin must be used with caution because of the unreliability of his facts.

Diehl, Edith. Bookbinding, Its Background and Technique. New York, Rinehart & Co., Inc., 1946. Vol. I: History, etc. has a lengthy bibliography.

Dioscorides, Pedanius, of Anazarbos. The Greek Herbal of Dioscorides. Edited by Robert T. Gunther. Oxford, printed by J. Johnson for the author at the University Press, 1934.

Diringer, David. The Hand Produced Book. London, Hutchinson & Co., 1953.

---- The Illuminated Book: Its History and Production London, 1958.

Dodd, George. "A Day at a Bookbinder's." Days at the Factories. Ser. I--London. London, Knight, 1843. pp. 363-384.

The Dolphin. No. 2. "A Journal of the Making of Books." New York, Limited Editions Club, 1935.

duBois, H.P. Historical Essay on the Art of Bookbinding. New York, Bradstreet Press, 1883.

French, Rogers, Lehmann-Haupt. Bookbinding in America. Portland, Me., The Southworth Anthoensen Press, 1941. Repr. 1967

Duff, E. Gordon. "The Bindings of Thomas Wotton." The Library. 3rd series, Vol. 1, 1910. pp. 337-347.

---- The Printers, Stationers, and Bookbinders of Westminster and London from 1476 to 1535. Cambridge, 1906.

Du Halde, P. "Of the Paper, Ink and Pencils, also of the Printing and Binding the Chinese Books." The General History of China, Including an Exact and Particular Account of Their Customs, Manners, Ceremonies, Religion, Arts, and Sciences. London, 1736. 4 vols. In vol. II, pp. 415-436.

Dutton, M.K. Historical Sketch of Bookbinding as an Art. Norwood, Mass., Holliston Mills, 1926. Beginnings in Italy, France, England and America.

Ede, Charles (ed.). "Hand Binding--The Art of the Book." Studio, 1951.

----"Commercial Binding--The Art of the Book." Studio, 1951.

247

Faraday, Michael. "On the Ventilation of Lamp Burners." Royal Institution Lecture April 7, 1843, in which he names combustion products as one source of leather decay.

Farleigh, John. "Sydney Cockerell--Bookbinder." The Creative Craftsman. G. Bell, 1950. Chap. 6, pp. 91-102.

Fletcher, W. Y. Bookbinding in France. London, Seeley & Co., 1894. A short but good history of French binding by a former Assistant Keeper of Printed Books in the British Museum.

Flower, Desmond. "Some French contributions to the art of the book." Signature. New series 7:7-16, 1948.

Folmsbee, Beulah. A Little History of the Horn Book. Boston, The Horn Book, Inc., 1942.

Forbes, R. J. Studies in Ancient Technology. Vol. 5 (Leather). Leiden, E. J. Brill, 1957.

Gansser, A. "The Early History of Tanning." CIBA Review. Basle, 1950.

Gansser-Burckhardt, A. "Leather Making in Antiquity and Its Preservation." Journal American Leather Trades Chemists Assoc. 49 (1954).

Gauffecourt, Capperonnier de. Traite de la Reliure des Livres. La Molte, France, 1763. Only 25 copies of this first book on bookbinding were printed.

"Gauffered Edges 16th Century, Method or Technique." Stone's Impressions. Vol. IV, 1934-1935.

Gelb, I. J. A Study of Writing. Second Revised Edition, Chicago, University of Chicago Press-Phoenix Books, 1963.

Gibson, Strickland. "The Localization of Books by Their Bindings." Transactions of the Bibliographical Society. 1906-1907.

---- Early Oxford Bindings. London, Oxford University Press, 1903. Printed for the Bibliographical Society. Contains photographs of beautiful old leather-covered books.

---- Abstracts from the Wills and Testamentary Documents of Printers, Binders, and Stationers of Oxford 1493-1638. London, Oxford University Press, 1903.

Golden Book, The. Chicago, Pascal Covici, 1927.

Goldschmidt, Ernst Philip. Gothic and Renaissance Bookbinding. Illustrated from the author's collection. 2 v. London, Boston and New York, 1928. One of the classics on history of bookbinding. Superb references, extremely readable.

Goldschmidt, E.P. The Printed Book of the Renaissance. Amsterdam, Gérard Th. van Heusden 1966. Three lectures on type, illustrations and ornament; many illustrations.

Gottlieb, T. K.K. Hofbibliothek. Bucheinbände. Vienna, 1910.

Gray, G.J. A Note Upon Early Cambridge Binders of the Sixteenth Century. Cambridge, 1900.

---- The Earlier Cambridge Stationers and Bookbinders and the First Cambridge Printer. London, Bibliographical Society, 1904.

Gray, G.J. and Palmer, W.M. Abstracts from the Wills and Testamentary Documents of Printers, Binders and Stationers of Cambridge from 1564 to 1699. 1915.

(Grolier) Bookbindings from the Library of Jean Grolier. London, The Trustees of the British Museum 1965. Biography of Grolier; the men who bound his books; the stamping tools of the various craftsmen.

Gruel, L. Manuel Historique et Bibliographique de l'Amateur de Reliures. Paris, Gruel and Engelmann 1887. Contains much general information although some of the author's conclusions are open to question.

Grycz, J. On the History and Techniques of the Book. Wroclaw (Poland) 1951. In Polish, but of value because of 106 illustrations.

Guild of Women-Binders. The Bindings of Tomorrow. A record of the work of the Guild and the Hampstead Bindery. Critical introduction by G. Elliott Anstruther. 1902.

Gutenberg Documents, The. New York, Oxford University Press, 1941.

Hamanova, P. A History of Bookbinding from the Beginning to the End of the 19th Century. Prague, Orbis 1959. 161 illustrations.

Hannett, John. An Enquiry into the Nature and Form of the Books of the Ancients; with a History of the Art of Bookbinding. 6th ed. London, Simpkin, Marshall, 1865.

Hanson, T.W. Book Handbook. 1948.

Harrison (Rev. Canon F.) Treasures of Illumination. English Manuscripts of the Fourteenth Century (c.1250 to 1400), 24 colored reproductions, 4to, 1937.

Harrison, T. The Bookbinding Craft and Industry: An Outline of its History and Technique. Pitman, 1926, and 2nd ed. 1930.

Harper, Joseph Henry. The House of Harper. New York, Harper, 1912.

Harthan, John. Bookbindings. London, H.M.S.O. 1950. This Victoria and Albert Museum illustrated booklet is a concise summary of the evolution of book decoration in the Near East and Europe.

Hedberg, Arvid. Stockholms Bokbindare 1460-1880. 2 v. Stockholm, 1949-1960. A 751-page history of Swedish binding, illustrated by 165 plates and many photographs and drawings in the text.

Hermann, H.J. Die Illuminierten Handschriften und Inkunabeln der Nationalbibliothek in Wein. Leipzig, 1930. (248 facsimile reproductions)

Hessel, Alfred. A History of Libraries. Metuchen, N.J., The Scarecrow Press, 1955.

Hevesy, André de. La Bibliothèque du Roi Matthias Corvin. Paris, 1923.

Highet, Gilbert. "The Wondrous Survival of Records." Horizon. 5(2), 1962.

History of Bookbinding, The 525-1950. An exhibition held at the Baltimore Museum of Art, November 12, 1957, to January 12, 1958. Baltimore, Md., published by the Trustees of the Walters Art Gallery, 1957.

History of Technology. London, 1956.

Hobson, Geoffrey Dudley. Blind-stamped Panels in the English Book Trade, c. 1485-1555. Bibliographical Society, 1944.

---- English Binding Before 1500. Cambridge, Cambridge University Press, 1929. (Sandars lectures, 1927.)

---- "Further Notes on Romanesque Bindings." The Library, 4th series, 15(2):161-211, September, 1934.

----Maioli, Carnevai and Others. London, 1925. The author shows that "Carnevari" bindings were executed for the Italian collector Pierluigi Franesi (1503-1547).

---- "Parisian Binding, 1500-1525." The Library, 4th series, II(4):393-474, March 1931. Panel stamps of devotional pictures.

---- "Some Early Bindings and Binders' Tools." The Library, 4th series, 19:202-246, 1938.

Hobson, A. R. A. French and Italian Collectors and their Bindings. Illustrated from examples in the library of J. R. Abbey. Oxford, 1953, pp. 5-20 including "Grolier's Mottoes."

---- The Literature of Bookbinding. London, Cambridge University Press, 1954.

Hoe, Robert. A Lecture on Bookbinding as a Fine Art. Delivered before the Grolier Club, Feb. 26, 1885. Illus. New York, The Grolier Club, 1886.

Horne, Herbert Percy. The Binding of Books. 2nd ed. London, Kegan, Paul, 1915. An essay on the history of gold-tooled bindings.

Howe, Ellic. List of London Bookbinders, 1648-1815. Bibliographical Society, 1950.

Howe, Ellic and Child, J. The Society of London Bookbinders, 1780-1951. Sylvan Press, 1952.

Humphreys, Henry Noel. The Origin and Progress of the Art of Writing. London, 1853.

---- The Illuminated Books of the Middle Ages: An Account of the Development and Progress of the Art of Illumination, from the fourth to the seventeenth centuries, 1849.

Husung, Maximilian Joseph. Bucheinbände aus der Preussischen. Staatsbibliothek zu Berlin in historischer Folge erläutert. Leipzig, 1925.

----"Geschichte des Bucheinbandes." Handbuch der Bibliothkswissenschafs herausgegeben von Fritz Milkau, Leipzig, 1: 666-716, 1931.

Hutner, J. C., Englische Miscellen Band 6. Tubingen, 1802.

Ivins, W. M., Jr. The Arts of the Book. New York, The Metropolitan Museum of Art, 1924.

Jackson, Holbrook. The Anatomy of Bibliomania. New York, Charles Scribner's Sons, 1932.

James, M. R. The Wanderings and Homes of Manuscripts. New York, The MacMillan Co., 1919.

Johnson, Elmer D. Communication. Metuchen, N. J., The Scarecrow Press, 1960. An introduction to the history of the alphabet, writing, printing, books and libraries.

251

---- A History of Libraries in the Western World. Metuchen, N.J.,
The Scarecrow Press, 1965.

Johnston, Edward. Writing and Illuminating and Lettering. London, Pitman, 1945.

Kenyon, Sir Frederick G. Ancient Books and Modern Discoveries.
Chicago, The Caxton Club, 1927. History of lettering and illumination.

---- Books and Readers in Ancient Greece and Rome. 1948.

Kepes, Gyorgy and others. Graphic Forms: The Arts as Related
to the Book. Cambridge, Mass., Harvard University Press,
1949.

Ker, Neil Ripley. Fragments of Medieval Manuscripts Used as
Pastedowns in Oxford Bindings with a Survey of Oxford Bindings, c. 1515-1620. Oxford, Oxford Bibliographical Society,
1954.

Koops, Matthias. Historical Account of the Substances Which Have
Been Used to Describe Events, and to Convey Ideas, from the
Earliest Date to the Invention of Paper. London, Printed by
T. Burton, 1800.

Kup, Karl. A Fifteenth-Century Girdle Book. New York, New
York Public Library, 1939.

"La Reliure Romantique." Connaissance des Artes. No. 19 (September 15, 1953.) Description and illustration of elaborate
bindings of the 18th and 19th centuries.

La Reliure, Ancienne et Moderne. Recueil de 116 Planches. Paris,
1878.

Labarte, J. Histoire des Arts Industriels au Moyen Age. Paris,
1864-1866.

Lamacraft, C.T. "Early Bookbindings from a Coptic Monastery."
The Library. 4th series, 20(2):214-233, September 1939.

Lamb, C.M., ed. The Calligrapher's Handbook. London, Faber
and Faber, (1956). Illus. Though designed for the practicing
calligrapher of today, this contains historical material of interest to the preservationist. See also, pp. 199-223, S.M.
Cockerell's "The Binding of Manuscripts."

Lecky, Margaret. "Of Books and Bindings." Creative Crafts,
June/July 1960. An introduction to fine binding by one of the
foremost binders in America and a lecturer in Art at UCLA.

Lee, Marshall. Books for Our Time. New York, Oxford University Press, 1951.

Lehmann-Haupt, French and Rogers. Bookbinding in America.
Portland, Me., 1941. Three essays. A must for every librarian. (Repr. by Bowker, New York, 1967)

Lehmann-Haupt, Hellmut. Gutenberg and the Master of the Playing Cards. New Haven, Yale University Press, 1966. Author
proposes that Gutenberg pioneered in printed illustrations as
well as movable type.

Lehmann-Haupt, with Wroth and Silver. The Book in America.
New York, R.R. Bowker Co., 1951.

Leighton, Douglas. Modern Bookbinding, a Survey and a Prospect.
London, London School of Printing, 1935. Fifth annual J.M.
Dent Memorial Lecture, 1935.

Lejard, André (ed.). The Art of the French Book. London, 1947.
Well illustrated history of French book production from early
manuscripts to the present time.

Lelande, Joseph Jérôme Le Francais de. Art de Faire le Papier.
Paris, Desaint et Saillant, 1761.

Lesné. Poème Didactique en Six Chants. Paris, 1820. A poem
about bookbinding by a bookbinder.

Levey, Martin. "Chemistry of Tanning in Ancient Mesopotamia."
Journal Chemical Education, 34 (1957).

---- "Mediaeval Arabic Bookmaking." Transactions American Philosophical Society, 52 (1962) Part IV.

---- et al. "An Eleventh Century Arabic Work on Bookbinding."
ISIS, 47 (1956).

Lister, Raymond. How to Identify Old Maps and Globes. Hamden,
Conn., Archon Books, 1965. Contains much information on
history of maps and map making, and a useful appendix on the
use of water marks in dating old maps and documents.

Li Shu-hua. The Spread of the Art of Paper Making. Taipei,
Taiwan, National Historical Museum, 1960. Text in English
and Chinese.

Locke, Leland. The Ancient Quipu or Knot Record. New York,
The American Museum of Natural History, 1923.

Louisy, M.P. Le Livre et les Arts Qui S'y Rattachent. Paris,
Librairie de Fermin-Didot et Cie, 1887. Includes chapters on
history of paper, parchment and bookbinding in France to the
end of the 18th century.

Lucas, Alfred. Ancient Egyptian Materials and Industries. 3rd ed. rev. London, Edward Arnold and Co., 1948.

Ludwig, Emil. The Nile. New York, Pyramid Books, 1963.

Madan, F. Books in Manuscript. London, 1893.

Marwick, Claire S. An Historical Study of Paper Document Restoration Methods. Unpublished master's thesis, The American University, 1964.

McCarthy, W. H., Jr. "Outline of the History of Bookbinding." The Dolphin, (3):447-468, 1938.

McLean. Victorian Book Design. 1963.

McMurtrie, Douglas C. The Book. 3rd rev. ed. New York, Oxford University Press, 1957. The story of printing and book making.

---- "The First American Bookbinder." Bookbinding Magazine, VI(6):22, June 1927.

Maskell, Alfred. Ivories. London, Methuen, 1905.

Maskell, William. Ivories Ancient and Mediaeval. London, Chapman and Hall, 1875.

Mason, William A. A History of the Art of Writing. New York, 1920.

Matthews, Brander. Bookbindings Old and New. London, George Bell & Sons, 1896. Discusses early binding, the late 19th-century binders and 19th-century commercial binding, including a lengthy section on printed paper covers.

"Meander and the Mummy." Time, 82:63, 66 (October 11, 1963). Describes briefly the work of the Institut de Papyrologie in the Sorbonne. Recently a long scroll of papyrus recovered from the wrappings of a mummy was identified as part of an unknown play of Meander.

Michel, Marius. Essai sur la Decoration Exterieure des Livres. Paris, 1878.

Middleton, Bernard C. A History of English Bookbinding Techniques. London, Hafner Publishing Co., 1963. An excellent history plus much technical information.

Milik, J. T. "Copper Document from Cave IV, Qumran," Bibl. Archaeology 19 (September 1956).

Miner, Dorothy, (ed.). The History of Bookbinding 525 AD to 1950

AD. Baltimore, Walters Gallery of Art, 1950. Illustrated catalog.

Mitchell, William S. A History of Scottish Bookbinding, 1432-1650. Edinburgh and London, Oliver & Boyd, 1955. A list of Scottish binders and a bibliography are appended.

Mitius, O. "Frankische Lederschnittbande des XV. Jahrhunderts; ein burgeschicchtlicher Versuch." Sammlung bibliothekswissenschaftlicher Arbeiten, Heft 28 (2te ser. Heft 11) Leipzig, 1909.

"Modern Book Production." The Studio, 1928.

Morrison, David. Bookbinding; Its History and Improvement, 1841.

Neil, R. K. Paste Downs in Oxford Bindings, 1954.

Nixon, Howard M. "Binding and Binders." Talks on Book Collecting. P.H. Muir (ed.) London, Cassell and Company, Ltd., 1952.

---- "Grolier's Binders." The Book Collector. London, 1960, 45-51, 165-70.

---- "Grolier's 'Chrysostom.'" The Book Collector. London, 1962. pp. 64-70.

---- Roger Powell and Peter Waters. Privately published, Peterborough, Hants, England, 1966. Describes the work of these two master craftsmen.

Nordhoff, Evelyn H. "The Doves Bindery." Chap-Book, 4:353-370, March 1, 1896. A short illustrated account of one of the finer binderies.

Ogg, Oscar. The 26 Letters. New York, 1948.

Oldham, J. B. Blind Panels of English Binders. Cambridge, Cambridge University Press, 1958.

Orcutt, William Dana. "The Art of the Book: A Review of Some Recent European and American Work in Typography, Page Decoration and Binding." London, The Studio, 1914.

---- In Quest of the Perfect Book. New York, 1926.

---- The Kingdom of Books. Boston, 1927.

P'an Chi-hsing. "The Earliest Specimen of Paper Made of Plant Fiber." Wen Wu II (1964). Describes paper unearthed in China in 1957 that was made in 206 B.C.

"Parchment Patients." Newsweek, 61:90, April 8, 1963. Tells

about the Vatican's institute for the scientific restoration of
books.

Pinner, H. L.   The World of Books in Classical Antiquity. 1948.

Poole, J. B. and Reed R.   "The Preparation of Leather and Parchment by the Dead Sea Scrolls Community." Technology and
Culture. 3 (1962).

Pollard, A. W. , (ed.).   Bibliographica. 3 v. London, 1895-97.
Papers on books, their history and art.

Pollard, Graham.   "Changes in the Style of Bookbinding." The
Library, June 1956.

---- "The Construction of English Twelfth-Century Bindings." The
Library, March 1962.

Pope, A. Upham (ed.).   A Survey of Persian Art. 6 vols. London, 1938-1939.   The best known account of Persian binding is
an article by E. Gratzl in Vol. III of this work.

Power, John.   Handy Book About Books, 1870.

Prideaux, S. T.   Bookbinders and Their Craft. London, 1903.

---- "Characteristics and Peculiarities of Roger Payne, Binder."
Magazine of Art, pp. 607-613, September 1898.

---- An Historical Sketch of Bookbinding. London, Lawrence &
Bullen, 1893.   Excellent bibliography of early French, German
and English sources.   He contends that marbled paper is of
Turkish origin.

Putnam, George Haven.   Books and Their Makers During the Middle Ages. 2 vols. New York, 1962.   A study of the production and distribution of literature from the fall of the Roman
Empire to the close of the 17th century.

Ramsden, Charles T.   Bookbinders of the United Kingdom Outside
London. London, Batsford, 1954.

---- French Bookbinders, 1789-1848.   Printed for the author by
Lund Humphries, 1950.

---- London Bookbinders, 1780-1840.   London, Batsford, 1956.

Rawlings, Gertrude Burford.   The Story of Books. New York,
Appleton, 1902.

Researches Concerning Jean Grolier, His Life and His Library...
Edited by Baron Roger Portalis.   Translated and revised by
Carolyn Shipman.   New York, The Grolier Club, 1907.   Cited

as "Shipman."

Rhein, Adolf. "Einband-Pressendruck vor Guttenberg." Archiv für Buchgewerbe und Gebrauchsgraphik, 73:283-286, 1936.

Rogers, Joseph V. 'The Rise of American Edition Binding." in Bookbinding in America. Hellmut Lehmann-Haupt 1941.

Rollins, Cary Purington. "A Survey of Contemporary Bookmaking." The Dolphin, no. 2, 1935, pp. 259-329.

Roquet, Antoine Ernest. Les Relieurs Francais (1500-1800). Biographic critique et anecdotique, précédée de l'histoire de la communauté des relieurs et doreurs de la ville de Paris et d'une étude sur les styles de reliure, par Ernest Thoinan (Pseud.) Paris, 1893.

Sachs. Eygentliche Beschenbung aller Stande auf Erden. Frankfort, 1568.

Sadleir, Michael. Evolution of Publishers' Binding Styles, 1770-1900. London, Constable, 1930.

Samford, C. Clement. The Bookbinder in Eighteenth-Century Williamsburg. Williamsburg, Colonial Williamsburg, 1964.

Sayce, R. Primitive Arts and Crafts. Cambridge, England, 1933. Articles on early paper making.

Schmieder, Eberhard and Kellner, Ernst. Schrift Und Buch. Leipzig, L. Staackman Verlag, 1939. A delightful illustrated treatise on books and printing. Knowledge of the language is not essential.

Stark, Lewis. "Branded Books from Mexico." New York Public Library Bulletin, August 1942.

Stedman, E.H. Bluegrass Craftsman. Lexington, Kentucky, 1959. Reminiscences of an early 19th-century paper maker.

Stevenson, J.H. 'The Fifteenth-century Scots Binding of the Haye Manuscript." Edinburgh Bibliographical Society, Journal, 6:77-82, 1901-1904.

Stonehouse, J.S. The Story of the Great Omar, 1933.

Storm, Colton and Peckham, Howard. Invitation to Book Collecting. New York, Bowker, 1947.

Streeter, Burnett Hillman. The Chained Library: A Survey of Four Centuries in the Evolution of the English Library. London,

MacMillan and Co. , 1931.

Subira, O.V. "Three Hundred Years of Paper in Spain." Wilmington, Del., The Paper Maker 34 (1965).

Sullivan, Sir Edward. The Book of Kells. London, Studio Publications 1942. The story of a medieval book.

Targ, William, (ed.). Bouillabaisse for Bibliophiles. Cleveland, The World Publishing Co. , 1955.

Taylor, Isaac. History of the Transmission of Ancient Books to Modern Times. Liverpool, Edward Howell, 1875.

Thoinan, E. Les Reliures Francais (1500-1800). Biographie Critique et Anecdotique, precedee del'Histoire de la Communaute... et d'une Etude sur les Styles de Reliure. Paris, Paul, Huard & Guillemin, 1893.

Thompson, Elbert A. , and L.S. Fine Binding in America. Urbana, Ill. , Beta Phi Mu, 1956.

Thompson, James Westfall. The Mediaeval Library.

Thompson, Lawrence S. Bibliopegia Fantastica. New York, New York Public Library, 1947. A description of many unusual and "freak" bindings on books. Contains many references to other articles on bookbinding curiosities.

Tooke, Mary A. "History of the Art of Bookbinding." The Art Journal. London, 1876.

---- "History of Bookbinding." American Bibliopolist. 2 :176, 220, 316.

Tschudin, W. Fr. "Oldest Methods of Paper Making in Far East." Chemical Abstracts. 53 (1959).

Tsien, Tsuen-hsuin. Written on Bamboo and Silk; the Beginning of Chinese Books and Inscriptions. Chicago, University of Chicago Press, 1962.

Tuer, A. History of the Horn Book. London, 1896.

Ure, Andrew. Dictionary of Arts, Manufactures and Mines. London, 1843.

Uzanne, O. L'Art dans la Decoration Extérieure des Livres en France. Paris, 1898.

---- La Reliure Moderne. Paris, 1887.

Valéry, Paul and others. Paul Bonet. Paris, Librairie Auguste

Bleizot, 1945.

Van Hoesen, Henry Bartlett. "History of Writing." Bibliography, Practical, Enumerative, Historical. New York, 1928, pp. 259-315.

Victoria and Albert Museum, London. A Picture Book of Bookbinding. Part 1: Before 1550; Part II: 1550-1800, London, 1933.

Voorn, H. "Papermaking in the Moslem World." Paper Maker, 28 (1959).

Weckbach, H. "On the History of Heilbronn Paper Mills." Papiergeschichte (Mainz) 15 (5-6):53-59, 1965.

Weeks, L.H. History of Paper Making in the United States, 1900-1916. New York, The Lockwood Trade Journal Co., 1916.

Welsh, Peter C. Tanning in the United States to 1850. Washington, Smithsonian Institution, 1964.

Westley and Clarke. "A Day at the Bookbinders." Penny Magazine, 1842 (Supplement).

Wheatley, Henry B. Bookbinding, Considered as a Fine Art. London, Mechanical Art and Manufacture, 1880.

---- "The History and Art of Bookbinding." Journal of the Society of Arts. 28:449-466, 1880.

---- Remarkable Bindings in the British Museum. 62 plates. London, 1889.

Wiemeler, Ignatz. "Bookbinding, Old and New." The Dolphin, 1933.

Wilson, D.M. "An Anglo-Saxon Binding at Fulda." (Codex Bonifalianus) Antiquarian Journal, July/October, 1901.

Wilson, R.N.P. Books and Their History. London, T.C. and E. C. Jach Ltd. (n.d.) Juvenile but excellently done.

Wroth, L.C., (ed.). A History of the Printed Book. Being the Third Number of the Dolphin. New York, The Limited Editions Club, 1938.

Bindings

Abbey, J.R. An Exhibition of Modern English and French Bindings from the Collection of J.R. Abbey. (Arts Council Catalogue.) London, 1949.

Adams, Charles M. "Illustrated Publishers' Bindings." Bulletin of the New York Public Library. 41:607-611, 1937.

Aga-Oghu, M. Persian Bookbindings in the 15th Century. Ann Arbor, Michigan, 1935.

An Exhibition of Hand Bookbinding, Casemaking, Restoration, Calligraphy and Illumination and Hand-decorated Paper. New York, The Guild of Bookworkers, 1959. Examples of fine bookbinding by some of today's professionals and amateurs.

Arts Council, An exhibition of modern English and French bindings from the collection of Major J.R. Abbey. Arts Council, 1949.

Barwich, F.G. A Book Bound for Mary, Queen of Scots: being a description of the binding of a copy of the Geographia of Ptolemy printed in Rome 1490, with notes on other books bearing Queen Mary's insignia. Bibliographical Society, 1901.

Blanc, Charles. "La Reliure." Gazette des Beaux Arts. October/November, 1880.

Bookbinding from the Library of Jean Grolier. Oxford, The Alden Press, 1965.

Bookbinding in Great Britain 16th to 20th Century. London, Maggs Brothers Ltd. (Catalog no. 893) 1964. Many photographs of fine bindings, identified as to time and binder. Illustrates changes in bookbinding style over the years.

Bosquet, E. La Reliure. Paris, 1894.

Bouchot, H. De la Reliure. Paris, 1891.

---- Les Reliures d'Art à la Bibliothèque Nationale. Paris, 1888.

Brassington, W. Salt. Historic Bindings at the Bodleian Library, Oxford. Reproductions and descriptions of 24 books. London, Sampson, Lowe, Marsten, 1892.

Briggs, Victor H. & Ernest L. Twentieth-century Cover Designs. Plymouth, Mass., 1902.

Brun, Robert. "Bindings." The Art of the French Book. P. Elak, 1947, pp. 141-164. A. Léjard, editor.

Catalogue of Ornamental Leather Bookbinding, Executed in America Prior to 1850. New York, Grolier Club.

Condit, C.W. American Binding Art. The Twentieth Century. New York, 1961. Quarto volume with 134 illustrations.

Contemporary Books, 1950. E.I. duPont de Nemours & Co., 1950.

Craig, Maurice. Irish Bookbindings 1600-1800. London, Cassell & Co., Ltd. 1954.

---- "Irish Parliamentary Bindings." The Book Collector, 2(1): 24-38, Spring 1953.

Cundall, J. "Ancient and Modern Bookbinding." Journal of the Franklin Institute, 45:211.

Davenport, Cyril. Beautiful Books. London, 1929.

---- Cameo Book-Stamps. 1911.

---- Cantor Lectures on Decorative Bookbinding. London, 1898.

---- Early London Bindings. London, The Queen, 1891.

----'Encyclopaedia Brit." Article on Bookbinding. London, 1902.

---- English Embroidered Bookbindings. 1899.

---- Royal English Bookbindings. New York, The MacMillan Co., 1896.

---- Royal English Bookbindings. London, Seeley and Co., Ltd., 1896.

Derome, L. La Reliure de Luxe. Paris, 1888.

De Ricci, Seymour. Signed Bindings in the Mortimer L. Schiff Collection. 4 vols. New York, Schiff, 1935. In Volume I-III (French Binding) and Vol. IV (English Binding) there are 315 plates and many reproductions of binders' tickets. 413 bindings in chronological order. 300 specimens of binders' stamps and binders' tickets.

De Bois, Henri Pène. American Bookbindings in the Library of Henry William Poor. Jamaica, N.Y., Marion Press, 1903.

Duff, E.G. "Early Stamped Bindings." in Prideaux's Historical Sketch of Bookbinding. London, 1893.

Fletcher, W.Y. English Bookbindings in the British Museum. London, Kegan Paul, 1895. 66 fine plates in gold and colors.

---- Foreign Bookbindings in the British Museum. London, 1896. Contains 65 colored plates of bindings, selected for their beauty and historical interest.

Fournier, Edouard. L'Art de la Reliure en France. Paris, Gay, 1864.

261

Gibson, Strickland. Early Oxford Bindings. Bibliographical Society Illustrated Monograph, No. 10. Oxford, 1903.

---- Some Notable Bodleian Bindings, 12th-18th Centuries. Oxford, 1904.

Gold-Tooled Bindings. Oxford University, Bodleian Library, 1951.

Goldschmidt, E. Ph. Gothic & Renaissance Bookbindings Exemplified and Illustrated from the Author's Collection. 1928. 2 v. 4to., with 115 plates, of which 4 are colored. Repr. 1967.

---- "Some Cuir-ciselé Bookbindings in English libraries." The Library, 4th series, 13(4):337-365, March 1933.

Guigard, J. Nouvel Armorial du Bibliophile. (2 vols.) Paris, 1890. A guide for the lover of heraldic bindings, with numerous facsimiles.

Guigard, J. and Brin, T. Exposition de la Société de la Reliure Originale, accompagnée d'une présentation de reliures ayant appartenu à Jean Grolier. Paris, Bibliotheque Nationale, 1959.

Harrison, Thomas. "Contemporary Bindings: a Commentary." The Penrose Annual, 44:71-74, 1950.

Harthan, John P. Bookbindings. (Victoria and Albert Museum) 2nd ed. London, Her Majesty's Stationery Office, John Wright and Sons.

Hayward, J. F. Silver Bindings from the J. R. Abbey Collection. 1955. With numerous illustrations of bindings.

Hobson, G. D. Bindings in Cambridge Libraries. Cambridge, 1929.

---- Thirty Bindings. London, The First Edition Club, 1926. Photographs and descriptions of thirty 15th-18th century European bindings selected from the First Edition Club's Seventh Exhibition.

Hoe, Robert. One Hundred and Seventy-Six Historic and Artistic Bookbindings. (2 vols.) New York, Dodd, Mead and Co., 1895. Etchings and lithographs of fine bindings dating from the 15th century.

Holmes, R. R. Specimens of Royal, Fine, and Historical Bookbinding Selected from the Royal Library, Windsor Castle. W. Griggs, 1893.

Holmes, Thomas James. "The Bookbindings of John Ratcliff and Edmund Ranger, Seventeenth-Century Boston Bookbinders." Proceedings of the American Antiquarian Society. 38:31-50, 1928.

Kyster, Ankar. Bookbindings in the Public Collections of Denmark. Vol. 1. Copenhagen, The Royal Library, 1938.

Land, William G. "Further Notes on Ratcliff and Ranger Bindings." Proceedings of the American Antiquarian Society. 39: 302-306, 1929.

Larson, S. and Kyster, A. Danish 18th-Century Bindings 1730-1780. Copenhagen, 1903. 102 plates of Danish bindings.

Mansfield, Edgar. Modern Design in Bookbinding. London, Peter Owen, 1966. Illustrations (with technical notes) of work by the foremost technical designer of fine bindings. Includes essay on the history of fine binding by the British Museum's Howard Nixon.

Masterpieces of French Modern Bindings. New York, Services Culturels Français, 1947.

Matthews, Brander. Bookbindings, Old and New. London, George Bell & Sons, 1896.

Matthews, William. Modern Bookbinding Practically Considered. New York, The Grolier Club, 1889. A lecture delivered before the Grolier Club, March 25, 1885.

Michel, Marius. La Reliure Française Commerciale et Industrielle depuis l'Invention de l'Imprimerie. Paris, 1881.

Michon, Louis-Marie. La Reliure Française. Paris, Larousse, 1951.

---- Les Reliures Mosaïquées du 18e siècle. Paris, Société de la Reliure Originale, 1956.

Mosaic Bookbindings. A Catalogue of an Exhibition. New York, The Grolier Club, (January 23-February 22, 1902) References on pp. 46-48.

Nixon, Howard M. The Broxbourne Library. London, 1957. 125 illustrations showing styles and designs of bookbinding from the 12th to the 20th century.

---- Broxbourne Library Styles and Designs of Bookbindings from the Twelfth to the Twentieth Century. 1956. 118 illustrations of bindings in the text, many full-page.

---- Royal English Bookbindings in the British Museum. London, 1957.

Oldham, J.B. English Blind Stamped Bindings. Cambridge University Press, 1952. The only satisfactory classification of these bindings.

263

---- Shrewsbury School Library Bindings. Oxford, 1943.

Oliver, E., and Hermal, G., and Roton, R. de. Manuel de l'Amateur de Reliure Armoriées Français. Paris, 1924-1938. Contains 2625 plates on French heraldic bindings.

Paton, Lucy A. Selective Bindings From the Gennadius Library. Cambridge, 1924.

Prideaux, S. T. An Historical Sketch of Bookbinding with a Chapter on "Early Stamped Bindings" by E. Gordon Duff. London, Lawrence & Bullen, 1893.

---- Modern Bookbindings, Their Design and Decoration. London, Constable, 1906. Modern English and French bindings.

---- "Some Scottish Bindings of the Last Century." Magazine of Art. January 1895, pp. 10-14.

Quaritch, Bernard. A Catalogue of Fifteen Hundred Books. Remarkable for the Beauty or Age of Their Bindings. London, Quaritch, 1839. Catalogs by booksellers such as Quaritch are excellent sources for illustrations of fine bindings. They are always carefully identified.

---- Facsimiles of Choice Examples of Historical and Artistic Bookbinding in the 15th and 16th Centuries. 103 plates printed in gold and colors. London, Quaritch, 1889. 4to.

Ramsden, C. T. French Bookbinders 1789-1848. London, 1950. Forty plates.

Richardson, H. S. Examples of Ancient Bookbindings. A portfolio of rubbings in the possession of the Art Library of South Kensington Museum. 1860.

Rolland, F. H. Exposicion de Encuadernaciones Espanolas Siglos XXI al XIX. 61 reproductions of bindings, some in color; illustrations in the text, Madrid, 1934.

Rye, Reginald Arthur, et al. Historical and Armorial Bookbindings. Exhibited in the University Library; Descriptive Catalogue. University of London, 1937.

Sarre, F. Islamic Bookbindings. London, Kegan Paul, 1923.

Schjoldager, A. Bokbind ag Bokbindere I Norge inntil 1850. Oslo, 1927. Norwegian bookbinding.

Schmidt, A. Bucheinbände aus dem XIV-XIX. Jahrhundert in der Landesbibliothek zu Darmstadt. Leipzig, 1921. The author pays particular attention to German 16th-century bookbindings.

Sjogren, Arthur. Svenska Kunkliga och furstliga Bokagaremarken.
Stockholm, 1915. Many plates of Swedish Royal bindings.

Techner, J.J. Reliures. Paris, 1861. (Accompagnée de Planches
à l'eau-forte par Jules Jacquemart - Folio).

Thoinan, E. Les Relieurs Francais, 1500-1800. Paris, 1893.

Thomas, Henry (Sir). Early Spanish Bookbindings. London, The
Bibliographical Society, 1939. Devoted to the 11th to 14th-
century Madejar bindings decorated in blind.

Toldo, Vittorio de. L'art Italien de la Reliure du Livre. Milan,
1924. Thirty-seven illustrations of the development of binding
styles in Italy from the 15th to 20th century.

Tuckett, C., Jr. Specimens of Ancient and Modern Bookbinding.
London, 1846. 4to. Eight plates selected chiefly from the Library of the British Museum.

Weale, W.H.J. Bookbindings and Rubbings of Bindings in the National Art Library, South Kensington. London, 1894-1898. 2 v.

---- "English Bookbinding in the Reign of Henry VII and Henry VIII."
Journal of the Royal Society of Arts. 37(1893):309-317, March
1, 1889.

Weber, Carl. A Thousand and One Fore-edge Paintings. Water-
ville, Me., Colby College Press, 1949.

Weill-Quillardet, Pierre-André and Lucie. Exhibition of Contemporary French Bookbindings and Illustrations. London, Ambassade
de France, 1956.

MATERIAL

General

Barrow, W.J. "New Device Tests Performance of Library Bindings." Book Production, March 1964, pp. 60-62.

---- Permanence/Durability of the Book. Richmond, W.J. Barrow
Research Laboratory, 1963.

Coleman, D.G. Woodworking Factbook. New York, Robert Speller,
1966. A handbook of basic information on wood.

Employing Bookbinders of America. Research Division. Special
bulletins on glue, book cloth, pyroxlin-treated fabrics, imitation gold leaf. New York, 1933.

Encyclopaedia Brittanica.

265

Encyclopedia, Americana.

Gallo, F. "Experimental research on resistance to biological agents of materials used in book restoration. Part 5. " Istituto di Patologia del Libro Bolletino 24(1-4):95-105, 1965. Tests on plastic films and discussion of their properties. (abstracted in Art and Archeology Technical Abstracts 6(2): 1966).

Grant, Julius. Books and Documents: Dating, Permanence and Preservation. London, Grafton & Co. , 1937.

Greathouse, A. G. and Wessel, C. J. Deterioration of Materials. New York, Reinhold Publishing Corporation, 1954.

Groome, G. T. Bookbinding Materials. Washington, D. C. , U. S. Government Printing Office.

Henley, N. W. Henley's Twentieth Century Book of Formulas, Processes and Trade Secrets. New York, N. W. Henley, 1946.

Huber, L. R. "Materials and Methods in Book Finishing and Repairing. " American Library Association Bulletin, 49, 1955. pp. 326-30. An appraisal of newer materials developed for the repair of books, such as pressure-sensitive tapes, adhesive cloths, plastic tapes and the like, which reports properties the more conservative will perhaps question.

Lamb, C. M. , (ed.). The Calligrapher's Handbook. London, Faber & Faber Ltd. Articles on pigment, ink, skins, gilding, binding of manuscripts, binding.

Library Handbook of Genuine Trade Secrets and Instructions, The. London, Foyles, 1923.

Nikitin, N. I. The Chemistry of Cellulose and Wood. New York, Davey, 1966. Translated from the Russian.

Nitz, H. Die Materialien für Buch und Bucheinband. 2nd ed. Halle, Wilhelm Knapp, 1950.

Scriven, Margaret. "Preservation and Restoration of Library Materials. " Special Libraries, 47:439-448, December 1956. Includes list of materials used in preservation and restoration.

Taylor, Isaac. History of the Transmission of Ancient Books to Modern Times. Liverpool, Edward Howell, 1875. Chapter on materials of ancient books.

"Trial Data on Painting Materials. " Technical Studies in the Field of the Fine Arts. Cambridge, Fogg Museum (vol V:1, VI:2, VI:3, VII:4, VIII:1, IX:4). Includes lengthy description of solvents, inks, colors and other materials used in conservation.

Exotics

Anna, Sister M., O.S.F. "Bark Cloth Making Among the Baganda
of East Africa," Primitive Man. Washington, D.C., 9(1), 1936.

Boynton, R.S. Chemistry and Technology of Lime and Limestone.
New York, Interscience, 1966.

Brady, G.S. Materials Handbook. New York, 1937. General information on stone.

Brigham, W.T. "Ka Hana Kapa; the Making of Bark-cloth in Hawaii." Bernice P. Bishop Museum, Memoirs. Honolulu, 1911.
v. 3.

Bühler, A. and Naumann, W. "Bark Fabrics of the South Seas."
CIBA Review. Basle, 33:1166-1203, 1940.

Chhabra, Bahadur Chand. "Seals of Ancient India." Indian Archives
14:36-49, Jan. 1961/Dec. 1962.

Ebers, Georg, "The Papyrus Plant." Cosmopolitan. XV:677-682,
1893.

Filliozat, J. "Manuscripts on Birch Bark and their Preservation."
Indian Archives 1, 1947.

Hunt, G.M. "The Behavior of Wood." Research 11, 1953.

Imberdis, Le P. and Jean, S.J. Papyrus, sive Ars Conficiendae,
Papyri... Le Papier, ou l'Art de Fabriquer le Papier. Traduction par Augustin Blanchet, Paris, C. Beranger, 1899.

Lucas, Alfred. Ancient Egyptian Materials and Industries. 3rd ed.
rev. London, Edward Arnold & Co., 1948.

Mitraux, Alfred. "Bark Cloth" in J. Steward (ed.) Handbook of
South American Indians. 5:67-68, 1949.

"Papyrus." The Encyclopaedia Britannica. Vol. XX.

Pliny, Natural History. vol. XIII Lib. II. Description of papyrus.

Raven, H.C. "Bark Cloth Making in the Central Celebes." Natural
History Magazine, vol. XXXIII, 1932.

Tachudin, Peter. "Papyrus." The Paper Maker. Wilmington,
Del, 1965. No. 1, pp. 3-15. illus.

Theophrastus. Inquiry Into Plants. Cambridge, Mass., Loeb Classical Library (n.d.). The earliest accurate description of
papyrus.

Leather

Bowker, Roy Clement and Geib, M.N.V. Comparative Durability of Chrome and Vegetable Tanned Leather. Washington, D.C., Government Printing Office, 1925. 1 p. 1. 267-286. U.S. Bureau of Standards, Technological paper no. 286.

Chivers, C. The Relative Value of Leathers and Other Binding Materials. Bath, Chivers Ltd., 1911. Pamphlet, illustrated by diagrams and microphotographs.

Cockerell, Douglas. "Leather for Bookbinding." Journal of the Society of Arts. London, 48:401-407, 1900.

Cobham, The Rt. Hon. Viscount, and Wood, Sir Henry Trueman. Leather for Bookbinding, Report of the Committee on. London, George Bell & Sons, 1905. Eleven plates, diagrams, leather samples, index.

Davenport, Cyril. "Leather as Used in Bookbinding." The Library, vol. X, 1898.

Davis, Charles Thomas. The Manufacture of Leather. Philadelphia, 1885.

Davy, Humphry. The Collected Works of Sir Humphry Davy. Edit. John Davy. Vol. 2. London, 1839. Sections describe leather.

Dussance, H. A New and Complete Treatise on the Arts of Tanning, Currying and Leather-dressing. Philadelphia, 1865.

Fiske, R.E. "Bookbinding Leather." Harvard Library Notes. March 1940. Reports on a series of leather tests. Also a bibliography of articles on leather in the 1920's and 1930's.

Frey, R.W. "Comparative Permanence of Chrome and Vegetable Leathers." Journal of American Leather Chemists Association. 29:489-511, 1934.

Gansser, A. "The Early History of Tanning." Ciba Review 81: 2938-2962, August 1950.

Green, G.H. "Leather Science: Some Recent Developments." Research. London, 11, 1958.

Hannigan, M.V., et al. "Evaluation of the Relative Serviceability of Vegetable and Chrome Tanned Leather for Bookbinding." Journal American Leather Chemists Assoc., 60(9), 1965.

Hide and Leathers Blue Book. Chicago, 1906, 1936, 1937.

Houghton, George C. "Leather, Tanned, Curried and Finished."

In part 3, "Special Report on Selected Industries," in vol. 9 of Twelfth Census of the United States (1900) Washington, 1902.

Howes, F.N. Vegetable Tanning Materials. London, Butterworth, 1953.

Hulme, E., Wyndham, E., et al. Leather for Libraries. By E. W. Hulme, J.G. Parker, A. Seymour-Jones, C. Davenport and F.J. Williamson. London, The Sound Leather Committee of the Library Association, 1905. Samples of leather on inside of covers.

Julia de Fontenelle, J.S.E., and Malepeyre, F. The Arts of Tanning, Currying and Leather Dressing. Edit. and transl. by Campbell Morfitt, Philadelphia, 1852.

Kantrowitz, M. and Groome, G. Bookbinding Leather. Washington Government Printing Office (1948). (G.P.O-P.I.A. Joint Research Bulletin, bindery series, no. 5) Pam.

Kennedy, David H., The Art of Tanning Leather. New York, 1857.

Lalande, Jérôme Le Francais de, "Art du Tanneur." Descriptions des arts et metiers. Vol. 38. Paris, Academie des Sciences, 1764.

"Leather for Bookbinding." Library Association Record. London, 1900. Vol. 2, p. 250-253.

"Leather for Libraries." Library Association Record. London, 1905.

MacBride, David. "Instructions to Tanners." Philosophical Transactions of the Royal Society of London. Vol. 68, part 1, pp. 111-130, 1778.

Martin, Thomas. The Circle of the Mechanical Arts. London, 1813.

McCloy, Shelby T. French Inventions of the Eighteenth Century. Lexington, Ky, 1952.

Mitton, R.G., Turner J.N. "A Study of Mould Growth on Chrome Tanned Leather and the Associated Changes in Physical Properties." J. Soc. Leather Chem., 39:343-358, 1955.

Modern American Tanning. 2 vols. Chicago, 1902-1910.

O'Flaherty, F., et al. The Chemistry and Technology of Leather. New York, Reinhold, 1965. 4 vols.

---- "Leather and Its Care." Leather Manufacturer. 71, No. 3, 1954.

Page, R.O. "The Mechanism of Vegetable Tanning." Journal Society Leather Trade Chemists. 37, 1953.

Parker, James Gordon. "Leather." The Encyclopaedia Britannica. 11th ed. vol. XVI.

Parker, J. Gordon. "Leather for Bookbinding." Soc. of Arts Journal. London, 50:25-35, 1902. Details on the 1901 Committee Report.

Phillips, H. "The Chemistry of Leather." Journal of the Royal Society of Arts. 102(4934):824-875, September 17, 1954.

Poole, J.B. and Reed, R. "The Preparation of Leather and Parchment by the Dead Sea Scrolls Community." Technol. and Cult. 3(1):1-26, 1962.

Proctor, Henry R. The Making of Leather. Cambridge, University Press. New York, Putnam's, 1914. 153 pp. illustrated and indexed.

Progress in Leather Science 1920-1945. London, British Leather Manufacturer's Research Association, 1946.

The Romance of Leather. New York, Tanners' Council of America. 1937.

"Report of the Committee on Leather for Bookbinding." London, Society of Arts Journal, v. 49, 1901. This is the study that pinpointed acid as the cause of deteriorated leather.

"Royal Society of Arts, London, and the Worshipful Company of Leathersellers. Report of the Committee on Leather for Bookbinding." London, Society of Arts, 1905. 5 p. 1, 120 pp.

Vallancey, Charles (transl.). The Art of Tanning and Currying Leather. From the French of M. de Lalande and others. Dublin, 1773.

Veitch, F.P., et al. "Polluted Atmosphere a Factor in the Deterioration of Bookbinding Leather." Journal of American Leather Chemists Association. v. 21, 1926. Describes tests demonstrating the effect of sulphur dioxide on leather.

Ward, A.G. "Tanning in the United States to 1850." Nature, London, 206(4988):991-992, 1965.

Warner, John. "Modern Bookbinding Leathers." Library Association Record. London n.s. 7:153-164, 1929. Bibliography p. 163. Notes by W.D. John, p. 163-164.

Waterer, John William. "Leather." A History of Technology. v. 2 edit. by Charles Singer and others. London, 1956.

---- Leather and Craftsmanship. London, Faber and Faber Ltd.,
1950.

---- Leather in Life, Art and Industry. London, Faber and Faber,
1943.

Welsh, Peter C. Tanning in the United States to 1850. Washington,
Smithsonian Institution, 1964. Excellent descriptions of vegetable tanning processes that produced durable leather. Lengthy
bibliography.

Wilson, J. A. The Chemistry of Leather Manufacture. New York,
The Chemical Catalog Co., Inc., 1928. Highly technical treatise. Lengthy bibliographies after each chapter.

Parchment and Vellum

Fahey, Herbert and Peter. Parchment and Vellum. San Francisco,
1940.

"Parchment." American Archivist. 1:5,14,16,52,60,73 3:212 16:
119.

Ryder, Michael L. "Parchment--Its History, Manufacture and Composition." Society of Archivists, Journal. 2:391-399, April
1964. Abstract in American Archivist 28:117, January 1965.

Saxl, Hedwig. "Histology of Parchment." Technical Studies in the
Field of Fine Arts. v. 8, no. 1, 1939.

Thompson, D. J. "The DeClarea of the so-called Anonymous Be-
rensis." Technical Studies 1(1 & 2), 1932.

Thompson, Edward M. Sir. "Parchment and Vellum." Encyclopaedia Britannica, 1945.

Paper

A Handy Guide to Papermaking. Translated by Charles E. Hamilton, after the Japanese edition of 1798. Berkeley, The Book
Arts Club, 1948.

Alibaux, Henri. Les Premières Papeteries Françaises. Paris,
1926.

Alley, Harold R. "Japanese Handmade Paper Industry." Paper
Ind. 33:932-933, 1951. C.A. 46, 1952. Brief, well-illustrated
article dealing with establishments in the Ogawa region.

American Paper and Pulp Association. The Dictionary of Paper Including Pulps, Paper Boards, Paper Properties and Related

Papermaking Terms. 3rd ed. New York, 1965.

Armitage, F.D. Atlas of Paper Making Fibers. Epsom, England, Guildhall Publishing Co. Contains photomicrographs of fibers.

Baker, W.E.B. "Relationship of Impurities to Paper Permanence." Paper Trade Journal, 91(4):51-52, 1930.

Balston, T. James Whatman Father and Son. London, Methuen & Co., Ltd., 1957. Appendices contain much information on Whatman watermarks.

---- William Balston Paper Maker. London, Methuen, 1954. Considerable technical information on Turkey Mill paper.

Barker, E.F. "Swiss Mill Produces Paper Containing Substantial Quantities of Nylon." Paper Trade Journal 145(7):48-51, 1961.

Barrow, W.J. "Establishing Least Squares Regression Lines for Data of Aged Paper." Tappi 45(9):209A-210A, 1962. Two figures and bibliography.

---- The Manufacture and Testing of Durable Book Papers. Richmond, Virginia State Library, 1960.

---- Permanence-Durability of the Book-II. Test Data of Naturally Aged Paper. Richmond, W.S. Barrow Research Laboratory, 1964.

---- Permanent/Durable Book Paper. Richmond, Virginia State Library, 1960.

---- Physical Strength of Non-Fiction Book Papers, 1900-1949. Richmond, W.J. Barrow Research Laboratory, 1957.

Barrow, W.J. and Sproull, R.C. "Permanence in Book Paper." Science v. 129, April, 1959.

Blanchet, A. Essai sur l'Histoire du Papier. Paris, E. Leroux, 1900.

Blum, André. Les Origines du Papier, de l'Imprimerie et de la Gravure. Paris, 1935.

---- On the Origin of Paper. Translated from the French by Harry Miller Lydenberg, New York, 1934. Seventy-nine pages of which three or four are devoted to Asiatic paper. New York, R.R. Bowker Co., 1934.

Bojesen, C.C. and Alley, Rewi. "China's Rural Paper Industry." The China Journal. Vol. XXVIII, No. 5. Shanghai, China, May 1938. Eleven pages text, 33 illustrations.

272

Boxshus, J.P., et al. "Permanence of Paper." Tappi, 37 (Oct. 1954). Rag vs. wood pulp paper.

Britt, K.W., (ed.). Handbook of Pulp and Paper Technology. New York, Reinhold Publishing Co., 1964.

Burton, John O. Permanence Studies of Current Commercial Book Papers. Washington, D.C., Government Printing Office, 1931. U.S. National Bureau of Standards, "Research Paper," no. 349.

Buyn, K.E.C. "Paper Permanence." Bulletin Associated Tech. Ind. Pap. 5:231-238, 1951; C.A., 45, 1951.

Byrne, J. and Weiner, J. Permanence. Appleton, Wis., Institute of Paper Chemistry, 1965, 165 pp.

Calkin, J.B. Modern Pulp and Paper Making. New York, Reinhold Publishing Corp., 1957.

Chaudhary, Yadovrao S. Handmade Paper In India. Lucknow, India, J.S. Kumarappa on behalf of A.I.V.I.A., April 10, 1936. Eight pages text on paper making in India.

Church, Randolph W., (ed.). The Manufacture and Testing of Durable Book Papers. Richmond, The Virginia State Library, 1960. Based on the investigations of W.J. Barrow.

Clapp, Verner W. "Permanent/Durable Book Papers." ALA Bulletin, 57:847-852, October 1963.

Clapperton, George. Practical Papermaking. London, 1894. Now outdated but a good source of information on paper technology at the end of the 19th century.

Clapperton, R.H. Paper. Oxford, Shakespeare Head Press, 1934. An historical account of its making by hand from the earliest times down to the present day. Includes a facsimile reproduction of text and illustrations of Kamisuki Chohoki (a handy guide for paper makers) published in Japan in 1798. Illus. Plates.

---- Paper and its Relationship to Books. London, London School of Printing, 1935. The fourth of the J.M. Dent Memorial Lectures given at the London School of Printing, October 26, 1934.

Clappertorn, R.H. and Henderson, W. Modern Papermaking. London, Blackwell, 1952.

Corte, H. "Fundamental Properties of Paper." School Science Review. London, 47(162):331-344, 1966.

Crane, Ellery B. Early Paper Mills in Massachusetts, Especially Worcester County. Worcester, Mass., 1887.

Curwen Press. Specimen Book of Pattern Papers. London, 1928. Contains actual specimens of binding papers used in edition binding by this firm.

Dawe, Edward A. Paper and Its Uses, a Treatise for Printers, Stationers and Others. 160 pages, 26 illustrations, 34 specimens. London, 1914.

Dunbar, J. Notes on the Manufacture of Wood Pulp Papers. Leith, 1892.

Durability of Paper, The. London, Library Association, 1930. Report of a special committee. The cover is printed on a Grade 1-a stock, as specified in the report; the title-page and the postscript on a Grade 1-b; the text on a Grade 2 stock.

Dureau De La Malle, D. J.C. A. Le Papyrus et Fabrication du Papier Chez les Anciens. Paris, 1851.

Emerson, H.W. Monograph on Papermaking and Papier-mâché in the Punjab. Lahore, India, 1908.

Erfurt, Julius. The Dyeing of Paper Pulp. Translated from the German by Julius Hübner. London, 1901. 157 specimens of colored papers.

Evans, L. Ancient Paper Making. London, 1896.

Fairbanks, Thomas Nast. "A Generalization of the Manufacture of Paper, Modern Papermaking in Japan." Fifteen illustrations. Printed in The Dolphin, II:120-130, New York, 1935.

Fiber Identification. Identification of Wood and Fibers. (Tappi T8 SM61) New York, Technical Association of the Pulp and Paper Industry.

Fisher, L. E. The Papermakers. New York, Franklin Watts, Inc. 1965. An introduction to the craft, written for children. Excellent illustrations and clear, concise text.

Fox, C. J. J. "Paper." Encyclopaedia Britannica. 1945 ed.

Franklin, Benjamin. "Description of the Process to be Observed in Making Large Sheets of Paper in the Chinese Manner, with One Smooth Surface." (Read by Dr. Franklin, June 20, 1788.) Transactions of the American Philosophical Society. Vol. III, Philadelphia, 1793.

Gee, W. H. Monograph on Fibrous Manufactures in the Punjab. Lahore, India, 1891.

Goodwin, Rutherford. The William Parks Paper Mill at Williamsburg. (Read before the Bibliographical Society of America,

June 23, 1937.) Lexington, Va., 1939. Illustrated

Goto, S. Japanese Paper and Papermaking. Tokyo, 1958-60. Vol. I Northeastern Japan; Vol. II Western Japan.

Grand Carteret, J. Papeterie et Papetiers de l'Ancien Temps. Paris, 1913. Many illustrations.

Green, J. Barcham. Notes on the Manufacture of Handmade Paper. London, The London School of Printing (and Graphic Arts), 1936. A brief, well illustrated (drawings) monograph on making paper by hand as it is still practiced in England.

Griffin, R. B. and Little, A. D. The Chemistry of Paper Making. New York, 1894.

Hagen, Victor Wolfgang von. The Aztec and Maya Papermakers. New York, J. J. Augustin, 1944. 120 pp. 39 plates.

Halfer, Joseph. The Progress of the Marbling Art from Technical Scientific Principles. Translated by Herman Dieck. Buffalo, N.Y., 1893. 35 specimens of marbled papers.

Hanson, Fred S. "Resistance of Paper to Natural Aging." Paper World. February, 1939, pp. 1157-63.

Harpham, J. A., Reid, A. R., and Turner, H. W. "A New Cotton Fiber Pulp for Fine Papermaking." Tappi, 41:758-763, December, 1958.

Herring, Richard. Paper and Papermaking, Ancient and Modern. London, Longman, Brown, Green and Longmans, 1855. Four illustrations, 25 specimens. A good account of early 19th-century paper making by machine.

Higham, Robert R. A. A Handbook of Papermaking. London, Oxford University Press, 1963. An excellent handbook of practical information on the science and technology of paper making.

Hoernle, A. F. R. "Who Was the Inventor of Rag Paper?" Royal Asiatic Society Journal, October 1903.

Hofmann, Carl. A Practical Treatise on the Manufacture of Paper. Philadelphia, Henry Carey Baird Co., 1873. Paper making as it was known and practiced in the latter half of the 19th century.

Hunter, Dard. A Papermaking Pilgrimage to Japan, Korea and China. New York, 1936. Sixty-nine illustrations and 50 specimens.

---- Chinese Ceremonial Paper. Chillicothe, Ohio, 1937. Fifteen illustrations and 47 specimens.

---- "Fifteenth Century Papermaking." Ars Typographica. 3(1): 37-51, July, 1926.

---- "Hand-made Paper and Its Relation to Modern Printing." The Dolphin. No. 1. New York, Limited Editions Club, 1933.

---- "Laid and Wove." Smithsonian Institution Annual Report for 1921. Washington, D.C., 1922. pp. 587-593.

---- Old Papermaking. Chillicothe, Ohio, 1923. One hundred fourteen illustrations.

---- Old Papermaking in China and Japan. Chillicothe, Ohio, 1932. Thirty-six illustrations and 19 specimens.

---- Papermaking by Hand in India. New York, 1939. Eighty-four illustrations and 27 specimens.

---- Papermaking in Indo-China. Chillicothe, Ohio, Mountain House Press, 1947. Two mounted samples. Limited edition of 250 copies.

---- Papermaking in Pioneer America. Philadelphia, Pa., University of Pennsylvania Press, 1952.

---- Papermaking in Southern Siam. Chillicothe, Ohio, 1936. Eighteen illustrations and 4 specimens.

---- Papermaking, The History and Technique of an Ancient Craft. New York, Alfred A. Knopf, 1943. Revised and enlarged 1947. The best book on the subject. Fine bibliography. Contains all a librarian needs to know about paper.

---- Papermaking Through Eighteen Centuries. New York, W.E. Rudge, 1930. This is a more comprehensive treatment of the material in the author's Old Papermaking (1923). Excellent information on early paper; early papermakers and their products. Good introduction to the study of watermarks.

Imberdis, Jean. Papyrus, Sive Ars Conficiendae Papyri ... Le Papier, ou l'Art de Fabriquer le Papier. Traduction par Augustin Blanchet. Paris, C. Beranger, 1899.

Imberdis, J. Papyrus or the Craft of Paper. Holland, Hilversum, 1952.

Ingpen, Roger. "Decorated Papers." The Fleuron. No. 2 London, Office of the Fleuron, 1924. Paper samples.

Jarrell, T.D. "Effect of Atmospheric Humidity on the Moisture Content of Paper." Paper Trade Journal, 85(3):47-51, 1927. Illustrated.

Jarrell, T.D., Hankins, J.M., and Veitch, F.P. Deterioration of Book and Record Papers. U.S. Dept. of Agr., Tech. Bull. No. 541, 1936.

Jennett, Sean. "Endpapers." The Making of Books. 2nd ed. Faber, 1956. Chap. 20, pp. 406-10.

Jugaku, Bunshō. Hand Made Paper of Japan. Tokyo, Tourist Library, 1942. This is an earlier version of the author's 1959 book.

---- Paper Making by Hand in Japan. Tokyo, Meiji-Shobu Ltd. 1959. Current methods; bound-in samples; well illustrated; early history; bibliography of literature 1600 A.D. to present.

---- Washi-Danso. (Symposium on Japanese Handmade Paper.) Kyōto, Japan, 1936. Only vol. 1 published. Two illustrations, 20 specimens.

(Kamisuki Chohoki). Hand-made Papers on Japan. Tokyo, IIS Crafts, 1963. This catalog of paper samples contains an abridged reproduction (with English translation) of the 1798 illustrated classic Kamisuki Chôhôki (Handbook of paper making).

Kantrowitz, M. and Spencer, E.W. The Process of Marbling Paper. Washington, U.S. Government Printing Office, 1953. History plus good technical instructions and a lengthy bibliography by Dard Hunter.

Karabacek, Josef V. Das Arabische Papier. Vienna, 1887.

Kato, H. "Studies on Japanese Paper." Kami-pa Gikyoshi, 16, October 1962, pp. 835-847. In Japanese with English summaries. Environ. Eff. Mater. Equip. Abstr. 4(1):48, January, 1964, PDL-50180. 14. Chemical changes in Japanese paper by exposure. 15. Physical changes in Japanese paper by exposure.

Kay, J. Paper. London, 1893.

Keppel, R.A., et al. "Paper from Inorganic Fibers." Industrial Engineering Chemistry. 1, 1962.

Khaddari, Munnalal. Handmade Paper Industry of India. (in Hindustani). Kalpi, U.P., India, 1937. Textbook of the Kalpi Handmade Paper School.

Khoodke, S.B. Handmade Paper, All India Village Industries Association. Wardha, India, 1936. Indian papermaking as practiced in the Mohandas K. Gandhi School of Papermaking, Wardha. Cover printed on Indian paper.

Kozulina, O.U., and Barysnikova, Z.P. "Biological Resistance of Paper to Insect Attacks." Moscow, Stareniye bumagi, 68-74

1965. (Abstracted in Art and Archaeology Technical Abstracts, 6(2), 1966.)

Kimberly, Arthur E. and Emley, Adelaide L. A Study of the Deterioration of Book Papers in Libraries. Bureau of Standards Miscellaneous Publication No. 140. Washington, 1933.

Kiyofusa, N. Japanese Paper Making. Tokyo, 1954.

Kôgei (Crafts). Articles on Japanese Handmade Papers by Naoyuki Ohta, Kazu Makamura, Muneyoshi Yanagi, Bunsho Jugaku, Naokatsu Nakamura, T. Iwai, and Dr. Torajiro Naitô. Fourteen illustrations and 18 specimens. Published by Nippon Mingei Kyokwai, Tokyo, April 15, 8th Year of Showa.

Kunihigashi, Jihyoe (or Kunisaki, Jihei). Kamisuki Chôhô-Ki. (Papermakers' Treasury). Osaka, Japan, 1798. The oldest book in the Japanese language devoted to papermaking. Woodblocks by Tôkei Niwa. Reprinted in part in IIS Crafts Catalog (Tokyo 1963), and in full in color by Parkes, H.S. (1871) and Clapperton, R.H. (1934).

Kunisaki, Jihei. A Handy Guide to Papermaking. Berkeley, The Books Arts Club, University of California, 1948. After the Japanese edition of Kamisuki Chôhôki of 1798 with a translation by Charles E. Hamilton. Illustrated.

Labarre, E.J. Dictionary and Encyclopedia of Paper and Paper Making. Amsterdam, Swels and Zeitlinger, 1952. A technical reference of great importance. Contains a ten-page bibliography on paper and is indexed in English, French, German, Dutch, Italian, Spanish and Swedish.

Langwell, W.H. "Permanence of Papers." Tech. Bull. 29(2), 1952, Tech. Sec. of the British Paper & Board Makers' Assoc.

---- "The Permanence of Paper." Tech. Bull. Tech. Sec. Brit. Paper and Board Makers' Assoc. 30(6):170, December 1953.

---- "The Permanence of Paper in Temperate Climates." Tappi 38(9), September 1955.

---- "The Permanence of Paper Records." Library Association Record. 55:212-215, 1953.

Latour, A. and Schaefer, G. "Paper." CIBA Review No. 72. Basle, 1949, pp. 2630-2656.

Laufer, Berthold. Paper and Printing in Ancient China. Chicago, The Caxton Club, 1931.

Launer, Herbert F. Determination of the pH Value of Papers. Washington, National Bureau of Standards, 1939. Research Paper RP1205.

Launer, Herbert F., and Wilson, William K. "The Photo-chemical Stability of Papers." Paper Trade Journal, 116:28-36, February 25, 1945.

Le Clert, L. Le Papier. 2 vols. Paris, 1926. Colored frontpiece and many other plates and facsimiles. The finest work on the history and manufacture of paper in France.

Lenz, Hans. Mexican Indian Paper; Its History and Survival. Mexico, 1961. Translated from the Spanish by H. M. Campbell.

Lloyd, E. "Account of a Sort of Paper Made of Linum Asbestinum Found in Wales." Phil. Trans., Abr. III, p. 105. 1684.

Loring, Rosamond B. Decorated Book Paper. Cambridge, Harvard University Press, 1942. A classic description of all types of decorated paper with appendices of instructions for making these papers in the traditional manner. Illustrated with actual examples.

--- Decorated Book Papers. Cambridge, Harvard University Press, 1952. An excellent reprint of 1942 edition with additional biographical material by Walter Muir Whitehill, Dard Hunter and Veronica Ruzicka. Lacks the tipped-in samples of papers that are in the original edition.

---- Marbled Papers. An address delivered before the members of the Club of Odd Volumes, November 16, 1932. Twelve specimens of marbled and paste papers. Boston, 1933.

"Machine-Finish End Paper." Proposal for Furnishing Paper for the Public Printing and Binding, Beginning November 1, 1960. Washington, Government Printing Office, 1960. U.S. Congress Joint Committee on Printing.

Manufacture of Pulp and Paper, The. Prepared under the direction of the Joint Textbook Committee of Paper Industry of the United States and Canada. Third edition, Vol. V. New York, McGraw-Hill Book Co., 1939.

Manufacture and Testing of Durable Book Papers, The. Conducted by W. J. Barrow. Edited by Randolph W. Church, Richmond, 1960. Virginia State Library Publications, No. 13.

Means, P. A. Ancient American Paper Making. Reprinted from Isis, 35(99), pt. 1, 1944.

Monumenta Chartae Papyraceae Historiam Illustrantia; or collection of documents illustrating the history of paper. Helversum, Holland, Paper Publications Society, 1950-65. Vol. I-V-Watermarks; Vol. VI-English Papermills; Vol. VII-Ancient Basle Papermills; Vol. VIII-Austro-Hungarian Mills; Vol. IX-Paper Mills of Berne; Vol. XI-Tromanin's Watermark Album.

279

Moss, L.A. "Rag Stock vs. Wood Pulp." Paper and Paper Products 81, 8, August 1940; BIPC 11, 25.

Munsell, Joel. A Chronology of Paper and Paper-Making. Albany, J. Munsell, 1857. An excellent capsule review of the crafts of papyrus, parchment and paper making from 670 B.C. to the middle of the 19th century.

Murdock, H.R. "Tsuso-rice Paper." Paper Trade Journal. 136, February, 1953. A description of "rice paper," which is neither paper nor produced from rice.

Narita, Kiyofusa. Japanese Papermaking. Tokyo, Hokuseido Press, 1954. A concise account of history and technique of Japanese papermaking, intended for tourist information but of value in lieu of earlier but now out of print books on the subject.

---- "Sumi-nagashi." Paper Maker (U.S.) 24 (1955). History and production of a "marbled" type paper.

Nikitin, N.I. The Chemistry of Cellulose and Wood. New York, Davey, 1966.

Nyuksha, Y.P. "Changes in the Chemical and Mechanical Qualities of Paper Contaminated by Gimnoascus Setosus." Microbiology (Moscow) 29(2):276-80, 1960.

---- "Microscopic Study of Paper Stained by the Fungus Gimnoascus Setosus." Microbiology (Moscow) 29(I):133-136, 1960.

Okamura, S., and Inagaki, H. "Papylon-Synthetic Papers." Paper Making 136(5):74, 1958.

Page, D.H., et al. The Structure and Physical Properties of Paper. London, British Paper and Board Research Association, 1960.

"Paper." American Archivist. 3:102 18:92.

"Paper, Chemistry." American Archivist. 12:9.

"Paper, Dictionary of." American Archivist. 10:18.

"Paper, Marbled." American Archivist. 1:15.

"Paper, Rag." American Archivist. 1:3 12:9.

"Paper, Wood Pulp." American Archivist. 12:9.

Parkes, Harry S. Report on the Manufacture of Paper in Japan. London, 1871. Includes facsimile reproduction of Kamisuki Chôhôki (Handbook of paper making) Osaka, 1798.

Parley, Norman. "Enduring Paper." The Book-collector's Quarterly. London, 1931. no. 3, p. 29-38.

Pearson, R.S. The Indian Forest Records. Calcutta, India, 1916. Notes on the utilization of bamboo for the manufacture of paper-pulp. Two illustrations and folding map.

Peach, Geoffry. Hand Decorated Pattern Papers for Bookcraft. London, Dryad Press, 1931. A guide to the various methods of decorating paper.

Pizzetta, Jules. Historia de un Plfego de Papel. Madrid, Biblioteca Cientifica Recreativa (Circa 1900). History of paper, paper making, writing and writing materials, books and printing, bookmaking from the Spanish point of view.

Portfolio: The Annual of the Graphic Arts. Cincinnati, Ohio, Zebra Press, 1951. Article on "French Marble Papers" shows methods of making the papers and includes an actual example.

Pravilova, T.A., and Strel'tzova, T.N. "Types of Paper Suitable for Use in Restoration." New Methods for the Restoration and Preservation of Documents and Books. Moscow, 1960. Translation available from Department of Commerce, OTS, Springfield, Va.

Publisher's Library of Paper Samples. (6 vols.) Boston, S.D. Warren Paper Co., 1908. This is a handy reference for identifying early 20th-century book papers.

Rasch, Royal H. and Scribner, B.W. "Comparison of Natural Aging of Paper with Accelerated Aging by Heating." Bureau of Standards Journal of Research, 11:727-732, December 1933. Research Paper RP 620.

Rasch, Royal H. and Shaw, Merle B., and Bicking, George W. Highly Purified Wood Fibers as Paper-Making Material. Washington, Government Printing Office, 1931. U.S. National Bureau of Standards, Research Paper No. 372.

Richter, George A. "Relative Permanence of Papers Exposed to Sunlight." Industrial and Engineering Chemistry, XXVII, February, April 1935. pp. 177-185, 432-439.

Rossman, J. "Methods of Producing Insect Repellent Paper." Paper Trade Journal. 100:39,40, 1935.

Santucci, L. "Report on Paper Stability." Bollettino dell'Istituto di Patologia del Libro. Rome, 1963.

Schaefer, J.C. Attempts Towards Making Paper from Plants and Wood. (German) Regensbury, 1765.

Scribner, B.W. "Comparison of Accelerated Aging of Record Paper with Normal Aging for 8 Years." Journal of Research of the National Bureau of Standards. 23:405-413, September 1939. Research Paper RP 1241.

Shaw, Merle B., Bicking, George W., and O'Leary, Martin J. A Study of the Relation of Some Properties of Cotton Rags to the Strength and Stability of Experimental Papers Made From Them. Washington, Government Printing Office, 1935. U.S. National Bureau of Standards, Research Paper, RP764).

Shaw, Merle B., and O'Leary, Martin J. Effect of Filling and Sizing Materials on Stability of Book Papers. Washington, Government Printing Office, 1938. U.S. National Bureau of Standards, Research Paper RP1149.

Shigeru, S., Koichi, O., and Tadao, S. "Synthetic Fiber Papers. III Manufacture of Nylon Papers." Parupu Kami Kogyo Zasshi 12, 1958, pp. 385-392.

Siamese Papermaking. A lecture on the making of Khoi (Steblusasper) paper, by Phya Kasikan Banca (in Siamese language). This pamphlet was distributed at the cremation of Madame Aphiraksh Amphorsathan at Wat Amarintraram, 10th of February B.E. 2477, Bangkok, Siam.

Smith, J.E.A. A History of Paper. Holyoke, Mass., Clark W. Bryan & Co., 1882.

Stephenson, J.N., (ed.). The Manufacture of Pulp and Paper, A Textbook of Modern Pulp and Paper Mill Practice. New York, 1939. 3rd ed. Compiled by many writers prominent in American papermaking. The best work in any language on the technique of modern paper fabrication. Five volumes, exhaustive text, hundreds of illustrations, figures, etc.

Stevens, Richard T. The Art of Papermaking in Japan. New York, (privately printed) 1909. Reprinted by the Japanese in facsimile in 1943.

Stevenson, Louis Tillotson. The Background and Economics of American Papermaking. New York, 1940. Charts, etc.

Stonehill, W.J. Paper Pulp from Wood and Other Fibres. 1885.

Stratton, B.L. "Harvard University Press specifies a new paper for books." Publishers Weekly. New York, 179(6):94-96, 1961.

Studeny, John, Pollard, J.D., and Landes, C.G. Permanent Paper and Method of Making Same. U.S. Patent 2,492,821 filed Sept. 28, 1948, issued Dec. 27, 1949; BIPC 20 370.

Sung Ying-Hsing. T'ien Kung K'ai wu. 1634. The earliest Chinese book to deal with papermaking. Four wood block illustrations.

Sutermeister, Edwin. The Story of Paper-Making. Boston, The S. D. Warren Co., 1954.

"Syntosil--a New Paperlike Material." Textil-Rundschau 15:674-677, 1960.

Tindale, T. K., et al. The Handmade Papers of Japan. Tokyo and Rutland, Vt., 1952. Regarded by Dr. Bunsho Jugaku of Kōnan University in Japan as the best work on the subject.

Torrey, W. V., and Sutermeister, E. "A Brief Study of Some Old Papers." Paper Trade Journal, XCVI:45, 46, May 25, 1933.

Tsuchibayashi, S., Sakai, T., and Nagaosa, T. "Synthetic Fiber Papers. IV Manufacture of Nylon Fiber Paper." Parupu Kami Kogyo Zasshi 12:725-733, 1958.

The Papermakers. Cambridge, Twelve by Eight Press, 1965. Illustrations in color by Rigby Graham.

Veitch, Fletcher Pearre. Paper-making Materials and Their Conservation. Washington, Government Printing Office, 1911. U. S. Chemistry Bureau, Circular 41. First issued Dec. 31, 1908. Reprinted March 31, 1909, January 31, 1911.

Venkajee, Tekumalla. "Handmade Paper Industry in India." Paper Trade Journal. New York, October 28, 1926. Four pages of text and 12 illustrations.

Von Hagen, Victor Wolfgang. Aztec and Mayan Paper Makers. New York, J. J. Augustin, Limited Edition, 1943. Trade Edition, 1944. A scholarly study of the history and technique of ancient paper making in America. 32 plates. Samples bound in 1943 edition.

---- "Mexican Papermaking Plants." Journal of the New York Botanical Garden. Vol. 44, 1943.

Voorn, H. The Paper Mills of Denmark and Norway and Their Watermarks. Hilversum, 1959.

Wang, C. J. K. "Preliminary Report on the Fungous Flora. Pulp and Paper in New York." Tappi 44(II):785-788, 1961.

Watt, A. The Art of Paper Making. London, 1890.

Weeks, Lyman Horace. A History of Paper Manufacturing in the United States, 1690-1916. New York, The Lockwood Trade Journal Co., 1916.

Wheelwright, W.B. Paper Trade Terms. Boston, 1947. A useful dictionary.

"When Did Newspapers Begin to Use Wood Pulp Stock?" Bulletin of the New York Public Library. 33(10), 1929.

White, Oswald. Japanese Paper Making. London, H.M. Foreign Office, 1905.

Wiley, H.W., and Merrian, C.H. Durability and Economy in Papers for Permanent Records. Washington, U.S. Department of Agriculture, 1909. U.S. Department of Agriculture Report No. 89.

Wilson, William K., Harvey, Jack L., Mandel, John and Worksman, Thelma. "Accelerated Aging of Record Papers Compared with Normal Aging." Tappi 38:543-548, September, 1955.

Film, Tapes and Discs

"American Standard Specifications for Safety Photographic Film." PH1. 25-1956. Obtainable from American Standards Association, 70 East 45th St., New York, N.Y.

Bradley, John G. "Motion Pictures as Government Archives." J. Soc. Mot. Pict. Eng. 26:653, June, 1936.

Calhoun, J.M. "The Physical Properties and Dimensional Behavior of Motion Picture Film." J. Soc. Mot. Pict. Eng. 43:227-266, October, 1944.

Carver, E.K., Talbot, R.H., and Loomis, H.A. "Film Distortions and Their Effect upon Projection Quality." J. Soc. Mot. Pict. Eng., 41:88-93, July, 1943.

Clapp, V.W., and Jordan, R.T. "Re-evaluation of Microfilm as a Method of Book Storage." College and Research Libraries. 24, January, 1963. Reports that microfilming cost exceeds that of new construction.

Clerc, L.P. Photography Theory and Practice. 2nd ed. New York, 1937. Photographic materials.

Cobb, A.L. "Burning Characteristics of 'Safety' Film." Quarterly of the Nat. Fire Protection Assoc., 50:135-138, October, 1956.

Cummings, J.W., Hutton, A.C., and Silfin, H. "Spontaneous Ignition of Decomposing Cellulose Nitrate Film." J. Soc. Mot. Pict. and Tel. Eng. 54:268-274, March, 1950.

Hard, Herbert G. "What Do You Know About Recording Tape?" Radio and Television News, 59(2):111 ff, February 1958.

Harding, Bruce C. Microfilm, Its Use in Public Offices. Lansing, Michigan Historical Society, n. d.

Hazard in the Handling and Storage of Nitrate and Safety Motion Picture Film. Eastman Kodak Co., Rochester, N. Y. February, 1951.

Henn, R. W., and Wiest, D. G. "Properties of Gold-treated Microfilm Images." Photo Science Engineering, 10(1):15-22, 1966. Describes protective treatment. (Abstracted in Art and Archaeology Technical Abstracts, 6(2), 1966.

Hill, J. R., and Weber, C. G. "Stability of Motion Picture Films as Determined by Accelerated Aging." J. Soc. Mot. Pict. Eng. 27:677-690, December, 1936.

Latham, W. S. "A Study of Limitations of Magnetic Tapes." USN-USL Report No. 140, Audio Eng., September, 1952, pp. 19 ff.

---- "Tape Life." U. S. Navy Underwater Sound Laboratory, IRE Convention Record (1955) Nat'l. Conv. Audio III Seminar Magnetic Recording by the Engineer.

Literature Survey on the Properties of Plastics Influencing Their Stability in Storage. Battelle Memorial Institute. Contract W33-019-ORD-5333. Submitted May 31, 1946.

McCamy, C. S., and Pope, C. I. "Current Research on Preservation of Archival Records on Silver Gelatin-type Microfilm in Roll Form." National Bureau of Standards, Journal of Research, 69A:385-395, Sept. 1965.

(Microfilm) Microfilm Norms. Chicago, American Library Association, 1965. Contains pertinent standards of American Standards Association, National Microfilm Association and U. S. Government.

Nuckolls, A. H., and Matson, A. F. "Some Hazardous Properties of Motion Picture Film." J. Soc. Mot. Pict. Eng., 27:657-661, December 1936.

Radocy, Frank. Magnetic Tape as a Recording Medium. Audio Devices, Inc., New York.

Scribner, B. W. "Summary Report of Research at the National Bureau of Standards on the Stability and Preservation of Records on Photographic Film." National Bureau of Standards Miscellaneous Publication M162. May, 1939.

Some Plain Talk About Sound Recording Tape. Rochester, N. Y., Eastman Kodak Co., 1965.

285

Ink

"A Receipt for Making Writing Ink." Gentleman's Magazine, XXIII, May, 1753. p. 212.

Barrow, William J. "Black Writing Ink of the Colonial Period." The American Archivist, XI:291-307, October 1948.

---- Manuscripts and Documents: Their Deterioration and Restoration. Charlottesville, Va., University of Virginia Press, 1955. Covers the history of papers, inks and restoration methods. Lengthy information on ink, ink making, effect of ink on paper. Bibliography.

---- "New Non-acid Permanent Iron Ink." American Archivist 10: 338, 1947.

Blagden, "Some Observations on Ancient Inks." Trans. Roy. Soc. 77 (ii) (1787) p. 451.

Bowles, Reginald F. Printing Ink Manual. Cambridge, University Press, 1961.

Brecht, W., and Liebert E. "The Effect of Writing Inks on the Strength of Paper." Papier-Fabr./Wochbl. Papierfabr. 9:330 December 1943. BIPC 14, 363.

Carvalho, David N. Forty Centuries of Ink. New York, The Banks Law Publishing Co., 1904.

Gamble, W.B. Chemistry and Manufacture of Writing and Printing Inks. Reprinted from Bul. New York Public Library 29, 579, 625, 706 (1925). Bibliographic, with references to many United States and foreign patents.

Gode, P.K. "Recipes for Hair Dyes in the Naranitaka (c. 2nd Century A.D.) and their Close Affinity with the Recipes for Ink Manufacture (After A.D. 1000)." Reprinted from Bharatiya Vidya, XI (1950).

---- "Studies in the History of Indian Palaeography--Some Notes on the History of Ink Manufacture in Ancient and Medieval India and Other Countries." Reprinted from the Praeyavani, III, October, 1946.

"Inks." American Archivist. 1:55, 76, 142, 147 2:9 3:7, 102, 109, 209, 212. 4:130 10:106, 338, 345, 11:291.

"Inks." Article in Encyclopaedia Brittanica. 14th edition, 1929.

"Ink, Early Analyzed." American Archivist. 11:291.

Kantrowitz, Morris S., and Gosnell, Earl J. Alkaline Writing Ink.

Washington, Government Printing Office, 1947. Technical Bulletin No. 25.

Laurie, A. P. Pigments and Mediums of the Old Masters. New York, MacMillan, 1914. Ink recipes.

Lehner, S. Manufacture of Inks. Translated, with additions by W. T. Branut. Philadelphia, H. C. Baird & Co., 1892.

"Manuscript-marking Ink." American Library Assoc. Bulletin 56, April, 1962.

"Manuscript-marking Ink Being Tested." American Library Assoc. Bulletin 56, March 1962.

Mitchell, Charles A., and Hepworth, Thomas C. Inks, Their Composition and Manufacture ... 4th ed. London, C. Griffin & Co., Ltd. 1937.

Mitchell, C. A., and Wood, D. R. "Action of Molds on Ink in Writing." Analyst, 1938, pp. 93-148.

Munson, L. S. "The Testing of Writing Inks." J. Am. Chem. Soc. 28, 512-516 (1906).

Rupert, F. F. "Examination of Writing Inks." Ind. Eng. Chem. 15, 1923. pp. 489-493.

Schmitt, Charles A. "The Chemistry of Writing Inks." Journal of Chemical Education, XXI:413-414, August 1944.

Susumu, I. "Identification of Inks by Paper Chromotography." Science and Crime Detection. Japan, 8 No. 3, 1955.

Underwood, N. and Sullivan, T. V. Chemistry and Technology of Printing Inks. New York, D. Van Nostrand Co., 1915.

Vaultier, R. "The History of China Ink." Papetier. (Special Fall Issue 1957) No. 7.

Waters, Campbell E. Inks. Washington, U.S. Government Printing Office, 1940. U.S. National Bureau of Standards, Circular C426. The history and technology of writing ink with formulas. Section on restoration of faded writing ink. An excellent source of general information with a selective bibliography.

Weiss, Harry B. "The Writing Masters and Ink Manufacturers of New York City." Bulletin of the New York Public Library. LVI, August 1952, pp. 383-394.

Wiborg, F. B. Printing Ink. New York, Harper & Bros., 1925. An illustrated history with a treatise on the modern methods of manufacture and use of ink.

287

Zimmerman, E.W.   Iron Gallate Inks--Liquid and Powder. Washington, D.C., National Bureau of Standards Research Paper RP807, July 1935.

Zimmerman, E.W., Weber, C.G., and Kimberly, A.E.   "Relation of Ink to the Preservation of Written Records."   J. Research NBS 14 (1935) RP779. pp. 463-468.

                              Adhesives

"Adhesives for Book Repair."   American Archivist. 13:318   1:3.

Animal Glues.   Forest Products Laboratory Report 492 (1955).

Barrow, W.J.   Permanence/Durability of the Book--IV Polyvinyl Acetate (PVA) Adhesives for Use in Library Bookbinding. Richmond, W.J. Barrow Research Laboratory Publications, No. IV. (1965).

Belaya, I.K.   "Glue for the Restoration of Leather Bindings." Collection of Materials on the Preservation of Library Resources.   Moscow, 1958.   U.S. Department of Commerce, Office of Technical Service, Springfield, Va., 1964.

Bindery Glues.   Washington, D.C., U.S. Government Printing Office, n.d.   Research Bulletin B-3, Bindery Series.

Blomquist, Richard F.   Adhesives-Past, Present and Future. Philadelphia, American Society for Testing and Materials, 1963.

Bookbinding Pastes.   Washington, D.C., U.S. Government Printing Office, 1953.   Bindery Series No. 2.

Braude, Felix.   Adhesives.   New York, Chemical Publishing Co., 1943.   Theory and application.

Brooke, N.   "Laboratory Adhesives."   Journal Chemical Education. 31 (1954).

Clark, R.G.   "Waterproof Starch Adhesives."   Canadian Pulp and Paper Industries   14(4):88-90, 93, 1961.

De Bruyne, Norman Adrian, and Houwink, Roelof, Editors.   Adhesion and Adhesives.   New York, Amsterdam, London, Brussels, Elsevier Pub. Co., 1951.   Illustrated.

Delmonte, J.   The Technology of Adhesives.   New York, Reinhold Publishing Corp., 1947.

Fowler, George Herbert.   "Paste."   British Records Association, Tech. Section Bulletin.   London, No. 1, March 1938, p. 3. Mimeographed.   A formula for making paste of good adhesive qualities.

Gairola, T. R. "Pastes and Adhesives for Paper and Textiles." Journal of Indian Museums. 8, 1952.

Galbreich, E. I. "Adhesive Properties of Polyvinyl Alcohol." Leningrad, Saltykov-Shchedrin State Public Library, 93-95, 1963. (Abstracted in Art and Archaeology Technical Abstracts, vol. 6, 1966, No. 2).

Gray, V. R. "Understanding Adhesives." New Scientist. London, 19, 1963.

"Gum Arabic." Adhesives and Resins. 1, 1953.

Guttimann, W. H. Concise Guide to Structural Adhesives. New York, Reinhold, 1961. (Chapman & Hall, London).

Hunt, George M., and Jones, W. L. The Selection and Testing of Animal Glue for High-Grade Joint Work. Madison, Wis., Forest Products Laboratory, L26, 506.

Hurd, Joyce, Adhesives Guide, Research Report M. 39. British Scientific Instruments Research Association, London, 1959.

Iwasaki, Tomokichi. Scientific Preservative Methods for Cultural Properties. VIII. Adhesives for Repairs of Cultural Properties. Museum (Tokyo) No. 154 (1964). pp. 32-33. A general description of adhesives used for repairs.

Kantrowitz, M. S., et al. Bindery Glues. Washington, U.S. Government Printing Office, 1948. The manufacture, testing, preparation and storage of bookbinding glues.

---- Flexible Glues for Bookbinding. Washington, U.S. Government Printing Office, 1941. Technical Bulletin No. 24.

---- Miscellaneous Bookbinding Adhesives. Washington, U.S. Government Printing Office, 1953. Bindery series No. 4. Includes formulas for various adhesives.

Kishore, R., and Kathpalia, Y. P. "A Note on Dextrine Paste." Indian Archives, 9 (1955). p. 55. Gives recipe for a flour paste incorporating insecticidal poisons.

McLaren, A. D., and Seiler, Charles J. "Adhesion III. Adhesion of Polymers to Cellulose and Alumina." J. Polymer Sci. 4 1949) pp. 63-74.

Morris, J. "Gum Arabic." Adhesives and Resins. 1 (1953).

Piez, Gladys T. "Some Library Adhesives--A Laboratory Evaluation of P. V. A. 's." American Library Association Bulletin. 56:838-843, October 1962.

"Resinous Adhesives for Book Binders." Chemical Age, 69:547-548, 1953.

Skeist, Irving, editor. Handbook of Adhesives. New York, Reinhold Publishing Corp. , 1962.

Smith, Lee T. , and Hamilton, R.M. "Starch Adhesives." Chem. Eng. News. 22 (1944). A review presenting a history of the development and uses of starch adhesives, together with a discussion of adhesion theories, adhesive requirements for specific purposes and methods of determining the comparative properties of different types. 147 references.

Stout, G.L. , and Horwitz, M.H. "Experiments with Adhesives for Paper." Technical Studies, 3(1), 1934. Reports results of tests of the adhesive properties and resistance to deterioration of various adhesives.

Sutton, D.A. "Modern Natural Synthetic Glues and Adhesives." Journal Royal Society of Arts. III (1963).

Verrier, Lindsay. "A Pressure-cooked Non-moulding Adhesive Flour Paste." Nature. London, 164 (1949) p. 545. Lindsay Verrier claims this recipe gives a paste of uniform consistency which is not messy to make and is nonpoisonous.

Webb, R.F. "Modern Glues." Research. 13 (1960).

Wetherall, W.F. "Adhesives, Their Properties and Selection." Holtztechnologie (Leipzig) 5:15-20, 1964. A survey of synthetic adhesives.

Yabrova, R.R. "Polymethacrylate Emulsion--A New Glue for Book Restoration and Bookbinding." Collection of Materials on the Preservation of Library Resources. Moscow (1958). U.S. Department of Commerce, Office of Technical Services, Springfield, Va. (1964).

Boards

Kantrowitz, M. and Blaylock, F. Paper Boards for Bookbinding. Washington, U.S. Government Printing Office, 1950. Description of the manufacture of and standards for boards.

Cloth

Book Cloths, Buckrams and Impregnated Fabrics for Bookbinding Purposes Except Library Bindings, Commercial Standard CS57-40. 2nd ed. Washington, U.S. Government Printing Office, 1940. U.S. National Bureau of Standards.

Bowyer, W. "Publishers' Binding Cloth." The Book Collector's

Quarterly. (6):57-59, April 1932.

Consult, C. Flax and Its Products. Belfast, 1862.

Cook, J. G. Handbook of Textile Fibres. 2nd ed. Watford, Herts, England, Merrow Publishing Co., Ltd. 1960.

Cushman, M. P. "Book Cloths and the Adoption of Standard Tests." Publishers Weekly. April 4, 1936, pp. 1427-1432. A talk given at a book clinic of the American Institute of Graphic Arts.

Dictionary of Bookcloth. London, Thomas Goodall & Co., 1944. Spiral-bound sample sheets.

Emery, Irene. The Primary Structures of Fabrics. Washington, The Textile Museum 1966. This volume clears the way for greater understanding of the confused realm of textile classification and terminology. Basic information on bark, papyrus and fibrous materials.

"Impact Wear Test for Bookcloths Described in Laboratory Report." Patra News. No. 94, October 1958, 1-2.

Kantrowitz, M. S., et al. Pyroxylin Treated Book Cloths. Washington, Government Printing Office, 1948. G. P. O. -P. I. A. Joint Research Bulletin, bindery series No. 7. Pam.

Leggett, W. F., The Story of Linen. New York, Chemical Publishing Co., Inc. 1945.

---- The Story of Silk. New York, Lifeline Editions, Inc. 1949.

Leighton, Douglas. "Canvas and Bookcloth: an Essay on Beginnings." The Library. 5th series, Vol. 3, June 1948, pp. 39-49.

Making of Bookbinding Fabrics; Being an Illustrated Story Showing the Various Processes Required to Transform Raw Cotton into a Finished Bookbinding Fabric. Norwood, Mass., Holliston Mills, about 1951.

Moore, A. S. Linen. London, 1914.

"Nomenclature of Nineteenth-century Cloth Grains." The Book Collector. 2(1):54-58, Spring 1953.

Schaefer, G. "Flax and Hemp." CIBA Review. No. 49. Basle, 1945. pp. 1762-1795.

Spoor, H., and Ziegler, K. "Chemistry and Fine Structure of Natural Silk." Angewandte Chemie. Weinheine, Germany 72 (1960).

"Technical Note on Silk Chiffon." Archives and Manuscripts.

291

Australia Library Association. June 1956. Discusses shrinking.

"The Influence of Contaminants on the Water Repellency of Fabrics." Am. Dyestuff Reptr. 52:P1059-P1067, December 1963. American Association of Textile Chemists and Colorists, Northern Piedmont Section.

Weibel, A.C. Two Thousand Years of Textiles. New York, Pantheon Books, 1952. Published for the Detroit Institute of Arts.

Woodhouse, T. The Finishing of Jute and Linen Fibers. London, 1928.

Woolman, M.S., and McGowan, E.B. Textiles. New York, The MacMillan Co., 1943.

Gold Stamping

Barnes, Richard H. Gilding and the Making of Gold Leaf. Philadelphia, Butler and Ferrigno Lithographic Co., 1962.

Hobson, Kenneth. "Some Notes on the History and Development of Bookbinder's Stamps and Tools." Print. 8(4), December, 1953.

Kantrowitz, M., and Blaylock, F. Bronze Stamping Leaf. Washington, U.S. Government Printing Office, 1952. Research Bulletin B-6, Bindery series.

Whiley, George M. Leaves of Gold: An Account of the Ancient Craft of Goldbeating and its Development into a Modern Industry. Privately printed, 1951.

Sewing

Castellini, Luigi. "Hemp." CIBA Review. No. 5, 1962.

Consult, C. Flax and Its Products. Belfast, 1862.

Hemp. Washington, U.S. Government Printing Office. U.S. Plant Industry Bureau Bulletins 46 and 221.

Linen, Jute and Hemp Industries. Washington, U.S. Government Printing Office. U.S. Foreign and Domestic Commerce Bureau, Special Agents Series No. 74.

Menzi, K., and Bigler, N. "Identification of Bast Fibers (Flax, Hemp, Ramie, Jute)." CIBA Review. No. 123:33-36. Basle, 1957.

Schaefer, G. "Flax and Hemp." CIBA Review. No. 49, pp. 1762-1795. Basle, 1945.

Select Essays: Containing the Manner of Raising and Dressing Flax and Hemp. Also the Whole Method of Bleaching or Whitening Linen-Cloth. Philadelphia, Printed by Robert Bell, 1777.

Miscellaneous Materials

Alexander, S. M. "Medieval Recipes Describing the Use of Metals in Manuscripts." Marsyas. New York, 12, 34-51, 1966.

American Library Association. Library Technology Project. Permanence and Durability of Library Catalog Cards. A study conducted by W. J. Barrow for the Library Technology Project. Chicago, American Library Association, 1961. LTP Publications, No. 3.

Barrett, O. W. "Roach-proof Book Varnish." Philippine Agricultural Review. 6:49, 1913.

Barry, T. H. Natural Varnish Resins. London, Ernest Benn Ltd., A history.

Block, S. S. "A Protective Lacquer for Books." Florida Public Library Newsletter. v. 3, pt. 9, 1949.

Colwall, Daniel. "An Account of the Way of Making English Green-Copperas." Royal Society of London, Philosophical Transactions, XII (1678) pp. 1056-1059.

Kashima, M., and Nose, Y. "Physiochemical Investigation of Rust Preventive Oil." Proceedings, National Association of Corrosion Engineers, Houston, Texas, 612-623, 1963.

Kimberly, A. E., and Hicks, J. F. G. Light Sensitivity of Rosin Paper-sizing Materials. Washington, D. C., National Bureau of Standards Research Paper 372.

Kowalik, R., and Czerwinska, E. "Sizes Used in Paper-Making and Paper Binding." BLOK Notes Muzeum Michiewicza. Warszawie, 1960. pp. 153-154.

Leggett, William F. Ancient and Medieval Dyes. Brooklyn, N. Y., Chemical Publishing Company, 1944.

Radley, J. A. Starch and Its Derivatives. London, Chapman and Hall, 1953.

Fungicides, etc.

Block, S. S. "Chemicals for Fungus Control." Chem. Week Rep. 26, 1952.

Christol, S. J. , and Haller, H. L. "The Chemistry of DDT--A Review. " Chemical Engineering News, 23, 1945.

Dahl, Sverre, et al. "Studies in Leather Fungicides. " Journal American Leather Chemists Association, 53, 1958.

Dyte, C. E. "Preliminary Tests of an Insecticidal Lacquer Containing Malathion. " Pest Technol. 2, 98, 1960.

Frear, D. E. H. Pesticide Handbook. 13th ed. State College, Pa. College Science Publishers, 1961.

---- Pesticide Index. P. O. Box 798, State College, Pa. , College Science Publishers, 1961.

Heimpel, A. M. "Bacterial Insecticides. " Bacter. Rev. 24, 266, 1960.

Holnes, R. F. G. "Use of Formaldehyde as a Fumigant. " British Records Association Bulletin. no. 14. 1942.

Insecta-Lac, the Improved Insecticidal Lacquer. 105 Tonbridge Road, Maidstone, Kent, England, Sorex (London) Ltd. 1956.

Kenaga, E. E. "Some Biological Chemical and Physical Properties of Sulphuril Fluoride as an Insecticidal Fumigant. " J. Econ. Entomol. 50, 1, 1957.

Moss, A. A. "DDT. " Museum Journal, 46, 1946.

Price, M. D. "Progress with Insecticidal Resins. " Pest Technol. 4, 187, 1961.

Reddish, G. F. Antiseptics, Disinfectants, Fungicides and Sterilization. London, H. Kimpton, 1957.

Roan, C. C. "What's New Among the Fumigants?" Pest Control, 30(7):9, 1962.

Solvents

Doolittle, Arthur K. Technology of Solvents and Plasticizers. New York, London, John Wiley, 1954.

Durrans, T. H. Solvents. London, Chapman & Hall Ltd. 1950.

Jordan, Otto. Technology of Solvents. London, Leonard Hill, 1937.

Mellan, Ibert. Industrial Solvents. New York, Reinhold Publishing Co. , 1950.

294

Synthetics

"A Guide to Man-Made Fibers." New Scientist. 13, 1962.

Barker, E. F. "Swiss Mill Produces Paper Containing Substantial Quantities of Nylon." Paper Trade Journal. 145(7):48-51, 1961.

Brydson, J. A. Plastic Materials. A comprehensive introduction to history, properties, structure, use, etc. of plastics. Princeton, N. J., Van Nostrand, 1966.

Golding, Brace. Polymers and Resins. New York, Van Nostrand, 1959.

Gruetzner, M. K., and Shay, J. J. "Acrylic Resins in Aerosol Surface Coatings." Paint Varnish Prod., 52:40-44, May 1962.

Haynes, William. Cellulose, The Chemical that Grows. Garden City, N. Y., Doubleday & Co., 1953.

Heuser, The Chemistry of Cellulose. New York, Wiley, 1946.

Jorner, J. "Photochemistry of Cellulose Acetate." Polymer Science. 37, 1959.

Maranyl, Nylon Soluble Polymers. London, Imperial Chemical Industries Information Service Note 611.

Mason, J. P., and Manning, J. F. The Technology of Plastics and Resins. New York, Van Nostrand, 1945. Illustrated. See especially the sections on cellulose (pp. 150-162), acrylic resins (pp. 239-259), and Polyvinyl acetate (pp. 272-278).

Morrison, J. A. S. Plastics in the Printing and Bookbinding Industries. London, London School of Printing and Kindred Trades, 1948.

Okamura, S., and Inagaki, H. "Papylon-Synthetic Papers." Paper Making. 136(5):74, 1958.

Ott, Emil, editor. Cellulose and Cellulose Derivatives. New York, Interscience Publishers, Inc., 1946.

Polyvinyl Acetate (PVA) Adhesives for Use in Library Binding. Richmond, Va., W. J. Barrow Research Laboratory, 1965.

Roff, W. J. Fibres, Plastics and Rubbers. London, Butterworths, 1956.

Schildknecht, C. E. Vinyl and Related Polymers. New York, Wiley, 1952.

Shigeru, S., Koichi, O., and Tadao, S. "Synthetic Fiber Papers,

295

III Manufacture of Nylon Papers." Parupu Kami Kogyo Zasshi
12:385-392, 1958.

Stannett, Vivian. Cellulose Acetate Plastics. London, Temple
Press, 1950.

---- Cellulose Acetate Plastics. New York, Chemical Publishing
Co., 1951.

Synthetic Materials Used in the Conservation of Cultural Property.
Rome, Intern. Centre for the Study of the Preserv. and the
Restor. of Cult. Property, pp. 67, 1963. Scientific description of synthetic adhesives, varnishes, resins, etc. with manufacturers and trade names.

'Syntosil--a New Paperlike Material." Textil-Rundschau 15:674-677,
1960. Anonymous.

Tsuchibayashi, S., Sakai, T., and Nagaosa, T. "Synthetic Fiber
Papers, IV Manufacture of Nylon Fiber Paper." Parupu Kami
Kogyo Zasshi, 12:725-733, 1958.

Werner, A. E. A. "New Materials in the Conservation of Antiquities." Museum Journal, 64, 1964. Discusses wide range of
synthetic materials.

---- "Technical Notes on a New Material in Conservation."
Chronique d'Egypte. 33(66), 1958. On soluble nylon.

Zaguliaeva, Z. A. "Biological Resistance of Some Methylcellulose
Grades for Paper Restoration Work." Moscow, Stareniye
bumagi, 112-116, 1965. (Abstracted in Art and Archaeology
Technical Abstracts, 6(2), 1966.

ENEMIES
General

Animals Injurious to Books. London, Science Museum 1938. Science Library Bibliographical Series No. 377.

Archer, John. "A Ten Year Test of Bindings." New York Public
Library Bulletin. 40(2), 1936.

Arts, Society of. Report on the Deterioration of Paper. London,
1898.

Baker, W. E. B. "Relationship of Impurities to Paper Permanence."
Paper Trade Journal, 91(4):51-52, 1930.

Barrow, W. J. "An Accelerated Aging Study of Several Writing
Papers. Re-evaluation of Data." Tappi, 47:105-107, February
1964.

296

---- "Migration of Impurities in Paper." Archivum. 3:105-108, 1953. Tables and bibliography. The migration of impurities from non-cellulosic material, acidic material from ground wood papers, acid from writing ink, and other materials is considered.

Basu, Purnendu. "Enemies of Records." Indian Archives. 4, 1950. Names time, fire, water, light, heat, dust, humidity, air pollution, fungi, vermin, acts of God and people.

---- "Common Enemies of Records." The Indian Archives. 5(1): 1950.

Belaya, I. K. "The Action of Certain Antiseptics on Paper." Collection of Materials on the Preservation of Library Resources. Moscow, 1958. English translation available. U.S. Department of Commerce, OTS, Springfield, Va.

---- "The Action of Short Wave Ultrawave Irradiation by Bacteriocidal Lamps on Paper." (ibid).

Blades, W. The Enemies of Books. London, Elliot Stock, 1888. Reprinted, 1902.

Blank, M. G., and others. "Aging of Restored Paper." Moscow, Stareniye bumagi, 57-67, 1965. Describes effects of water, chloramine, magnesium carbonate, etc. on new and old paper. (Abstracted in Art and Archaeology Technical Abstracts, 6(2), 1966.)

Brooks, C. E. P. "Climate and the Deterioration of Materials." Quarterly Journal of the Royal Meteorological Society. 72:87-97, 1946.

Chakravorti, S. K. "Effect of 'Gammaexane' on the Durability of Paper." Nature, 163(607), 1949.

Chesebrough, T. W. "Death of Books." University Quarterly. 2: 284.

Cheshire, A. "The Aging of Leather." Journal International Society of Leather Trades Chemists. 30, 1946.

Church, R. W. Deterioration of Book Stock; Causes and Remedies. Two Studies on the Permanence of Book Paper. Richmond, Virginia State Library, 1959. Studies conducted by W. J. Barrow.

Clapp, Verner W., Henshaw, Francis H., and Holmes, Donald C. "Are Your Microfilms Deteriorating Acceptably." Library Journal, 80(6):589-595, March 15, 1955.

Dahl, S., and Kaplan, A. M. "Laboratory and Field Exposure Stud-

297

ies of Leather Fungicides." J. Amer. Leather Chemists Assoc. 51(3):118-136, 1956.

---- "The Effects of Fungicides on Deterioration of Leather." J. Amer. Leather Chemists Association. 52(11):611-621, 1957.

"Destroyers of Early Books." Hogg's Instruction. 3:220.

Deterioration and Preservation of Book Material Stored in Libraries, The. Garston, Eng., Building Research Station, 1949. Note no. D.62.

De Zeih, C.J. "Effects of Nuclear Radiation on Cork, Leather and Elastomers." U.S. Atomic Energy Commission, D 2-1819, 1957.

Frey, R.W., et al. "The Decay of Bookbinding Leathers." in Jour. of Amer. Leather Chemists Assoc. 26:461-482, 1931.

Galbraich, E.I., and others. "Some Properties of Paper Restored with the Help of Synthetic Polymers." Part II. Leningrad, O sokhranenii bumagi, 42-61, 1963. Reports the action of sulphur dioxide, light, etc. on plastic coatings. (Abstracted in Art and Archaeology Technical Abstracts, 6(2), 1966.

Gallo, A. "Libri mallati." Accademie e biblioteche d'Italia. 10:334-335, 1936.

---- Le Malattie del Libro. Milano, Mondadori, 1935.

---- "Patologia e Terapia del Libro." Enciclopedia Poligrafica. Vol. 1 monograph 3, Roma, Editrice Raggio, 1951.

---- 'The Pathology of Books." East and West. 1:54-58, 1950. Illustrated. The Director of the Istituto di Patologia del Libro in Rome reviews the afflictions to which books are subjected.

Greathouse, G.A., and Wessel, C.J., et al. Deterioration of Materials. New York, Reinhold Publishing Corp., 1954. Discusses the climatic, chemical, physical and biological agents of deterioration. Outlines protective methods for wood, paper, textiles, cordage, leather, plastics, rubber and paints and varnishes.

Greenwood, F.W.P. "Uses and Abuses of Books." Christian Examiner. 10:240.

Grove, L.E. "Paper Deterioration--An Old Story." College and Research Laboratories. 25, September 1964.

Guarnieri, A.C. Notas sôbre o problema do môfo nos livros. São Paulo, Universidade de São Paulo, 1948.

298

Hamilton, Robert M. "The Library of Parliament Fire." The American Archivist, XVI:141-144, April 1953.

Hanson, Fred S. "Resistance of Paper to Natural Aging." The Paper Industry and Paper World. Chicago, 1939.

Herzberg, W. "Destruction of Paper by Writing Ink." Paper Trade Journal, 76(10), March 8, 1923.

Hill, F.P. "The Deterioration of Newspaper Paper." American Library Associatioi Bulletin. 4: 1910. Also Library Journal, 35: 1910.

Hill and Weber. "Stability of Motion Picture Films as Determined by Accelerated Aging." Jour SMPE. XXVII(6):677 ff, December, 1936.

Innes, R. Faraday. The Deterioration of Vegetable-Tanned Leather in Storage. London, 1931. Illustrated. Reprinted from the Journal of the International Society of Leather Trades' Chemists for October, 1931.

Jarrel, T.D., Hankins, J.M., and Veitch, F.P. Deterioration of Book and Record Papers. U.S. Department of Agriculture, Technical Bulletin No. 541, November 1936. An early proof of the necessity for positive action to save paper records in libraries and archives.

---- Deterioration of Paper as Indicated by Gas Chamber Tests. Washington, U.S. Department of Agriculture Bulletin No. 605, 1938. Reports investigation that showed the effects of sulphur dioxide in paper deterioration.

Kathpalia, Y.P. "Deterioration and Conservation of Paper. I: Biological Deterioration." Indian Pulp and Paper, 15, July 1960.

---- "Deterioration and Conservation of Paper. III: Chemical Deterioration." Indian Pulp and Paper, 16, November 1961.

---- "Deterioration and Conservation of Paper. II: Physical Deterioration." Indian Pulp and Paper, 15, January 1961.

Kimberly, A.E., and Emley, A.L. A Study of the Deterioration of Book Papers in Libraries. Washington, U.S. Government Printing Office, 1933. National Bureau of Standards. Miscellaneous publication no. 140.

Langwell, W.H. "The Permanence of Paper Records." Library Association Record. 55:212-215, July 1953.

Lawrence, Virginia. "Preservation of Manuscripts." Manuscripts, 6, 1954. A warning on effects of light, heat, moisture.

Lewis, Harry F. "The Deterioration of Book Paper in Library Use." American Archivist, 22:309-322, 1959.

Nyuksha, J.P. "Changes in Alkali-soluble Fraction of Paper Fibers as the Result of Some Physical and Chemical Actions." Leningrad, O sokhraneii bumagi, 69-87, 1963. Reports the effect of water, alcohol, formaldehyde, hypochlorite, etc. on mildewed paper. (Abstracted in Art and Archaeology Technical Abstracts, 6(2), 1966.)

---- "Some Causes of Book Damage." Moscow, Priroda, 11:94-95, 1955. Discusses dust, sulphur dioxide, moisture, insects, fungi.

"Paper, Diseases of." American Archivist. 1:165.

Perl'stein, E. Ia. "Changes in the Physical and Mechanical Properties of Paper as a Result of Natural Aging." Moscow, Stareniye bumagi, 148-149, 1965.

---- "Step-solubility of Paper in Caustic Soda Solutions." Moscow, Stareniye bumagi, 30-45, 1965.

Permanent/Durable Book Paper, Summary of a Conference Held in Washington, D.C., September 16, 1960. Richmond, The Virginia State Library, 1960. Sponsored by the American Library Association and the Virginia State Library. A good presentation of the problem of paper deterioration and a comparison of suggested solutions.

Pravilova, T.A. "Aging of Paper." New Methods for the Restoration and Preservation of Documents and Books. Moscow, 1960. U.S. Department of Commerce, Office of Technical Services, Springfield, Va. 1965.

Scarone, Arturo. El Libro y sus Enimigos. Montevideo, 1917.

Schoeller, V. "Concerning the Yellowing of Paper." Freiburg, West Germany, Mitteilungen der Arbeitsgemeinschaft der Archivrestauratoren, 6, 54-57, 1960 and 7, 59-68, 1960. (Abstracted in Art and Archaeology Technical Abstracts 6(2), 1966.)

Sée, Pierre. Les Maladies du Papier Piqué. Paris, Dion et Fils 1919.

Shaw, Merle B., and O'Leary, Martin J. Effect of Filling and Sizing Materials on Stability of Book Papers. Washington, U.S. Government Printing Office, 1938. U.S. National Bureau of Standards Research Paper RP1149.

---- Study of the Effect of Fiber Components on the Stability of Book Papers. Washington, U.S. Government Printing Office, 1936. U.S. National Bureau of Standards Research Paper RP 949.

Shearon, Will H., Jr. "The Old Grey Book." Industrial Engineering Chemistry, 49:25A-26A, November, 1957.

Sinha, S.N. "Loss of Mechanical Strength of Paper Due to Aging." Indian Print & Paper 11, 31, 1946; BIPC 17, p.299.

Sugimatsu, A., Senda, S., and Harada, Y. "Degradation of Cellulose by Gamma Irradiation." Kogyo Kagaku Zasshi 62:576. citato dal Chem. Abstracts 57, 15391 g.

Suri, V.S. "Some Hints on the Health of Contents of Libraries." Indian Librarian. March 1954, pp. 147-153.

Takamuru S., Miyamato, Y., and Hachihama, Y. "Effect of Gamma Irradiation on the Hydrolysis of Cellulose." Kogyo Kagaku Zasshi 64, 2027, 1961. citato dal Chem. Abstracts 57, 3663 a.

Vely, V.C., Gallagher, N.D., and Neher, M.B. "Effect of Gamma Radiation on Leather and Pickled Calfskin." Journal Amer. Leather Chemists Assoc., 55:202-219, 1960.

Walton, Robert P. Causes and Prevention of Deterioration in Book Materials. New York, The New York Public Library, 1929.

Weber, Charles G., et al. "Effects of Fumigants on Paper." Washington, Bureau of Standards Journal of Research 15, September, 1935.

Wilson, W.K., and Forshee, B.W. "Degradation of Cellulose Acetate Films." SPE Journal 15, February 1959.

Wilson, W.K., Harvey, J.L., Mandel, John, and Worksman, Thelma. "Accelerated Aging of Record Papers Compared with Normal Aging." Tappi, 38(9):543-548, September 1955.

Yabrova, R.R. "Artificially Accelerated Aging of Paper." Collection of Materials on the Preservation of Library Resources. Moscow, 1958. U.S. Department of Agriculture, OTS, Springfield, Va., 1964.

Zimmerman, Elmer W., Weber, Charles G., and Kimberly, Arthur E. Relation of Ink to the Preservation of Written Records. Washington, U.S. Government Printing Office, 1935. U.S. National Bureau of Standards, Research Paper RP779.

People

Adams, R.G. "Librarians as Enemies of Books." Library Quarterly, 7:317-331, 1937.

"Adhesive Tape, Damage From." American Archivist. 16:122.

Hatson, C.W. "Abuse of Books." Southern Magazine. 9:536.

Land, Robert H. "Defense of Archives Against Human Foes." American Archivist. 19:121-138 April, 1956.

Weber, C.G., et al. "Effects of Fumigants on Paper." Journal of Research, National Bureau of Standards. 15(3):271, 1935.

Air

Carroll, J.F., and Calhoun, J.M. "Effect of Nitrogen Oxide Gases on Processed Acetate Film." Jour. Soc. Mot. Pict. and Tel. Eng. 64:501-507, September 1955.

Denmead, C.F. Air Pollution by Hydrogen Sulphide From a Shallow Polluted Tidal Inlet, Auckland, New Zealand. Proc. of the Clean Air Conference, Vol. 1, 1st Technical Session Paper No. 4, 1962. Held at Sydney, Australia, February 19-21, 1962.

Environmental Effects on Materials and Equipment, Section A. Washington, Preservation from Deterioration Center, Division of Chemistry and Chemical Technology, National Academy of Sciences-National Research Council, 1962 to present.

Frey, R.W. "Gaseous Pollution of the Atmosphere; a Cause for Leather Decay." Library Journal, 57:405-414, 1938.

Greenburg, L., et al. "Corrosion Aspects of Air Pollution." American Paint Journal, 39, 1955.

Hudson, F.L., et al. "Atmospheric Sulphur and Durability of Paper." Journal Society of Archivists, 2, 1961.

---- "The Pickup of Sulphur Dioxide by Paper." Journal of Applied Chemistry, 14, October 1964.

Iwaski, Tomokichi. "Scientific Preservative Methods for Cultural Properties. V. Air Pollution." Museum. Tokyo, No. 143, 1963, pp. 28-29.

Jacobs, M.B. The Chemical Analysis of Air Pollutants. New York, Interscience Publishers, Inc. 1960.

Kimberly, A.E. "The Deteriorative Effect of Sulphur Dioxide upon Paper in Atmospheres of Constant Humidity and Temperature." Journal of Research. 8, Washington, Bureau of Standards, 1932.

Kowalik, R., and Sadurska, I. "Micro-organisms Destroying Paper, Leather and Wax Seals in the Air of Archives." Acta Microbiologica Polonica, 5(1/2):277-284, 1956.

Marsh, Arnold. "Smoke, the Problem of Coal and the Atmosphere."

302

The Destruction of Property. London, Faber and Faber, 1947. Ch. 6, pp. 94-107. Illustrated.

McCabe, L.C. "Atmospheric Pollution." Industrial Engineering Chemistry. 48, 1953.

Meetham, A.R. Atmospheric Pollution, Its Origins and Prevention. New York, MacMillan 1964. 3rd edition.

Parker, A. "The Destructive Effects of Air Pollution on Materials." Chemical Abstracts. 52, 1958.

Salvin, V.S. "The Effect of Atmospheric Contaminants on Light Fastness." Journal Society of Dyers and Colourists. 79:687-696, December 1963. Celanese Fibers Co., Charlotte, N.C.

Schreiber, Walter T., Bullock, Austin L., and Ward, Wendell L. "Resistance of Partially Acetylated Cotton Fabric to Nitrogen Dioxide and to Hydrogen Chloride." Textile Res. Journal. September 1954, pp. 819-822.

Thomson, Gary. "Air Pollution--A Review for Conservation Chemists." Studies in Conservation, 10(4), 1965. Should be read by all librarians.

Veitch, F.P., et al. "Polluted Atmosphere a Factor in the Deterioration of Bookbinding Leather." Amer. Leather Chemists Assoc. Journal. Easton, Pa., 21:156-176, 1926. Also reprinted separately.

Vernon, W.H.J. "Second Report to the Atmospheric Corrosion Research Committee." Transactions of the Faraday Society. 1927. Effect of atmosphere on metals.

Light and Darkness

Allison, J.P. "Photo-degradation of Polymethyl methacrylate." Journal Polymer Science, Easton, Pa., Part A-114:1209-1221, 1966.

Apps, E.A. "The Fading of Printed Matter." Paper and Print. 31, 1958.

Balder, J.J The Discoloration of Coloured Objects Under the Influence of Daylight, Incandescent Light, and Fluorescent Light. Leiden, Netherlands Museum Association, 1956. In English.

Brommelle, N.S. "The Russell and Abney Report on the Action of Light on Water Colours." Studies in Conservation. Vol. 9, no. 4, November 1964. An analysis of the often quoted but not readily accessible 19th-century pioneer work on the effect of light on color.

303

Brommelle, N., and Harris, J.R. "Museum Lighting, Part 2."
Museums Journal 61, 1961. Effect of light on deterioration.

Cooper, B.S. "Fluorescent Lighting in Museums." Museums Journal III, 1954. An examination of the effect of light on materials.

Feller, Robert L. "The Deteriorating Effect of Light on Museum Objects." Museum News. Technical Supplement 42(10):i-viii, 1964. 5 charts, 49 references.

Giles, C.H. "The Fading of Colouring Matters." Journal of Applied Chemistry, London, 15:541-550, 1965.

---- "The Fading of Coloring Matters." Curator, New York, 9(2): 95-102, 1966.

Harrison, L.S. "Evaluation of Spectral Radiation Hazards in Window-Lighted Galleries." Recent Advances in Conservation. London, Butterworth, 1963.

---- Report of the Deteriorating Effects of Modern Light Sources. New York, The Metropolitan Museum of Art, 1954.

Kato, H. "Studies on Japanese Paper." Kami-pa-Gekyoshi. 16, October 1962. Discusses paper deterioration due to light. English summary.

Launer, Herbert F., and Wilson, William K. "The Photochemical Stability of Papers." Paper Trade Journal, CXVI:28-36, February 25, 1943.

Lodewijks, J. "The Influence of Light on Museum Objects." Recent Advances in Conservation. London, Butterworth, 1963. Describes the damage to cellulose by ultraviolet light and to colors by visible light.

McLaren, K. "The Spectral Regions of Daylight Which Cause Fading." Journal, Society of Dyers and Colorers. 72, 1956.

Mohrberg, W. "The Yellowing and Resistance to Aging of Paper." Bulletin Institute of Paper Chemistry. 23, 1952-1953. Effect of light on paper ingredients.

Norton, J.E. "A Study of the Variables Encountered in Natural Light Fading." American Dyestuff Reporter, 46:861-883, 1957.

"Problems of Artificial Lighting." In Icom News. 3(1), 1950

Rabek, J.F. "The Effect of UV-light on Polymers." Warsaw, Wiadomosci chemiczne, 20:291-300, 355-372, 435-447, 1966. (Abstracted in Art and Archaeology Technical Abstracts 6(2), 1966.

Richardson, A. "On the Action of Light on Water Colours." Report British Association of Advanced Science, 58:641-642, 1888.

Richter, G. A. "Relative Permanence of Papers Exposed to Sunlight." Industrial and Engineering Chemistry 27, February/April 1965.

Russell, W. J., and Abney W. Action of Light on Water Colours. London, H.M.S.O. 1888. A report to the Science and Art Department of the Committee of Council on Education.

Senebier, J. Memoires Physico-chemiques sur l'Influence de la Luminière Solaire. Geneva, 1782 (vol. 3).

Thomson, Garry. "Visible and Ultraviolet Radiation." Museums Journal 57, 1957.

van Beek, H. C. A., and Heertjes, P. M. "Fading by Light of Organic Dyes on Textiles." Studies in Conservation. 11(3), August 1966.

Vely, V. C., Gallagher, N. D., and Neher, M. B. "Effect of Gamma-radiation on Leather and Pickled Calfskin." Journal American Leather Chemists Association. 55:202-19, 1960.

Wilson, William K., and Harvey, Jack L. "Effect of Light on Coated Groundwood Papers." Tappi 36(10):459-461, 1953.

Heat and Moisture

Ambler, H. R., and Finney, C. F. "Brown Stain Formed on Wet Cellulose." Nature, 179:1141, 1957.

Belaia, I. K. "Aging of Cotton and Flax Fiber Papers under the Simultaneous Influence of Heat and Humidity." Moscow, Stareniye bumagi, 46-56, 1965. (Abstracted in Art and Archaeology Technical Abstracts, 6(2), 1966.

Block, S. S. "Humidity Requirements for Mold Growth." Engineer. Progress. University of Florida VII(10):287-293, 1953.

Block, S. S., Rodriguez-Torrent, R., Cole, M. B., and Prince, A. E. "Humidity and Temperature Requirements of Selected Fungi." Developments in Industrial Microbiology. New York, Plenum Press, 1962. Vol. 3, pp. 204-216.

Bowes, J. H., et al. "Action of Heat and Moisture on Leather." Journal Amer. Leather Chem. Assoc. 56, 1961.

Brooks, C. E. P. "Climate and the Deterioration of Materials." Quarterly Journal of the Royal Meteorological Society, 72:87-97, 1946.

Carson, F. T. Effect of Humidity on Physical Properties of Paper. Washington, U.S. Government Printing Office, 1944. National Bureau of Standards Circular C. 445.

Crook, D. M., and Bennett, W. E. The Effect of Humidity and Temperature on the Physical Properties of Paper. February 1962. The British Paper and Board Industry Research Association.

Hamlin, Arthur T. "The Libraries of Florence--November 1966." American Library Association Bulletin, February 1967.

Jarrell, T. D. "Effect of Atmospheric Humidity on the Moisture Content of Paper." Paper Trade Journal 85(3):47-51, 1927. Illustrated.

Kimberly, Arthur E. "Deteriorative Effect of Sulphur Dioxide Upon Paper in an Atmosphere of Constant Humidity and Temperature." Bureau of Standards Journal of Res. 8:159-171, February 1932.

Lassen, Leon. Influence of Temperature on Relative Humidity within Confined Spaces with and without a Desiccant. FPL Report R1498 (1945). Tables and chart.

Little, A. H., and Clayton, J. W. "Photochemical Tendering and Fading of Dyed Textiles at Different Humidities." Journal Soc. Dyers and Colourists. 79:671-677, December 1963. Shirley Institute, Manchester, England

Richter, George A., and Wells, Frank L. "Influence of Moisture in Accelerated Aging of Cellulose." Tappi, 39(8):603-608, August 1956.

Rose, C. D., and Turner, J. N. "Mold Growth on Leather as Affected by Humidity Changes." Journal Society of Leather Trades' Chemists. 35, 1951.

Rubinstein, Nicolai. "Libraries and Archives of Florence." Times Literary Supplement, December 1, 1966, page 1133.

Tribolet, Harold W. Flood Damage to Florence's Books and Manuscripts. Chicago, The Lakeside Press, 1967.

Yabrova, R. R. "Influence of Temperature and the Air Humidity on the Aging of Paper." Chemical Abstracts, 54, 1960.

Insects

Animals Injurious to Books. 3rd ed. London, 1938. Science Museum. Science Library Bibliographical Series no. 377.

Back, E. A. Book-Lice or Psocids. Washington, U.S. Government Printing Office, 1922.

---- Bookworms. Washington, U.S. Department of Agriculture, 1940.

---- "Book Worms." The Indian Archives. 1(2), 1947.

---- "Book Worms." Smithsonian Institution Annual Report. Washington, U.S. Government Printing Office, 1939. An excellent summary with 18 illustrations of the insects dangerous to books.

Ballou, H.A. Insect Pests of the Lesser Antilles. Bridgetown, Barbados, Advocate Co., 1912. Imperial Department of Agriculture for the West Indies. Great Britain. Pamphlet Series no. 71.

Boyer, J. "Insect Enemies of Books." Scientific American. 98:413-414, 1908.

British Museum, Economic Series: "The Cockroach." No. 12, 1951; "Clothes Moths and House Moths." No. 14, 1951; "Furniture Beetles." No. 11, 1954. Economic Leaflets: "Silver Fish and Firebrat." No. 3, 1957; "Psocids, Book Lice, etc." No. 4, 1940.

Broadhead, E. "The Book-Louse and Other Library Pests." British Book News. March, 1946, pp. 77-81.

Clothes Moths and Carpet Beetles: How to Combat Them. Washington, U.S. Government Printing Office, 1953.

Clothes Moths and House Moths; Their Life-History, Habits and Control. 5th ed. London, 1951. British Museum (Natural History).

Cockroaches--How to Control Them. Washington, U.S. Government Printing Office, 1958.

Collins, P.B. Household Pests; Their Habits, Prevention and Control. London, Pitman, 1936.

Feytaud, Jr. "Les Insectes Ravageurs d'Archives; Comment les Combattre?" Archives, Bibliotheques, Collections, Documentation. 1952, No. 6, pp. 147-156.

Fullaway, D.T. "Termites, or White Ants, in Hawaii." Hawaiian Forester and Agriculturist. 23:68-88, 1926.

Gahan, C.J. Furniture Beetles; Their Life History and How to Check or Prevent the Damage Caused by the Worm. London, British Museum, 1920. Natural History Department. Economic Series No. 11.

Gallo, A. "La Lotta anti-Termitica in Italia." Bolletino dell Istituto de Patologia del Libro. 11:3-34, 1952.

Gallo, F. "Fatti e Misfatti del Pesciolino d'Argento." Bolletino dell Istituto de Patologia del Libro, 13, 1954.

Godwin, A. J. H. "Insects and Human Culture in Africa." Scientia. 43:324-329, 1958.

Golledge, C. J. "The Insect Pests of Books. Library Association Record. 7:240-242, 1929.

Hagen, H. A. "Insect Pests in Libraries." Library Journal, 4: 251-274, 1879.

Harris, W. V. Termites: Their Recognition and Control. London, Longmans, 1961.

Hickin, N. E. Woodworm: Its Biology and Extermination. Leatherhead, Surrey, 1954.

Hinton, H. E. "The Ptinidae of Economic Importance." Bulletin of Entomological Research, 31:331-381, 1941.

Hoffman, W. A. "Rhizopertha Dominica as a Library Pest." Journal of Economic Entomology. 26:293-294, 1933.

Houlbert, C. V. Les Insectes Ennemis des Libres. Paris, Picard, 1903.

Howard, L. O., and Martlett, C. L. The Principal Household Insects of the United States. Washington, U. S. Government Printing Office, 1896.

Hughes, A. W. McKenny. "Insect Pests of Books and Paper." Archives. 7, 1952. The British Records Association, 1 Lancaster Place, London, W. C. 2.

"Insect Attacks on Wood." Review. 28: 725-726, 829-830, 1955.

"Insects, Damage From." American Archivist. 16:377.

Jepson, F. P. "Sitadrepa Damages Books." Fiji Department of Agriculture Annual Report. 1919.

Kalshoven, L. G. E. "Book-Beetle in the Netherlands Indies." Entomologische mededeelingen van Nederlandsch-Indie. 4:10-16, 1938.

Kimberly, A. E. "Insect and Bacterial Enemies of Archives." American Archivist, 11:246-247, 1948.

Kofoid, C. A., et al. Termites and Termite Control. Berkeley, University of California Press, 1946.

Laing, F. "Borkhausenia pseudospretella and Other House Moths."

Entomologist's Monthly Magazine, 68:77-80, 1932.

Lepigre, A. L.   Insectes du Logis et du Magasin.   Alger, Insectarium Jardin d'Essai, 1951.

Light, S. F.   Termites and Termite Damage.   Berkeley, University of California, 1929.   College of Agriculture Circular No. 314.

Lindsay, E.   "The Biology of the Silverfish.   Ctenolepisma Longicaudata Esch. with Particular Reference to Its Feeding Habits."   Proc. Zool. Soc. Victoria.   Vol. 52.

Mallis, A.   "The Silverfish."   Pest Control and Sanitation.   1(1), 1946.

Marshall, M.   "The Termite Menace."   Technical Studies, 4(3), 1936.

McDaniel, E. I.   Cockroaches, Silverfish, and Book-Lice.   East Lansing, Michigan State College, 1934.   Agricultural Experiment Station Circular Bulletin 101.

McKenny Hughes, A. W.   "Insect Pests of Books and Paper."   Archives, 7, 1952.

Morita, H.   "Some Observations of the Silverfish, Lepisma saccharina."   Proc. of the Hawaiian Entomological Soc. 6:271-273, 1925.

Nyuksha, Y. P.   "Changes in the Chemical and Mechanical Qualities of Paper Contaminated by Gimnoascus Setosus."   Microbiology (Moscow) 29(2):276-80, 1960.

---- 'Microscopic Study of Paper Stained by the Fungus Gimnoascus Setosus."   Microbiology (Moscow) 29(I):133-136, 1960.

O'Connor, Rev. J. F. X.   Facts About Bookworms.   London, Suckling & Co., 1898.   Their history in literature and their damage in libraries.

Peignot, E. F.   "Insectes Qui Rongent les Livres."   Dictionnaire Raisonne de Bibliologie.   Paris, Villeir, 1802.

Perotin, Y.   "Le Probleme des Termites et Autres Agents Destructeurs aux Archives de la Reunion."   Arch. Dept. Réunion.   Paris, 1953.

Petrova, G. I.   "Insects in Book Storerooms."   Collection of Materials on the Preservation of Library Resources.   Moscow, U.S.S.R. State Library, 1953.   English translation available from U. S. Department of Commerce, OTS, Springfield, Va.

Plenderleith, H. J.   "Insects Among Archives."   British Records

Association Bulletin. No. 18, 2-6, 1945.

Robinow, B. H. "Books and Cockroaches; An Attempt to Cope with the Menace." South Africa Libraries, 24(2):40-42, 1956.

Silverfish and Firebrats. Washington, U. S. Government Printing Office, 1957.

Skaife, S. H. Dwellers in Darkness. London, Longmans, 1955.

Snyder, T. E. Our Enemy the Termite. Ithaca, N. Y., Comstock Publishing Co., 1935.

---- Our Enemy the Termite. 2nd ed. London, Constable, 1948.

Stored Grain Pests. Washington, U. S. Government Printing Office, 1962. Farmers Bulletin No. 1260. Includes identification of pests known to attack books and paper.

Terlecki, E. "Book Scorpions." Bibliotekarz. 21, 1954.

Termites in the Humid Tropics. Paris, UNESCO, 1960.

Termites, Wood-borers and Fungi in Buildings. Report of the Committee on the Protection of Building Timbers in South Africa Against Termites, Wood-boring Beetles and Fungi. Pretoria, South African Council for Scientific and Industrial Research, 1950. National Building Research Institute.

Wahls, A. "Woodboring Pests and Their Remedies." Munich, Maltechnik, 72:18-23, 1966. (Abstracted in Art and Archaeology Technical Abstracts, 6(2), 1966.

Watson, J. R. "A Tropical Bookworm in Florida." Florida Entomologist. 26(4):61-63, 1943.

Weiss, H. B., and Carruthers, R. H. Insect Enemies of Books. New York, New York Public Library, 1945.

---- Insect Pests of Books. New York, 1936.

Fungi

Abrams, Ed. Microbiological Deterioration of Organic Materials. Washington, U. S. Government Printing Office, 1948. Bureau of Standards Misc. Publication 188.

Armitage, F. D. The Cause of Mildew on Books and Methods of Preservation. London, Printing, Packaging and Allied Trades Research Association. PATRA Bulletin No. 8, 1949.

Barghoorn, E. S. "Histological Study of the Action of Fungi on

Leather." Journal Amer. Leather Chem. Assoc., 45:688-700, 1950.

Barr, P. "Mildew in Libraries--Prevention and Treatment." New Jersey Library Bulletin, 13:123-129, 1945.

Beckwith, Theodore D., Swanson, W.H., and Iiams, Thomas Marion. "Deterioration of Paper; The Cause and Effect of Foxing." University of California, Los Angeles, Publ. Biol. Sci., 1(13): 299-356, pls. 13-20, 1940.

Belyakova, L.A. "The Mold Species and Their Effect on Book Materials." Collection of Materials on the Preservation of Library Resources. Moscow, 1958. English translation available from Department of Commerce, OTS, Springfield, Va.

Block, S.S., Rodriguez-Torrent, R., Cole, M.B., and Prince, A.E. "Humidity and Temperature Requirements of Selected Fungi." Developments in Industrial Microbiology. New York, Plenum Press, 1962. 3:204-216, 1962.

Bracken, A. The Chemistry of Micro-organisms. London, Pitman and Sons, 1955.

Brown, A.E. "Report on the Problems of Fungal Growth on Synthetic Resins, Plastics and Plasticizers." U.S. Office of Scientific Research and Development Report 6067, 1945.

Czerwinska, E., Sadurska, I., and Kozlowska, D. "Actinomycetes Damaging Old Manuscripts and Documents." Acta Microb. Polon. 2:160-163, 1953.

Czerwinska, E., and Kowalik, R. "Penicillia Destroying Archival Papers." Acta Microb. Polon., 5(1-2):299-302, 1956.

Flieder, F. "Etude de la Résistance Biologique des Procédés de Renforcement des Documents Graphiques." Studies in Conservation. London, 1963. Mme. Flieder's findings on the resistance of reinforced paper to mold.

---- "Lutte Contra Les Moisissures des Materiaux Constitutifs des Documents Graphiques." Studies in Conservation. London, 1961. Summarizes Mme. Flieder's investigation of molds and preventive measures.

Gallo, F. "Biological Agents Which Damage Paper Materials in Libraries and Archives." Recent Advances in Conservation. London, Butterworths, 1963.

Gascoigne, J.A., and Gascoigne, M.M. Biological Degradation of Cellulose. London, Butterworths, 1960.

Harmsen, L., and Vincentsnissen, T. "Bacterial Attacks on Wood."

Berlin, Holz-Roh und Werkstoff, 23:389-393, 1965. (Abstracted in Art and Archaeology Technical Abstracts, 6(2), 1966.)

Henn, R.W., and Wiest, D.G. "Microscopic Spots in Processed Microfilm: Their Nature and Prevention." Photographic Science and Engineering 7:253-261, September/October, 1963.

Iiams, T.M., and Beckwith, T.D. "Notes on the Causes and Prevention of Foxing in Books." Libr. Quart. 5(4):407-418, 1935.

Inouye, Y., Iizuka, Y., and Tazima, T. "Studies on Leather Fungi. I. Morphology and Enzyme Activity of the Leather Fungi. II. Selection of the Test Strains and the Antifungal Action of Phenolic Compounds. III. The Antifungal Activity of Organic Mercury Compounds." Bull. Jap. Assoc. Leather Tech. 3:95-100, 1957; 4:163-168, 1958.

Kanagy, J.R., et al. "Effects of Mildew on Vegetable-Tanned Strap Leather." Journal of Research, National Bureau of Standards. 36, 1946.

Kowalik, R. Micro-organisms Destroying Paper, Leather and Wax Seals, Pathogenic for Man. Warsaw, Muzeum Mickiewicza, 1960.

---- Micro-organisms That Destroy the Archival Papers. Warsaw, Prace Placowek Naukowo Badawczy Ministerstwa Przemyslu Chimiczenego Zeszyt 2/52.

Kowalik, R., and Sadurska J. "Micro-organisms Destroying Leather Bookbindings." Acta Micr. Polon. V:1-2, 285-90, 1956.

---- "Micro-organisms Destroying Paper, Leather and Wax Seals in the Air of Archives." Acta Microbiologica Polonica. 5(1/2): 277-284, 1956.

Leutritz, John Jr. "The Effect of Fungi and Humidity on Plastics." ASTM Bulletin, No. 152, 88 ff, TP 140, May 1958.

Levi Della Vida, M. "I microorganismi nemici del libro." Accad. Bibl. Italia, 10(4):234-250, 1936.

McCamy, C.S., and Pope, C.I. Summary of Current Research on Archival Microfilm. Washington, U.S. Government Printing Office, 1965. National Bureau of Standards Technical Note No. 261. Summarizes all the information available up to 1965 on microfilm spots. Includes recommendations for storage and handling.

"Mildew." American Archivist. 1:11.

Minier, D.W. "Mildew and Books." Library Journal, 57:931-936, 1932.

Mitchell, C.A., and Wood, D.R. "Action of Molds on Ink in Writing." Analyst, pp. 63-111, 1938.

Mitton, R.G., and Turner, J.N. "A Study of Mould Growth on Chrome Tanned Leather and the Associated Changes in Physical Properties." Journal Society of Leather Chemists. 39:343-358, 1955.

Moutia, A. "Sitodrepa panicea L. Infesting Books." Mauritius Department of Agriculture Annual Report. 1932. Published 1933.

Nishira, H. "The Tannin-decomposing Enzyme of Molds. V. Paper Chromatographic Analysis of Tannase Formation." Hakko Kogaku Zasshi. 37: 85-89.

Nishira, H., and Mugibayashi, N. "Tannin Decomposing Enzyme of Molds. XI. Formation of Tannase by Various Molds on Wheat Bran Medium." Hyogo Noka Daigaku Kenkyu Hokoku Nogeikaku Hem. 4:113-116, 1960.

Nyuksha, J.P. "Changes in the Chemical and Mechanical Qualities of Paper Contaminated by Gimnoascus Setosus." Microbiology. Moscow, 29(2):276-280, 1960.

---- "Microscopic Study of Paper Stained by the Fungus Gimnoascus Setosus." Microbiology 29(1):133-136, 1960.

---- "Mycoflora of Books and Paper." Botanicheskii Zhurnal. 41(6):797-809, 1956. Translated by D.A. Sinclair, Ottawa, 1958.

---- "Physical Investigation of Gimnoascus Setosus Eidam." Microbiologiya, 22(1):15-22, 1953 and 3:306-312, 1957. Reports on one of the most common book pests. (Abstracted in Art and Archaeology Technical Abstracts, 6(2), 1966.)

---- "The Action of Bacterial Irradiation on Fungi Spores." Moscow, Microbiologiya, 22(2):678-681, 1953. (Abstracted in Art and Archaeology Technical Abstracts, 6(2), 1966.)

---- "Experimental Pigmentation of Paper Samples by Fungi." Moscow, Stareniye bumagi, 82-93, 1965. (Abstracted in Art and Archaeology Technical Abstracts, 6(2), 1966.)

Plenderleith, H.J. "Mould in the Muniment Room." Archives, 7:13, 1952.

Rose, C.D., and Turner, J.N. "Mold Growth on Leather as Affected by Humidity Changes." Journal Soc. of Leather Trades' Chemists, 35:37-42, 1951; C.A. 45, 1951, 8283d.

Siu, Ralph G.H. Microbial Decomposition of Cellulose, With Special Reference to Cotton Textiles. New York, Reinhold Publishing Corp., 1951.

Smirnowa, B.I. Problems of Micro-organisms in Parchments. Moscow, U.S.S.R. Academy of Sciences, 1962.

Tate, Vernon D. Checklist of Information About Microscopic Spots on Microfilm. Distributed at the 28th annual S.A.A. meeting October 6-10, 1964. Society of American Archivists, 1964.

Wang, C.J.K. "Preliminary Report on the Fungus Flora Pulp and Paper in New York." Tappi 44(II):785-788, 1961.

Wiest, D.G., and Henn, R.W. "Microscopic Spots; a Progress Report." (Abstract) National Micro-News, 70, 249-264, June 1964.

Acid

Barrow, W.J. "Acidity: An Undesirable Property in Paste and Mending Tissue." American Archivist, 30:190-193, January, 1967.

Bishop, William W. "One Problem for 1950--Woodpulp Paper in Books." Bookmen's Holiday. New York, New York Public Library, 1943. pp. 407-415.

Cause and Prevention of Decay in Bookbinding Leather, The (two reports). London, St. Bride's Institute, 1933 and 1936. Findings of the Printing Industry Research Association and the British Leather Manufacturer's Research Association.

Chene, M. "Unfavorable Influence of Acidity on Paper and Board Quality." Bulletin, Association Tech. Ind. Papetiere 5, 74, 1947; BIPC 18, 771.

Hoffman, W.F. "Deterioration of Paper by Excessive Acidity." Paper Trade Journal 88(12):59-60, 1929.

---- "Effect of Residual Acid on Rate of Deterioration of Paper." Paper Trade Journal 86(9):58-60, illus., 1928.

"Ink, Acidity." American Archivist. 10:338   11:291   12:11.

Jarrell, T.D., Hankins, J.M., and Veitch, F.P. The Effect of Inorganic Acids on the Physical Properties of Waterleaf Rag Bond Paper. Washington, U.S. Government Printing Office, 1932. U.S. Department of Agriculture Technical Bulletin No. 334.

"Paper, Acidity." American Archivist. 6:151   12:9.

Report of the Committee on Leather for Bookbinding. London,

314

Royal Society of Arts, 1905.   Covers the sources of leather de-
cay--mainly acid.

Zaguliaeva, Z.A.   "The Influence of Acidity on Fungi Growth in
    Paper." Moscow, Stareniye bumagi, 75-81, 1965.   (Abstracted
in Art and Archaeology Technical Abstracts, 6(2), 1966.)

Conservation
General

Abridgement of Specifications Relating to Books, Portfolios, Card
    Cases A.D. 1768-1866. H.M. Patent Office, London, 1870.

Alden, J.E.   "Why Preserve Books?" Catholic Library World, 30:
    267-272, 1959.   An attempt to explore reasons other than the
    obvious ones for the preservation of books as physical objects.

American Library Association, Library Technology Project.   Perma-
    nence and Durability of Library Catalog Cards.   A study con-
    ducted by W.J. Barrow for the Library Technology Project.
    Chicago, American Library Association, 1961. (LTP Publica-
    tions, No. 3.)

Archer, H. Richard, (ed.) Rare Book Collections.   Chicago, Amer-
    ican Library Association, 1965.   Some theoretical and practical
    suggestions for use by librarians and students on the subjects of
    the nature and importance of rare books; the rare book library
    and the public; housing and equipment; care, maintenance and
    storage.

Bach, C.H., and Oddon, Y.   Petit Guide Du Bibliothecaire.   4th
    ed.   Paris, Bourrelier, 1952.

Barrow, W.J.   "New Device Tests Performance of Library Bind-
    ings." Book Production, 79:60-62, March 1964.

Baughman, Roland.   "Conservation of Old and Rare Books." Li-
    brary Trends,   4:3, 239-247, 1956.

Beljakova, L.A., et al.   "Book Preservation in U.S.S.R. Libra-
    ries." UNESCO Bulletin for Libraries, 15, July 1961.

Belov, G.A.   "New Techniques, New Materials, and New Experi-
    ences Concerning Restoration of Documents and Seals, Preser-
    vation of Maps and Plans, and Photography Since 1950."
    Archivum, 10:72-80, 104-105, 1960.   Abstract in American
    Archivist, 26:256, April 1963.

Belyakova, L.A., and Kozulina, O.V. (editors).   Collection of Ma-
    terials on the Preservation of Library Resources No. 3.   Mos-
    cow, 1958.   Translated from the Russian by Israel Program for
    Scientific Translations for National Science Foundation, Wash-

315

ington. Available from Department of Commerce, OTS, Springfield, Va.

Bhargava, K. D.   Repair and Preservation of Records.   New Delhi,
National Archives of India 1959.

"Books and Documents."   American Archivist, 10:188.

Brandi, Cesare.   "Il Fondamento Teorico del Restauro."   Bolletino
Istituto Centrale Restauro I, 1950.   Theoretical considerations
and the importance of the esthetic point of view.

Buck, R. D.   "An Experiment in Co-operative Conservation."   Studies in Conservation II, No. 3, 1956.

Capell, H. W.   "The Preservation and Repair of Old Books."
British and Colonial Printer, 148(1160):192, 200, 1951.

"Care and Conservation in the Home."   Toledo Museum of Art.
Museum News, 8(3), 1965.

Care of Records in a National Emergency, The.   Bulletin No. 3 of
the National Archives, Washington, U. S. Government Printing
Office.

Casford, E. L.   "Periodicals; Their Use and Preservation."   Wilson
Library Bulletin, 13:593-596, 1939.

Chasse, J.   Conservation des Documents.   (Instructions sommaires
pour l'organisation et le fonctionnement des bibliothèques pub-
liques, 3) Paris, Ministère de l'Education Nationale, Direction
des Bibliothèques de France, 1954.

Chastukin, V.   "Scientific Research on Book Hygiene"   Bibliotekar
No. 9, Dec. 1948.

Clark, John Willis.   The Care of Books.   Cambridge, Cambridge
University Press, 1901.

Clayjus, F. H.   "The Prevention of Damage to Books and Manuscripts."   Allgemeine Paper- Rundschau 16 (1956),   Bull. Inst.
Pap. Chem., 27, 1956-1957.

Cobden-Sanderson, T. J.   Industrial Ideals and the Book Beautiful.
London, 1901.

Collis, I. P.   "Technical Care of Records; Document Conservation
in the Local Repository."   Archives, 6:4-7, March, 1963.

"Comité pour les Laboratoires de Musées.   Groupe de Travail pour
l'Etude de la Conservation des Materiaux Constitutifs des Documents Graphiques."   Paris, Bibliothèque Nationale.   (19-21
mai 1960) Pieces Jointes. 1-3.   International Council of Museums.

Condon, Edward Uhler. Preservation of the Declaration of Independence and the Constitution of the United States. Washington, U.S. Government Printing Office, 1951. NBS Circ. 505,16 pp.

Constable, W.G. "Curators and Conservation." Studies in Conservation I(3), 1954.

---- "Curatorial Problems in Relation to Conservation." Bulletin Fogg Museum of Art, 10, 1946.

David, Charles. "The Conservation of Historical Source Material." American Documentation, 7:76-82, April, 1956.

Deterioration and Preservation of Book Material Stored in Libraries, The. Garston, Building Research Station, 1949. (Note No. D. 62). Great Britain. Department of Scientific and Industrial Research.

Edlund, P.E. "The Continuing Quest: Care of Library of Congress Collections." Library Journal 90, 1965. Care of books, maps, manuscripts, film, tape, etc.

Ellis, R.II. "An Archivist's Note on the Conservation of Documents." Journal of the Society of Archivists, 1(9):252-254, 1959.

---- "Latest Information for the Private Owner and Smaller Repository." Archives 4, 1963. (Archive repair.)

Erastov, D.P. "Potentialities of Electronographic Methods in Document Investigation." Moscow, Stareniye bumagi, 133-144, 1965. (Abstracted in Art and Archaeology Technical Abstracts, 6(2), 1966.)

---- "Additional Data on the Investigation of Experimental Paper Samples by Means of Optical Methods." Moscow, Stareniye bumagi, 153-156, 1965.

Fitzpatrick, John C. Notes on the Care, Cataloging, Calendaring and Arranging of Manuscripts. Washington, U.S. Library of Congress. Division of Manuscripts, 3rd ed. Government Printing Office, 1928.

Fitzsimmons, N. "Emergency Measures and Museums." Museum News 43(6), 1965. (Suggested wartime measures.)

Geigy (J.R.) A.G. "Protecting Organic Materials from the Effects of Ultraviolet Radiation and Oxidation." British patent 991,320, May 5, 1965. (Uses additives to plastic formulas.)

"General Library Conservation." Library Journal, 90(3), 1965.

Grant, Julius. Books and Documents: Dating, Permanence and

Preservation. London, Grafton and Co., 1937. (The section on preservation is devoted to preventive rather than curative measures.)

Greathouse, G.A., and Wessel, C.J. Deterioration of Materials, Causes and Preventive Techniques. New York, Reinhold Publishing Corp., 1954.

Grove, L.E. "Predictability of Permanence in Perfect Library Bindings." College and Research Libraries 22:341-344, Sept. 1961.

---- "What Good Is Greenland?" New thinking on book preservation and temperature. Wilson Library Bulletin 36:749, 1962.

Guha Roy, K.K. "How to Preserve Books." Modern Librarian, 9:79-87, 1939.

"Handling Prints, Drawings, Books." Museum News, 43, 1964.

Harrison, T. "The Care of Books." The Book-collector's Quarterly, 3:1-14, London 1931.

Harrison, W.R. Suspect Documents, Their Scientific Examination. New York, Frederick Praeger, 1958.

Hawthorne, J.O., et al. "Method of Protecting Material Against the Effects of Light." Prevention of Deterioration Abstracts, 18, 1960. Protection by chemical treatment.

Held, J.S. A Preliminary List of Basic Reference Works in the Fine Arts. New York, American Group, International Institute for Conservation, 1966.

Hobbs, John L. Local History and the Library. London, Andre Deutsch, 1962. With a foreword by H.M. Cashmore. Partial contents: manuscript records, pp. 55-77; local records, the present position, pp. 78-96; care and treatment of archives, pp. 97-113. Includes bibliography.

"How Long Do Books Last?" (Abstract) Bulletin Institute of Paper Chemistry 30, 1959-1960.

Iiams, Thomas M. "Preservation of Rare Books and Manuscripts in the Huntington Library." Library Quarterly, II: October, 1932.

India, Imperial Record Department, New Delhi. Notes on Preservation of Records. Simla, Government of India Press, 1941.

Instructions for the Preservation of Books. Achimota, University College of Ghana Library, 1956.

318

Johnson, Charles. The Care of Documents and Management of Archives. London, Society for Promoting Christian Knowledge, 1919.

Kathpalia, Y.P. "Care of Books in the Libraries." Indian Archives, 9:147-154, 1955.

Keck, Caroline. "History and Philosophy of Conservation." Bulletin American Group (IIC) 5, 1964.

---- "Technical Assistance; Where to Find it; What to Expect." Curator, 8(3), 1965.

Keck, C., and Keck, S. "Conservation in the U.S.A.: a Scandal." Art News, 57, 1958.

Keyes, D.M. "Alternatives to a New Library Building." College and Research Libraries, 22, Sept. 1962.

Kimberly, Arthur E. "Recent Developments in Record Preservation." Indian Archives 3:69-72, 1949.

Kimberly, A.E., and Scribner, B.W. Summary Report of the Bureau of Standards Research on Preservation of Records. Washington, Bureau of Standards Miscellaneous Publication No. 144, 1934. This is a milestone in American library conservation studies and an excellent point of departure for a detailed study of the overall problem.

Kingery, Robert E. "The Extent of the Paper Problem in Large Research Collections and the Comparative Costs of Available Solutions." Permanent/Durable Book Paper. Summary of a conference held in Washington, September 1960. Sponsored by the American Library Association and the Virginia State Library. Richmond, The Virginia State Library, 1960, pp. 37-38.

Lamb, C.M., (ed.). The Calligrapher's Handbook. London, Faber and Faber, Ltd. Contains useful information for librarians on ink, skins, paper, gilding and manuscript binding.

Land, Robert H. "Defense of Archives Against Human Foes." American Archivist, 19:121-138, April 1956.

Lewis, Harry F. "Research for the Archivist of Today and Tomorrow." The American Archivist, XII, 9-17, January 1949.

---- "The Deterioration of Book Paper in Library Use." American Archivist 22, 1959.

Lovett, Robert W. "Care and Handling of Non-Governmental Archives." Library Trends, 5:380-389, January 1957. A bibliography is included.

---- "Care in the Handling of Manuscripts and Archives." In American Association of Law Libraries, Institute for Law Librarians, Proceedings: Literature of the Law-Techniques of Access. South Hackensack, N.J., Rothman & Company, 1962, p.17-22.

Lucas, A. Antiques, Their Storage and Preservation. London, 1924.

Ludwig, H. "Some Hints on the Care and Treatment of Graphics, Drawings, etc." Neue Museumskunde, Leipzig, 3:158-160, 1960.

Melía, J.A. "La Conservación de Libros y Manuscritos." In: Universidad Nacional Autónoma de México, Anuario de biblioteconomía y archivonomía, pp. 81-97. Universidad Nacional Autónoma de México, 1962.

"New Rx for Old Books Offered by Vatican Institute." Library Journal, 88(12), 1963. Vitamins for paper.

Nyuksha, J.P. "To Preserve for Centuries." Moscow, Bibliotekar 12:38-40, 1963. Describes restoration practices at the State Public Library, Leningrad.

---- "Lighting Appliance for Book Restoration." Moscow, Bibliotekar, 10:41-42, 1956. A lighting device for use between book pages.

Petrova, L.G. "Requirements for the Preservation of Book Collections in the Book Storerooms of the Lenin State Library." In: Collection of Materials on the Preservation of Library Resources, (Moscow, 1953). U.S. Department of Commerce, Office of Technical Services, Springfield, Va., 1964.

---- "Instructions for Dusting Book Collections and for Leaf-by-Leaf Treatment of Damaged and Dirty Books." (ibid.)

---- "Instructions for Inspecting Book Collections." (ibid.)

Petrova, L.G., (ed.), and Belyakova, L.A., (ed.). Collection of Materials on the Preservation of Library Resources. Moscow, U.S.S.R. State Library 1953-1958. Translation available from U.S. Department of Commerce, Office of Technical Services, Springfield, Va.

Plenderleith, Harold James. "Preservation of Museum Objects in War-time." Nature (London), 152:94-97, 1943.

---- "The New Science of Art Conservation." UNESCO Courier 18, 1965. Some conservation techniques and the work of the Rome Centre.

Plumbe, W.S. The Preservation of Books. London, Oxford Press, 1964.
320

Pollak, H. "Dehumidification for the Preservation of Documents." *Mechanical World*, 1961, Aug. pp. 268-270; Sept. pp. 302-304.

"Preservation of Books--Examination of the Problem." *Library Journal*, 91(1 and 2), 1966.

"Preservation of Records in Libraries." *Science*. New York, 79 (2043):176, Feb. 23, 1934. A summary of the U.S. Bureau of Standards studies.

"Protection of Documents." *American Archivist*. 1:142 14:372 15:280 16:125, 181, 234 17:110, 370 19:122, 130, 134 20:36.

Ranbir, Kishore. "The Preservation of Rare Books and Manuscripts." *The Sunday Statesman*, March 1, 1959.

Ranganathan, S.R. *Social Bibliography or Physical Bibliography for Librarians*. Delhi, India, University of Delhi, 1952. 348 pp. (Library Science Series, No. 4.)

Rawlins, F.I.G. "Science in the Care of Museum Objects. *Museums Journal*, 54, 1955.

----- "Scientific Methods in the Care of Works of Art." *Research*, London, 11, 1958.

----- "The Scientific Outlook in Conservation." *Museums Journal*, 61, 1961.

Rorimer, J.J. *Ultraviolet Rays and Their Use in the Examination of Works of Art*. New York, Metropolitan Museum of Art, 1931.

Sanders, J.P. "The Preservation of Manuscripts and Bindings." *Library Journal*, 1932, pp. 936-938. Also appeared in *Science*, 1932, No. 76, pp. 277-278.

Santucci, L. "The Application of Chemical and Physical Methods to Conservation of Archival Materials." *Recent Advances in Conservation*. London, Butterworths, 1963. A review of the history of the scientific approach to conservation with detailed bibliographic references.

Schulz, H.C. "The Care and Storage of Manuscripts in the Huntington Library." *Library Quarterly*, 5:78-86, January 1935.

Schubert, H., and Brommelle, N. "Cooperation for Conservation in Great Britain." *Museums Journal* 61, 1961.

Scribner, B.W. *Preservation of Newspaper Records*. Washington, U.S. Government Printing Office, 1934. (National Bureau of Standards Miscellaneous Publication No. 145.)

321

---- "Preservation of Records in Libraries." Library Quarterly, 4:371-383, 1934.

Scriven, Margaret. "Preservation and Restoration of Library Materials." Special Libraries, (N.Y.), 47(10):439-448, 1945.

Sherwood, P.W. "Corrosion Inhibitors." Australian Paint Journal, 6(11):31-33, 35, 37, 1965.

Spawn, Willman. "The Conservation of Books and Papers." Ontario Library Review, 46, 5-7, 1962.

Spyers-Duran, Peter. Moving Library Materials. Chicago, American Library Association, 1965. A 63-page monograph on the problem of moving books from one building to another.

Standard for the Protection of Records 1963. Boston, National Fire Protection Association 1963. Fire protection.

Subramanian, R. "Chemical Conservation" in Handbook of Museum Technique. Madras, Government of Madras 1960. Includes treatment of paper.

Suri, V.S. "Care and Preservation of Old and Rare Materials in Libraries." Indian Librarian, pp. 8-13, March 1954.

---- "Some Hints on the Health of Contents of Libraries." Indian Librarian, pp. 147-153, March 1954.

Tauber, M.F., (ed.). "Conservation of Library Materials." Library Trends 4, January 1956.

---- Technical Services in Libraries. New York, Columbia University Press, xvi, 1954. See Chapters 15-17, "Conservation of Library Materials."

Tests and Procedures for Books and Book Components. Hoboken, N.J. United States Testing Company, 1957.

Turner, Robert W.S. "To Repair or Despair?" American Archivist, 20:319-334, October 1957.

Usilton, Bertha M. Subject Index to Technical Studies in the Field of Fine Arts. Pittsburgh, Tamworth Press, 1965. Key to the wealth of information in the ten volumes (1932-1942) of the Fogg Museum's important work.

Warren, Jenney. "Permanence and Durability; Different Qualities and Needs." Publishers' Weekly, 185(5):121,124, February 3, 1964. Comments on the Barrow reports by the director of S. D. Warren Co.

Werner, Anthony E. "The Preservation of Archives." Journal of the Society of Archivists, 1:282-288, October 1959.

Williams, E.C. "Magnitude of the Paper Deterioration Problem as Measured by a National Union Catalog Sample. " College and Research Libraries 23, Nov. 1962.

Williams, Gordon R. "The Preservation of Deteriorating Books, Part I, The Problem; Part II, Recommended Solution. " New York, Library Journal, 91:51-56, 189-194, Jan. 1966. A report for the Association of Research Libraries committee on preservation.

Wood, G.W. "Books and Documents: Protection from Insect Damage. A Survey of the Problem and Methods of Control. " Pesticides Abstracts and News Summary Section A, 2, Maggio 1956.

Wood, L.A., and Moyer, R.C. "Proper Care of Test Records. " Trans IRE-PGA, July 1952, pp. 4ff.

Yabrova, R.R. "The Prevention of Aging of Books and Newspapers. " Collection of Materials on the Preservation of Library Resources, Moscow 1953. English translation available from The National Science Foundation, Washington, D.C., 1964.

Your Book Collection: Its Care. Albany, N.Y., New York State Library. Library Extension Division, 1957. Illus.

Zaehnsdorf, E., and Hutchins, C.J. "The Care and Preservation of Books. " The American Book Collector, I(1), January 1932.

Zigrosser, C., and Gaehde, C.M. A Guide to the Collecting and Care of Original Prints. New York, Crown Publishers, 1965.

Environment Control

Denninger, E. "Problems of Climate and Climate Control. " (In buildings.) West Germany, Nachrichtenblatt der Denkmalflege in Baden-Württemberg, 8(3):64-65, 1965. (Abstracted in Art and Archaeology Technical Abstracts, 6(2), 1966.

Environmental Effects on Materials and Equipment. (Abstracts Section A). Washington, Prevention of Deterioration Center, National Academy of Sciences--National Research Council, 1945-1965.

Franizitta, G. "Relative Humidity in Rooms and Its Dependence Upon the Thermal Regime. " Milan, La Termotecnica, No. 5, 283-286, 1966. (Abstracted in Art and Archaeology Technical Abstracts, 6(2), 1966.)

Hughson, R.U. "Controlling Air Pollution. " Washington, Chemical

323

Engineering News, 73(8):71-90, 1966.

Air Conditioning

"Air Conditioning and Lighting from the Point of View of Conservation." Museums Journal 63(1-2), 1963.

Air Conditions and the Comfort of Workers. Industrial Health Series No. 5. New York, Metropolitan Life Insurance Company, 1930.

Amdur, Elias J. "Humidity control--Isolated Area Plan." Museum News, 43:58-60, 1964, one chart; Technical Supplement No. 4, Part II. Detailed information about applying this concept to existing structures as well as to new construction. An alternative when total air-conditioning is not feasible.

Beach, R. F., and Martin, W. H. "Union Theological Seminary Airconditions Its Library." College and Research Libraries, 18: 297-301, 1957. Practical experience and conclusions in the air-conditioning of an existing library building; of value to the librarian considering such a step.

Belaya, I. K. "Instructions on the Use of Bactericidal Circulation Devices for the Disinfection of Air in Libraries." Collection of Materials on the Preservation of Library Resources. Moscow, 1958. U. S. Department of Commerce, OTS, Springfield, Va., 1964.

Brommelle, N. S. "Air-conditioning and Lighting from the Point of View of Conservation." Museums Journal 63(1-2):33-36, 1965.

Buck, Richard D. "A Specification for Museum Air Conditioning." Museum News 43:53-57, 1964; Technical Supplement, No. 4, Part I; one chart, seven references. Applies equally to libraries and archives.

Carr, D. S., and Harris, B. L. "Solutions for Maintaining Constant Relative Humidity." Ind. Eng. Chem. 41:2014, 1949.

Cecil, Raymond J. "Libraries: a Survey of Current Lighting Practice." Light and Lighting, 55:228-241, August 1962.

Chan Kai Meng. "A De-humidifier for the Personal Library." Malayan Library Journal, 1(2):13, 1961.

Dauphinee, G. S., Munkelt, F. H., and Sleik, H. Air Conservation Engineering. New York, W. S. Connor Engineering Corp., 1st ed., 1944.

Kaplun, E. A. "Stringent Air-conditioning Control for Library's Rare Works." Heating, Piping and Air-conditioning, 36(2):103-

105, February 1964. Describes two air-conditioning systems installed to fit the exacting requirements of the Berg collection in the New York Public Library.

Keally, F., and Meyer, H.C. "Air-conditioning as a Means of Preserving Books and Records." American Archivist, 12:280-282, 1949.

Kimberly, A.E., and Emley, A.L. A Study of the Removal of Sulphur Dioxide from Library Air. Washington, U.S. Government Printing Office, 1933. U.S. Bureau of Standards Miscellaneous Publication 142.

Macintyre, J. "Air-conditioning for Mantegna's Cartoons at Hampton Court Palace." Technical Studies 11(4), 1934.

Measurement of Humidity. London, National Physical Laboratory, 1953.

"Modern Trends in Conservation." Museums Journal, 60, 1961.

Padfield, Tim. "The Control of Relative Humidity and Air Pollution in Showcases and Picture Frames." Studies in Conservation, 11(1), February 1966.

Plenderleith, H.J. The Conservation of Antiquities and Works of Art. London, Oxford University Press, 1956.

Plenderleith, H.J., and Philippot, P. "Climatology and Conservation in Museums." Museum (UNESCO) 13, 1960. Much useful data for small establishments as well as large organizations.

Pollak, H. "Dehumidification for the Preservation of Documents." Mechanical World, 1961, August, pp. 268-270; September pp. 302-304.

Rawlins, F.I.G. "The Control of Temperature and Humidity in Relation to Works of Art." The Museums Journal XLI, 1942.

Sourwein, G.K. "Air Conditioning for Protection." Heating, Piping and Air Conditioning, 13:311, May 1941. Atmosphere control from the point of view of a rare book custodian.

Stokes, R.H., and Robinson, R.H. "Standard Solutions for Humidity Control at 25°C." Ind. Eng. Chem., 41:2013, 1949.

"Stolow on Air-Conditioning." Museum News. Nov./Dec. 1965.

Stout, George L. "Air Conditioning in Storage." W.A.M. News Bull. & Calendar, 17:29-31, 1952, illus.

Thomson, Garry. "Air Pollution--A Review for Conservation Chemists." Studies in Conservation, 10(4), 1965. The Journal of the International Institute for Conservation of Historic and Artistic Works.

Tottle, H. F. "Strong-room Climate." Archives, 2:387-402, 1956.

Housekeeping

Kowalik, R. , and Sadurska, I. "Disinfection of Infected Stores in Rooms in Archives, Libraries and Museums." Istituto di Patologia del Libro Bolletino, 24(1-4):121-128, 1965. (Abstracted in Art and Archaeology Technical Abstracts, 6(2), 1966.)

Krogh, August. "The Dust Problem in Museums and How to Solve It." Museums Journal, 47:183-188, 1948.

Morrill, R. C. "Dust-proofing Exhibits by Air Pressure." Curator 5, 1962.

Sander, H. J. , and Colwell, R. E. "An Electric Heat Pump for All-year Heating and Cooling in Libraries." Library Journal 79 (22), 1954.

Lighting

Elenbaas, W. Fluorescent Lamps and Illumination. Paris, Dunod, 1963.

Holway, Alfred N. , and Janeson, Dorothea. Good Lighting for People at Work in Reading Rooms and Offices. Boston, Division of Research, Graduate School of Business Administration, Harvard University, 1947.

Jordan, Robert T. "Lighting in University Libraries." UNESCO Bulletin for Libraries, 17:326-336, November/December 1963.

Keyes, D. M. "Library Lighting." Library Journal 86, Dec. 1, 1961.

"Lighting." Museums Journal 63(1-2), 1963.

"Plastic Filters Reduce Light Damage in Museums." Plastics Industry 13, December 1955.

"Plastic Light Filters." Museums Journal, 55, 1956.

Plexiglass Ultraviolet Filtering Formulation. Philadelphia, Rohm & Haas Co. , 1963. Bulletin PL612 discusses filters for fluorescent lights and windows.

"Protection of Record and Exhibit Material Against Light." U. S. National Bureau of Standards, Paper Section. News Bulletin, June 1937.

Protective Display Lighting of Historical Documents. Washington, Government Printing Office, 1953. U.S. National Bureau of Standards, Circular 538.

Scott, H.P. "Lighting and Protection for an Art Museum." Electrical Construction and Maintenance, 35, 1956.

Use of Fluorescent Lighting in Museums. Paris, ICOM, 1953.

Housing

Bean, Donald E. "Library Construction." Illinois Libraries, 46: 181-186, March 1964.

Beers, R.J. "High Expansion Foam Fire Control for Records Storage." Fire Technology, May 1966.

Bleton, Jean. "The Construction of University Libraries: How to Plan and Revise a Project." UNESCO Bulletin for Libraries, 17:307-315, 345, November/December 1963.

Bond, Horatio. A "First Book" on Fire Safety in the Atomic Age. Boston, Mass., National Fire Protection Association, 1952, 72 pp., illus.

Bradley, J.G. "Film Vaults: Construction and Use." J. Soc. Mot. Pict. Eng., 53:193-206, August 1949.

Burchard, John E., et al. Planning the University Library Building. Princeton, N.J., Princeton University Press, 1949. xvii illus.

Chapman, J.M. "Stepping up Security." Museum News, 44(3), 1965.

Dominge, Charles Carroll, and Lincoln, Walter O. Building Construction as Applied to Fire Insurance and Inspecting for Fire Underwriting Purposes. 4th ed. Philadelphia, New York, 1949.

"Emergency Measures." Museum News 43(6), 1965.

"Fire." Museum News, 44(9), 1966.

Fire Protection Handbook. 12th edition. Boston, National Fire Protection Association 1962. This bible of fire protection includes chapters on behavior of fire, housekeeping practices, fire hazards of material, building protection, building equipment.

Francis, Sir F. "Security." Museums Journal 63(1-2):28-31, 1963.

Gondos, Victor. "Archival Buildings--Programing and Planning."

American Archivist, 27:467-483, October 1964.

Hemphill, B. F. "Lessons of a Fire." Library Journal 87,
1962. Baltimore County, Md., branch library.

Horner, James W., Jr. "Planning the New Library: Archer
Daniels Midland Company Research Library." Special Libraries, 55:36-40, January 1964.

Howard, Richard Foster. Museum Security. American Association
of Museums, 1958. (American Association of Museums, Publications new series, No. 18.)

Keally, Francis. "An Architect's View of Library Planning." Library Journal, 88:4521-4525, Dec. 1, 1963. Many of the observations are applicable to archival buildings.

Keck, C. K., and others. A Primer on Museum Security. Coopers-
town, N. Y., New York State Historical Association, 1966.
Much information of use to librarians.

MacGregor, W. D. The Protection of Buildings and Timber Against
Termites. London, H. M. Stationery Office, 1950. Great
Britain. Department of Scientific and Industrial Research.
Forest Products Research Bulletin No. 24.

Metcalf, Keyes D. Planning Academic and Research Library Buildings. New York, McGraw Hill Book Company, 1965. A study
sponsored by the Association of Research Libraries under a
grant by the Council on Library Resources.

National Fire Protection Association, Boston, Mass., 1960. Protection of Records, NFPA, No. 232. Minimum fire protection
requirements for vaults and records rooms, treatment of water-
soaked and charred records, and the role of records management in achieving protection against fires.

Noblecourt, André F. "The Protection of Museums Against Theft."
Museum, XVII(4), 1964. The entire issue of this UNESCO journal is devoted to the protection of museum objects against fire
and theft. Much of the information is applicable to rare book
libraries and archives.

Nye, William. "Trends in Rare Book Library Facilities." College
and Research Libraries, 24, Sept. 1963. Discusses handling,
storage, and conservation.

Plumbe, Wilfred J. "Climate as a Factor in the Planning of University Library Buildings." UNESCO Bulletin for Libraries,
17:316-325, November/December 1963.

Probst, T. "Electronic Eyes and Ears on Guard." Museum News,
44(3), 1965.

---- "Fire Detection--Fire Protection." Museum News 44(9), 1966.

Protecting the Library and Its Resources: A Guide to Physical
   Protection and Insurance. American Library Association, Library Technology Publication No. 7, 1967.

"Protection From Fire." American Archivist, 1:179 11:165 14:
   157.

Protection of Cultural Property in the Event of Armed Conflict.
   Paris, UNESCO 1958.

Protection of Records, Standard No. 232-1963.   Boston, National
   Fire Protection Association, 1963.

Sanchez Belda, Luis. "Construction of Archives Buildings in the
   Last Ten Years." UNESCO Bulletins for Libraries, 18:20-26,
   January/February 1964. Includes pictures and plans.

"Security." Museums Journal, 63(1-2), 1963.

Simon, Louis A., Gondos, Victor, Jr., and Van Schreeven, William
   J. Buildings and Equipment for Archives. Washington, 1944.
   (Bulletins of the National Archives, No. 6.)

Strickland, Robert. "An Inexpensive Alarm System for the Small
   Museum." Museum News, 43, 1965. (Also useful for libraries.)

"Thiefproofing Museums." UNESCO Courier 18, 1965.

Thomas, Anthony. Library Buildings of Britain and Europe; An International Study With Examples Mainly From Britain and Some
   From Europe and Overseas. London, Butterworth, 1963. Includes plans, photographs, and bibliography for each building.

Ulveling, Ralph A. "Problems of Library Construction." Library
   Quarterly, 33:91-101, January 1963. Many of the general observations are applicable to archives buildings.

Wheeler, J.L. The Small Library Building. Chicago, Small Libraries Project, Library Administration Division, American Library Association.

Storage

Archer, H. Richard. "Display and Exhibit Cases." Urbana, Ill.,
   Library Trends, 13:474-480, April 1965.

Barrow, W.J. "Archival File Folders." American Archivist,
   28(1):125-128, 1965. Table and bibliography. Two file folders
   with properties which make them suitable for archival use.
   Test data on physical strength, aging, pH and fiber composition.

Coleman, R.A., and Peacock, W.H. "Ultraviolet Absorbers." Lancaster, Pa., Textile Research Journal, 28:784-791, 1958.

Collison, R.L. Modern Storage Equipment and Methods for Special Materials in Libraries. 72 Worsley Road, London, N.W. 3: Collison, 1955.

Dabney, Virginius. "New Ways to Permanent Files." Saturday Review. May 9, 1964, pp. 67-68.

Feller, R.L. "Standards of Exposure to Light." Bulletin American Group, International Institute for Conservation, 4(1), 1963.

Gondos, Victor, Jr. "A Note on Record Containers." American Archivist, 17:237-242, July 1954.

Hill, J.F. "Storage in University Library Buildings." UNESCO Bulletin for Libraries, 17:337-345, November/December 1963.

Kimberly, Arthur E. "New Developments in Record Containers." American Archivist, 13:233-236, July 1950.

Kimberly, A.E., and Hicks, J.F.G. A Survey of Storage Conditions in Libraries Relative to the Preservation of Records. Washington, National Bureau of Standards, Miscellaneous Publication No. 128, 1931.

Langwell, W.H. "The Protection of Paper and Parchment Against Dampness in Storage." London, Society of Archivists Journal, 3:82-85, Oct. 1965.

Minogue, A.E. "The Use of Transparent Plastics for the Protection of Manuscripts." Manuscripts. New York, 8, 1956. Envelopes etc., not lamination.

Piez, Gladys T. "Archival Containers--A Search for Safer Materials." American Archivist, 27:433-438, July 1964.

Rider, Fremont. Compact Book Storage. New York, Hadham Press, 1949. Some suggestions toward a new methodology for the shelving of less-used research materials.

Rieger, Morris. "Packing, Labeling, and Shelving at the National Archives." American Archivist, 25:417-426, October 1962.

Thirsk, J.W. "The Storage of Newspapers and Periodicals." The Treatment of Special Material in Libraries, by R.L. Collison. London, Aslib, 1957.

Thomson, G., (ed.). Recent Advances in Conservation. London, Butterworths, 1963. These contributions to the 1961 Rome Conference of the International Institute for Conservation of Historic and Artistic Works include articles on museum climate,

fungicides and insecticides, and education and training of conservators. Detailed bibliographies.

Wallace, J. H. Modern Storage Methods for Records. University
of Sydney, 1957.

Williams, W. O. "Shelving of an Aluminum Alloy." Archives.
London 2, 1949-1952.

Wilson, William K. Selection, Use and Storage of Records for the
International Geophysical Year. Washington, National Bureau of
Standards Report 5321, 1957.

Storage (Maps)

Abelson, Nathaniel. "A Method for Filing Rolled Wall Maps."
Special Libraries Association, Geography and Map Division,
Bulletin No. 15:10-12, February 1954. Describes the UN way
of filing wall maps by putting screw eyes on the inner map rod
and hooks at about 3-inch intervals on a 19-foot long 2x4
fastened on a wall 9 feet above the floor.

Allen, Francis S. "Maps in the Library." Illinois Libraries,
Springfield, Ill., 23(10):3-5, 1941. Summarizes the map storage problem.

Bahn, Catherine, "Map Libraries: Space and Equipment." Special
Libraries Association, Geography and Map Division, Bulletin
No. 46:3-17, December 1961.

Collison, Robert Lewis. Modern Storage Equipment and Methods
for Special Materials in Libraries. Hampstead, Eng., 1955.
A foreword by J. G. Davies. Advocates roller shelves for large
folio atlases and shallow drawers for maps. Issued in connection with an exhibition of modern storage equipment and methods
for special libraries in London, January 1955. Includes names
and addresses of exhibitors.

Hill, J. Douglas. "Map and Atlas Cases." Urbana, Ill., Library
Trends, 13:481-487, April 1965.

Jong, G. de. "De Kaartenverzaneling." Bibliotheekleves. Rotter-
dam, 33:267-281, 1948. Illustrated. A general treatise on the
care of maps in a library. Includes bibliography.

Josephson, A. G. S. "The Care of Maps at the John Crerar Library."
Chicago, American Library Association Bulletin, 16(4):263,
July 1922. Maps are filed in special boxes.

Le Gear, C. E. Maps; Their Care, Repair and Preservation in Libraries. Washington, Library of Congress, 1956. A must reference for all curators of map collections. Lengthy bibliogra-

phy plus detailed instructions on processing, filing, preservation, repair and storage.

Lewis, Willard P. "The Care of Maps and Atlases in the Library." Library Journal. New York, 55:494-496, 1930. Considers various types of map filing equipment.

Nelson, Peter. "Maps and Atlases." American Library Association. Pamphlets and Minor Library Material. Chicago, 1917, pp. 23-29. Also A. L. A. Manual of Library Economy, Chapter 25. A summary of the acquisition, processing and care of maps in libraries.

Parsons, Francis H. "The Care of Maps." Library Journal. New York, 20(6):199-201, June 1895. A good general discussion, based on early experiences with the map collection of the U.S. Coast and Geodetic Survey.

Phillips, Philip Lee. Notes on the Cataloging, Care and Classification of Maps and Atlases, Including a List of Publications Compiled in the Division of Maps. Rev. ed. Washington, Government Printing Office, 1921. Amplified from his earlier contributions.

---- "Preservation and Record of Maps in the Library of Congress." Library Journal. New York, 25(1):15-16, January 1900. A brief outline of the care of maps at the Library of Congress.

Potterf, Rex M. "The Map Collection in the Public Library. Acquisition, Cataloging and Care of the Collection." Wilson Library Bulletin. New York, 19(4):270-272, December 1944.

Raisz, Erwin J. "Preservation and Cataloging of Maps." General Cartography. New York, McGraw-Hill Book Company, 1938. pp. 342-345. Concerned primarily with university and college map collections.

Ristow, Walter W. "The Library Map Collection." Library Journal. New York, 67(12):552-555, June 15, 1942. A resume of acquiring, processing and preserving maps.

Selva, Manuel. Guía para organización fichado 7 catalogación de mapotecas. Buenos Aires, J. Suarez 1941. Chapter 2, pp. 53-62, relates to the care and preservation of maps.

Skelton, Raleigh A. "The Conservation of Maps." Society of Local Archivists. Bulletin No. 14. London, October 1954, pp. 13-19. A discussion of map storage and use problems in general, and the British Museum's plans and practices in particular.

Smither, Reginald E. "The Treatment of Pamphlets, Maps, Photographs and Similar Items." Library World. London 15:195-199, 1912-1913. A general discussion of non-book materials in a

British library. Recommends that maps be dissected, mounted and folded to book size. Less satisfactory ways of handling them are to roll them, bind them or keep them in portfolios.

Steckzén, Birger. "Storage and Preservation of Maps in Swedish Military Archives." Indian Archives. New Delhi, 4(1):14-19, 1950. Illustrated. Describes also the classification, cataloging and indexing of the collection. Includes a floor plan of the map depository.

"Storage and Conservation of Maps, The." Geographical Journal. 121:182-189, June 1955. A report prepared by a committee of the Royal Geographical Society 1954. A review of ideal standards of map conservation for the guidance of map curators.

"Storage of Maps." Library Journal. New York, 39:936, December, 1914. Published also in American Library Annual, 1914-1915. p. 220. Describes a map case designed by Dr. Charles Warren Hunt, Secretary of the American Society of Civil Engineers, for the Society's map collection in New York.

Winkler, J. Fred. "Cartographic Record Filing in the National Archives." American Archivist. Cedar Rapids, Iowa, 12:382-385, 1949. Contains useful suggestion for anyone planning the installation of map filing equipment.

Pest Control (Insects and Rodents)

Araujo, R. L. "Notas e Informacões; Notas sobre Insectos que Prejudicam Livros." Biologico. São Paulo, 1:32, 1945.

Armitage, F. D. "Prevention of Damage to Paper, Books and Documents, by Insect Pests." PATRA Journal, 8(2):40-49, 1944.

Barnhard, C.S. "How to Control Cockroaches with Dry Ice Fumigation." Pest Control 31 no. 2:30 (1963).

Becker, G. "Tests on the Effectiveness of Synthetic Contact Insecticides Against Four Termite Species." Berlin, Holz-Roh und Werkstoff, 23:467-478, 1965. (Abstracted in Art and Archaeology Technical Abstracts, 6(2), 1966.

Block, S.S. "Protection of Paper and Textile Products from Insect Damage." Industrial and Engineering Chemistry, 43(7):1558-1563, 1951.

British Standard Code of Practice CP3 - Chapter X (1950). Precautions Against Vermin and Dust. London, British Standards Institution, 1950.

Chakravorti, S. "Formaldehyde as a Preventive Against Bookworm." Science and Culture, 9:251-252, 1943.

Control of Termites with Dieldrin and Protection of Buildings from Attack. Shell Company of West Africa, Ltd., 1958. Agricultural Circular No. 4.

Cristol, Stanley J., and Haller, H.L. "The Chemistry of DDT--A Review." Chem. Eng. News, 23:2070-2075, 1945; C.A., 40: 666, 1946.

Current Pest Control Recommendations. Washington, U.S. Armed Forces Pest Control Board. December 1963. Technical Information Memorandum 6.

Donskoi, A.V., and others. "Disinfection of Books in an Electric Field of High Frequency." Leningrad, Saltykov-Shchedrin State Public Library, 28-34, 1959. (Abstracted in Art and Archaeology Technical Abstracts, 6(2), 1966.)

Evans, D.M. Protection of Books Against Insects. Leatherhead: Printing, Packaging and Allied Trades Research Association, 1949. Bulletin No. 9.

Gahan, C.J. Furniture Beetles; Their Life History and How to Check or Prevent the Damage Caused by the Worm. London, British Museum, 1920. British Museum Natural History Department, Economic Series, No. 11.

Gallo, P. "Problems in the Use of Insecticides on Occupied Premises." Recent Advances in Conservation. London, Butterworths, 1963.

Gay, F.J. "Soil Treatments for Termite Control in Australia." Building: Lighting: Engineering. August 1963.

Goodhue, Lyle D., Cobb, Raymond L., and Cantrel, Kenneth E. Repelling Insects. Bartlesville, Okla., Oct. 22, 1963. Phillips Petroleum Co., U.S. Pat. 3,108,037.

Graveley, F.H. "Paraffin Wax as a Protection Against Termites." Journal of the Bombay Natural History Society, 45(3):439-440, 1945.

Gupta, R.C. "How to Fight White Ants." The Indian Archives, 8(2), 1954.

Hall, I.N. "Microbial Control of Insects." Agricultural Chemistry, 14:45-112, 1959.

Harris, W.V. Termites; Their Recognition and Control. London, Longmans, 1961.

Hutson, J.C. "Preservation of Book Covers from Cockroaches." Ceylon Department of Agriculture Report on the Work of the Entomological Division, 1932.

"Insects, Protection From." American Archivist. 1:87,111,214 2:21 3:141, 212 6:38,197 7:159 11:246 16:377.

Jepson, F. P. "Preventing Injury to Books by Cockroaches. Fiji Department of Agriculture Report on the Work of the Division of Plant Pest Control, 1934.

Kirk-Othmer, "Insecticides and Fungicides." Paper Fillers. New York, Interscience Encyclopedias, Inc., 1947.

Kleindienst, T. Note d'Information sur la Protection des Collections Contre les Insectes et les Champignons ou Moisissures. Paris, Direction des Bibliotheques de France, 1953.

Kozulina, O. V. "Insect Control Methods Used in Moscow Libraries." UNESCO Bulletin for Libraries, 15:200-202, 1961.

Lepesme, P. La Protection des Bibliotheques et des Musées contre les Insectes et les Moisissures. Paris, Presses documentaires, 1943.

MacGregor, W. D. "The Protection of Buildings and Timber Against Termites." Forest Products Research Bulletin, 1950. London, H. M. S. O. No. 24, 1950.

"Making Binding Insect Proof." Bookbinders Monthly, 10(7):2, 1929.

McKenny Hughes, A. W. "Protection of Books and Records from Insects." Indian Archives, 7(1), 1953.

Moncrieff, R. W. Mothproofing. London, Leonard Hill Ltd., 1950.

Mori Hachirō, "Studies on the Control of Insects Noxious to Ancient Art Materials. 1. On the insecticidal methods with reduced pressure." Sci. Pap. Japn. Antiques. No. 1, pp. 30-32, January 1951.

Noirot, C., and Alliot, H. La Lutte contre les Termites. Paris, Masson, 1947.

Nyuksha, J. P. "Disinfection of Books in Chambers." Saltykov-Shchedrin State Public Library, Leningrad, 5-27, 1959. Reviews various methods of book disinfection. (Abstracted in Art and Archaeology Technical Abstracts, 6(2), 1966.)

Opfell, John B., et al. "Penetration by Gases to Sterilize Interior Surfaces of Confined Spaces." Applied Microbiology. Pasadena, Calif., Dynamic Science Corp., January 1964. 12:27-31.

Pence, R. J. "Control of Powder-post Beetles." California Agriculture 10: September 1956. Infra-red radiation.

"Precautions Against Vermin and Dust." British Standard Code of

Practice CP3. London, British Standards Institution, 1950.
Chapter X.

"Protection Against Spoilage by Micro-organisms, Insects, Mites
and Rodents. " British Standard Packaging Code. London, 1951.
British Standards Institution. British Standard 1133, Section 5.

Robinow, B. H. "Books and Cockroaches; An Attempt to Cope with
the Menace. " South African Libraries, 24(2):40-42, 1956.

St. George, R. A., et al. Subterranean Termites; Their Prevention
and Control in Buildings. Washington, U. S. Government Printing Office, 1958. Department of Agriculture Home and Garden
Bulletin No. 64.

Sakharova, T. V. On the Question of Quantities of Rat Poison Required for Rat Extermination in Cities. (in Russian). Tr.
Tsentr. Nauchn. Issled. Dezinfektsion. Inst. 14:291-294, 1961.

Silverfish and Firebrats; How to Control Them. Washington, U. S.
Government Printing Office, 1957.

Snyder, T. E. Control of Non-subterranean Termites. Washington,
U. S. Government Printing Office, 1958. Department of Agriculture Farmer's Bulletin No. 2018.

Snyder, T. E., and Zetek, S. Effectiveness of Wood Preservatives
in Preventing Attack by Termites. Washington, U. S. Department of Agriculture, 1943. Circular No. 683.

Stored Grain Pests. Washington, U. S. Government Printing Office,
1962. Farmers Bulletin No. 1260. Includes information on
control of beetles known to infest libraries.

Tiunin, K. "A Vacuum Gas-chamber for Disinfection in the State
Ethnographic Museum in Warsaw." Ochrana Zabytkoa, War-
saw, 19(1):77-79, 1966. (Abstracted in Art and Archaeology
Technical Abstracts, 6(2), 1966.)

Tooke, F. G. C. "The Use of Preservatives Against Wood-destroying
Insects. " Farming in South Africa. 1943, pp. 235-240.

Townsend, H. G. "Insecta-lac: New Roach Killer Brushes on Like
Paint. " Pest Control 30(2):40, 1962.

Van Grenou, B., et al. Wood Preservation During the Last 50
Years. Leiden, A. W. Sijthoff, 1951.

Wolcott, G. N. Termite Repellents; A Summary of Laboratory
Tests. Puerto Rico, 1947. University of Puerto Rico Agricultural Experiment Station Bulletin 73.

Wood, G. W. "Books and Documents; Protection from Insect Damage. A Survey of the Problem and Methods of Control." Pesticides Abstracts and News Summary, Section A., Insecticides. 2(2), 1956.

Pest Control (Mildew)

Abrams, Edward. Microbiological Deterioration of Organic Materials; Its Prevention and Methods of Test. Washington, U. S. Government Printing Office, 1948. National Bureau of Standards Miscellaneous Publication No. 188.

Armitage, F. D. The Cause of Mildew on Books and Methods of Preservation. London, Printing & Allied Trades Research Association, 1949. PATRA Bulletin No. 8.

Barr, P. "Mildew in Libraries--Prevention and Treatment." New Jersey Library Bulletin, 13:123-129, 1945.

Beljakova, L. A. "Fungus Control in the Lenin State Library." UNESCO Bulletin for Libraries, 15:198-200, 1961.

Betto, E. The Bacterial and Fungicidal Activity of Ethylene Oxide in Vacuum Fumigation. Milan, Istituto di Patologia Vegetale dell'Universita di Milano, 1960. (Booklet No. 52.) (Abstracted in Art and Archaeology Technical Abstracts, 6(2), 1966.)

Bhandari, N. D., Agarwal, P. N., Nigam, S. S. and Raman, R. S. "Urea-Formaldehyde Resin Treatment for Protection of Woolen Fabrics Against Micro-organisms and Insects." Indian Journal Technol. 1:255-256, June 1963. Indian Defense Research Lab. Stores, Kanpur.

Block, S. S. "Humidity Requirement for Mold Growth." Engineering Progress. University of Florida, VII(10), 1953.

Buchanan, Estelle D., and Earle, Robert. Bacteriology. 4th ed. New York, The MacMillan Company, 1938.

Dahl, Sverre. "Prevention of Microbiological Deterioration of Leather." Journal Am. Leather Chemists. Assoc., 51, 1956.

Deribere, M. "The Pathology of the Book and the Use of Ultraviolet Rays." Papetérie, 73:719-721, 1951.

"Heater Units Prevent Mildew in Book Stack." Electrical World. 107:574, 1937.

Hetherington, D. C. "Mold Preventive for Bookbindings." College and Research Libraries, 7:246, 1946.

Iiams, T. H., and Beckwith, T. D. "Notes on the Causes and Prevention of Foxing in Books." The Library Quarterly, V(4),

October 1935. This report pinpoints the causes of foxing and suggests preventive measures, but has little to say about removing foxing stains.

Kurir, A. "The Possibility of Destroying Termites with Atomic Waste." Holzforschung Holzverwertung. 15, 1963.

Mechalas, B. J. "Microbiological Pest Control." Pest Control 29. No. 10, 20, 1961.

Niukska, I. P. "High Frequency Currents as Instruments of Mold Control on Books." Moscow, Bibliotekar. pp. 35-36, 1949.

Plumbe, W. J. "Protection of Books Against Mildew." Malayan Library Journal, 1(2):11-13, 1961.

Reddish, G. F. Antiseptics, Disinfectants, Fungicides and Sterilization. London, H. Kimpton, 1957.

Rybakova, S. G. "Control of Mold Fungi on Books." Collection of Materials on the Preservation of Library Resources. Moscow, 1953. U. S. Department of Commerce, Office of Technical Services, Springfield, Va., 1964.

---- "Preservation from Molding of the Glue Used for the Binding and Restoration of Books." Moscow, Bibliotekar. pp 39-40, 1949. In Russian.

Schley, Donald G., and others. "Simple Improvised Chambers for Gas Sterilization with Ethylene Oxide." Applied Microbiology, 8:15, 1960.

Leather

Belaja, I. K. "Preservation of Leather Bindings at the Lenin State Library in the U. S. S. R." UNESCO Bulletin for Libraries, XIII:125-126.

Beljakova, L. A. "Protection of Leather-bound Books from Mold Attack." Collection of Materials on the Preservation of Library Resources. Moscow, 1958. U. S. Department of Commerce, Office of Technical Services, Springfield, Va., 1964.

Beljakova, L. A., and Kozulina, O. V. "Book Preservation in the U. S. S. R. Libraries." UNESCO Bulletin for Libraries, XV: 198-202.

Breillat, Pierre. "Rare Books Section in the Library." UNESCO Bulletin for Libraries, XIX:174-194, 251-263.

"Caring for Your Collections: Metals and Leather." History News. American Association for State and Local History, 1962. Technical Leaflet 1, Illustrated.

Causes and Prevention of the Decay of Bookbinding Leather, The.
London, Printing Industry Research Association, 1933.

Dahl, S. "The Effects of Fungicides on Deterioration of Leather."
Journal American Leather Chemists Assoc., 52(11):611-621,
1957.

Frey, R.W., and Beebe, C.W. "Preliminary Experiments on Prevention of Leather 'Red Rot'." American Leather Chemists
Association Journal, 29: October, 1934.

Frey, R.W., and Veitch, F.P. Preservation of Leather Bookbindings. Washington, U.S. Government Printing Office, 1930,
U.S. Department of Agriculture Leaflet No. 69.

Innes, R.F. "The Preservation of Bookbinding Leathers." Library
Association Record, 52(12):458-461, 1950.

"Leather Preservation." American Archivist. 1:114 9:228 16:
116,125.

Lollar, R.M. "Para-nitrophenol as a Fungicide for Leather."
Journal Society Leather Trades Chemists, 49, 1954.

Meldrum, R.S. "Rotproofing of Leather." Chem. Products, 12
(1):4-6, 1948.

Missar, Margaret du F. Preservation and Treatment of Old Leather
Bindings. Washington, National Trust Publications.

"New Wax for Bookbindings." UNESCO Bulletin for Libraries, 13:
99, 1959. (CIRE 212).

Plenderleith, H.J. "The Preservation of Leather." Museums Journal. London, 27:217-218, 1928.

---- The Preservation of Leather Bookbindings. London, British
Museum, 1946. Illustrated.

Rogers, J.S., and Beebe, C.W. Leather Bookbindings, How to
Preserve Them. Washington, U.S. Department of Agriculture,
1956.

Veitch, Fletcher Pearre. The Care of Leather. Washington, U.S.
Government Printing Office, 1920. U.S. Department of Agriculture. Farmer's Bulletin 1183.

Veitch, F.P., and Frey, R.W. Preservation of Leather Bookbindings. Washington, U.S. Government Printing Office, 1930.
U.S. Department of Agriculture, Leaflet No. 69.

339

Paper

American Library Association Committee, "Preservation of Newspapers." American Library Association Bulletin, 6:116, 1912.

Annow, G. L. "Paper Preservation: New Hope for Survival."
Medical Library Association Bulletin 53:384-387, July 1965.

Anthony, Donald C. "Caring for Your Manuscripts and Related Material." Hobbies Magazine, 68(8):110-111, 126, 1964.

Barrow, W. J. "An Evaluation of Document Restoration Processes."
American Documentation 4:53-54, April 1953.

---- Stabilization of Modern Book Papers. Richmond, 1958. A preliminary report.

Buyn, K. E. C. "Paper Permanence." Bulletin Assoc. Tech. Ind.
Papetiere. 5:231, 1951. BIPC 22, 30.

Chakravorti, S. "Vacuum Fumigation: a New Technique for Preservation of Records." Science and Culture No. 11, 1943-44.

Church, Randolph W. "Is There a Doctor in the House?" Publishers' Weekly. 175(76):78-80, January 5, 1959. An essay on
the problems of paper conservation.

---- "Perish the Paper, Perish the Book, Perish the Thought: An
Inquiry." Publishers' Weekly. 172:54-58, Sept. 2, 1957.

Clapp, Anne F. "Curatorial Works of Art on Paper Supports."
Intermuseum Conservation Assoc. Newsletter. 3, June 1965.
Care of prints and pictures.

Clarke, Carl D. Pictures; Their Preservation and Restoration.
Butler, Md., Standard Arts Press, 1959.

Dabney, Virginius. "New Ways to Permanent Files." Saturday Review, 47(19):67-68, May 1964. Discusses new permanent/dur-
able papers.

Fitzpatrick, John C. Notes on the Care, Cataloging, Calendaring,
and Arranging of Manuscripts. Washington, 1913. Other editions were published in 1921, 1928, and 1934. A description of
the practices of the Division of Manuscripts, Library of Congress, this work is still important for the observations on arranging and flattening.

Grove, Lee E. "Paper Deterioration--An Old Story." College and
Research Libraries, 25:365-374, Sept. 1964.

---- "The Conservation of Paper." Museum News. 42(2):15-20,
1963. Illustrated. A summary of Barrow's work on perma-

nent/durable book paper and spray deacidification. Bibliography.

India, Imperial Record Department, New Delhi. Notes on Preservation of Records. Simla, Government of India Press, 1941.

Jaffar, S. M. "Protection of Paper." M. J. Pakistan 4, April, 1952, ICOM News 5:33, October/December, 1952.

Jayme, G., and Rohmann, E. M. "Use of Infrared Spectroscopy in Examining Pulp and Paper." Darmstadt, Papier, 19(10A):719-728, 1965. (Abstracted in Art and Archaeology Technical Abstracts, 6(2), 1966.

Kane, Lucile M. "A Guide to the Care and Administration of Manuscripts." Bulletin of the American Association for State and Local History. II(11), Sept. 1966. Contains a short but excellent section on manuscript preservation. Selective bibliography on care and administration of manuscripts.

Kremer, Alvin W. "The Preservation of Wood Pulp Publications." College and Research Libraries, XV:205-209, April, 1954.

Langwell, W. H. "The Preservation of Paper Records." Archives. II(11), Lady Day, 1954.

Launer, Herbert F. Determination of the pH Value of Papers. Washington, U. S. Government Printing Office, 1939. U. S. National Bureau of Standards, Research Paper RP1205.

Lee, H. N. "Established Methods for Examination of Paper." Technical Studies in the Field of the Fine Arts. IV(1-2); 1935. Description of the commonly used methods by which the constituents of paper may be determined.

---- "Improved Methods for the Examination of Paper." Technical Studies, IV(2), 1935.

Lovett, Robert W. "Care and Handling of Non-Governmental Archives." Library Trends, 5:380-389, January 1957. A bibliography is included.

Ludwig, H. "Some Hints on the Care and Treatment of Graphics, Drawings, etc." Neue Museumskunde, Leipzig, 3:158-160, 1960.

Lydenberg, Henry M. "On the Preservation of Manuscripts and Printed Books." Library Journal 53:712-716, September 1928.

---- "Preservation of Modern Newspaper Files." Library Journal, 40:240, 1915.

Minogue, Adelaide E. "Physical Care, Repair and Protection of Manuscripts." Library Trends, 5:344-351, January 1957.

Norton, Margaret C. "Handling Fragile Manuscripts." Illinois Libraries, 29:410-413, 460-464, November/December 1947.

Oregon State Public Welfare Commission. Drying of Flood Damaged Records of Marion County Welfare Office. Salem, 1965. 10 p.

Peckham, Howard H. "Arranging and Cataloging Manuscripts in the William L. Clements Library." American Archivist. 1:215-229, October 1938. Instructions for handling manuscripts in bulk.

Plenderleith, H.J., and Werner, A. "Technical Notes on the Conservation of Documents." Journal of the Society of Archivists, 1, April 7, 1958.

Plett, T.M. Microscopic Methods Used in Identifying Commercial Fibers. Washington, U.S. Government Printing Office. National Bureau of Standards Circular C 423.

Pravilova, T.A., et al. "Effect of a High-Frequency Electromagnetic Field on Paper." New Methods for the Restoration and Preservation of Documents and Books. Moscow, 1960. U.S. Department of Commerce, Office of Technical Services, Springfield, Va. 1964.

Redstone, L.S., and Steer, F.W. Local Records; Their Nature and Care. London, G. Bell and Sons Ltd., 1953.

Rossiter, Henry Preston. "On the Care of Prints." Print Coll. Q. 30:33-40, March 1950. Recommendations are made on the care and handling of fine prints. Describes injuries caused by the cutting of margins, the abrasive action of dirt and dust, careless handling, damp air, water drip and poor mounts.

Schraubstadter, Carl. Care and Repair of Japanese Prints. Cornwall-on-Hudson, N.Y., Idlewild Press, 1948. Illustrated.

Schulz, H.C. "The Care and Storage of Manuscripts in the Huntington Library." Library Quarterly, 5:78-86, January 1935.

Veitch, F.P. "Paper Specification." U.S. Department of Agriculture Report 89. 1909. This early study of durability and economy in papers for permanent records stressed the importance of atmosphere control long before the advent of air-conditioning.

Volina, T.L., and others. Protection of Cardboard from Biological Deterioration. Moscow, C.N.I.T.I., 1963.

Weber, C.G., et al. "Effects of Fumigants on Paper." Journal of Research, National Bureau of Standards, 15(3):271, 1935.

Werner, A.E.A. "The Conservation of Manuscripts." Research, 11, pp. 166-172.

----"The Preservation of Archives." Journal Society of Archivists, 1, 1955-1959. Discusses atmosphere control, deacidification and lamination.

Wilson, Norval F. "A New Stain for Identifying Papermaking Fibers." Pap. Ind. and Paper World, 27:215-216, 1945. C.A. 39, 1945. 3664.

Wilson, William K. "Record Papers and Their Preservation." The Capital Chemist, 6(2):46-51, February 1956.

Yabrova, R.R. "The Prevention of Aging of Books and Newspapers." Collection of Materials on the Preservation of Library Materials. Moscow, 1953. U.S. Department of Commerce, Office of Technical Services, Springfield, Va., 1964.

Cloth

Columbus, J.V. "Washing Techniques Used at The Textile Museum." in Bulletin of the American Group, International Institute for Conservation, 7(2), May 1967.

Martin, A.R. "Dry Cleaning Museum Textiles." in Bulletin of the American Group, International Institute for Conservation, 7(2), May 1967.

Parchment and Vellum

Gairola, T.R. "Preservation of Parchment." Journal of Indian Museums, 14-16, 1958-1960.

Wachter, Otto. "Reflections on the Theme of Parchment Restoration." Allgemeiner Anzieger für Buchbindereien. Stuttgart, 75(5), 1962. In German.

Exotic Materials

Bleck, R.D. "Conservation of Bronzes According to Thouvenin." Leipzig, Neue Museumskunde 9:47-50, 1966. (Abstracted in Art and Archaeology Technical Abstracts, 6(2), 1966.)

Cotton, J.B. "Control of Surface Reactions on Copper by Means of Organic Reagents." Proceedings, National Association of Corrosion Engineers, Houston, Texas, 590-596, 1963. (Abstracted in Art and Archaeology Technical Abstracts, 6(2), 1966.)

Cupr, V., and Pelikan, J.B. Elements of the Conservation of Metals in Museums. Prague, National Museum, 1964.

Gladstone, R. "Guide to Marble Care." The New York Times,

343

Section 2, D 27, Nov. 27, 1966. How to remove stains, and polish.

Lewin, S. Z. "The Preservation of Natural Stone 1839-1965." Art and Archaeology Abstracts, 6(1), 1966. A thorough review of the literature on the conservation of stone.

Mori, Toru, and Asano, Ikno. "Prevention of Decay and Insect Damage in Wood." Scientific Papers on Japanese Antiquities and Art Crafts. 1951.

Murphy, J. F., and Amore, C. J. "Protective Oxides on Metal Surfaces." French patent 1,426,811 Jan. 28, 1966. Describes a soap solution.

Schlegal, M. "Tarnish-preventing Transparent Lacquer or Plastic Coatings for Silverware." German patent 1,207,244, December 16, 1965.

Schulz, F. "Practical Hints on the Treatment and Care of Coins and Medals --." Neue Museumskunde, Leipzig, 4:174-178, 1961.

Tulka, J., and Cerveny, L. "Inhibition of the Corrosion of Silver, Copper and Their Alloys by Sulphur Compounds." Czech patent 115,779, August 15, 1965.

Film, Tape and Discs

American Standard Practice for Storage of Microfilm. PH5.4-1957. New York American Standards Association 1937.

Archives Handbook Series No. 3: Microfilm Procedures. Denver, Colorado, Division of State Archives and Public Records 1964. Contains basic information on care of film and equipment.

Ballou, H. W. Guide to Microreproduction Equipment. Annapolis, National Microfilm Association, 1959.

Brown, H. G. "Problems of Storing Film for Archival Purposes." British Kinematography, 20:150-162, May 1952.

Calhoun, J. M. "Air Conditioning in Storing and Handling Motion Picture Film." Heating and Ventilating, 46:66-69, October
. 1949.

Clapp, Verner W., Henshaw, Francis H., and Holmes, Donald C. "Are Your Microfilms Deteriorating Acceptably?" Library Journal, 80(6):589-595, March 15, 1955.

Clerc, L. P. Photography: Theory and Practice. 2nd ed. New York, 1937. Care of photographic materials.

344

Crabtree, J.I., and Ives, C.E. "The Storage of Valuable Motion Picture Film." Journal Soc. Mot. Pict. Eng. 15:289-305, Sept. 1930.

Davidson, Helen L. "Handling Pictures and Audio-Visual Materials in Company Libraries and Archives." Special Libraries, 53: 326-329, July/August 1962.

État des Microfilms de Securité Conservés aux Archives Nationales. Paris, French National Archives, 1962.

Evaluation of Record Players for Libraries. Series II, Chicago, Library Technology Project, American Library Association, 1964.

Filing Negatives and Transparencies. Rochester, N.Y., Eastman Kodak Co., 1960. Kodak Pamphlet P-12.

Gallo, F. "About the Conservation of Microfilms." Rome, Istituto di Patologia del Libro, Bolletino, 24(1-4):107-110, 1965. (Abstracted in Art and Archaeology Technical Abstracts, 6(2), 1966.)

Gifford, Woodland and Dahl. "A Method for Testing Quality of Phonograph Records." Modern Plastics. 34(12):140 ff, August 1957.

Hawken, W. R. Photocopying from Bound Volumes. Chicago, American Library Association, 1962. An evaluation of twenty commercial book-copying devices.

Hill, J.R., and Weber, C.G. Evaluation of Motion-Picture Film for Permanent Records. National Bureau of Standards, Miscellaneous Publication M158, 1937.

Hutchison, G.L., Ellis, L., and Ashmore, S.A. "The Surveillance of Cinematographic Record Film During Storage." Report No. 2/R/48. Chemical Research and Development Establishment and the Department of the Government Chemist, Ministry of Supply (British), February 1948. See Journal Soc. Mot. Pict. & Tel. Eng., 54:381-383, March 1950. Appendix C.

Lewis, Chester M., and Offenhauser, W.H. Microrecording. New York, Interscience Publishers, 1956.

"Microfilm Preservation." Washington, Chemistry, 39(9):28-29, 1966. Summarizes National Bureau of Standards findings on microfilm blemishes. Recommends storage procedures.

Mo Och Domsjo Altiebolag. "Anticurl Treatment for Photographic Paper." Netherlands patent application 6,401,434, August 19, 1965. Gives permanent anticurl to photographs. (Abstracted in Art and Archaeology Technical Abstracts, 6(2), 1966.)

345

Noll, D. F. "The Maintenance of Microfilm Files." American Archivist. 13:129-134, 1950.

Offenhauser, W.O., Jr. "16mm Sound Motion Pictures." Interscience, Preservation and Recording, Chap. XI, pp. 355-363, 1949.

Peele, David. "Bind or Film: Factors in the Decision." Library Resources and Technical Services, 8:168-170, Spring 1964.

Pickett, A.G., and Lemcoe, M.M. Preservation and Storage of Sound Recordings. Washington, Library of Congress, 1959. The results of a protracted study financed by the Rockefeller Foundation to fill a gap in the basic research in the field of library conservation. Highly technical, with a lengthy bibliography for specialists.

Porter, James D. "Sound in the Archives." American Archivist. 27:327-336, April 1964. Includes sections on the storage and processing of magnetic tape.

---- Use and Storage of Magnetic Tape Sound Recordings as Public Records. Oregon State Library 1963. Oregon State Library State Archives Division, Bulletin No. 6, Publication No. 27.

"Protection by Microfilming." American Archivist, 15:221.

Radocy, Frank. "Tape Storage Problems." Journal Audio Eng. Soc., 5:32ff, 1957.

Ryan, J.V., Cummings, J.W., and Hutton, A.C. "Fire Effects and Fire Control in Nitrocellulose Photographic-Film Storage." Building Materials and Structures Report 145, U.S. Department of Commerce, April 2, 1956.

Schuursma, R.L. "The Sound Archives of the University of Utrecht." Recorded Sound, No. 15, pp. 246-250, July 1964.

Scribner, B.W. Summary Report of Research at the National Bureau of Standards on the Stability and Preservation of Records on Photographic Film.

Selsted and Snyder. "Magnetic Recording; A Report on the State of the Art." Trans IRE. pp. 137ff, September/October 1954.

Standard for Storage and Handling of Cellulose Nitrate Motion Picture Film, NFPA No. 40. Boston, National Fire Protection Association, 1953.

Standards of the National Board of Fire Underwriters for Storage and Handling of Cellulose Nitrate Motion Picture Film as Recommended by the National Fire Protection Association. N.B. F.U. Pamphlet No. 40, November 1953. Obtainable from

National Board of Fire Underwriters, 85 John St., New York, N.Y.

Storage and Preservation of Microfilms. Rochester, N.Y., Eastman Kodak Company, 1965. Kodak Pamphlet P-108.

Storage and Preservation of Motion Picture Film. Rochester, N.Y.,
Eastman Kodak Co., 1957.

Storage of Cellulose Acetate Motion Picture Film. National Board
of Fire Underwriters Special Interest Bulletin No. 283. (September 25, 1950). Obtainable from National Board of Fire Underwriters, 85 John St., New York, N.Y.

Storage of Microfilms, Sheet Films and Prints. Rochester, N.Y.;
Eastman Kodak Co., 1946.

Storage of Microfilms, Sheet Films and Prints. Rochester, N.Y.;
Eastman Kodak Co., 1951. Safety film base and paper base materials only.

Storage of Processed Color Film. Rochester, N.Y.; Eastman Kodak Co., 1962.

Testing and Evaluation of Record Players for Libraries, The.
Chicago, American Library Association, 1962. A report based
on studies by Consumers Research, Inc.

Weber, C.G., and Hill, J.R. "Care of Slide-Films and Motion
Picture Films in Libraries." Journal Soc. Mot. Pict. Eng.,
27:691-702, December 1936.

In the Tropics

Ballou, H.A. "Book Protection." Tropical Agriculture, 3:212-213,
1926.

Boustead, W.M. "The Surface pH Measurement and Deacidification
of Prints and Drawings in Tropical Climates." London, Studies in Conservation 9(2):50-58, 1964.

Brooks, C.E.P. "Climate and the Deterioration of Materials."
Quarterly Journal of the Royal Meteorological Society, 72:87-97,
1946.

Compton, K.G. "Corrosion in the Tropics." Transactions of the
Electro-Chemical Society, 1947, p. 705.

Control of Termites with Dieldrin and Protection of Buildings from
Attack. 1958. Shell Company of West Africa Ltd. Agricultural
Circular No. 4.

347

Coremans, P. "Preservation of the Cultural Heritage in Tropical Africa." Tokyo, Museum, 18(3):168-182, 1965. Discusses the influence of climate on deterioration.

Cundall, F. "The Preservation of Books in the Tropics." Handbook of Jamaica. Kingston, Government Printing Office, 1926.

Doe, Brian. "Notes on Museum and Art Gallery Lighting in the Tropics." Studies in Conservation. 10(2), May 1965.

Edwards, W.H. The Preservation of Wooden Buildings in the Tropics, with Special Reference to Conditions Existing in Jamaica. Kingston, 1939.

Flieder, Francoise. "La Protection des Documents Graphiques dans les Pays Tropicaux." Cahiers de la Maboke. Paris, July 1963.

Gay, F.J. "Soil Treatment for Termite Control in Australia." Building; Lighting and Engineering, August 1963.

Graveley, F.H. "Paraffin Wax as a Protection Against Termites." Journal of the Bombay Natural History Society, 45:439-440, 1945.

Harris, J. "Notes on Book Preservation in West Africa." WALA News, 2(4):102-105, 1956.

Kalshoven, L.G.E. "Book-beetles in the Netherlands Indies." Entomologische Mededeelingen van Nederlandsch-Indie. 4:10-16, 1938.

Keller, G.W. "Preventing Fungus and Bacteriological Attack in the Tropical Monsoon Period." Chemical Abstracts, 53, 1959.

Kennedy, R.A. "Conservation in the Humid Tropical Zone." Museum News, 38, 1960.

---- Conservation in the Wet Tropics. Technical Bulletin of the Museums Association of Middle Africa. Bulletin No. 1, 1959.

Kleindienst, T. Note d'Information sur la Protection des Collections contre les Insectes et les Champignons ou Moisissures. Paris, Direction des Bibliotheques de France, 1953.

Kowalik, R., Czerwinska, E. "The Preservation of Organic Coatings in Tropical Conditions." Acta Microbiologica Polonica, 9:59-60, 1960.

Leonard, John M., and Pitman, A.L. "Tropical Performance of Fungicidal Coatings; A Statistical Analysis." Indust. Eng. Chemistry, 43, 1951.

348

Lepesme, P. La Protection des Bibliothèques et des Musées contre les Insectes et les Moisissures. Paris, Presses Documentaires, 1943.

Mould-proofing Treatment and Mould Resistance Test for Leathers for Use in Tropical Conditions. Milton Park, Egham, British Leather Manufacturers' Research Association, 1950.

Noirot, C., and Alliot, H. La Lutte Contre les Termites. Paris, Masson, 1947.

Operation Tropical Wet. Environmental and Microbiological Observations. Panama Canal Zone, Republic of Panama, (November/ December 1960). Washington, U.S. Detroit Arsenal, Center-line, Mich. (C. Bruce Lee). May 1962.

Plenderleith, H. J. "Mould in the Muniment Room." Archives, 7:13, 1952.

Plumbe, W. J. "Preservation of Library Materials in Tropical Countries." Library Trends, 8:291-306, 1959. A short history of insect damage and methods of control and preservation going back to ancient Greece and Rome. Description of methods of preservation used in many modern tropical countries.

---- "Protection of Books Against Mildew." Malayan Library Journal, 1(2):11-13, 1961.

---- "Storage and Preservation of Books, Periodicals and Newspapers in Tropical Climates." UNESCO Bulletin for Libraries, 12:156-162, 1958. A select bibliography.

---- The Preservation of Books in Tropical and Sub-Tropical Countries. London, Oxford University Press, 1964.

---- "Tropical Librarianship." Library Review, 99:161-166, 1951.

"Protection of Documents in Tropics." American Archivist. 3:212 6:197 7:159 15:379 17:54.

Rauschert, Mansfred. "Paper and Writing Materials in Moist Tropical Regions." Allgem. Papier-Rundschau, 1957, pp. 48-50. There is an abstract in The Paper Industry, May 1957.

Report on Plastics in the Tropics. 14. Low-Pressure Glass-Fibre Laminates Bonded With Polyester Resins. Great Britain Ministry of Aviation. Report TIL(BR)631; ...ASTIA Doc. 407178, 1962. Laminates, ester polymers, glass, fiber, weathering, climate (dry), climate (tropical, rainy), marine.

Reports on Plastics in the Tropics. 15. Protected Polythene. Great Britain Ministry of Aviation. Report TIL(BR)632; ...ASTIA Doc. 407511, 1962. Ethylene polymers, weatherproofing, carbon

black, weathering, climate (tropical, rainy), climate (dry),
marine.

Robinow, B. H. "Books and Cockroaches; an Attempt to Cope with
the Menace. " South African Libraries, 24(2):40-42, 1956.

Shipley, Sir A. E. "Enemies of Books. " Tropical Agriculture,
2:223-224, 1925.

Termites in the Humid Tropics. Paris, October 1960. UNESCO.
Proceedings of the New Delhi Symposium jointly organized by
UNESCO and the Zoological Survey of India.

Termites, Wood-borers and Fungi in Buildings. Report of the
Committee on the Protection of Building Timbers in South Africa
Against Termites, Wood-boring Beetles and Fungi. Pretoria,
South African Council for Scientific and Industrial Research,
1950. National Building Research Institute.

Termite-proofing of Timber for Use in the Tropics. Forest Products Research Leaflet. Great Britain, 1944. No. 38.

Tropic Proofing; Protection Against Deterioration Due to Tropical
Climates. London, H.M.S.O., 1949. Great Britain. Ministry
of Supply and Department of Scientific and Industrial Research.

Williams-Hunt, P.D.R. Preserving Books and Prints in the Tropics. Kuala Lumpur, Museums Department, Federation of Malaya, 1953. Museums Popular Pamphlet No. 3.

Wood, G.W. "Books and Documents; Protection from Insect Damage. A Survey of the Problem and Methods of Control. "
Pesticides Abstracts and News Summary. Section A., Insecticides, 2(2), 1956.

Repair and Restoration
General Repair

Adam, Paul. Das Restaurieren alter Bücher; Wiederherstellungs-
arbeiten en alten Buchern, Einbänden, auch Manuskripten sowie
Ausführungen über das notwendige Verstandnis für die Technik
des Buches zur Beurteilung von Zeit und Herkunft alter Einbände. Halle, Saale; W. Knapp, 1927.

---- "Das sinngemässe Restaurieren alter Einbände. " Zeitschrift
für Bücherfreunde. Jhrg. 7:499-506, Bielefeld, 1904.

All the King's Horses. 350 East 22nd St., Chicago, R.R. Donnel-
ley & Sons Co.

Almela Meliá, Juan. Manual de Reparación y Conservación de
Libros, Estampas y Manuscritos. Mexico, 1949. Illustrated

with facsimiles. Instituto Panamericano de Geografia e Historia. Comisiön de Historia. Publicacion 10. Manuales de técnia de la investigaciön de la historia y ciencias afines, 2.

Ambler, George H. Water Damaged Files, Papers and Records; What to Do About Them. Royal Oak, Mich, Document Reclamation Service, Inc. 1963.

Archivschule Marburg. Die Archivtechnische Woche der Archivschule. Vom. 26, Marburg, 1957.

Arnsberger & Rheinboldt, Offenbach a.M. Wissenswertes über die verschiedenen Sorten Leder für Bucheinbände; ihre Herkunft, Gerbung, Färbung, Narbung, Haltbarkeit u. Verwendung. Offenbach a.M.: Selbstverlag, 1928.

Bahmer, Robert H. "Recent American Developments in Archival Repair, Preservation and Photography." Archivum, 10:59-71, 1960. Abstract in American Archivist, 26:256, April 1963.

Belen'Kaya, N.G. "Methods of Restoration of Books and Documents." New Methods for the Restoration and Preservation of Documents and Books. Moscow, 1960. Translated U.S. Department of Commerce, Office Technical Services 64-11054. An outstanding summary of traditional as well as new techniques for paper restoration as practiced in Russia, Europe and the U.S.

Belov, G.A. "New Techniques, New Materials and New Experiences Concerning Restoration of Documents and Seals, Preservation of Maps and Plans and Photography since 1950." Archivum. 10:72-80, 1960.

Bhargava, K.D. Repair and Preservation of Records. New Delhi, National Archives of India, 1959.

Blaquière, Henri. "La Restauration: Un des Moyens de Sauvetage des Archives Communales." La Gazette des Archives. Paris, 50, 1965.

Brandi, Cesare. "Il Fondamento Teorico del Restauro." Boll. Ist. Centrale Restauro. 1:5-12, 1950.

Chakravorti, S. "Preservation of Archives." Modern Librarian, 13:101-104, 1943.

Cunha, George M. "Soluble Nylon; a New Tool for Restorationists." Guild of Bookworkers' Journal, 4(2), Winter 1965-1966.

Deterioration and Preservation of Book Material Stored in Libraries, The. Garston, Building Research Station, 1949. Note No. D. 62, Great Britain. Department of Scientific and Industrial Research.

Ellis, Roger. The Principles of Archive Repair. London, London
  School of Printing and Graphic Arts, 1951.

France-Lanord, A. "How to 'Question' an Object Before Restoring
  It." Paris, Archeologia 6:8-13, 1965. Stresses the importance
  of collaboration among conservator, curator and scientist.

Grabor, I.A. Academician, (ed.). Problems of Restoration and
  Conservation of Objects of Art. Moscow, Academy of Arts,
  1960. A methodical guide. Text in Russian but 70 interesting
  illustrations. Lengthy summary and review in Studies in Conservation. 8(2), 1963.

Grünewald, Max. "Über die Pflege des Buches in hygienischer
  Beziehung." Schweizerisches Gutenbergmuseum. Bern, Jhrg.
  15:91-92, 1929.

Guha, Roy K.K. "How to Preserve Books." Modern Librarian,
  9:79-87, 1939.

Harrison, T. "The Care of Books." Book-collector's Quarterly,
  3:1-14, 1931.

Haslam, W. Library Handbook of Genuine Trade Secrets and Instructions. London, Foyles, 1923.

---- The Book of Trade Secrets, Recipes and Instructions for Reno-
  vating, Repairing, Improving and Preserving Old Books and
  Prints. London, J. Haslam & Co. Ltd. 1910.

Hensel, Evelyn. "Treatment of Nonbook Materials." Library
  Trends. 2:187-198, October 1953. Bibliography is included.

Hummel, Ray O., Jr. and Barrow, W.J. "Lamination and Other
  Methods of Restoration." Library Trends 4(3):259-268, 1956.

Jenkinson, Sir Hillary. "The Principles and Practice of Archive
  Repair Work in England." Archivum II:31-41, 1952.

Kathpalia, Y.P. "Care of Books in Libraries." Indian Archives,
  9:147-154, 1955.

Khovkina, K. Kh. "Recommendations of a Restorer." Leningrad,
  Saltykov-Shchedrin State Public Library, 33-40, 1958. Practical advice for beginners.

---- The Simplest Operations in Book Restoration. Leningrad,
  State Public Library, 1954. A 16-page practical guide for librarians (in Russian).

Kimberly, Arthur E. "Repair and Preservation in the National Archives." American Archivist, 1:111-117, July 1938.

Kremer, Alvin W. "The Preservation of Wood Pulp Publications." College and Research Libraries, 15:205-209, April 1954.

Langwell, W. H. The Conservation of Books and Documents. London, Pitman, 1957.

Mahmood, A. "Preservation Methods." Granthalaya. 1955. pp. 58-65.

McLendon, V. I. Removing Stains from Fabrics. Washington, U.S. Government Printing Office, 1959. Department of Agriculture Home and Garden Bulletin No. 62.

Million Charms of Empress Shotoku, The. Chicago, The Lakeside Press, 1966. A collection of tales about the preservation of rare books and documents at the Lakeside Press.

Minogue, Adelaide E. The Repair and Preservation of Records. Bulletins of the National Archives, Number 5, Washington, 1943. Includes a classified bibliography on causes and prevention of deterioration of paper, leather and binding.

---- "Treatment of Fire and Water Damaged Records." American Archivist, 9:17-25, January 1946.

Moscow. Collection of Materials on the Preservation of Library Resources. Moscow, 1953. English translation available from Department of Commerce, Office of Technical Services, Springfield, Va. Many informative articles on Russian preservation and restoration methods.

---- New Methods for the Restoration and Preservation of Documents and Books. Moscow, 1960. Translation available from Department of Commerce, Office of Technical Services, Springfield, Va. More information on research in restoration and conservation in Russia.

Moyano, L. "The Restoration of a Collection of 16th-century Drawings in the Cabinet des Estampes, Liege." Musées de Belgique Bulletin, 3:202-205, 1960-1961. Describes technique used for chalk drawings.

Pallenberg, Corrado. "Restoration of Ancient Books." Catholic Market 3:82-83, July/August, 1964. Describes Institute for the Scientific Restoration of Books, Rome.

Petrova, L. G. "Procedure for the Restoration of Books, Other Printed Matter and Manuscripts." Collection of Materials on the Preservation of Library Resources. Moscow, 1953. U.S. Department of Commerce, Office of Technical Services, Springfield, Va., 1964.

Plenderleith, H. J. "La Conservation des Estampes, Dessins et

Manuscrits." Mouseiôn. XXIX-XXX:81-104, 1935; XXXIII-
XXXIV:199-227, 1936. An early work of the author, most of
which is included in his later The Conservation of Antiquities
and Works of Art. 1956.

Pravilova, T.A. and Strel'tzova, T.N. "Types of Paper Suitable
for Use in Restoration." New Methods for the Restoration and
Preservation of Documents and Books. Moscow, 1960. U.S.
Department of Commerce, Office of Technical Services, Springfield, Va., 1964.

Redstone, L.J. and Steer, F.W. Local Records, Their Preservation and Care. London, G. Bell and Sons Ltd. 1953.

"Repair Center." American Archivist. 9:182.

"Repair, Checks On." American Archivist. 20:326.

"Repair in National Archives Bulletin." American Archivist. 7:
202 9:320.

"Repair Methods." American Archivist. 1:1, 20, 22, 51, 53, 56, 59, 66,
70, 111 2:21, 144, 115 3:212 6:151 7:202 8:120 9:17, 320
10:57 13:404 14:176, 280, 363 15:272 16:118 17:105 19:71
20:319, 327, 329 25:243, 353 26:257, 469.

"Restoration Methods." American Archivist. 1:16, 147 6:151 16:
115, 120, 335 17:370.

"Restoration of an Ancient Manuscript." The Library of Congress
Quarterly Journal. Washington, X:13-17, November, 1952.

"Restoration of Tracing Paper." New Methods for the Restoration
and Preservation of Documents and Books. Moscow, 1960.
U.S. Department of Commerce, Office of Technical Services,
Springfield, Va., 1964.

Salvaging and Restoring Records Damaged by Fire and Water.
Washington, D.C., Federal Fire Council, 1963.

Santucci, L. "Restoration, Conservation and Durability of Paper;
Some Chemical and Physical Problems." Bollettino, Istituto di
Patologia dell Libro, 1-2, 1959.

Scott, Alexander. "Romance of Museum Restoration." Journal of
the Royal Society of Arts. 80:488-498, 1932. Interesting account of unusual restorations of museum artifacts.

Scriven, Margaret. "Preservation and Restoration of Library Materials." Special Libraries, New York, 47(10):439-448, 1956.

Spawn, William. "The Conservation of Books and Papers." Ontario Library Review, 46:5-7, 1962.

Still, John S. "Library Fire and Salvage Methods." The American Archivist, XVI:145-153, April 1953.

Thompson, Daniel V. (trans.) The Craftsman's Handbook. New Haven, Yale University Press, 1933. Modern edition New York, Dover Publications, Inc. 1954. An accurate translation of Cennini's 15th-century Il Libro dell Arte.

Trey, E. Kh. "Methods of Restoration and Present Condition of the Ostromirovo Gospel." Leningrad, Saltykov-Shchedrin State Public Library, 49-96, 1958.

Tribolet, Harold W. "Trends in Preservation." Library Trends, 13(2). The director of the Department of Extra Binding at the Lakeside Press discusses recent developments in library conservation.

Turner, R.S. "To Repair or Despair?" American Archivist, 20: 319-329, Oct. 1957.

U.S. National Archives. The Rehabilitation of Paper Records. Washington, D.C., 1950. Staff Information Paper, No. 16.

"Water and Fire Damaged Books and Records, Treatment of." American Archivist, 5:129 9:17 16:141,149.

Werner, Anthony E. "The Preservation of Archives." Journal of the Society of Archivists, 1:282-288, October 1959.

Williams, Howard D. "Records Salvage After the Fire at Colgate University." American Archivist, 27:375-379, July 1964.

Paper Testing

Lanner, H.F. Determination of the pH Value of Papers. Washington, Government Printing Office, 1939. (Bureau of Standards Research Paper RP1205.)

Lee, H.N. "Established Methods for Examination of Paper." Technical Studies, 4(1), 1935.

Tests and Procedures for Books and Book Components. Hoboken, N.J. United States Testing Co., 1957.

Mildew Damage

Almela Meliá, Juan. Higiene y terapeutica del libro. Mexico, D.F.: Fondo de Cultura Ecônomica, 1956. Illustrated.

Belyakova, L.A. "Choice of Antiseptic for Mold Control on Book Glue." Collection of Materials on the Preservation of Library

355

Resources. Moscow, 1958. English translation available from Department of Commerce, Office of Technical Services, Springfield, Va.

---- "Effect of Ultraviolet Radiation by Bactericidal Lamp on Spores of Mold Fungi. " (ibid.).

---- "Instruction for Use of Sodium Pentachlorophenate as Glue Antiseptic. " (ibid.).

----"The Resistance of Fungi to Fungicides. " (ibid.).

---- Fungus Control in the Lenin State Library. " UNESCO Bulletin for Libraries, 15:198-200, 1961.

---- "Gamma Radiation as a Disinfecting Agent. " Environ. Eff. Mater. Equip. Abst. 2:117, 1962.

Betto, E.   The Bacterial and Fungicidal Activity of Ethylene Oxide in Vacuum Fumigation.   Milan, Istituto di Patologia Vegetale dell'Universita di Milano, 1960.   (Abstracted in Art and Archaeology Technical Abstracts, 6(2), 1966.)

Helwig, H.   "Books Infected by Mold: Possibilities for Disinfection and Preservation. " Das Papier, Darmstadt, 7, July 1953.

Holnes, R. F. G.   "Use of Formaldehyde as a Fumigant. " British Records Association Bulletin, No. 14, 1942.

Hubner, P. H.   "Les Maladies du Papier et Leur Traitment. " Mouseion. XXVII-XXVIII, 1934.   A unique method for restoration of mildewed paper utilizing ultra-violet light and other electric illumination to kill mold and mildew and reduce stains, followed by sizing with glue and coating with cellulose acetate. Not recommended for rare books and manuscripts.

Petrolva-Zavgorodnyaya, et al.   "Disinfection of Books and Documentary Materials by a High-Frequency Electromagnetic Field. " New Methods for the Restoration and Preservation of Documents and Books.   Moscow, 1960.   U.S. Department of Commerce, Office of Technical Services, Springfield, Va. , 1964.

---- "The Effect of High-Frequency Electromagnetic Fields on Paper-destroying Mold Fungi. " (ibid.).

"Portable Fumigation Chamber. " Museum News, 44(6), 1966.

Santucci, L.   "Rigenerazione dei documenti III. " Istituto di Patologia dell'Libro Bollettino 18(3-4), 1959.   On foxing.

Sykes, G.   Disinfestation and Sterilization.   London, Spon, 1958.

"Vacuum Fumigation Unit. " Wilson Library Bulletin, 38, 1963.

Describes the Vacudyne Corp. unit.

Winge-Heden, K. "Ethylene Oxide Sterilization Without Special Equipment." Acta Pathologica et Microbiologica Scandinavica, 58, 1963. Uses plastic bags.

Yadow, V. L. "A Portable Fumigation Chamber for the Small Museum." Museum News, 44(6), 1966.

Zagulyaeva, Z. A. "The Lethal Effect of High Frequency Currents on Cellulose-destroying Mold Fungi." New Methods for the Restoration and Preservation of Documents and Books. Moscow, 1960. U.S. Department of Commerce, Office of Technical Services, Springfield, Va., 1960.

Insect Damage

Basu, M. "Preservation of Books Affected with Insects." Science and Culture, 7:617, 1942.

Beattie, W. R. The Use of Hydrocyanic Gas for Exterminating Household Insects. Washington, U.S. Division of Entomology, 1902. Bulletin No. 31, new series.

Blew, J. Oscar, Jr., and Kulp, John W. Comparison of Wood Preservatives in Mississippi Post Study. Research Note FPL-01. February 1964. U.S. Forest Service. Forest Products Lab., Madison, Wis.

Bollaerts, D., Quoilin, J., and van den Bruel, W. E. "New Experiments on the Application of Micro-Waves to the Destruction of Insects Hiding in Wooden Materials." In French with English summary. Staat Gent. 26:1435-1450, 1961. Mededel. Landbouwhogeschool Opzoekingssta.

Bryan, J. "Methods of Applying Wood Preservatives." Forest Products Research Records, 9,1946.

Chakavorti, S. "Vacuum Fumigation--A New Technique of Preserving Records." Science and Culture, 9(2):77-81, 1943.

Coaton, W. G. H. "Toxic-smoke Generator for Termite Control." Farming in South Africa, September 1947.

Cotton, R. T., and Roark, R. C. "Ethylene Oxide as a Fumigant." Industrial and Engineering Chemistry, 1928.

Ebeling, W., and Wagner, R. "Rapid Desiccation of Drywood Termites with Inert Sorptive Dusts and Other Substances." Journal Econ. Ent. 52:190-207, 1959.

Gray, H. E. "Vikane--A New Fumigant for Control of Dry Wood

357

Termites." Pest Control 28:43-46, 1960.

Kozulina, O. V. "Dermistid Book Pests and Measures for Their Extermination." Collection of Materials on the Preservation of Library Resources. Moscow, 1958. U.S. Department of Commerce, Office of Technical Services, Springfield, Va., 1964.

---- "Instructions for Use of DDT Preparations in the Extermination of Book Pests." (ibid.).

Lepigre, A. L. Technique de la Désinsectisation. Paris, P. Lechevalier, 1947.

Liberti, Sal. "A New Fumigant for Disinfestation with Lindane as a Base." Bollettino, Istituto di Patologia dell Libro. 1-2, 1959. Smoke fumigation.

Petrova, G. I. "Insects in Book Storerooms and Control Measures." Collection of Materials on the Preservation of Library Resources. Moscow, 1953. English translation National Science Foundation, Washington, 1964. A thorough, scientific study of the insect problem in libraries and ways to control it.

Petrova, L. G. "Instructions for the Use of DDT Preparations Against Insect Infestation of Books." Collection of Materials on the Preservation of Library Resources. Moscow, 1953. U.S. Department of Commerce, Office of Technical Services, Springfield, Va., 1964.

Plenderleith, H. J. "Bookworm; Treatment by Carbon Disulphide." British Records Association Bulletin. No. 19, p. 8, 1948.

---- "Protection of Records Against Bookworm." British Records Association Bulletin. No. 11, 1940.

Stewart, D. "Precision Fumigation for Drywood Termites with Vikane." Pest Control 30(2):24, 1962.

"Vacuum Fumigation Unit for Destroying Insects and Mold in Graphic Records." Wilson Library Bulletin. 38:246, November, 1963.

Walker, J. F. Formaldehyde. American Chemical Society Monograph, 1944. Includes instructions for fumigation with this chemical.

Cleaning Paper

Beaufort, Thomas Richard. Pictures and How to Clean Them; To Which are Added Notes on Things Useful in Restoration Work. London, J. Lane, 1926 xi.

Gunn, Maurice J. Print Restoration and Picture Cleaning. London,

1922.

Longo, L., et al. "Experiments on a Method for Cleaning Discolored Paper Manuscripts." Istituto di Patologia del Libro Bollettino. 18(3-4), 1959.

Third Report of the Department of Scientific and Industrial Research on the Cleaning and Restoration of Museum Exhibits. London, H.M.S.O., 1926. Extremely valuable advice on the cleaning of prints and water colors.

Bleaching

"Bleaching." American Archivist. 1:76.

Bibikov, N.N., and Filippova, N.A. "The Electrochemical Method of Restoration of Library Materials." Leningrad, State Public Library, 35-46, 1959. Describes bleaching techniques. (Abstracted in Art and Archaeology Technical Abstracts, 6(?), 1966.).

de Fulvio, Silvano and Longo, Luigi. "Use of Ozone for Bleaching of Browned Paper in Book Restoration." Bollettino, Istituto di Patologia dell Libro. 19, 1960.

Filippova, N.A. "Methods of Removing Ink Spots from Paper." Leningrad, Saltykov-Shchedrin State Public Library, 23-32, 1958. (Abstracted in Art and Archaeology Technical Abstracts, 6(2), 1966.)

Flieder, F. "Chemical Bleaching of Mildew Spots on Old Papers." Association Technique de l'Industrie Papetière Bulletin. Paris, 4, 1960. Comparison of 26 bleaching agents. In French

---- Studies of Chemical Bleaching of Stains in Old Paper. Paris, Laboratoire de Cryptogamie 1961. In French.

Gettens, Rutherford John. "Bleaching of Stained and Discolored Pictures on Paper with Sodium Chlorite and Chlorine Dioxide." Museum. Paris, 5:116-130, 1952. C.A. 46:9385e, 1952.

Keck, Sheldon. "A Method of Cleaning Prints." Technical Studies in the Field of Fine Arts. V(1), 1936. Cambridge, Mass., Fogg Art Museum. Describes an effective method for reducing stains in paper without leaving harmful residual chemicals in the paper.

Pravilova, T.A., and Istrubcina, T.W. "The Bleaching of Documents on Paper with Sodium Chlorite." Moscow-Leningrad, USSR Academy of Sciences, 1962, pp. 5-27. Illustrated, diagrams, 22 references. Problems of the conservation and restoration of paper and parchment.

Santucci, L. "Chemical Restoration of Documents." Bollettino Istituto di Patologia del Libro. 12(3), 1953.

Santucci, L., and Wolff, C. "Rigener Azione dei Documenti IV." Rome, (ibid. December, 1963). A scientific report on their method for the revival and stabilization of iron inks.

Yabrova, R.R. "Instructions for Removal of Ink Stains and Stamping Ink Stains from Paper." Collection of Materials on the Preservation of Library Resources. Moscow, 1958. U.S. Department of Commerce, Office of Technical Services, Springfield, Va., 1964.

---- "Removal of Dyes from Paper." (ibid.).

Deacidification

Barrow, W.J. "Deacidification and Lamination of Deteriorated Documents, 1938-1963." American Archivist. 28:285-290, April 1965.

---- Manuscripts and Documents; Their Deterioration and Restoration. Charlottesville, Va., University of Virginia Press, 1955. Deacidification techniques.

---- Permanence-durability of the Book. Richmond, Va., 1963. Deacidification of a book by spraying. The stability of polyvinyl acetate adhesives. Development of performance standards for library binding.

---- Permanence-durability of the Book--III. Spray Deacidification. Richmond, Va., 1964. Research Laboratory. Illustrated.

Blanc, M.C., and Nyuksha, J.P. "On the Stabilization of Paper with Calcium and Magnesium Carbonates." Leningrad, O sokhranenii bumagi, 61-69, 1963. Reports favorably on the Barrow process.

Istrubtsina, T.V., and Pravilova, T.A. "Conservation of Paper Documents by Buffering." Probl. Dolgovechnosti Dokumentov i Bumagi, Akad. Nauk USSR Lab. Konservatsii i Restavratsii Dokumentov. pp. 71-81, 1964. Chemical Abstracts. 62, 2911, 1965.

Kathpalia, Y.P. "Deterioration and Conservation of Paper IV: Neutralization." Indian Pulp and Paper, 17, October 1962.

Langwell, W.H. "The Vapour Phase Deacidification of Books and Documents." Journal of the Society of Archivists. 3, April 1966.

Raff, R.A., Herrick, I.W., and Adams, M.F. "Archives Docu-

ment Preservation. " Northwest Science. 40(1), 1966. A report on a technique for simultaneously deacidifying and strengthening paper by impregnating it with artificial resins.

Smith, R.D. "Paper Deacidification: A Preliminary Report. " The
Library Quarterly. 36(4), October 1966. Reports preliminary
investigation on a new approach to the preservation of deteriorating paper.

Sizing

Belen'Kaia, N.G., and others. "The Use of Methyl-cellulose for
the Restoration of Archival and Library Materials. " Moscow,
Stareniye bumagi, 94-111, 1965. Reports usefulness of the material for sizing paper and fixing ink. (Abstracted in Art and
Archaeology Technical Abstracts, 6(2), 1966.)

Daniel, J.S. "Sizing Paper." December 13, 1960. U.S. pat.
2,964,445.

Kowalik, R., Czerwinska, E. "Sizes Used in Paper-making and
Paper Binding, Their Deterioration and Preservation. " Blok
Notes Muzeum Mickiewicza. Warsaw. 1960. pp. 153-154.

Langwell, W.H. "The Preservation of Unstable Papers. " Archives.
London, 4, 1949-1952. Emphasis on gelatin sizing.

"Sizing. " American Archivist. 1:4,9,64.

Mending Paper

Bolsée, J. "La Restauration des Documents aux Archives Gener-
ales du Royaume. " Archives Bibliothèques et Musées de
Belgique, XXIe Anee. 1950, No. 1, pp. 3-10.

Collis. "Document Conservation in the Local Repository. "
Archives. 6, 1963. Tips for small library conservators.

Gear, James L. "The Repair of Documents--American Beginnings. "
American Archivist. 26, pp.469-475, 1963.

"Inlaying Paper." American Archivist. 16:123.

Jentink, R.L. "Notes on the Use of Mending Tapes on Paper. "
Bulletin American Group IIC. 2, 1961. How to undo the damage.

Kathpalia, Y.P. "Deterioration and Conservation of Paper. Part V,
Restoration of Documents. " Indian Pulp and Paper. 17, April
1963, pp. 565-573. Environ. Eff. Mater. Equip. Abstr. 4,
1964, p. 158. POL-49812.

Minogue, Adelaide E. "Some Observations on the Flattening of Folded Records." American Archivist, 8:115-121, April 1945.

Nyuksha, J.P. "Application of Paper Pulp in Restoration Work." Leningrad, Saltykov-Shchedrin State Public Library, 41-48, 1958. Describes necessary apparatus.

---- "Restoration of Books and Documents by Application of Paper Pulp." Leningrad, Saltykov-Shchedrin State Public Library, 47-56, 1959. Gives details of technique.

"Paper, Restoration." American Archivist. 16:120.

"Paper, Splitting." American Archivist. 1:20 16:121.

Smith, L. Herman. "Manuscript Repair in European Archives." American Archivist. 1:1-22, 51-77, January, April 1938. Paper mending.

Stout, G.L., and Horwitz, M. "Experiments with Adhesives for Paper." Technical Studies. III(1), 1934.

Wachter, Otto. "Paper Repairing Processes." Allgemeiner Anzieger für Buchbindereien. Stuttgart, 7(9), 1958. In German.

Welch, C.E. "Repair of Documents." Assistant Librarian. 53: 53-55, 1960.

Williams, G., and Tribolet, H. "More Hints on the Preservation of Manuscripts." Manuscripts. 13, 1961.

Yabrova, R.R. "Instructions for the Reinforcement and Restoration of Documents with Polymethylacrylate Emulsion." Collection of Materials on the Preservation of Library Resources. Moscow, 1958. U.S. Department of Commerce, Office of Technical Studies, Springfield, Va., 1964.

---- "Treatment of Paper with Certain Polyacrylate Resins." (ibid.).

Lamination

Barrow, William J. "An Evaluation of Document Restoration Processes." American Documentation. 4:50-54, April 1953. Silk tissue and lamination processes with full exposition of the latter.

---- "The Barrow Method of Laminating Documents." Journal of Documentary Reproduction. 2:147-151, June 1939.

---- Barrow Method of Restoring Deteriorated Documents. Richmond, Va., The author, 1965. 19 p.

Belen'kaya, N.G. "Methods of Restoring Books and Documents."

New Methods for the Restoration and Preservation of Documents
and Prints. Moscow, 1960. Translated U.S. Department of
Commerce, Office of Technical Services 64-11054. Includes a
summary of lamination practices in Europe and America and
reviews the pros and cons of lamination.

Belen'kaya, N.G., and others. "On Some Properties of Laminated
Papers." Moscow, Stareniye bumagi, Laboratory of Conservation and Restoration of Documents, 117-27, 1965. (Abstracted
in Art and Archaeology Technical Abstracts, 6(2), 1966.)

Boak, R.I. "Putting New Life in Old Volumes." Publisher's
Weekly. The Arbee Company's president writes on lamination
and book preservation.

Broadman, Joseph. Cellulose Acetate Sheetings as Used for the
Preservation of Permanent Records; a Critical Analysis. New
York, 1946. Gives reasons why cellulose acetate cannot be con-
sidered a permanent plastic.

Chakrovorti, S.A. "A Review of the Lamination Process." Indian
Archives. I:304-312, 1947.

Darlington, Ida. "The Lamination of Paper Documents." Journal
Society of Archivists. I, 1955-1959. English techniques.

de Valinger, Leon Jr. "Lamination of Manuscripts at the Delaware
State Archives, 1938-1964." American Archivist. 28:290-293,
April 1965.

Evans, D.L. "The Lamination Process, A British View." British
Records Association, Technical Section, Bulletin. 18:10-14,
October 1945.

Gear, J.L. "Lamination After 30 Years: Record and Prospect."
American Archivist. 28:293-297, April 1965.

---- "The Repair of Documents--American Beginnings." American
Archivist. 26:469-475, October, 1963.

Goel, O.P. "Repair of Documents with Cellulose Acetate on a
Small Scale." The Indian Archives. 7:162-165, 1953.

Hummel, Ray O., Jr., and Barrow, W.J. "Lamination and Other
Methods of Restoration." Library Trends 4(3):259-268, 1956.

Kathpalia, Y.P. "Hand Lamination with Cellulose Acetate." American Archivist 31(3), 1958.

Kremer, A.W. "NBS Study of Lamination Completed." Library of
Congress Information Bulletin. 16, 1957. Summary of study
and findings.

"Lamination." American Archivist. 1:114 2:22 4:200 6:37,151,
259 9:227,320 16:122 20:320,324,329,332.

"Laminator for Maps." American Archivist. 15:81.

"Laminators." American Archivist. Arbee Co. 20:180 Barrow
4:68 10:203 13:413 14:364 20:321.

Langwell, W.H. "The Postlip Duplex Lamination Processes." Society of Archivists Journal. 2:471-476, October 1964.

Nixon, H.M. "Lamination of Paper Documents with Cellulose Acetate Film Foil." Archives. No. 2, 1949. The British Records
Association, 1 Lancaster Gate, London, W.C. 2.

Piez, G.T. "Laminator for Libraries." ALA Bulletin. 53, March
1961.

Procedures and Equipment Used in the Barrow Method of Restoring
Manuscripts and Documents. Richmond, Va., State Library
Building, 1958.

"Putting New Life in Old Volumes." Publisher's Weekly. July 19,
1965. Commercial lamination.

Scribner, B.W. Protection of Documents With Cellulose Acetate
Sheeting. Washington, Government Printing Office, 1940. U.S.
National Bureau of Standards, Miscellaneous Publication M168.

Tollenaar, D. "L'Acetate de Cellulose et la Lamination des Documents." Archivum. II:51-53, 1952.

Werner, A.E. "The Lamination of Documents." Journal of Documentation. 20:25-31, March 1964.

Wilson, W.K., and Forshee, B.W. Preservation of Documents by
Lamination. Washington, U.S. National Bureau of Standards,
1959. Monograph No. 5.

Ink Revival

Almy, L.H. "Restoration of Faded Ink Writings." Abstract Review. 249, September 1958.

Arias, A. Charro. "New Method for Restoring Falsified or Faded
Documents." Farm. nueva. Madrid, 7:480-485, 1942. Chem.
Zentr. I:1916, 1943. CA 38 m 4065, 1944.

Davis, Raymond. Action of Charred Paper on the Photographic
Plate and a Method of Deciphering Charred Records. Washington, Government Printing Office, 1922. U.S. Bureau of Standards. Scientific Papers, No. 454.

Erastov, D. P. "Control of Operating Conditions in Reproduction Technique for Highlighting Faded Images." New Methods for Restoration and Preservation of Documents and Books. Moscow, 1960. U. S. Department of Commerce, Office of Technical Services, Springfield, Va., 1964.

"Faded Writing." Archives. Michaelmas, December 1949. Methods employed at the Public Records Office of England to restore faded writing. Very brief.

Hamilton, D. H. "The Repair of Autographs." Hobbies Magazine. 63, November 1958.

Hilton, Ordway. An Evaluation of Chemical Methods for Restoring Erased Writing Ink. London, Swindon Press Ltd. 195? This short paper is primarily for examiners of questioned documents but contains general information on ink revival useful for librarians.

"Ink, Restoration of." American Archivist. 1:16.

Jones, G. A. "Decipherment of Charred Documents." Nature. 147: 676-677, 1941. Infrared illumination.

Kishore, Ranbir. "Preservation of Pencil Writing." Indian Archives. 6:34-38, 1952. Chart.

Kom'arek, Karel. "Restoration of Faded Ink Writings." Chemical Abstracts. 54, 1960.

Lyublinskii, V. S. "Two Different Cases of Restoration of Faded Text." New Methods for the Restoration and Preservation of Documents and Books. Moscow, 1960. U. S. Department of Commerce, Office of Technical Services, Springfield, Va., 1964. Describes use of photoanalytical methods for deciphering faded texts.

Murry, H. D. "Examination of Burnt Documents." Nature. 148: 199, 1941. Immersion in silver nitrate.

Radley, J. A., "Deciphering of Charred Documents." Analyst. 75: 628-629, 1950. C. A. 1951, 914i.

Shoichi, N. "Restoration of Erased Ink Writings with Iron Complex." Science and Crime Detection. Japan, 8, 1955.

Taylor, W. D., and Walls, H. J. "A New Method for the Decipherment of Charred Documents." Nature. 147:417, 1941. A combination of chemical treatment and photography.

Waters, C. E. Inks. Washington, U. S. Government Printing Office, 1940. National Bureau of Standards Circular C426. Includes section on ink revival.

Yabrova, R.R. "Instructions for Removing Ink Stains and Stamping Ink Stains from Paper." Collection of Materials on the Preservation of Library Resources. Moscow, 1958. U.S. Department of Commerce, Office of Technical Services, Springfield, Va., 1964.

Zimmerman, Elmer W., Weber, Charles G., and Kimberly, Arthur E. Relation of Ink to the Preservation of Written Records. Washington, U.S. Government Printing Office, 1935. U.S. National Bureau of Standards, Research Paper RP 779.

Leather Repair

Belaya, I.K. "Instructions for Restoring Leather Bindings." Collection of Material on the Preservation of Library Resources. Moscow, 1958. U.S. Department of Commerce, Office of Technical Services, Springfield, Va., 1964.

---- "Instructions for Softening Vegetable and Chrome Tanned Leather Bindings." (ibid.).

---- "Softening Leather Bindings." (ibid.).

Frey, R.W., and Veitch, F.P. Preservation of Leather Bookbindings. Washington, Department of Agriculture, 1933. Leaflet No. 69.

Plenderleith, H.J. "Laboratory Notes: The Preservation of Bookbindings." British Museum Quarterly. London, 3:77-78, 1927.

Parchment and Vellum

Audsley, G.A. Guide to Illuminating on Vellum and Paper. London, Rowney, 1911.

"Parchment Stretcher." American Archivist. 1:7,15 9:330.

"Repair of Parchment." American Archivist. 1:5,14,52,60,73 3:212,213 16:119.

Skordas, Gust. "The Parchment Stretcher at the Maryland Hall of Records." American Archivist. 9:330-332, October 1946.

Wachter, Otto. "On the Stretching and Flattening of Old Parchment." Allgemeiner Anzeiger für Buchbindereien. Stuttgart, 71, 1958. No.1. In German.

---- "The Restoration of the Vienna Dioscorides." Studies in Conservation. 7, 1962. Detailed report on repairs to an early sixth-century illustrated parchment manuscript.

366

Allgemenier Anzeiger für Buchbindereien. Stuttgart, Buchbinder-
Verlag. 5(14a) Christophstrasse 9, Fernruf 94215. General information for bookbinding.

All the Kings Horses. Chicago, The Lakeside Press. Description
of work by the Extra Bindery of this publishing firm.

"Bookbinding." American Archivist. 3:267 16:115.

Chytil, Dr. K., and Borovsky, F.A. Bucheinbande vom XVIII,
Jahrhundert Bis in Die Neveste Zeit. Prague, Kunstyewer-
bliches Museum, 1904. Descriptive text on bookbinding in
German and Hungarian.

Dana, John C. Bookbinding for Libraries. Chicago, Library Bureau, 1906. The librarian's point of view on bookbinding at the
turn of the century

de Haas, Hendrik. De Boekbinder. Dordrecht, 1806. Complete
description of everything related to this art, partly taken from
the best known foreign works and augmented with the theory and
practice of the best domestic artists and artisans.

Domesday Rebound. London, H.M.S.O., 1954. Detailed description of the restoration of two of the Domesday Books.

Gould, F.C. Mechanization of Bookbinding, Being Lecture Three of
the 16th Series of Craft Lectures Given in Stationers' Hall on
Friday, 17th December, 1937.

Grimm, Francis W. A Primer to Bookbinding. Boston, Houghton
Mifflin Co., 1939.

Halliday, John. Bookcraft and Bookbinding. London, Pitman, 1951.
Illustrated.

Harrison, T. The Bookbinding Craft and Industry; An Outline of Its
History, Development and Technique. London, Pitman, 1930.
2nd ed. Illustrated.

Hasluck, P.N. Bookbinding. Philadelphia, David McKay, 1903. A
digest of information on binding which originally appeared in the
British weekly journal Work. Interesting sections on marbling
paper, tree calfing leather, and gold blocking.

Ignatz Wiemeler, Modern Bookbinder. New York, Museum of Modern Art, 1935.

Jennett, Seán. The Making of Books. 2nd ed. Faber, 1956.

Johnson, Pauline. Creative Bookbinding. Seattle, University of Washington Press, 1963.

Leighton, D. Modern Bookbinding; a Survey and a Prospect. London, School of Printing, 1935.

Kinder, Louis H. Formulas for Bookbinders. East Aurora, N.Y., The Roycrofters, 1905.

MacDougall, G. Some Research Problems in Bookbinding. London, 1935.

Mansfield, Edgar. Modern Design in Bookbinding. London, Peter Owen, 1966. A book on the technique and theory of creative bookbinding by the president of the Guild of Contemporary Bookbinders.

---- "New Directions in Modern Bookbinding." Graphis, XV:350-357, August, 1959.

"Methods and Materials for Electronic Case Making." Part I. Material. Bookbinding and Book Production. 57:32-33, June 1953. Part 2. Machines. 58:33-34, July, 1953. Part 3. Decorating. 58:48-51, August 1953. Part 4. 58:50, September 1953.

Modern Book Production. The Studio, 1928.

Philip, Alex J. The Business of Book-binding: For Librarians, Publishers, Students, Binders, and the General Reader. 2nd ed. Gravesend, England, Alex. J. Philip, 1935. Originally published in 1912. Entirely rewritten, 1934. British practice. Includes samples of leather, cloth and leather-cloth.

A Rod for the Back of the Binder. Chicago, Lakeside Press, 1928. Describes fine binding as done by this company in the 1920's.

Theory and Practice of Bookbinding. Washington, U.S. Government Printing Office, 1950.

Tomlinson, C.J. Cyclopedia of Useful Arts and Manufactures. 1852. Early methods of bookmaking.

Tribolet, Harold W. "Binding and Related Problems." American Archivist. 16:115-126, April 1953. Except for lack of information on deacidification, a good summary of what should and should not be done to valuable books.

Vaughan, A.J. Modern Bookbinding. London, Charles Skelton Ltd. 1929. One of the best 20th-century volumes on the combination of hand and machine binding for high quality workmanship.

---- Modern Bookbinding. Leicester, Raithby, Lawrence, 1946.

368

Wheatley, H.B. "The Principles of Design as Applied to Bookbinding." Journal of the Royal Society of Arts. 36(1840):
359-377, February 24, 1888.

"Why Not Do Your Own Binding?" Reproduction. 1:10-11, April,
1964.

Williamson, Hugh. Methods of Book Design. Oxford University
Press, 1956.

Hand Binding

Adams, Charles. "Notes on Marbling Paper." Bulletin New York
Public Library. July 1947.

Banister, Manly. Pictorial Manual of Bookbinding. New York,
1958.

Battershall, Fletcher. Bookbinding for Bibliophiles. Greenwich,
Conn., The Literary Collector Press, 1905.

Bean, Florence O. Bookbinding for Beginners. Boston, School
Arts Publishing Co., 1914. A teaching manual for use in elementary school handcraft classes.

Bookbinders' Complete Instructor in All Branches of Bookbinding.
Peterhead, 1823.

Bookbinders' Manual. London, 1832.

Brade, L., and Winkler, E. Het Geillustreerde Boekbindersboek.
Leyden, 1861. The illustrated book for the bookbinder. Complete instructions in bookbinding. Describes French, English
and German accomplishments in this profession, with instructions for the making of various marbled and other edges, also
gilding. Tells about latest machines, with 76 very good recipes
and many woodcuts.

Buffam, Clara. Hand Bound Books. Providence, R.I., 1935.

Cockerell, D. Bookbinding and the Care of Books. 5th ed. London,
Pitman, 1953.

---- Some Notes on Bookbinding. London, Oxford University Press,
1929. This small volume is a sequel to Douglas Cockerell's
Bookbinding. Hard to find but well worth looking for.

Cockerell, Sydney M. Marbling Paper. Hitchin, Herts, England,
Russel Bookcrafts, 1947. Pamphlet.

---- Marbling Paper as a School Subject. Hitchin, England, July
1934. One specimen of marbled paper.

---- "The Binding of Manuscripts." The Calligraphers Handbook. (Lamb, C.M., ed.) London, Faber and Faber Ltd.

Combed Pattern Papers. Leicester, England, Dryad Leaflet No. 107. Instructions for decorating paper.

Cowie. Bookbinders Manual. London, Strange, 1868. Full descriptions for leather and vellum binding, also directions for gilding book edges. Lists bookbinders' charges for the mid-19th century.

Crane, W.J.E. Bookbinding for Amateurs. London, Gill, 1885. Descriptions of the various tools and detailed instructions for their use. Well illustrated.

de Recy, Georges. Decoration du Cuir. Paris, Ernest Flammarion (ed.) 1905.

Diehl, Edith. Bookbinding, Its Background and Technique. New York, Rinehart, 1946. Two volumes. Illustrated. Vol. 1 comprises a history of the craft; Vol. 2 a manual of hand binding.

Diringer, David. The Hand Produced Book. 1953.

Domesday Rebound. London, H.M.S.O., 1954. A description of the rebinding of the Domesday Books.

Dudin, L'Art du Relieur et Doreur de Livres. Paris, 1772. This early book on bookbinding and gold tooling has 112 pages of text and 16 plates. It was written for the Academie Royale des Sciences.

---- L'Art du Relieur. Nouvelle édition, augmentée ce tout de qui a été écrit de mieux sur ces mattières en Allemagne, en Angleterre, en Suisse, en Italie, &c. Par J.E. Betrand. Two explanatory plates, Paris, 1820. Extract from the "Description Générale des Arts e Métiers."

Ede, Charles. "Hand Binding." The Art of the Book. Studio, 1951.

Eggeling, Arthur. Bookbinding by Hand. New York, Eggeling Bookbindery, 1925.

Fahey, Herbert and Peter. Finishing in Hand Bookbinding. San Francisco, printed and published by Herbert and Peter Fahey, 1951.

Goodwin, Bancroft L. Pamphlet Binding. Chicago, United Typothetae of America, 1925. Typographic technical series for apprentices. Part 5, No. 20.

Grimm, F.W. A Primer on Bookbinding. Boston, Houghton Mifflin Co., 1939. An introductory text for young people.

Groneman, Chris H. General Bookbinding. Bloomington, Ill., McKnight and McKnight, 1946. A high school level manual of instruction. Calls for simplest of tools and equipment.

Halfer, J. Art of Marbling and Treatment of the New Bronze Colours. 2nd ed., 1904.

---- The Progress of the Marbling Art; with a Supplement on the Decoration of Book Edges. Buffalo, N.Y., American Bookbinder Co., 1893. Many specimens of marbled papers.

Halliday, J. Bookbinding as a Handwork Subject. New York, E.P. Dutton and Company, n.d.

Harnett, John. Bibliopegia or the Art of Bookbinding in All Its Branches. By John Andrews Arnett (pseud.) London, Groombridge, 1835.

Harrison, T. Fragments of Bookbinding Technique. London, 1950.

Hatchards & Zaehnsdorf, Notes on the Art of Bookbinding. London, Hatchards, 1952. Pamphlet.

Hewitt-Bates, J.S. Bookbinding. Leicester, 1962. Illustrated instructions for the neophyte.

---- Bookbinding for Schools: A Textbook for Teachers and Students in Elementary and Secondary Schools and Training Colleges. Peoria, Ill., Manual Arts Press, 1935.

Hewitt-Bates, James Samuel, and Halliday, J. "Three Methods of Marbling." Dryad Leaflet No. 74. Leicester, England, Dryad Press, n.d.

Jaugeon, "L'Art de Reliure les Libres." This forms the fifth part and completion of a great work, Description et Perfection des Arts et Metiers. The manuscript has never been printed. It was begun in 1693 and finished in 1704. The part relating to binding has 42 pages of text, and two explanatory plates; these last were used later on by Dudin in his "Art du Relieur et Doreur des Livres," which appeared in 1772. This is the first technical work on binding known.

Johnson, Pauline. "Decorative Covers." Craft Horizons. XLV:20-23, August 1954.

Kantrowitz, N., and Spencer, E.W. The Process of Marbling Paper. Washington, U.S. Government Printing Office, 1953. (G.P.O.-P.I.A. Joint Research Bulletin, Bindery series No. 1.) Printing Industry of America. Much information on evolution of

371

the process with useful formulas and a lengthy bibliography by Dard Hunter.

Kitson, Edward. Bookbinding. New York, Dover Publications, 1954.

Klinefelter, Lee M. Bookbinding Made Easy. Milwaukee, Wis., Bruce Publishing Co., 1935.

Le Moine, Simone. Manuel Practique du Reliure. Paris, Dunod, 1960.

Lewis, Arthur William. Basic Bookbinding. New York, Dover Publications, 1957.

Loubier, Hans. Der Bucheinband. Leipzig, 1926.

"Marbled Paper." American Archivist. 1:15.

Martin, Complete Instructions in all Branches of Bookbinding, 1823.

Mason, John. Bookbinding. London, 1936. 36 illustrations in a 62-page pamphlet of the basic steps in bookbinding.

---- Gold and Colour Tooling. Dryad Leaflet No. 105. Leicester, Eng., Dryad Press, n.d.

Mathews, William. Bookbinding. New York, E.P. Dutton & Co., Inc., 1929. A manual for amateurs.

---- Modern Bookbinding Practically Considered. New York, 1889.

Nathan, M. The Decoration of Leather. New York, 1905. From the French of Georges de Recy.

Nicholson, J.B. A Manual of the Art of Bookbinding. Philadelphia, Pa., Bair and Company, 1856. Reprinted in 1902. A practical manual on fine hand binding.

Oswesley, N. The Whole Art of Bookbinding. London, 1811. This is the earliest English book on the subject of bookbinding. Contains recipes for sprinkling, marbling and coloring leather in addition to forwarding and finishing instructions.

Palmer, E.W. A Course in Bookbinding for Vocational Training. New York, Employing Bookbinders of America, 1927. Part I, Elementary Section, was all that was ever printed.

Parry, H. The Art of Bookbinding. 1818.

---- The Whole Art of Bookbinding. 1811.

372

Pearce, W. B. Practical Bookbinding. Marshall, 1906.

Perry, K. F., and Baab, C. T. The Binding of Books. Peoria,
Ill., The Manual Arts Press, 1940.

Pleger, John J. Bookbinding. Chicago, Inland Printer Co., 1924.
Contains section on marbling, edge gilding and printed fore
edges.

---- Gilt Edging, Marbling and Hand Tooling. Chicago, Inland
Printer, 1914.

Pointer, Wallace. "Rebinding the Klencke Atlas." British Museum
Quarterly. London, 1961. Discusses problems in handling a
book five feet tall.

Pratt, Guy A. Let's Bind a Book. Milwaukee, Wis., Bruce Publishing Co., 1940.

Process of Marbling Paper, The. Washington, U. S. Government
Printing Office, 1953. GPO-PIA Joint Research Bulletin B-1.
Many recipes, detailed instructions, lengthy bibliography.

Smith, F. R. Bookbinding. New York, Pitman Publishing Corp.,
1929.

Thrift, Tim. Modern Methods in Marbling Paper, a Treatise for
the Layman on the Art of Marbling Paper for Bookbinding...
Including a Description of Several Practical Methods with Illus-
trative Samples of Marbled Effects. Winchester, Mass., The
Lucky Dog Press, 1945.

Town, Laurence. Bookbinding by Hand for Students and Craftsmen.
London, Faber & Faber, 1951. The style of presentation and
excellent drawings in this book make it of particular value to
beginners.

Verstage, K. A., et al. Hints on Marbling. London School of
Printing, 1940.

Watson, Aldren A. Hand Bookbinding: A Manual of Instruction.
New York, Reinhold Publishing Corp., 1963.

Wolf-Le Franc M., and Vermuyse, Ch. La Reliure. Paris, Bail-
liere et Fils, 1957.

Wood, Stacy H. Bookbinding. New York, Merit Badge Series,
B. S. A., 1940.

Woodcock, John. Binding Your Own Books. London, Penguin
Books, n. d. Puffin Picture Book 104.

Woolnough, C. W. The Whole Art of Marbling as Applied to Paper

and Book Edges. Contains a full description of the materials
used and the method of preparing them. 82 page text; 38 examples of surface-decorated paper. London, 1881. (This and
Halfer's books are the most comprehensive works on the subject in the English language.)

Zaehnsdorf, Joseph W. The Art of Bookbinding. London, Bell,
1880. An illustrated manual of forwarding and finishing by one
of the great binders.

---- The Art of Bookbinding: a Practical Treatise. Bell, 1925.
A standard work first published in 1880.

Zaehnsdorf Ltd. Notes on the Art of Bookbinding. 1952.

Library Binding

Ayer, T.P. "A Schedule for Binding and Rebinding." Library
Journal, pp. 621, 856-7, November 15, 1937.

Bailey, Arthur L. Library Bookbinding. White Plains, N.Y.,
Wilson, 1916.

Callender, T.E. The Library Bindery and its Administration.
London, North Western Polytechnic, School of Librarianship,
1954. Occasional papers, No. 4.

Clough, Eric A. Bookbinding for Libraries. London, 1957.

Coutts, Henry T., and Stephen, George A. Manual of Library
Book-binding: With Specimens of Leathers and Cloths, Forms
and Illustrations. (Libraco Series.) London, Libraco Ltd,
1911.

Dana, J.C. Notes on Bookbinding for Libraries. Chicago, Library
Bureau, 1906.

Development of Performance Standards for Library Binding, Phase
I. Chicago, American Library Association, Library Technology
Publication No. 2, 1965. A preliminary study.

Development of Performance Standards for Binding Used in Libraries, Phase II. Chicago, American Library Association,
1967. Presents three provisional standards (durability, workmanship and openability) developed by the American Library Association Library Technology Project.

Drewery, R.F. Library Binderies. Library Association, 1950.
Library Association Pamphlet No. 3.

Feipel, L.N., and Browning, F.W. Library Binding Manual.
Chicago, American Library Association, 1951. Well presented

information on library binding procedures.

Handbook for Library Binding. Boston, Library Binding Institute, 1963. Advice and assistance for librarians.

Letterpress Bookbinding Terminology. London, Master Bookbinders' Association, 1928.

Observations on Library Binding with Special Reference to the Unsewn Method. British Federation of Master Printers, 1950. Library Binders' Memorandum, No. 1.

Philip, Alex J. The Business of Bookbinding. Gravesend. A. Philip, 1935. Specimens of book cloths. 2nd ed.

Preparing Material for the Bindery. Los Angeles, Pacific Library Binding Company, 1938.

Standard for Library Binding. Boston, Library Binding Institute, 1963. The latest standard for all library binding, including pre-library bound books as well as rebinding used books and binding of periodicals.

Weiss, D.A. "Library Binding and the Purchasing Agent." Library Binder, 3:15-19, 1955.

---- "Facts and Fallacies on Library Binding." Library Journal, 82(1):15-20, January 1, 1957.

---- "Working with a Library Binder." Sci-Tech News 19(1), Spring 1965. Recommendations for librarians by the Executive Director of the Library Binding Institute.

Commercial Binding

A Modern Library Bindery, a Description of the Work of the Firm --B. Riley & Co., Ltd. 1909-1949. Huddersfield, England, Riley, 1949.

Adams, John. The House of Kitcat, a Story of Bookbinding, 1798-1948. London, Kitcat, 1948.

British Manufacturing Industry Series, 1877. Volume on printing and bookbinding.

Control of Warp in Book Covers. Washington, Government Printing Office, 1948. G.P.O.-P.I.A. Joint Research Bulletin, Bindery Series, No. 8.

Crown Agents for Oversea Governments and Administrations. Standard specification No. 40. Binding of Books. London, 1954.

Ede, Charles. "Commercial Binding." The Art of the Book. Studio, 1951.

Esdaile, Arundell. "Binding" in Student's Manual of Bibliography. 3rd ed. rev. by R. Stokes. Allen & Unwin and the Library Association, 1954. Chap. 6, pp. 190-227.

Gerring, C. Notes on Bookbinding. Nottingham, Frank Murray, 1899. Illustrations of Birdsall & Chivers' bindings.

Harrison, T. Bookbinding for Printers. Association of Teachers of Printing and Allied Subjects, 1949. ATPAS Handbook for Teachers, No. 2.

Helwig, Hellmuth. Handbuch der Einbandkunde. Vol. I, n.p., 1953.

Madagan, J.R. Bookbinding Methods and Aids for the Printing Trade. Charlotte, N.C., Washburn Printing Co., 1952.

Mason, John. Bookbinding and Ruling. Pitman, 1933. The art and practice of printing, Vol. 5.

---- A Practical Course in Bookcrafts and Bookbinding. London, B.T. Batsford, n.d. (Preface, 1935). Fuller and more detailed than his introductory book, Bookbinding (London, Warne, 1937).

---- Edition Case Binding. Pitman, 1946. Printing Theory and Practice. No. 23.

---- Letterpress Bookbinding. Pitman, 1946. Printing Theory and Practice, No. 21.

Monk, J. Leonard, and Lawrence, W.F. Textbook of Stationery Binding; A Treatise on the Whole Art of Forwarding and Finishing Stationery Books, Including Chapters on Ruling, Marbling, Leather and Papers. Leicester, Raithby, Lawrence, 1912.

Mordy, C.H. Loose-leaf Binding, Being the Fifth Lecture of the Stationers' Company and Printing Industry Technical Board. 1930-1.

Plan for a Good Book, An Illustrated Guide Book Describing the Methods and Equipment Used in Better Book Manufacturing. Chicago, John F. Cuneo Company, 1951.

Pleger, J.J. Bookbinding and its Auxiliary Branches. Chicago, 1914.

---- "Loose-leaf Binders." Bookbinding. Chicago, Ill., Inland Printer, 1924, pp. 261-268.

---- Pamphlet Binding, Punching, Crimping and Quarter Binding. Chicago, Inland Printer, 1914.

Rollins, Carl Purington. "A Survey of Contemporary Bookmaking." The Dolphin, (2):259-329, 1935.

Siegel, A. "Modern Methods of Loose-leaf Construction." Bookbinding and Book Production, 1951.

Whetton, Harry. Practical Printing and Binding. London, Odhams Press, 1955.

Unsewn Bindings

Clough, Eric A. Perfect Binding, a New Development. Vinyl Products Ltd., 1949. Internal Sales Circular, No. 16. Reprinted from the Library Association Record, October 1948.

Flexiback Thermoplastic Binder, The. Book Machinery Co., Model E instruction manual. (circa 1950).

Grove, Lee E. "Adhesive Bookbinding: A Practice Reviewed." Library Resources and Technical Services. 6:143-160, Spring 1962.

"New Trends in Vinyl Binding." Book Production, 68:40, 1958.

"Summary of 'Adhesive' Binding Techniques." Bookbinding and Book Production, August 1952, pp. 35-36.

"Thermoplastic Unsewn Binding." British Printer, 66:78-79, May/June 1954. On the Flexiback binder.

"Unsewn Binders." Paper & Print (Summer 1951), pp. 205-206.

Upton, P.G.B., and Busby, G.E. The Strength of Unsewn Binding. Leatherhead, PATRA, 1951. Interim report, No. 63.

Vaughan, A.J. "Letterpress Binding." Practical Printing and Binding. 2nd ed. Odham Press, 1955. Chap. 31, pp. 381-412. Harry Whetton, editor.

Book Repair

All the King's Horses. Chicago, The Lakeside Press, 1954. Illus. Also published serially in abridged form as H.W. Tribolet's "Arts of Book Repair and Restoration." in Book Production, v. 67-8, 1958.

Basu, M.N. "Preservation of Books." Indian Librarian, June 1953, pp. 17-20.

377

Belen'kaya, N. G. , and others. "The Use of High Frequency Magnetic Field for the Separation of Stuck-together Documents and
Book Pages. " Moscow, Stareniye bumagi, 128-131, 1965.
(Abstracted in Art and Archaeology Technical Abstracts, 6(2),
1966.)

Belen'kaya, N. G. , and Strel'tsova. "Application of Methylolpoly-
amide Glue PFE-2/10 in the Restoration and Seamless Reinforcement of Books and Documents. " in New Methods for the
Restoration and Preservation of Documents and Books. Moscow,
1960, U.S. Department of Commerce, Office of Technical Services, Springfield, Va. , 1964.

Beljakova, L. A. , and Kozulina, O. V. "Book Preservation in
U.S.S.R. Libraries. " UNESCO Bulletin for Libraries, 15:
198-202, July 1961.

Beyerman, J. J. "Een nistekend conserveringsmiddel voor leren
banden. " Nederlands Archievenblad, 67:30-31, 1963. An unusual means of preserving books. Abstract in American Archivist 27:526, Oct. 1964.

"Books, Care and Repair. " American Archivist. 1:22 10:57
11:280 18:394.

Book Mending. New York, Remington Rand. circa 1948. Remington Rand Library Bureau.

Bro-Dart Industries. Modern Simplified Book Repair. Newark,
N. J. , Bro-Dart Industries (195-) Illus. Means of utilizing
polyvinyl acetate emulsions, acrylic resin lacquers and other
products.

Buck, M. S. Book Repair and Restoration. Philadelphia, Nicholas
L. Brown, 1918.

Byrne, Brooke. Mending Books Is Fun. Minneapolis, Minn. ,
Burgess Publishing Company, 1956. Lightly written, but useful for small circulation libraries with limited budgets.

Cockerell, Sydney M. The Repairing of Books. London, 1958.
An important manual on book repair by one of England's foremost binders.

Demcobind: A Practical Manual of Mending Books. May be obtained free from Demco Library Supplies, Box 1488, Madison,
Wis. ; Box 1722 New Haven, Conn. ; or Box 852, Fresno, Calif.

Douglas, Clara and Lehde, Constance. Book Repairing: New Ideas
from the Mendery. Seattle, University of Washington Press,
1940.

Fores, Jean. "How Texts and Bindings Are Repaired at the Bibliotheque Nationale." Arts et Metiers Graphiques, No. 63, 1939.

Gardner, A. "The Ethics of Book Repairs." The Library. 5th series, 9(3):194-198, September 1954.

Gaylord Bros., Inc. Bookcraft; an illustrated manual describing the Gaylord unit method of book repair. Syracuse, N.Y.; Stockton, Calif., 1947. 32 pp., illus.

Horton, Carolyn. "Treating Water-Soaked Books." International Institute for Conservation News, London, II(2):14, July 1962.

---- "Saving the Libraries of Florence." Wilson Library Bulletin, June 1967.

---- Cleaning and Preserving Bindings and Related Materials. Chicago, American Library Association, 1967. Part I of American Library Association's Technology Program on book preservation.

"How to Use Adhesives Effectively and Economically." Book Production. March 1935.

Huntting, H.R. Book Mending. Springfield, Mass., Huntting Company.

Hutchins, C.I. "The True Art of Restoration of Books and Bindings." Bibliophile. London, 1:301-306, 1908.

Lawrence, V.N. "The Case Against Plastic Tape." Manuscripts. New York, 8, 1956.

Lydenberg, Harry Miller, and Archer, John. The Care and Repair of Books. 3rd rev. ed. New York, R.R. Bowker Company, 1945. 123 pp., 2 pls.

---- The Care and Repair of Books. New York, R.R. Bowker Company, 1960. An updating of the 1945 edition by John Alden, Keeper of Rare Books, Boston Public Library.

Morgana, Mario. Restauro dei Libri Antichi. Milano, Hoepli, 1932, xvi, illus. (Manuali Hoepli). The standard Italian work in the field.

Norton, P.H. Handbook on Book Repairing. Rev. ed. St. John and Red Cross Hospital, Library Department, 1952.

Nyuksha, J.P. "Modern Methods of Restoration of Books and Manuscripts." Bibliotekar, Moscow, 12:64-66, 1958.

Tribolet, Harold W. "Art of Book Repair and Restoration." Book Production 67, March-September 1958.

Wachter, Otto. "The Restoration of Persian Lacquer Bindings."
Allgemeiner Anzeiger für Buchbindereien. Stuttgart, 72, No.
7, 1959. In German.

Williams, G. R. "The Preservation of Deteriorating Books: An
Examination of the Problem with Recommendations for a Solution." Library Journal 91, Jan. 1, 1966 and 91, Jan. 15,
1966.

Yabrova, R. R. "The Effectiveness of Book Reinforcement by Polymethylacrylate Emulsion." Collection of Materials on the Preservation of Library Resources. (Moscow, 1958). U. S. Department of Commerce, Office of Technical Services, Springfield, Va., 1964.

Map Repair

Almela Melia, Juan. Manual de Reparacion y Conservacion de
Libros, Estampas y Manuscriptos. Mexico, D. F., 1949. (Pan
American Institute of Geography and History. Publication No.
95.) Pages 65-66 relate specifically to maps, although the entire work is applicable to map care and preservation.

"A New Mounting Cloth for Cloth Backing Maps, Records and
Charts." Canadian Surveyor. Ottawa, 7(8):21, 1942, illus.
Describes "Charte Cloth," which can be ironed on a map.

Brown, A. G. "Protective Surfacing of Maps and Charts." Canadian Chemistry and Process Industries. Toronto, 30:27-28, 1946.
Contains several formulas for plastic coatings developed during
the war.

Brown, Lloyd A. Notes on the Care and Cataloging of Old Maps.
Windham, Conn., Hawthorne House, 1940.

Fowler, George Herbert. "Maps." British Records Association,
Technical Section. Bulletin. London, 4:4-7, January 1939.
Describes the handling and mounting of maps in the British
Public Records Office. Reprinted in its Bulletin No. 16, 1946,
p. 23-26.

(Globes) "The Repair of Globes." A lecture first given at the
meeting of the Internationale Vereinigung Meister der Einbandkunst held at the Royal Library, Stockholm, September 1966.
Reprints available from U. K. Group, International Institute for
Conservation, c/o National Gallery, London. Excellent description of the repairing of globes as it is done in the British Museum.

Heawood, E. "The Use of Watermarks in Dating Old Maps and
Documents." Geographical Journal 63, 1924.

Hirsh, A. A. "Heavy-Duty Mounting for Maps." Water and Sewage

Works, 111:117, March 1964.

Kramer, Fritz. "Map Mounting Procedure." Journal of Geography. Chicago, 51:21-23, January, 1952. Gives step-by-step directions for mounting a multisheet wall map and lists the equipment needed.

Lynn, Lyman D. "The Care of Special Materials in the U.S. Coast and Geodetic Survey Library." Special Libraries. New York, 31:396-400, November 1940. Describes the care of charts.

Mackin, J. Hoover. "A Method of Mounting Maps." Science. New York, n.s. 84:233-234, 1936.

"Maps; Care and Use." American Archivist. 1:105 3:9 4:190, 283 9:20,161 10:5,59 12:283,425 13:135.

"Maps; and Globes." Museums Journal. 63(2), 1963.

Maughan, Edwin K. "Binding Maps for Easy References." American Association of Petroleum Geologists. Bulletin 37(2):2051-2054, 1953, map, illus. Describes a method of binding large maps into a post binder for convenient reference and storage.

Schmitz, Julia M. "Mounting Maps on Plywood." Wilson Library Bulletin. New York, 15:765-767, 1940-41.

Stanford, Edward. Methods of Map Mounting with Illustrations. London, E. Stanford, 1890.

Thiele, Walter. "The Care of Maps." Official Map Publications. Chicago, American Library Association, p. 294-295, 1938. Advocates filing maps in shallow horizontal drawers.

Throop, Vincent M. "A Method of Mounting Maps." Science. New York, 78(2016):149-150, August 18, 1933. The mounting of maps on cloth at Syracuse University.

Restoration of Manuscripts

Barrow, William J. "Restoration Methods." (For paper.) American Archiv. 6:151-154, 1943.

---- Manuscripts and Documents, Their Deterioration and Restoration. Ann Arbor, Mich., University Microfilms, Inc., 1959.

---- Procedures and Equipment Used in the Barrow Method of Restoring Manuscripts and Documents. Richmond, Va., 1961, 14 pp., one plate and bibliography.

---- Barrow Method of Restoring Documents. Richmond, Va., by the author, 1965. 19 pp.

Belov, G.A. "New Techniques, New Materials and New Experiences Concerning Restoration of Documents and Seals, Preservation of Maps and Plans and Photography since 1950." Archivum, 10:72-80, 1960.

Bhargava, K.D. Repair and Preservation of Records. New Delhi, National Archives of India, 1959, 39 pp.

Bolsée, J. "La Restauration des Documents aux Archives Génerales du Royaume." Archives, Bibliothèques et Musées de Belgique, XXIe (Anée, 1950), 3-10.

Botha, C. Graham. Report of a Visit to Various Archive Centres in Europe, United States of America and Canada. Pretoria, Government Printing and Stationery Office, 1921. Contains information on manuscript repair.

Durye, Pierre, (ed.). Pathologie des Documents et Leur Protection aux Archives de France. Paris, Archives de France 1961. A bulletin of information on restoration, shop outfitting, repairs with tissue, protection from sun, conservation, fumigation and lamination. Each article is written by a foremost French authority on the subject.

Fitzpatrick, John C. Notes on the Care, Cataloging, Calendaring and Arranging of Manuscripts. 3rd ed. Washington, Government Printing Office, 1928. The sections on repairing and mounting apply equally to maps.

Guide International des Archives. Paris, Institut International de Cooperation Intellectualle, 1934. Information on manuscript repair in France.

Haslam, W. The Library Handbook of Genuine Trade Secrets and Instructions for Cleaning, Repairing and Restoring Old Manuscripts, Engravings and Books. London, W. & G. Foyle, Ltd., 1923.

Jenkinson (Sir Hilary). A Manual of Archives Administration. P. Lund Humphries & Co., Ltd. London, 1937. Includes manuscript repair.

Kimberly, Arthur E. "The Preservation of Records." Technical Association of the Pulp and Paper Industry, Technical Association Papers. New York, 22(1):337-341. Describes successive steps in the restoration of manuscripts including lamination.

Lydenberg, Henry M. "On the Preservation of Manuscripts and Printed Books." Library Journal, 53:712-716, September 1928.

"Manuscript Preservation in Old Northwest." American Archivist 1:142.

382

"Manuscript Repair in European Archives." American Archivist 1:1, 51   14:363.

Plenderleith, H. J.   "Technical Notes on Unwrapping of Dead Sea Scrolls." in Barthelemy, D. and Milik, J. T., Discoveries in the Judean Desert.   London, Clarendon Press 1955.

Plenderleith, H. J., and Werner, A. E. A.   "Technical Notes on the Conservation of Documents." Journal Society of Archivists, 1, 1955-1959.   Advice on latest techniques by two experts.

"Protection of Manuscripts." American Archivist.   14:233   19:121.

"The Restoration of Archive Documents." Figaro Littéraire.   February 9, 1952. ICOM News 5, Aug. 1952.

Prints and Drawings

Bonnardot, A.   Essai sur l'Arte de Restaurer les Estampes et les Livres. Paris, 1858.   First mention of the use of pulp for repairing damaged paper. Repr. by B. Franklin, N. Y., 1966.

Bradley, Morton C.   The Treatment of Pictures.   Cambridge, Mass., Art Technology, 1950. 433 pp., illus.

Buck, Richard D.   "Conservation and Mounting of Drawings." ICOM News, 2:5-6, Feb. 1949 (in French); pp. 11-12 (in English).

Plenderleith, H. J.   The Conservation of Prints, Drawings and Manuscripts. London, 1937.

"Protection of Pictures." American Archivist.   17:25.

"Repairing Engravings." American Archivist.   1:22, 63.

Schraubstadter, Carl.   Care and Repair of Japanese Prints. Cornwall, N. Y., Idlewild Press, 1948.   A compendium of safe methods for cleaning, repairing and remounting of Japanese prints as done by Japanese craftsmen.

Wachter, Otto.   "The Restoration of a Color Lithograph." Allgemeiner Anzieger für Buchbindereien. Stuttgart, 69(10), 1956. In German.

Wan-Dan-Chua.   "The Conservation of Prints." Blok-Notes, 1955. Warsaw, Muzeum Mickiewicza.

Seals

Fleetwood, Gustav.   "The Conservation of Medieval Seals in the Swedish Riksarkiv." American Archiv. 12:166-174, 1949.

Tr. and condensed from Meddelanden från Svenska Riksarkivet
for år 1946.

Galbreich, E. I. "Restoration of a 15th-Century Lead Seal." Leningrad, Saltykov-Shchedrin State Public Library, 91-93, 1963.

Jenkinson, Hilary. "Some Notes on the Preservation, Moulding
and Casting of Seals." Antiquaries Journal, (Society of Antiquaries of London) IV:388-403, 1924.

"Repair of Seals." American Archivist. 1:9, 55 12:166, 169, 266.

Sitwell, H. D. W. "Matrix of an Ancient Seal Found in the Chapel
of St. Peter ad Vincula, H. M. Tower of London." Archives,
5:88-89, 1961. American Archivist, 26:397, July 1963.

Repair of Exotic Materials

Berce, R. "Metal Preservation in Museums." Archeologia Aus-
triaca 18, 1955.

Bhargava, K. D. Repair and Preservation of Records. New Delhi,
Archives of India 1959. Care and repair of birch bark, palm
leaf, paper, ink, leather.

Bhowmik, S. "Conservation of Palm-leaf Manuscripts." Baroda
Museum and Picture Gallery Bulletin 19, 1965-1966.

Bosov, N. N. , and Trey, E. N. "Restoration of a Manuscript on
Birch Bark." Leningrad, Saltykov-Shchedrin State Public Library, 57-60, 1965.

Bryan, J. "Methods of Applying Wood Preservatives." Forest
Products Research Records, 1946, No. 9. Great Britain, Department of Scientific and Industrial Research.

"Conservation of Cuneiform Tablets, The." British Museum Quarterly, 23(2), 1961.

Crawford, V. E. "Ivories from the Earth." Bulletin, Metropolitan
Museum of Art 21, 1962. Preservation techniques.

Filliozat, Jean. "Manuscripts on Birch Bark and Their Preservation." Indian Archives 1:102-108, 1947.

Gairola, T. R. "Preservation of a Bone Object." Ancient India,
10 and 11, 1954 and 1955.

Giraud, V. C. M. "Removal of Rust and Calamine from Ferrous
Metals." Chemical Abstracts, Washington, No. 20, 19735b,
1961.

Hunt, G. M. , and Garrett, G. A. Wood Preservation. New York,

McGraw-Hill, 1953.

Jacquiot, C., and Keller-Vaillon. La Préservation des Bois. Paris, Hermann, 1951.

Khovkina, K.H. "The Work of a Restorer on Oriental Manuscripts." Leningrad, Saltykov-Shchedrin State Library, 61-66, 1959.

Kishor, Ranbir. "Preservation and Repair of Palm Leaf Manuscripts." Indian Archives, 14:73-78, January 1961/December 1962.

Kumar, Virendra. "Preservation of Bark and Palm-leaf Manuscripts." Herald of Library Science, 2:236-241, October 1963.

Nair, G.S. "Preservation of a Wooden Object from the Government of Nepal." Journal Indian Museums, 17-20, 1961-1964.

Nordstrand, Ove K. "Some Notes on Procedures Used in The Royal Library, Copenhagen, for the Preservation of Palm-leaf Manuscripts." Studies in Conservation, III(3):135-40, 1958.

Organ, R.M. "The Conservation of Cuneiform Tablets." British Museum Quarterly 23(2):52-57, 1961.

Packard, Elizabeth. "The Cleaning of a Babylonian Tablet." Technical Studies VIII(2), 1939.

Parkinson, D.E. "The Preservation of Cuneiform Tablets." Museum News 27, March 1950. Reviews general practices for preheating, firing, washing and coating clay tablets.

Pelikán, J.B. "Conservation of Iron with Tannin." Studies in Conservation, 11(3), 1966. Reports on a means for preserving rusted iron by painting with chemicals that convert oxides to insoluble protective films.

"Repair of Papyrus." American Archivist. 1:14,62.

Ritornello, V. "Composition for the Removal of Oxide Coatings from Precious Metals and Alloys." Washington, Chemical Abstracts, 63, 13, 17639C, 1963.

Rawlins, F.I.G. "The Cleaning of Stone Work." Studies in Conservation, 3(1), 1957.

"Stone Preservative." Building Research Station Watford, Herts., England. Digest 128, Nov. 1959.

Sujanova, O. "Contribution to the Problem of Removal of Black Deposits from Sandstone." Prague, Zprávy Památkové Pece, 74-81, 1963. (Abstracted in Art and Archaeology Technical Abstracts, 6(2), 1966.)

Todd, Wm. "A Vacuum Process for the Preservation of Bone and Similar Material." Technical Studies IX(4), 1940.

"Wood Deterioration and Treatment." Technical Studies in the Field of Fine Arts, V:64-66, 1936-37.

Film, Tape and Discs

De Mitri, C. "The Preservation of Color in Mounted Color Prints." Journal of Photographic Science. London, 8 Nov.-Dec., 1960. Protecting color photographs.

Gallo, F. "About the Conservation of Microfilm." Istituti di Patologia del Libro Bolletino, 24(1-4):107-10, 1965.

Handling Repair and Storage of 16mm Films. Kodak Pamphlet D-23. Rochester, New York, Eastman Kodak Co., 1965.

Henn, R.W., and Mack, B.D. "A Gold Protective Treatment for Microfilm." Photo Science Engineering, 9(6), 1965.

Hutchinson, Ellis and Ashmore. "The Surveillance of Cinematograph Record Film During Storage." Journal of Applied Chemistry, 8:24ff, January 1958.

Keiler, J.A., and Pollakowski, G. "Restoration of Silver Images on Black and White Films." East German Patent 36,078, May 25, 1965. (Abstracted in Art and Archaeology Technical Abstracts, 6(2), 1966.)

Lindgren, E. "The Permanent Preservation of Cinematograph Film." Proc. Brit. Soc. International Bibliography, 5:97-104, 1943.

McCamy, C.S. Inspection of Processed Photographic Records for Aging Blemishes. Bureau of Standards Handbook 96. Washington, USGPO 1964.

Ostroff, E. "Restoration of Photographs by Neutron Activation." Washington, Science, 154(3745):119-123, 1966.

Prevention and Removal of Fungus on Processed Films. Kodak Pamphlet E-22. Rochester, N.Y., Eastman Kodak Company, 1961.

Ravensway, Charles van. "An Improved Method for the Restoration of Daguerrotypes." Image 5, 1956. Rochester, N.Y., Eastman Kodak Company.

Wiest, D.G., and Henn, R.W. "Microscopic Spots in Processed Microfilm--Their Nature and Prevention." Photographic Science and Engineering, 7(5):253-261, 1963.

386

Repair in the Tropics

Blackie, W.J. "Preservation of Books in the Tropics." Agricultural Journal of Fiji. 3(2):84,85, 1930.

Boustead, W.M. "The Conservation of Works of Art in Tropical and Sub-Tropical Zones." Recent Advances in Conservation (ed. G. Thomson), London, Butterworths, 1963.

----'The Surface pH Measurement and Deacidification of Prints and Drawings in Tropical Climates." Studies in Conservation, 9(2), May 1964.

Browne, F. "The Preservation of Books in Hot Climates." Scientific American Supplement 1903, Vol. 56.

---- "The Preservation of Books in Hot Climates." Scientific American Supplement 1908, Vol. 65.

Chan Kai Meng. "A De-humidifier for the Personal Library." Malayan Library Journal, 1(2):13, 1961.

Cundall, F. "The Preservation of Books in the Tropics." Handbook of Jamaica. Kingston, Government Printing Office, 1926.

Gwam, Lloyd C. The Preservation of Archives in Tropical Countries. Ibadan, Nigeria, National Archives Headquarters, 1964.

Harris, J. "Notes on Book Preservation in West Africa." WALA News, 2(4):102-105, 1956.

Instructions for the Preservation of Books. Achimota, University College of Ghana Library, 1956.

Lefroy, H.M. "Preserving Books in the Tropics." Agricultural News. Barbados, 8:367, 1909.

Plenderleith, H.J. "Bookworms; Treatment by Carbon Disulphide." British Records Association Bulletin, No. 19, p. 8, 1948.

Plumbe, W.J. The Preservation of Books in Tropical and Sub-Tropical Countries. Kuala Lumpur, Oxford University Press, 1964. One of the best sources of information. Lengthy bibliography.

Savage, E.A. "The Preservation of Books in the Tropics." Appendix I in The Libraries of Bermuda, the Bahamas, the British West Indies, British Guiana, British Honduras, Puerto Rico, and the American Virgin Islands. London, Library Association, 1934.

Shipley, Sir A.E. "Bookbinding in the Tropics." Tropical Agriculture, 1926. 3:141.

Williams-Hunt, P.D.R. Preserving Books and Prints in the Tropics. Kuala Lumpur, Museums Department, Federation of Malaya, 1953.

Precautions in the Use of Chemicals

Allan, H. "Safe Practice With Solvents." Chemical Age 73, 1955.

Amor, A.J. "The Toxicity of Solvent, I - II." Paint Manufacturing. 20, 1950

Barnes, J.M. "Control of Health Hazards Associated with the Use
of Pesticides" in R. L. Metcalf's Advances in Pest Control
Research. New York, Interscience Publishers 1957.

---- "Toxic Hazards of Certain Pesticides to Man." Bulletin,
World Health Organization 8:419-490, 1953.

Brown, A.W. Insect Control by Chemicals. New York, Wiley and
Sons, 1951.

Edson, E. F. "Applied Toxicology of Pesticides." Pharmacy Journal 185:361-367, 1960.

Entomological Report--Dieldrin (compound 497). Shell Chemicals,
Ltd., 1957.

Foulger, J.H. "A Practical Approach to Protection of Laboratory
Personnel from Toxic Materials." Journal Chemical Education, Washington 42(4):A285-289, 1965.

Frear, D.E.H. Pesticide Handbook. 13th ed. Pennsylvania,
College Science Publishers, 1961.

Gallo, Fausta. "Biological Agents Which Damage Paper Materials
in Libraries and Archives." Recent Advances in Conservation.
London, Butterworths, 1963.

Gallo, Piero. "Problems in the Use of Insecticides on Occupied
Premises." Recent Advances in Conservation. London, Butterworths, 1963.

Hayes, W.J. "The Toxicity of Dieldrin to Man." Bulletin, World
Health Organization, 20:891-912, 1959.

"Hygienic Guide Series." Detroit, Mich., American Industrial Hygiene Association. Gives details on toxicity and other hazards of industrial chemicals.

Jasser, A. "Without Knowing It, YOU May Be Killing Yourself." Graphic Arts Monthly, 1962. Hazards of solvents.

Mellan, Ibert. Industrial Solvents. 2d ed. New York, Reinhold Publishing Company, 1950. 764 pp. illus. The nature of solvents. Safe handling of solvents.

Plunkett, E. F. Handbook of Industrial Toxicology. New York, Chemical Publishing Company, 1966. Discusses hazards, tolerances, symptoms and precautions.

(Precautions) "The Editor's Column." Washington, Analytical Chemistry, 38(12):93A-95A, 1966. Discusses importance of precautions in use of common solvents, particularly benzene and carbon tetrachloride.

Toxicité des Pesticides pour l'Homme. World Health Organization. Study Group Report No. 114, Geneva 1956.

Weber, C. G., et al. "Effects of Fumigants on Paper." Journal of Research, National Bureau of Standards, 15(3):271, 1935.

Whitney, W. K. "Fumigation Hazards as Related to the Physical, Chemical and Biological Properties of Fumigants." Pest Control, 29(7):16, 1961.

Wood, W. S. "Use, Storage and Disposal of Flammable Solvents." Industrial Engineering Chemistry, 51, 1959.

Abstract Journals

"Abstracts" in Technical Studies in the Field of the Fine Arts. Fogg Art Museum, Cambridge, Mass., 1932-1942.

Abstracts of the Technical Literature on Archaeology and The Fine Arts. London, International Institute for the Conservation of Historic and Artistic Works, 1955 to 1966. (IIC Abstracts) Includes author and subject indices.

APCA Abstracts. Pittsburgh, Pa., Air Pollution Control Association, in cooperation with the U.S. Public Health Service and the Library of Congress, 1956 to present.

Art and Archaeology Technical Abstracts. (Formerly IIC Abstracts) New York, Institute of Fine Arts, New York Univ., 1966 cont.

Gettens, R. J., and Usilton, B. M. Abstracts of Technical Studies in Art and Archaeology. Washington, Freer Gallery of Art,

1955. Information on world-wide literature from 1943 to 1952. Includes sections on paper, papyrus, books, leather, parchment, ink, adhesives, solvents, agencies of deterioration, protection and fire prevention.

Preservation from Deterioration Abstracts. Washington, Prevention of Deterioration Center, Division of Chemistry and Chemical Technology, National Academy of Sciences--National Research Council, 1946 to 1961/62.

Bibliographies

Adhesives. (4 vols.) Appleton, Wis., The Institute of Paper Chemistry; 1963-64. (Vol. I theory and testing; Vol. II paper.)

Air Conditioning: Catalog of Technical Reports. Washington, U.S. Department of Commerce, Office of Technical Services, 1958.

Bibliography on Leather, Hides and Shoes. Washington, U.S. Department of Commerce 1961. (Office of Technical Services SB-483)

Bibliography on Magnetic Recording Systems. Washington, U.S. Department of Commerce, 1963. (Office of Technical Services SB-471, Revised)

Bibliography on Pest Control. Washington, Department of Commerce, 1962. (Office of Technical Services SB-486)

Grenberg, Yuri I. Bibliographic Index of Russian Literature on Restoration and Conservation. Moscow, Central Laboratory of Restoration and Conservation of Works of Art, 1961-1965. 2,467 abstracts of articles from the Russian literature including paintings, drawings, printed books, manuscripts, sculpture, etc.

Perrella, Renato, (comp.). Bibliografia delle Pubblicazioni Italiane Relative all Archivistica. Roma 1963. Confined to works published in Italy and primarily of interest to archivists, but it contains a section on conservation and restoration of archives as practiced in Italy.

"Repair Bibliography." American Archivist. 1:22, 59, 61, 70, 77.

Smith, Lee T., and Hamilton, R.M. "Starch Adhesives." Chemical Engineering News 22, 1944. A review, plus bibliography of 147 references.

Snyder, T.E. Bibliography of Termites. Washington, Smithsonian Institution, 1956.

U.S. Library of Congress. Reference Department. Safeguarding Our Cultural Heritage; a Bibliography on the Protection of Museums, Works of Art, Monuments, Archives, and Libraries in Time of War. Compiled by Nelson R. Burr. Washington, U.S. Government Printing Office, 1952. 117 pp.

(World Health Organization). "Select Bibliography on the Toxicity of Pesticides to Man and Animals 1953-1955." Bulletin World Health Organization 16:1219-1241, 1957.

Bibliographies - Paper

Bibliography on Paper. Washington, U.S. Department of Commerce 1963. Office of Technical Services SB-515.

Grove, L.E. "Conservation of Paper." Museum News 42:15-20, October 1963. Includes bibliography.

Hunter, Dard. The Literature of Papermaking 1390-1800. Chillicothe, Ohio, 1925. 48 pages of text, 20 illus., 23 facsimile title pages.

Kantrowitz, Morris; Spencer, Ernest W., and Simmons, Robert H. Permanence and Durability of Paper, an Annotated Bibliography of the Technical Literature from 1885 A.D. to 1939 A.D. Washington, Government Printing Office, Division of Tests and Technical Control, Technical Bulletin, 1940, No. 22.

"Paper, Bibliography." American Archivist. 4:50 10:187.

Paper in Its Relation to Printing. Appleton, Wis., The Institute of Paper Chemistry, 1962. Almost 2,000 references on paper.

Permanence of Paper. Appleton, Wis., The Institute of Paper Chemistry, 1964. An annotated bibliography containing most of what has been published on the permanence of paper.

Surface, H.E. United States Government Publications Pertaining to Pulp and Paper. New York, 1910 (reprinted from Paper, October 4, 1916).

Weiner, Jack. Bibliography of Papermaking, 1951-1955. New York, Technical Association of the Pulp and Paper Industry, 1957.

Bibliographies - Book

"Bibliography of Book Production." Book Production Magazine 78: 76a December 1963.

Bookbinding bibliography in Edith Deihl's Bookbinding, Its Background and Technique. New York, Rinehart & Company, 1946.

Deuel, Leo. Testaments of Time. New York, Alfred A. Knopf, 1965. Includes a lengthy bibliography of sources of information on early records.

Duehmert, Anneliese. Buchflege. Stuttgart, Max Hettler, 1963.
A bibliography of the literature in several languages on the
care and repair of books. Over 2000 entries.

Freer, Percy. Bibliography on Modern Book Production. Jo-
hannesburg, Witwaterstrand University, 1954. Chap. 11, pp.
229-248.

Hobson, A.R.A. The Literature of Bookbinding. London, Cambridge University Press 1954.

Hobson, G.D. "Books on Bookbinding." in Book Collector's Quarterly, No. 7, pp. 70-84, July/Sept. 1932.

List of Books and Articles Relating to Bookbinding to Be Found in
the Library. New York, Grolier Club 1907.

Mejer, Wolfgang. Bibliographie der Buchbindereiliteratur. Leipzig, Verlag K. Hiersemann 1925. Lists 2,691 titles in seven
languages on binding history and technique, the enemies of
books, and bookbinding materials.

Plumbe, Wilfred. Storage and Preservation of Books, Periodicals
and Newspapers in Tropical Climates. Paris, UNESCO 1964.
A select bibliography.

Prideaux, S.T. "A Bibliography of Bookbinding." The Library.
Vol. 4, 1892.

---- An Historical Sketch of Bookbinding. London, 1893. Over 600
bibliographical entries in appendix.

St. Bride Foundation Institute - "Catalogue of the Periodicals Relating to Printing and Allied Subjects in the Technical Library
of the St. Bride Institute." (With an introduction by Ellic
Howe, 1951.) This publication lists 27 periodicals that relate
wholly or partly to bookbinding.

Walton, R.P. "Causes and Prevention of Deterioration in Book Materials." New York Public Library Bulletin, 33(4), 1929. A
compendium of much of the published data (1858-1929) on book
preservation, deterioration of leather, leather preservation
recipes and acidity in leather; out-of-date but interesting.

Bibliographies - Air Pollution

Bibliography on Air Pollution and Purification. Washington, U.S.
Department of Commerce 1963. (Office of Technical Services
SB-448; revised with supplement.)

Kingsley, K. "Air Pollution Review, 1956-57." Industrial Engineering Chemistry 50, 1958. (261 references.)

Murk, Janet B. "Sources of Air Pollution Literature." Industrial Engineering Chemistry, 47, 1955.

Richardson, Marie S. "Bibliography on Air and Water Pollution." Special Libraries 57, July/August 1966.

International Journals

Bulletin for Libraries. UNESCO, Place de Fontenoy, Paris VII. Many articles on preserving books and other library materials.

Museum. A quarterly review published by UNESCO, 19 Ave. Kliber, Paris 16. Many articles of interest to librarians.

Studies in Conservation. The quarterly journal of the International Institute for Conservation, c/o National Gallery, Trafalgar Square, London.

American Journals

American Archivist. The quarterly journal of the Society of American Archivists.

Annual Report of the Council on Library Resources, Inc., 1025 Connecticut Avenue, N.W., Washington, D.C.

Bookbinding Magazine. New York, 1925 to 1936. This was continued as Bookbinding and Book Production, 1936 to 1954.

Bookbinding and Book Production. 1936 to 1954. This was continued as Book Production.

Book Production, New York, 1955 to January 1965. This was continued as Book Production Industry.

Book Production Industry. New York, February 1965 to present.

Book Production. New York, 1955 to date.

Bulletin of the New York Public Library.

Bulletin of the American Group, International Institute for Conservation.

Craft Horizons, American Craftsman's Council, 16 East 52nd St., New York, N.Y. 10022

Guild of Book Workers Journal. Published three times a year by the Guild of Book Workers, 1059 Third Avenue, New York, N.Y.

Library Journal. New York, 1826 to present. Nearly every number in early issues had something on bookbinding. Many articles
of conservation interest in current issues.

Library Quarterly. University of Chicago Press. A journal of investigation and discussion in the field of library science.

Library Trends, published by Graduate School of Library Science,
University of Illinois, Urbana, Ill.

Tappi, (paper). New York, Journal of the Technical Association of
the Pulp and Paper Industry.

Technical Studies in the Field of the Fine Arts. Cambridge, Fogg
Art Museum Quarterly from 1932 to 1942. Original contributions included articles on paper, adhesives, vellum, ink,
leather, conservation techniques etc. Also abstracted over 450
articles in other journals.

British Journals

Annual Reports of the Master Bookbinders Association. London,
19th century.

Bookbinders' Trade Circular. London. Oct. 1850 to Nov. 1877.
(All published.) This was the organ of the London Consolidated
Society of Journeymen Bookbinders.

Bookbinder, The. London, 1887 to 1890. (A Trade Journal continued as the British Bookmaker.)

British Bookmaker, 1890 to 1894. (This was absorbed by the
British Printer in 1894.)

Bookbinding Trades Journal. Manchester, 1910 to 1912.

British Museum Quarterly, The. Published by Trustees of British Museum. Occasional articles on books, prints and maps.

Library, The. Series 1-3, London, 1889-1919; series 4. Transactions of the Bibliographical Society, London, 1920 (cont.).

Transactions of the British Bibliographical Society.

Transactions of The Royal Society of Arts, London.

Occasional articles appear in The Book Collector, the Bowater Pa-
pers, The British Printer, Graphis, The Library, Paper and
Print, The Penrose Annual, Print in Britain, and Printing
World.

Others

Allgemeiner Anzeiger für Buchbindereien. Stuttgart (current)

Archiv für Buchbinderei. Halle, 1902.

Blok-notes Museum Mickiewicza. (Mickiewicz Museum Note Book)
A journal for all museum material. Summaries in English.

Bollettino Dell' Istituto di Patologia del Libro. The journal of the
Institute of Book Pathology in Rome contains articles of importance to all librarians and archivists. English summaries;
well documented; lengthy bibliographies.

Das Falzbein. Monalsschrift für den Nachwuchs in Buchbinderinge-
werb. Buchbinder-Verlag, Stuttgart, April 1948 to March 1951
(all printed). (The "bone folder"--guidance for men in bookbinding.)

Jahrbuch der Einbandkunst. 4 Vols. Leipzig, 1927-1937.

Index

Abstracts 242, 389
Acid 14ff, 75ff, 176, 182, 314
  effect on leather 175
  effect on materials 23, 56
  migration of 78
  sources of 76, 78
  tanning 23
Acidity, determination of 122
Acrylic resin 42
Adhesives 38ff, 288
  casein 155
  seal repair 153
  suppliers 205
  synthetic 155, 177
Aerosols 57, 176, 180
Air conditioning 80, 81, 82, 176, 324
Air contamination 55ff, 302
Air filtration 81
Alden, John 122, 148
Alexandrian Library 3
Alum 50
  effect on paper 28
Alum-rosin size 50, 77, 175, 177
Alum tawed skin 22
American Group Internationa Institute for Conservation 191
American Library Association 119, 146, 160, 192, 213
  Library Technology Project 147
Ammonia 56
Ammonium sulphide 138
Antichlor 129
Archer, H. Richard 241
Archive repair 183ff
Archives of France 196
Archives of India 197
Art and Archaeology Abstracts 242
Asian Restoration Centers 196
Association of Research Libraries 176, 193
Atmosphere control 80, 81, 82, 156, 302

Atmospheric contamination 176
Austrian National Museum 141

Backing material 208
Bacteria 74
Bannister, Manly 144
Bark 1, 19, 59, 60
  paper 32
  preservation 108
  repair 154
Barrow Research Laboratory 42, 133, 193
Barrow, W.J. 52, 132, 133, 176
Baynes-Cope, David 132
Bedbugs 71
  control 95
Beetles 3, 70
Belan'kaya, N.G. 240
Belgian Restoration Centers 196
Bhargava, K.D. 157
Bibliographies 390ff
Bibliography 239ff
Bibliotheque Nationale 146, 196
Binderies 160
Binding, bibliography 367ff
  cloth 147
  early practices 5ff
  equipment 160
  judging 159
  leather, repair of 144, 159
  origin of 5
  paperback 148
  techniques 10, 11
  unsewn 148
  vs. restoration 119
Bindings, bibliography 259
Black millboards 44
Bleach formulas 201
Bleaches 129
Bleaching 13, 77, 129, 359
  manuscripts 149
Blind stamping 8
Boards, acid free 177, 290
  book 10, 43, 145
  repair of 146

404